Other Words

A Writer's Reader

David Fleming

and the
UMass Amherst Writing Program
Editorial Collective

Leslie Bradshaw

John Gallagher

Emma Howes

Jason Larson

Morgan Lynn

Brian Mihok

Staci Coleman Mitchell

A'Dora Phillips

Megan Trexler

and

Peggy Woods

Kendall Hunt
publishing company

All royalties from the sale of this book go to support educational initiatives of the University of Massachusetts Amherst Writing Program, including publication and celebration of our students' writing, professional development of our teachers, and other special projects.

Kendall Hunt
publishing company

www.kendallhunt.com
Send all inquiries to:
4050 Westmark Drive
Dubuque, IA 52004-1840

Table of Contents

Introduction

Welcome to *Other Words,* an anthology of contemporary nonfiction prose in English. Collected here are 32 essays by some of the most talented writers of our time, culled from some of the best journals, magazines, books, and websites available, and treating some of the most important issues we face, both as individuals and as a society.

Although this book should appeal to all kinds of readers, it was designed primarily for students in college writing courses, especially first-year students. If that's you, we think you'll find here an instant companion for the start of your new life; a guide to help you join new conversations, confront new challenges, and try on new selves; a partner in this new phase of your education. You've embarked on a difficult, exciting journey, and we're proud to accompany you—at least for part of the way!

Some of the writing collected here may strike you, at first, as difficult or strange. A few of the pieces will seem almost unbearably sad or intense. Others you'll find sweet, informative, funny. Some you will immediately love; some you will feel more conflicted about; many will only grow on you over time. But all of them, we believe, are *alive,* each in its own way; and all will reward your attention. Each is the product of writerly skills that come from years of practice and hard work, from the deep and difficult effort of trying to represent a world, or worlds, in language; and each is also the product of what might be called "public desire," the longing to share one's experiences and concerns with strangers. *Reading* these essays will require work as well, but we think the effort will be worthwhile. In most cases, we think, it won't feel like effort at all.

The essays were also chosen because they can give you interesting things to think and talk about as you start this new phase of your life; because they can model for you new ways of using language that you can emulate in your own writing; and because they can provoke you to respond in writing about your own ideas and experiences. They can also help build community in your classroom by centering discussion among you and your peers; and, since students in other classes will likely be reading and talking about the same essays, we think they can help build community on your campus more generally.

Perhaps above all, we believe that reading these essays will broaden and enrich your life by giving you new words, new ideas, and new lives to think, talk, and write about. That' s what's behind our title, *Other Words,* which we mean to suggest several things at once: the different perspectives represented by these diverse authors (*others'* words); the multiple ways manifest here to talk about the "same" phenomena (*in other words* . . .); and the wholly different kinds of experience opened up by these very different pieces (each one another *world* entire).

The subtitle is multi-voiced too: this is *a writer's reader;* but then again, so are you.

On writing

If we have initially positioned you here as a *reader,* it's your development as a *writer* that this anthology really aims for; it's *your* texts that it's designed to support, and *your* writing skills that it's meant to practice. And that's as it should be, given the kind of course you're in and the nature of literacy in our time. Writing today is more complex, and more consequential, than ever. It's also more self-sponsored, more collaborative, more mediated, more malleable—in short, more *complicated*—even as it's also, in many ways, more fun. Writing has become *the* intellectual skill of our society.

Some observers even claim that we are witnessing, for the first time in history, the rise of a mass *writing* public, something qualitatively different from the mass *reading* publics of the past. From adolescence on, nearly everyone in our society now "texts," and does so almost constantly. There are now more occasions to write, more media to write with, more audiences to write for, more styles and venues to write in, more topics to write about, more opportunities to reflect on writing, than ever before. And it's not just our personal lives that are increasingly written: our economic, political, professional, and cultural worlds are now largely structured around written texts which ordinary people produce as well as consume. It is not too much of a stretch to say that the ability to make and circulate textual meaning (increasingly multi-authored, multimedia, and multi-lingual) is now one of the hallmarks of human *being.*

Unfortunately, we still often learn (both in school and out) that writing is simple, secondary, and subsequent; that it is little more than the deployment of graphic signs (one set, singular and fixed, per "language") for the purpose of visually representing one's thoughts and feelings; and that it is a basic skill that is, or should be, acquired once and for all early in one's education. From this point of view, writing is a rule-governed process, the results of which can be readily assessed by stable, determinate, formal criteria.

We know instinctively, of course, that this is untrue—or, at the very least, partial. Writing is enormously complex even for fluent writers—perhaps especially for fluent writers! It turns out that it is related to speech and thought but not reducible to them, that it has its own independent powers and pitfalls, and that it is a radically plastic phenomenon, capable of being used in a nearly infinite number of ways and situations for an almost impossibly wide range of purposes.

Think, for example, about the many kinds of writing *you* do every day, how different each is from the other, what complex factors are involved in that activity, and yet how useful, even pleasurable, it all is for you. Today, you may well have written a to-do list; a text message; a comment on a blog; an email or instant message; a wall post on Facebook; an e-vite for a party. Yesterday, or last year, you were likely writing personal statements for college applications, movie reviews for your school newspaper, poems for people you liked or loved, résumés and cover letters for jobs you wanted, song lyrics for your band, driving directions to your house, labels for your scrapbook, thank you notes to relatives, entries in your journal or diary. And then there's all the writing you do for school: from lecture notes to lab reports, research papers to essay exams, summaries and analyses to weekly response papers.

Now think about the wide range of purposes you accomplish with these texts, which you use to greet, to share, to respond, to request, to remind, to purchase, to collect, to sell, to impose, to plan, to analyze, to judge, to bind, to loose, to record, to fix, to complain, to report, to advertise, to plead, to honor, to propose, to apply, to recommend, to apologize, to promise, to borrow, to decline, to accept, to wonder, to dream, to flirt, to argue, to show off, to seduce, to demur, to grieve, to part. The list could go on indefinitely.

Finally, think about how you learned to accomplish through writing all these purposes: not by memorizing rules but by practicing the activity itself, in concrete situations, with other people, through trial and error, by observation and imitation, with feedback and response. The success of such writing was not measured by how few red marks you got from a teacher but by the extent to which you met your goals. It was successful if it was meaningful, effective, rewarding.

The fact is that in our society, ordinary people write all the time, using different resources and media to communicate with different audiences, in different languages and genres, for different reasons and goals. They know, instinctively, that writing is useful, that it's a way to make meaning for self and others, that it connects us to family, friends, acquaintances, and even self; but that it also allows us to converse with strangers, near and far, long gone and not yet born. They know that writing is multiple and contingent, dependent in each case on the writer's purposes, the expectations and needs of his or her audience, and the topics, problems, and subject matters they all (theoretically) share. In fact, each intersection of writer, reader, and topic is unique. An email message to a professor asking about tomorrow's homework assignment; a letter sent to an employer regarding a summer internship; an online profile posted to a social networking site—each of these texts asks you to represent yourself, your readers, and your topic in different ways; and the choices you make in those diverse situations can have important consequences for you and your world.

The drawing below, a version of what is often called "the rhetorical triangle," is a common way to represent the key factors involved in writing.

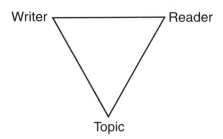

The triangle is a useful reminder that writing is always ultimately about *people* (who occupy two of its three corners!), their purposes, expectations, and needs, as well as their joint situation in a world of (presumably) shared problems, histories, objects. If we add TEXT and CONTEXT, the device can help us see that writing is also extraordinarily complex, always dependent on the linguistic, discursive, and rhetorical resources available to participants and the situations in which they find themselves and which writing, in part, helps to bring about. Learning to write well is learning to make good choices given all these factors and variables.

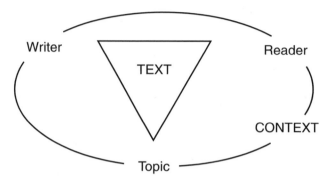

The good news is that you're already familiar with most of this, you're already accomplished as a writer in many situations, you already produce different kinds of texts to achieve different purposes in your life. As Dr. Benjamin Spock used to tell new mothers in *Baby and Child Care*: "Relax. You know more than you think you do."

But if you're already fluent in some kinds of writing, you're embarking now on a journey in which text-making is about to become much more complex and its stakes, much higher: you'll now be writing to pursue such challenging purposes as knowledge creation, career advancement, organizational change, community development, and personal transformation. You'll be using writing for intellectual inquiry, social justice, and artistic discovery—to name just some of the more demanding purposes that writers pursue in college and beyond. And this will require you to stretch your rhetorical muscles in new ways. Even more daunting, you'll find yourself in a society that needs you to be extraordinarily *flexible* as a writer, to switch back and forth among *multiple* literacies, to write with and for very different kinds of audiences with sometimes conflicting expectations and needs, to write in a variety of genres, styles, dialects, and even languages. You'll need to write not just for friends and family but for clients and consumers, employers and employees, regulators and lawyers, fellow citizens and government officials, your neighbors and people far away, the knowledgeable and the less so, the powerful and the oppressed.

School, if it sometimes misrepresents what writing is and how people acquire skill in it, can be a good site for practicing these hard kinds of writing. Courses like first year composition and advanced writing in the disciplines can embed literacy development in supportive communities of readers, writers, and thinkers with specific purposes to pursue and moves to practice. And if writing in general is infinitely particular, there are commonalities across these complex literate activities that school can isolate and exercise: it can protect less experienced writers as they learn to take on increasingly sophisticated challenges, providing them with low-risk opportunities to experiment, fail, and, thus, improve. More specifically, writing classes can develop in young writers the habits, skills, and attitudes needed to meet the demands of difficult rhetorical situations by providing them with 1) authentic <u>invitations to write</u>, motivations and exigencies that can exploit their desire to express themselves, discover new things, and communicate with others; 2) sufficient <u>time to write</u>, especially to generate ideas—ideas which may eventually be discarded or changed beyond recognition—as well as time to draft, revise, and edit language itself; 3) ample <u>resources for writing</u>: models, phrases, ideas, and materials to work with and learn from, including relevant writing tools and sources of information; 4) <u>response and feedback</u> from critical but helpful readers who can push writers to re-see and revise their work; and, finally, 5) <u>opportunities to circulate writing</u>, to see the effects of one's words on others and how meaningful, useful, even pleasurable, such "public" writing can be.

So, ironically, in introducing these texts meant above all to be *read,* we want to remind you how important your own *writing* is in learning to write. We want to encourage you to seek out communities and contexts in which you can develop your writing voices, practice your writing moves, and find readers for your written texts. That' s why it's so important in college to take classes that make space and time every day for writing; that provide peer readers who listen but also interrogate, who make suggestions but also honor your ownership of your ideas and style; and that publish your writing, making *it,* not the texts of professional writers, the center of the course. Many of the writers collected in this volume benefited from such scaffolding in school. We think you will, too.

On reading

If the central activity of the college writing class is *writing,* and the central text the *students'* own texts, why then use a reader of previously published essays by professional writers? why is the writing class a place not just to practice writing but also *reading?* why, for that matter, do most fluent writers *read* constantly, widely, and actively? does *reading* help people somehow *write?* and does *writing* make them somehow different kinds of *readers?*

Writers read for many reasons and benefit in many different ways from what and how they read. Imagine, for instance, that you're driving down the highway: it's hard not to read the signs along the way: road markers, travel advisories, commercial advertisements. We pass texts at 65 miles per hour, and, incredibly, we process them —a kind of accidental reading that is a common feature of a text-rich society like ours. Or imagine that you're walking to class, and there's an announcement written in chalk on the sidewalk outside your residence hall; there's a banner hanging above the entrance to the school's main administrative building; there's a sign taped to the door of one of your classroom buildings. You read those things whether you want to or not. And such reading affects you and, no doubt, your writing, too.

But sometimes reading is more personal: you get an invitation to read something from someone you know (an email in your inbox, a text message on your cell phone, a folded note taped to your door). This kind of reading requires a little more work on your part than just glancing up at a sign as it passes by; but you don't have to go out seeking such texts either—they come to you. You read them, in fact, mainly out of fellow-feeling, gratitude, love or desire for the person trying to contact you. Writers often read, in other words, because someone they know has asked them to, has asked them, implicitly or explicitly, to respond to their words. If the personal, hand-written letter sent through the mail has largely disappeared from our society, it has been replaced by multiple other forms of interpersonal textual connection, many of them digital. How many friends or family members have you written to today? How many messages have you received?

Sometimes, of course, we read more deliberately—not just as part of our daily dialogue with friends and family but as part of more substantial intellectual, creative, professional, political, and spiritual projects. In such cases, we actively seek out texts, usually from authors we don't even know—because we need information or advice, because we want to learn something, because we desire the pleasure that can only be had by immersing ourselves in someone else's prose. We buy a magazine, go to a website, click on a PDF, check out a book, browse the internet, broadcast a query, order a document. We read, that is, out of curiosity, need, desire. And this reading is often quite impersonal in the sense that we typically don't know the author at all. We read the text because of what' s *in* it. It's only later that we reflect on the fact that the text was written *by* someone *for* a particular purpose *in* a particular situation.

The academic life is at its heart a search for texts that can help us answer questions, solve problems, advance our understanding, satisfy our longings. Sometimes in that search for texts (for knowledge, information, theory, data, opinion, advice, instruction, pleasure) we find just what we're looking for. More often than not, the journey is circuitous, unpredictable, unfinished—and more exciting precisely for that reason.

Unfortunately, some reading in school doesn't allow for or exploit the freedom or excitement just described. Sometimes students read because they're told to. In writing classes like the one you're enrolled in, you were likely *assigned* to read essays in this book. Hopefully, your teacher, your classmates, your own intellectual curiosity will carry you some way in motivating you to do that reading and keep an open mind about it. Maybe your teacher's enthusiasm for a particular essay will be contagious, or a classmate you admire will tell you how interesting the piece is, or the title will capture your fancy. But if you're skeptical of the reasons to read these essays, the uses to which you can put them, here are a few things to consider.

First, reading other people's texts, not just those of your peers but those of experienced, accomplished, published writers, can give you things to talk about in your own writing: ideas, issues, problems, opinions, facts, and experiences that you can use in your own work, starting points to develop content for your own essays. Think about the issues treated in this book: friendship, gender, education, the environment . . . Granted, this class isn't *about* those things; it's a *writing* class, after all, one centered on YOUR ideas and experiences, as those are developed in your OWN thinking and writing. Still, reading can help you see what problems, themes, issues, and controversies are interesting and relevant to others. *Their* hopes, desires, experiences, opinions, and questions can propel you to think and write about similar or related topics.

As you're reading these essays, then, we hope you'll occasionally say to yourself: "Oh, you mean I can write about *that?*" Or, "I just thought of something *I'd* like to write about!"

Second, reading these texts can give you rhetorical models to emulate, ways of representing your own ideas, opinions, and experiences, patterns of language or discourse that you might use in your own work. Think about the many different styles of writing collected here. Some of these essays are funny; others serious. Some are short, some long. Some are "plain," others more inventive. Some are written in the first person, some in the second or third. Some deal with the past, others with the present or future. If any of these "ways with words" appeal to you, we encourage you to actively emulate them. Your teacher will talk with you about respecting the intellectual property of others; but we all learn a lot about writing from reading other writers, noticing what they do with language, and being inspired by them to try new things.

Third, reading these essays can provoke *direct* responses from you about the texts themselves. In other words, you might use these pieces, literally, as conversation partners, interacting with them in myriad ways. Perhaps the most common form of writing in the academy, in fact, is writing *about* other texts: summarizing, paraphrasing, quoting, analyzing, synthesizing, criticizing, and evaluating others' words. Such moves can be difficult, especially when the "original" text is difficult; but they are very important in higher education for good reason. One of the best ways to create and test knowledge, after all, is to build on the work of others. So we hope that you'll take up the implicit invitations of these authors and respond directly to their texts.

Fourth, since at least some of these essays will be assigned to your whole class, reading them can help build community in your classroom, can give you and your classmates something to share, "common" texts that can help you build relationships with your peers, even if those relationships are primarily intellectual in nature. Such relationships are especially valuable early in college and on large campuses where you don't know many people at first.

Those are all good reasons, we think, for using a book like this in a writing class. But there's another reason why we collected these essays for you—because we think you'll like them! Anthologies like this one, designed mainly for the classroom, sometimes fail to mention that reading can be *pleasurable;* that it can be enjoyable to lose oneself in another person's words, his or her representation of experience; that it can be satisfying to be carried along by a capable guide on a journey into another world, another life—to realize that you're seeing new things and thinking new thoughts. Reading, in other words, can be its own reward. In fact, *we* were drawn to these essays primarily because we liked them, because, apart from all the other motivations listed above, we found them to be illuminating, memorable, compelling. We felt like the hour or two we spent with each one made our lives different, better, richer.

Reading, after all, is first and foremost an <u>experience.</u> It takes place over time, requires (and rewards) concentration, and leaves you feeling as if you've lost track of yourself and the mundane concerns of your daily life, that you now inhabit someone else's world, that you're dwelling in their sentences and paragraphs and following along as they travel from idea to idea. It's a strange experience, one that is sometimes described as communicating with others while remaining alone, participating in dialogue while being quiet. In this sense, "losing track of yourself" may not be quite the right metaphor, at least not for nonfiction prose. In the best essays, readers *do* feel carried along by the stream of another's words; but, as Maryanne Wolf recently put it in her book *Proust and the Squid,* the secret at the heart of fluent reading is that the human brain can *both* process someone else's written words *and* entertain its own related thoughts at the same time. The combination of another person's ideas and your own, interacting in quiet and solitude, can be enormously powerful.

And here's the point we want to make: the activity just described can feed back into your own writing in an especially poignant way because to appreciate the reading experience that another writer has given *you* can leave you wanting to do the same for *others*. We *write* sometimes, in other words, because we *read:* because we want to pay forward the gift of that experience to other people.

On difficulty

If we encourage you, then, to approach reading these essays as an *experience,* and to give yourself up to its pleasures, that doesn't mean that the texts collected here will be light and easy for you. In fact, we think you'll find most of them quite challenging. Part of the reason for that is genre. Many of these pieces are nonfiction essays of the occasional sort, a kind of writing that you may not be very familiar with or practiced in. You've no doubt read lots of *stories* in your life. And you've also probably read lots of *textbooks*—a kind of nonfiction that tends to be mostly explanatory, synthetic, factual. You've also likely read lots of other kinds of expository and argumentative prose —instructions, opinions, reviews—to say nothing of the many informal and practical genres that we discussed earlier (email, résumés, etc.). But some of you may be less familiar with the *essay,* at least its non-school variety, which shares some characteristics with these other genres but has its own particular qualities as well. Like a story, an essay usually asks that you read from beginning to end, that you experience the text as a journey, an unfolding. But its characters and plot, if it has any, will be quite different from those of narrative. Like much expository and argumentative prose, on the other hand, an essay is usually "truthful," or at least tries to represent the world or some slice of it as it "really" is. But essays aren't usually something you can skim or reduce to a point. Neither story nor report, the essay is difficult to categorize, though that may be one reason it's so full of possibilities!

In addition, there is difficulty here in both form and content: many of these pieces are long, dense, complex. Some deal with painful topics. Some are written in a voice that may, at first, be off-putting to you. The pieces are also quite different from one another—in fact, we purposefully tried to include here a multiplicity of writers, styles, and subject matters. If after really working hard with one piece, you finally come to appreciate its style and substance, be careful: the next piece may force you to start all over again, as if you're entering a whole *other* world!

Here's some advice as you begin reading, based on our own experience with these essays and our own background as readers and writers.

Give yourself time to read these pieces. As we've tried to indicate, this isn't a text-book that you can skim; and the "chapters" aren't research reports from which you can extract thesis statements, or "op-ed" pieces that make their point early and can then be reduced to that claim. They're *essays*—many are long—most are challenging in one way or another—and all are meant to make you think, to stretch your mind, to reward your effort. You need time to do all that well.

Find a quiet place to read. If you're enrolled in a writing course, there's likely a community of readers and writers behind your work. That community is, we hope, lively and talkative, and you should know how important such sociality is to writing development. But reading these essays requires concentration. Now, everybody is different—some people can read while listening to music or watching television or carrying on a conversation with a friend. But you might want to try reading these pieces in a quiet place. We know that quiet is sometimes hard to find in college, especially if you're living in a residence hall. But it's hard for us to imagine really appreciating these essays without to some extent losing oneself in them.

Come with an open mind. Try to approach each essay as you would want someone to approach your own writing: willing to experience it on the writer's terms. We call this playing "the believing game," making one's first pass over an essay a sympathetic one. Let the essay take its course and follow it. Assume that the author is someone you'd want to listen to and his or her essay, something you're likely to learn from. Only then, after first believing, can you play "the doubting game," in which you engage the essay in a more questioning, even critical, spirit.

Re-read and annotate. Most of these essays will require (and reward) a second (or third) read. It's often only in that subsequent reading that many of us begin to think more actively about and with the piece at hand, often annotating the text while we read. Sometimes annotation is just putting a little penciled dot by a passage you really like or a question mark by one you don't understand. Sometimes you dog-ear a page where there's something that really inspired you. Sometimes annotations are more prominent: you highlight key phrases in colored ink or write notes in the margin. The key thing is to pay attention to what interests, inspires, puzzles, or provokes you.

Engage the text. Now, once you're re-read the piece and annotated key passages, start thinking more purposively about what you've read and how you might interact or engage with it substantively. Summarize the essay, or some part of it, in your mind. Reflect on what impressed or surprised you about it. Ask questions of it. Talk back to it. Try to figure out how it works. Discuss it with your roommate. Listen to what your classmates say about it. Debate it. Argue with it. Translate it. Apply it. Then re-read it, and think about it some more!

On writing again

Perhaps the most powerful kind of engagement you can have with these texts, of course, is to *write* about them. And that brings us back to where we started: with a society of text-makers and the increasingly central, increasingly diverse, activity of writing, which allows us to create and communicate meaning in so many ways for so many purposes. We hope this book of *readings* will help you build on the text-making skills you already have, adding to your repertoire new ways of *writing* that can help you inquire into yourself, interact with texts, add to conversations, and reflect productively on all of that.

And here's our last bit of advice for you. Have fun with the essays in this book! Be inspired by them, learn from them, argue with them, tell your friends about them! Carry this book around with you. Keep it by your bed. Slip it into your suitcase when you go home for the holidays. Return to it in the future, long after the semester in which it was required is over. Above all, read! Write! Enjoy!

Emily

Heather Abel

Here's the image: The hallway of Willets, a typical dorm built in the late fifties, when cinder block was appreciated, was quiet that late afternoon. The eight doors were closed; the shared hall phone—this was before cell phones or even room phones—dangled off the hook. Then, some life. Two pretty girls dragged out a CD player, its electrical cord stuck like a tail under the door. While Sinéad O'Connor sang, they began flailing their arms around, leaping and shimmying under the flickering fluorescent lights. This was a liberal arts school. These were liberal girls. Both bodies had taken ballet lessons; both bodies pushed to be sexy, and the result was somewhere between awkwardness and delight. The hall was narrow and long, and they ran the length of it. The song was on repeat.

That freshman fall, they danced often in this flailing, wafting way. They could do all sorts of things together that they would never have done alone. Once they danced shirtless and outside. They were singing a song, maybe the same Sinéad song, and it was raining. They'd been taking a walk and ended up in the college's wooded amphitheater, where years later, hardly speaking to each other, they would receive diplomas and graduate. It would rain then as well. This is the story of what happened in between.

Sometime during the first week of college, I don't remember when, I met Emily. I liked her because she was sweet to me. Midwestern sweet. And she was funny and impeccably pretty, but not in a way that would dampen me.

What I mean is that Emily and I were different in specific and obvious ways. I'd brought vintage dresses and velvet skirts to college. She wore pale blue shirts tucked into jeans. I already knew about Foucault. She could draw, write poetry, and sing like a starlet. The child of lefty academics, I was more worldly. The daughter of genuinely friendly people, she was kinder. As I saw it, she was the sparkly, shimmery skim of water. I sunk deeper, where the seaweed grows.

Perhaps as a result of growing up with two sisters—and sharing my mother with them—I had at a young age found a way to compete without competing. I would decide that certain things were mine and that I alone could claim them. In return, I'd abstain from other things. Early on, the color red was mine. Blue was my sister's, even though I quite liked it, so I would not choose the sweet blue sweater at the store. Later,

Nicaragua was mine. Marxism was also mine. Doc Martens were mine. Having best friends was mine. Having boyfriends was not mine. (This got confusing because I actually had a boyfriend through much of high school and into college, but I still didn't identify as someone with a boyfriend.) Discussing was mine. Making out was not mine. Apartheid was mine. Athleticism was not mine. Deep, difficult things were mine; I wasn't actually depressed, but I liked to talk animatedly about depression. Drinking games, TV, and one-liners were not mine. The environment was mine, both the outdoors (yes, I claimed the wide world) and the defense of the outdoors.

This is the thinking, I can say in retrospect, of a scared girl.

Because Emily and I had separate talents, I wasn't afraid we'd have to compete over something I cared about. Without this fear, we attained something I can only call equanimity, and it allowed us, at times, the buoyancy of a soap bubble. That's how I see it now, two girls dancing and singing and drawing and learning Foucault and talking about boys in code, all inside a soap bubble.

With our differences frozen in place, Emily and I could be practically the same. We were both girlie girls. Girlie like first-graders, trading stickers. We picked music, boys, shirts, and posters that were pretty as strawflowers. And we both wistfully and vehemently missed our moms. If college is a railroad away from your mother, we had both hopped the slow train. They'd been our first friends, our models of just how close you could get to someone.

The term *boyfriend* is coy, hiding all implications of intimacy or raunchiness. "Sure he's my boyfriend," you retort in eighth grade. "He's a boy and he's my friend." The term *best friend* is not coy. It puts the competition implicit in friendship right out there for everyone to see. It says that some friends are good, some are better, but all of these girls are left standing on the second step wearing silver medals, while only one girl wins first. Everything is in its understood place. That's why I liked having a best friend.

Of course, gaining a boyfriend is much more straightforward than winning a best friend: there's a first kiss. But becoming a best friend is also physical. Maybe you trade clothes. Maybe, with your fingers, you scoop white frosting off of a row of yellow cakes after everyone has left the dining hall. Maybe you describe in detail how you feel about giving blow jobs.

Or maybe, you lie on the grass, and with four feet in the air and your hips aligned, you compare the length of your legs. There's no way to describe an eighteen-year-old body fourteen years later, because at the time I thought mine was large and ungainly, and now I'm sure it was adorable. (My capacity for jealousy is huge; I am jealous of myself then.) And I don't remember Emily's body either, except that she's about four inches shorter than I and was comparably smaller, and we could wear some of the same clothes but not most. And at times I minded that. So, it's not that I thought that we had the same body exactly. Or that we didn't ever feel envious. It's just that I liked them both together.

I'm not talking sex. I'm talking familiarity and ownership. Sometimes when I saw her and she was beautiful, I thought I was seeing myself.

By the first snowfall, Emily was my best and I was hers. We walked on the thin crust to the faraway part of campus that held a frat-house-turned-feminist-center. I'd never lived in winter, and Emily taught me to wear tights and mittens and what chipmunks looked like. She also taught me to sing in tune. *We are self-sufficient, self-empowered women,* we sang. *But sometimes we get a little horny.* We didn't date boys that year, and this is one reason I think our own romance bloomed. Instead, we both had high school boyfriends who sent us letters. Instead, we rewrote a song from *Les Mis,* rhyming *horny* with *Californ-y,* and performed it to boys in a perverse flirtation.

A week later I was home for winter break. It was a day like a flirt, when Los Angeles flaunts its distance from the East. Bright blue sky behind feathery palm fronds. Robins alit on scarlet bougainvillea, the purple tips of jacaranda. I was lying next to my mom, on my parents' bed, trying to bring the coasts together by conjuring up snow and bare branches and every tiny thought I'd had since I last saw her. That's when the phone rang. I didn't pick it up right away. The world felt too full: somewhere there were mittens and here was my mother and outside, aloe plants; but perhaps we just remember fullness before emptiness. I sat cross-legged on the edge of the bed. *Is this Heather?* It was Emily. She was calling to tell me that her mother had a headache, and it turned out to be a brain tumor.

Emily's mother started dying for real in the beginning of sophomore year, and I took on the death like a project, with the self-importance and fervor I brought to protest the Gulf War: My job would be to carry Emily through this. When she returned home, I offered to audit her classes and take notes. I spoke to her teachers and the deans. I called her nightly. But mostly I spent a lot of time telling myself: Pretend it's your mom. How would you feel?

At the funeral, I sat next to Emily in the front row. I have no memory of her boyfriend or other friends. My job felt enormous, but I believed I would succeed. I did dishes all afternoon, staring out the window that had been cut out of the wall for Emily's mother, so that she could look at the woods while working.

Emily and I shared a room in a quad, and when she didn't return to school, my concern grew until it filled the space of her. In early December, my parents visited me for the first time, and we were walking through a portrait-lined lounge when my mother told me that her mother was very sick with cancer. *I'm sorry,* I said, not looking at my parents; I was staring at the faces of Swarthmore's founders, lovely pacifist ladies, full of sympathy I couldn't muster. *But I can't think about it now. I'm full up.* My grandmother had played favorites (it's a tradition in our family); my sister was hers. I was not. So, I reversed the equation. Emily's mother's death was mine. My grandmother's death was not.

This, as they said throughout college, was problematic. Emily's mother's death was hers. Or, perhaps, her mother's.

When the spring semester began and Emily returned, I developed a hierarchy of suffering among our roommates. I was at the bottom; my grandmother's cancer was an age-appropriate tragedy. Molly, who had just begun grappling with a history of sexual abuse, entered a claustrophobic and demoralizing relationship with a guy; she was easily several rungs above me. That winter, Tina learned that her father was HIV positive, and her high school boyfriend overdosed. She surpassed Molly. Emily was on top, the queen with the true, visceral horror. Her mother had gone, in a few short months, from being lovely and nurturing to bald and strange to dead. Since happiness was denied our quad that year, I decided that the person with the most suffering would likely receive the most love. I knew how pathetic and cruel this hierarchy was, but I also knew that, according to its rules, I'd lost, and it was up to me to take care of everybody.

I have to admit: for a while this gave me an incredible sense of resolve. I liked being busy all day in class, and then, the rush ended, I liked knowing I was needed. Most of all, I liked the time in between, the long, purposeful march to our dorm. I could see it, pretentious in stone and turrets but somehow still looking like an Elks' lodge, as I crossed the train tracks and then the vast lawn used by sports teams in the spring, now brown as tundra. One day, I carried ice cream, which made me hopeful. It was crucial to come home with a plan.

Up in our room, the afternoon light hit like a beacon, the slant call of a lighthouse.

In the center of the room were two single beds, pushed together. And on them, only a small part of Emily was visible to me: one arm and black shoes. The rest was hidden by her bedspread. On our windowsill were her sea green vases, and there were my Nicaragua posters hung on the wall, vestiges of the girls we were the year before, which seemed so silly now.

Also seeming silly: the ice cream. A pathetic gesture against grief so giant that you would wear shoes to bed. Still, I gingerly set it down on our two desks, also pushed together. I stood there. I wouldn't wake her.

What are you doing? She was annoyed, not asleep. *Um, I got some ice cream. Do you want it?*

No. Of course not. It was a stupid plan.

Should we take a walk to the creek?

No. I thought how in two years I'd grown to like this winter light, but I didn't say that. Emily didn't like it now.

Want to go to dinner? No. Order pizza? No. Emily! Tell me what's going on. Tell me how you feel. I don't know. Should I leave?

No.

The sun slipped west. *Can I turn on the lights? Is that okay?* Emily made an unsure noise. When the room was totally dark I switched on the overhead, and she pulled a pillow over her head. Sometimes, this was all there was all night.

But this evening, our friend came by. During the hours I'd spent trying to get Emily out of bed, she'd gone for a run, eaten dinner, put on a dress with cowboy boots. She told us about a party and said, *Please come, Emily, please come, sweetie.* Emily sat up. *I want to go.*

At the mirror, she pulled her hair back and loosed the one curl that would corkscrew the length of her forehead. It was her new hairstyle. I believed that after what she'd seen of her mother's body, after she'd bathed it and smelled it, Emily changed her own. She developed an attentiveness to her beauty that I lacked and that took all her energy. I didn't touch my hair; looking put-together was now Emily's. I thought: I need to study; I need dinner. But really, I was jealous. I had wanted to be the one who got her out of bed. I wanted her to wake up from depression because of me, because of how much I loved her.

On the way out the door, *Aren't you coming, Heather?*

I said no, so I can't say what happened at the party, how she suddenly unspun from her cocoon in our bed and became multi-syllabic and conversant, but I can describe how guys looked at her those days. We were no longer noticed together, those two pretty girls singing their smug song. She was noticed alone. I told myself I didn't care. I had one crush. He was an outdoorsy guy named Greg, and he seemed as untroubled and beautiful as a boy could be. I didn't flirt, exactly. Instead, I searched for Greg on campus and then ignored him or, if I felt brave, talked about plants. This was no time for frivolity: In L.A. people were rioting, burning stores; in New York, my grandmother was hurrying to finish her eighteenth mystery novel before dying; and in our room, Emily's sorrow shot up, tall, narrow, and awkward as a palm tree. But still, I had plans for him. After all, the outdoors were mine and, in my hopeful heart, the outdoorsy guy as well.

I'd been asleep for a while when Emily returned. First I heard her giggling in the hall, then she slammed the door behind her.

The next day, Emily and I walked at noon to the campus store. She'd said yes to gummi fish. She'd said no to lunch. All the way across the lawn she was telling me what she hated. Apparently she hated a lot. Her stupid classes, for one. How tired she was. She was so amazingly tired. This was obvious; her voice dragged and stalled, like a screen door on a foggy day, squeaking open, inching closed. She hated the stupid people at this school. The guys looked at her as tragic. The teachers treated her delicately. But she also hated how some people ignored it. How they blithely talked about their mothers. Like she wanted to hear about their mothers.

Before we reached the store, a guy from Emily's English class came scurrying up the hill, laden down like a hermit crab with the paraphernalia of a poet: an army satchel presumably chockfull of verse on one shoulder, a hat, an oversize suede jacket. All of him coffee-stained, but his face was lavish, dark featured and eyelashed like a girl's. He needed to talk to Emily about some poem he'd written. Only she would understand it.

Me? Smiling. She touched her curl. She looked radiant. *Sure, I'd love to.* For one flushed second, I hated her. Then I stopped myself.

Over the past ten years, this memory has calcified, so it's almost all I have from that time. I know that she started to be mean to me, to say sarcastic, cutting things, but I can't recite them. I know that she seemed angry at me for having so many things to do, but I can't describe how she showed this. I remember only the sense of failing at my job and not knowing why. I remember only that there were two Emilys. There was the drowning one, who turned to me, and there was the illuminated one, who everyone else saw.

This made me furious, but I turned the fury on myself, deciding the disparity was my fault. That past Thanksgiving, a few weeks after the funeral, I had sat between my aunt and mother on a sage green couch in my grandmother's elegant brownstone on the Upper West Side. I'd rarely felt so safe as then, sitting between these women. The aunt was a psychiatrist, and she was talking to me—in that intense, biannually intimate way of my family—about the death of my best friend's mother. She wanted me to know that, in mourning, Emily might come to despise me, not only because I had seen her at her most vulnerable but also because I'd participated in the event that was most hateful to her. So, as Emily walked with the poet to the dining hall, I held on to what my aunt had said, believing Emily shunned me because of my beneficence.

But I began to suspect Emily had another reason: My mom was alive. She was in London, in fact, and I memorized the calling card number and used it daily. She talked to me about concentric circles of grief. I always pictured the surface of a stump after the tree falls. The dead person is in the middle. The people close to the dead person are the first ring. The people close to the people close to the dead person are the second ring. My mother, presumably, was the third ring. The lesson was: We're all in this together.

Perhaps I wanted to join Emily in the center of the stump, because I spent that afternoon, like many others, nervously trying to imagine that I had lost my mother. And I could barely handle it. I didn't want my mother to die.

It's hard to write about this year because I'm embarrassed by it. Not because I couldn't save Emily but because I chose to do so by rushing up next to her, trying on her loss. Because I understood, on some level, that the equanimity of our perfect friendship relied on us having set things in common—like mothers—and I dared to think that I could equalize our experiences. These days I figure that the only way I could have assuaged Emily's sorrow would have been to go dancing with her, to distract her with guys or *90210* or drugs, joining her in the idiocy of grief rather than in its psychology. But to do that would have been to give up my role as the receptacle for her dark moods, really, to give up my role as best friend. I wasn't able to separate enough from her, just as I couldn't separate from my mother. And now I remind myself that this is what she'd been forced to do, and I'm embarrassed again.

In mid-February, I came home and the windows were open and she was listening to music. This wasn't normal. Greg had stopped by to ask me to help him organize an environmental conference. Finding Emily instead, he offered her the job. *We're meeting Thursday,* she said, smiling. *Probably you could help out, too.* I walked out the door.

Sometime the next week, Greg asked her out. Our roommates had helped set it up, and everyone was excited about Emily getting out, having a date. This time, I didn't just leave the room, I left the state, taking the bus to Connecticut for the weekend.

What drove me away was unspeakable: I felt competitive with someone whose mother died. I was jealous of how loss had changed her, making her more attractive, almost foreign. I wondered, was grief black and murky for her, or did she take some pleasure in the fact that men were adoring her and our roommates babying her? I was supposed to be the deep, dark one. Despair was my terrain. I'd believed we were going to get through this together by hunkering down and being sad and feeling things, all sorts of things, flushing them out of us. Then, if there was a party, we would go together, we would perform those public displays of secrecy that make having a best friend so thrilling: *We are self-sufficient, self-empowered women . . .*

God, I was angry. I was so angry I wrote in my journal what a foul person I was. *I am a BAD best friend,* I wrote in large letters across two pages of the book. *I am a*

BAD daughter. I am a BAD girlfriend. None of this was true, of course. I was a very good daughter and a devoted friend and nice enough to my boyfriend across the country. I only *wanted* desperately to feel free enough to be bad, to say: Fuck you, Emily, I need things too.

Of course the date didn't happen. Emily wasn't ready to desire anything. Her charm shone brightly but had an infantile attention span—suddenly, in the middle of a sentence, she'd be nowhere near us—and I'd gone to Connecticut for nothing. Except for this: On the bus ride home through wintered woods, I decided to stop eating.

This seemed very bad indeed. I believed anorexia to be one of the meanest things girls could do to each other. If being thin is a competition, I figured, the anorexics win unfairly. My approach was anthropological. I joked with my women's studies professors about the triteness of college eating disorders and carefully studied the habits of the anorexics in the dining hall. I interviewed them about exercise. They said: Run.

I didn't think it would last. I'd always harbored a strange terror of running. Athleticism was not mine. But it turned out, to my great surprise, that losing weight was a job I could handle.

It's untrustworthy to impose a narrative on something so murky. Why does a girl stop eating? But I'd venture that anorexia was my way out of all the anger I wouldn't admit to. I had been obsessing about Emily. I knew where she was at all times during the day. I knew when she might be alone and whether that might be a problem. I knew what time her classes began, and I knew if she wasn't getting out of bed to make them. This was how I cared for her. But she didn't care for my help.

It was simpler for me to starve myself than to tell Emily how pissed off I was about this. Dieting gave me something easier—and blessedly achievable—to obsess about. One week, instead of making sure she arrived at the dining hall, I searched for plain rice to eat. The next week, I stealthily went running even though I knew she was by herself. And while running I couldn't think so much about how my mother's death would feel right then, on a clear, windy day, with the first crocuses out. I thought: Holy shit, I'm running!

I ran and ran until finally, in late March, Tina turned to me and said, not very nicely: *You're starting to look just like Emily.* It's true. I've never, before or since, looked more like her; I shrunk out of my clothes and started wearing hers. But by then our equanimity was off, our friendship staggering like a drunk.

One night around that time, I was sitting in the college coffee shop with Greg, waiting for Emily to come plan the ecology conference. For fifteen lovely minutes I talked to him alone. I knew exactly where she was: listless with the covers up. For months I'd waited for her to get out of bed, and now I wanted her to stay there. Twenty minutes passed. Twenty-five. In came Emily, her hair perfect, her lateness excused by the sight of her.

By Emily's birthday, April 19, I'd lost twenty pounds. I promised her we'd do something exquisite. But then Greg asked me to go to a diner along the highway on the night of her birthday, and I told her, vaguely, that something had come up.

I remember listening to a sort of sexy song about a girl kissing a girl as I got dressed. I remember wearing Emily's smallest pants with my Doc Martens. She went to New York City for the night, and the next day I compensated by hosting a picnic on the lawn. It was a lofty spring day, pastel blooms everywhere. I felt the sweet breeze and considered that I'd cheated on my best friend.

If I had to find the moment I stopped trying to understand Emily, it would be this: Two weeks after that first date, I'd returned from my grandmother's funeral late in the evening, and I sat on the wet grass outside our dorm considering Emily and the other girls inside. Then I stood and walked to Greg's room and woke him up. *Take off your dress,* he told me, and I did. I was skinny and kissing Greg, who was huge. My body had nothing to do with Emily's body. It had to do with his body.

For most of my life I've had a rather remarkable memory for the unimportant detail. I would shock my friends by recalling what I wore on the first day of school from kindergarten to senior year. I would list off my activities for a series of fifteen Saturdays. I've recently realized that this was just an insomniac's party trick; I'd been memorizing these mundanities as I lay awake. But in any case, I've never cultivated such near-perfect recall as during the first days of dating Greg. For years I told myself the bedtime story of everything that happened those six weeks before summer. So it's extraordinary that I can't remember how Emily entered this time. I can't remember ever talking to her about my relationship. I've tried over and over again, and I can't.

Mostly I remember this: I was happy. I was so fucking happy.

It felt corrupt to be thrilled when Emily wasn't, as if I'd won this happiness at the fair and she'd lost it. My logic—the reasoning of my entire life then—was that it was cruel to be happier. That if something pleased me, it displeased someone else, and there went the friendship. That's why I don't remember spending time with Emily during those weeks. I wouldn't expose my happiness to her. I was hiding.

Why did I guiltily assume that, by dating a cute guy and being thin, I hurt her any more than she was already hurting? As I figure it, I learned some of this from my parents, who suggest that another person's joy can be so sharp it cuts you. Recently, my sister had a baby, and at a celebratory dinner that evening, my father asked if it was hard for me, being babyless and all, as if only one baby exists and she got it. There's something touching about this: the rotten side of each of us—our jealousies and hurts—was always attended to. But it generates a sense of scarcity. And this scarcity made me scared to want something and terrified when someone wanted what I had. (Thus my decision that there was only enough thinness, Nicaragua, joy, Marxism, or blue for one friend.)

It's false, of course. There *is* more than one baby or beauty or boyfriend. There's even, despite its exclusionary title, more than one best friend. The world is crowded and we are easily distracted. But in one crucial respect, this schema is true: There are simply not enough mothers to go around. This is what I learned when her mother died and Emily became furious. It confirmed what I'd been taught, and that frightened me. I worried that having a mother would become my weapon; it could wound. Wanting to give up something in exchange, I made everything scarce. I shrunk the world.

I am not a quick learner, so when, at the end of junior year, my mother was diagnosed with breast cancer, I did it again. I decided to move home and drive her here and there, joining her suffering and compensating for my health. Once again I was surprised when I was miserable. *I should be happy,* I wrote in my journal. *I have all this free time at home! I should learn something. Guitar lessons? Pottery classes? I* should *start my thesis.* I don't remember Emily calling or writing.

My mother lived, and in the years since her illness, I've been able to do all sorts of things with her. I stopped relying on her for reassurance. I started talking about writing with her. I watched her age. I worried about her. I've changed the rules of our friendship so many times she's dizzy. Emily hasn't done any of this with her mother. Unlike me, she didn't call her mom when beginning this essay to ask what she remembered. My mother said: *Honestly, it was disturbing, that fall after her mother died, when you called me so much and that poor girl had nothing.*

There is a dearth of mothers. It's the immovable fact of our friendship and of this essay. I tried to shift the balance, feeling bad for having things, giving up things I wanted, but it didn't work. I hate that helplessness.

The end of the story is quick. I spent the fall in Bogotá; she studied in Ireland in the spring. We met once, at New Year's in Ohio, smoking a cigarette out her attic window and kissing at midnight. It was a relief, both the day together and the year apart. We did share a house during senior year, along with three other girls, but we didn't have much of a friendship. Frankly, I don't know which it was: either she was elusive and unknowable, or I felt that to really know her would be to relinquish the happiness I'd scrounged. I'd feel guilty when she complained, angry when she was caustic after my mother's chemo ended. Then suddenly she would be delightful, and I grew tired of watching out for her moods.

I already had a new best friend. Luckily, I never competed with her like I did with Emily. But neither did I ever mistake her beauty for my own or take such a personal pleasure in her physical presence.

It wasn't like we never talked again; it wasn't that kind of breakup. It was just that sometimes she'd be sitting across from me at dinner, when she made it to dinner, and I'd miss her terribly. I missed my vision of her as buoyant, and I missed her vision of me as brilliant. It was a kind of heartbreak, the kind that makes you wish someone never existed, the kind that is entirely uncharitable. I was—and remain—puzzled by how soon I felt done with being charitable.

Except, I would never really be through caring for Emily. I remember one shining fall day during senior year. Greg, who had graduated, was visiting for the last time before we broke up. He'd just arrived on campus, and we'd barely talked, when Emily walked across the lawn. As she approached, his face lit up. *Hey lovely,* he said. I didn't feel mad or jealous. I just looked at her and thought, Why yes, she's the loveliest. That is hers.

Heather

Emily Chenoweth

My mother was my first best friend. We were each other's great confidantes, advocates, and allies, bound by a deep and sometimes ferocious love.

When my mother was dying, my best friend was Heather. There had been other intimates over the years, but Heather had eclipsed them. When she came to Ohio for my mother's funeral, she sat with me in the first pew—the royalty of the grieving—and held my hand through the eulogy and the hymns. My boyfriend sat somewhere in the back of the church, another indistinguishable mourner. It was November 1991, and Heather and I were nineteen.

I met Heather at Swarthmore College, when we were assigned rooms on the same freshman hall. My first impression of her centered on her hair, which was coppery brown and fell in uncombed but shiny waves almost to her waist. To me, it was a striking style: in the Midwest, girls wore their hair long only until their mothers let them cut, perm, and feather it into lacquered crests. Heather's hair made her look younger, more approachable; she was the kind of girl boys at my high school called a granola.

My father, in between unloading suitcases, was charming the new arrivals: You came from California all by yourself? he asked Heather. Heather smiled brightly: she had. My mother proclaimed her very brave—and her parents, too, she said, for letting her come so far alone. We stood for a moment in Heather's doorway and watched the other students filing past. Someone had set up a stereo already; *Rico Suave* poured into the hall.

Later, after all the families had waved good-bye, I went back to Heather's room, where she sat me down amidst the mess of her unpacking—the space would never fully recover from it—and pulled out a fat photo album. Here was Santa Monica High, she said, and here was the beach; here she was getting ready to go to a party, and there was her boyfriend with the grape boycott sign. She had dozens of friends, and a story for each—that one had joined the cheerleading squad as a joke; this one spent her summers in India; that one wrote passionate editorials for the school newspaper. Like currency, she counted the friends up; they were beloved and she missed them already. Then she told me that her high school best friend and her mother were both named Emily.

She closed the album and turned to face me. "Emilys have always been very important to me," she said.

"Heather" by Emily Chenoweth as appeared in *The Friend Who Got Away.* Reprinted by permission of the author.

I was shy and uncertain; Heather could not have crafted a more gentle invitation to friendship.

In those first days, smitten already, I watched her use this gift of instantaneous and effortless connection. "Oh, I was at the Greek Theatre when Jerry played 'Dark Star,'" she said to a hippie with bells jingling on her wrists. "I took campers all over the Sierra Madre," she might say to a boy wearing hiking boots. To the political, she was an activist; to the athletic, a dancer; to the academic, a straight-A student who'd decided, at the last possible minute, not to go to Harvard.

None of this was disingenuous—she was all those things. She was also the daughter of distinguished professors and the proud progeny of, as she put it, "a long line of atheist intellectual Jews," the girlfriend of Cesar Chavez's godson, and a family friend of Jackson Browne. She had been arrested while protesting at the nuclear testing site in Nevada and had given her name, at the police station, as Mother Jones. She had once cooked dinner with Jerry Garcia.

Meanwhile I'd been playing the violin, getting good grades, and lettering in sports in a shabbily picturesque small town, part of a family that had been blue-collar until a generation ago; I had nothing to compare to her range of experience. Perhaps this is why she offered as our bond the simple fact of my name. But, like me, Heather was also somewhat of an innocent. Neither of us had been allowed to watch TV, or stay out very late, or eat sugar cereal. Our teachers had loved us; our parents had enjoyed the relative ease of our raising. We had not done any real drugs or had any real sex to speak of.

The early weeks of college were marked by shifting alliances; coalitions were made, briefly nurtured, and then abandoned. Who knows exactly why Heather and I stuck? There is only to say that we did, and that we were, for the most part, inseparable from the beginning. Thanks to Heather, I became a vegetarian, hennaed my hair, boycotted Gillette products, bought Birkenstocks, stopped shaving my legs, joined the student environmental group, and spent long afternoons drinking tea at the Women's Center. Thanks to me, Heather drank at a few fraternity parties, occasionally wore lipstick, and began chewing with her mouth closed. Heather and I wore each other's clothes and jewelry; we cowrote a paper on Nicaragua; we fasted for Oxfam. We listened to Edie Brickell and bands with girls in them and the Philadelphia public radio station. When studying bored us, we wrote songs about the Swarthmore boys, and how none of them was handsome enough, and with the casual heartlessness of pretty eighteen-year-olds, we sang our favorites in front of them.

That first semester, we waited for the cold weather and then for the snow, I with a midwesterner's resignation to the months of gray skies, Heather with the voluble anxiety of a Southern Californian: women in L.A., she told me, shake out their minks the minute it drops below sixty. Her parents sent her her first ever winter coat in the mail—we made an appropriately big deal over this green woolen novelty, with its big fur-lined hood—but for the rest of her gear we went to the mall. We lifted sweaters and scarves off their hangers, holding them up: What do you think? Would I wear this? Would you?

By then we had gained the fifteen pounds everyone said we would, and there was only one pair of jeans (Heather's) between us that fit; most mornings involved a decision about who got to wear them. We'll eat better next semester, we promised ourselves.

I left Heather at the sweaters and wandered off to look at shoes. When I came back, bored, unable to find anything and reluctant to spend the money anyway, Heather was still flipping through the racks some fifteen feet away. Because there were mirrors everywhere around us, I saw her, in the yellow fluorescence of the juniors' section, from many angles at once. For one thrilling, vertiginous moment, I stared at her and I thought: What am I doing over there?

That winter, on New Year's Eve, my father walked into the kitchen for coffee and found my mother unconscious on the floor. He called an ambulance but told my younger brother and me that we shouldn't worry, that she had probably fallen and hit her head. At the hospital, before the nurses had even asked my father her name, she had a terrible seizure.

The subsequent MRIs were fuzzy—it was a portable machine—and the phrase "neurological problem" was proffered and repeated in low tones of concern. My mother woke aphasic and confused, which I insisted was a result of the drugs they'd given her to prevent further seizures, the first of which had laid her out on the kitchen tile and the second of which, in the ER, had almost killed her.

In the hospital gift shop, I bought her a little yellow chick; it peeped when squeezed. "Oh," my mother said, "look at the . . ." She turned it over in her hands. "Cat?" she asked me.

She had a biopsy when I was back at Swarthmore: it was an astrocytoma. Named for the star-shaped glial cells from which it grows, the astrocytoma is one of the most common types of brain tumors. Some are operable. My mother's was not.

Heather's empathy was immediate and genuine. She vowed to take care of me, and in those early months of my mother's illness, I still knew how to be grateful.

Had my mother remained healthy, I still might have lost my energy for activism—in protesting and do-gooding. My social conscience was not, by nature or nurture, highly developed, and I'd done what I could to encourage it. But after her diagnosis I abandoned all interest, except what remained as a guilt-inflected afterimage. Heather, on the other hand, had grown up playing games about world peace—of course she retained her commitment.

In February 1991, a few weeks after the United States invaded Iraq for the first time, Heather and some older students from the Swarthmore Political Action Committee decided that they should hang antiwar banners on the I-95 overpasses. Since this was illegal, they were going to do it at night—the night, as it happened, of a big college dance. My date, with whom I'd been set up, was ardent and eager, and because I did not return his affections I wanted Heather to grab a boy and come with us. I knew I ought to protest too—if not to express my outrage and fear then at least to preserve some of Heather's regard—but I couldn't summon either the decisiveness or the desire. I thought that the other students, whom I held in some thrall for their righteous passions and senior status, would be able to see right through the PEACE NOW T-shirt to the provincial moderate I feared I was. And anyway, there was a *chance* I'd have fun dancing.

When I saw that Heather wouldn't be swayed, I half hoped that she would encourage me to come along. But she was focused on the protest—not my participation in it—and her impatience was clear. "Why don't you just borrow my dress?" she said.

I knew which one she meant. It was a steely blue velvet minidress with a shirred empire waist, and I had long coveted it. "Thanks," I said. I opened her closet with a mixture of shame and relief.

When Heather left in someone's car, I put the dress on and admired myself in the mirror; I'd gotten thin again since my mother's diagnosis. I'd started borrowing a different pair of Heather's jeans—ripped, faded Levi's—which only I could fit into. (Before she became too impaired to kid around, my mother used to say, "Cancer— it's a great way to lose weight.")

Then I went and drank half a bottle of Southern Comfort with a girl from Tampa Bay. In a dining hall transformed by strobe lights and a rented sound system, I left my bewildered date standing on the dance floor as I ran outside and ducked into the bushes, where, weeping with humiliation, I threw up everything.

The night was clear and cold. Couples streamed in and out of the dance; the pale clouds of my breath formed and then vanished. I wiped my eyes and looked down— I'd vomited all over the snow and my shoes, all over the beautiful velvet and shiny lacquer buttons of Heather's perfect dress.

Spring came with a profusion of flowers. Magnolias blossomed all over campus, blood-red tulips bloomed outside the library, and the stately oaks that lined the path to the main administration building waved their green fingers. On the Beach, a soft, sloping lawn bordered by daffodils, students lay about and sunbathed, the adventurous girls topless. Someone was always playing music out a nearby dorm window, and we were young enough to still be moved: Van Morrison wanted to rock our Gypsy souls.

Heather and I sat with friends on the Beach to relax but took our tanning down to Swarthmore's little slice of woods, where on the edge of the forest, small-breasted and modest, we sunned in our bras. We put flowers in our hair and took pictures; in them we are wild-haired and smiling.

When I talked to my mother on the phone, there were long silences in which she groped for words. In the notes she sent me, her handwriting was uncertain, childish. P's became B's, and Z's were C's. The tumor was growing, branching out, but no one told her. This was a kindness—she truly didn't want to know. Probably I didn't want to know either, and for a while, I didn't. I wrote her back: "Hey, Mom, how are the radiation and chemo things treating you? Are you having any fun?" Really I wrote that.

Heather accepted the rhythm of my moods; she was giddy with me when I wanted to forget and sympathetic when I couldn't. Her responsiveness stood in marked contrast to that of others I confided in. A college administrator whose daughter had died of a brain tumor sat me down in his office and told me to quit wasting my emotional reserves. "Don't let yourself feel too bad right now," he said. "You have no idea the shit you're in for." When I went to the school counselor, she blew her nose throughout the session—she had a wet, nasty cold—and rolled her eyes at most of what I said. Only when it came time to book my next appointment did she show any sign of human warmth: Next Tuesday then, she said with a thin, wan smile. These people are supposed to make me feel better? I asked Heather one day at lunch.

That night she begged the keys to someone's car. She put me behind the wheel (she didn't have her driver's license), turned on the radio, and pointed me toward town: we went to McDonald's and CVS, and maybe an ice cream shop or a grocery store, and we stuffed ourselves senseless on french fries and Milky Ways and mint chocolate chip. We laughed because we were such disgusting pigs and because Heather had gotten food in her hair again. Drowning out the radio, we sang along to R.E.M.'s "Shiny Happy People." With Heather, I could remember what it was like to be happy.

In May, after classes ended, she came to Ohio to visit. I know this not because I recall the week itself but because my mother made a sign for her. She used colored pencils for the script; with a marker she drew three blue, wobbly hearts. "Welcome Home (ours is yours)," it said. "We're glad you're here Heather + Emily. Welcome Welcom. Be 'combel.'" She meant "comfortable."

I didn't want to go back to school sophomore year. The only consolation was that I was living with Heather. We'd gotten a suite with two D.C. girls, Tina and Molly—friends Heather had made for us—while Rebecca and Sasha, with whom we'd also become close, had found rooms down the hall. Flush with the excitement of co-ownership, Heather and I went to South Street and got pretty postcards and a Maxfield Parrish poster to pin up. We bought incense, and a red vase for flowers. Back in our room, we pushed three single beds together to make a giant, creaky raft. We slept on the outer two while the middle one accumulated papers, books, shirts, and socks—a precarious heap that we whispered over at night beneath the high ceilings, with the lights from the parking lot shining down on us.

Heather had a wonderful laugh, silly and infectious; it was one of the many things that drew people to her. She couldn't take a class without bonding with someone in it, couldn't join a group without stealing someone away to have dinner. She chummed around with a Colombian girl from New York City, a pretty military brat she'd met in the environmentalists' organization, a blond sophomore who was questioning her sexuality. In working on a video project for one of her courses, she became fast friends with not only the other students but the young and exotically hip professor.

I couldn't understand this at all. The way I saw it, I'd made my choice in the first few days of college; I was happy to know and love other people, but at some level, Heather would have been enough. And I was afraid—now that I spent so many of my days tearful and furious—that one of the new friends would replace me.

What distinguished me from these other girls, besides the fact that I was first, I wondered. I could not pretend to be as worldly or ambitious or comparatively untroubled as surely they were. College meant almost nothing to me then—my mother was *dying,* who cared about recycling, or sexism, or Literature of Conscience? I was convinced that every single connection Heather made cheapened the one she had made with me.

There is nothing more primitive and ordinary than the mating instinct, no easier social transaction than one of desire. I went a little boy crazy: I made lists of the ones who liked me; I dissected significant glances; I parsed casual conversations into snippets of promise. These activities passed beyond minor distractions into a carefully nurtured project to help me avoid thoughts of my mother's heartbreaking decline. I encouraged the affections of a poet and a lacrosse player; I went to parties. There, through a superficial smiling prettiness, an ability to charm and be charming, I felt relief.

One night at a party there were two boys circling, moving in and out of my orbit. Heather sighed volubly. "This is getting boring," she said. Maybe she found flirting hard, or a waste of time, or maybe she wondered why I wasn't thinking of my boyfriend in Chicago. But more likely I think she couldn't understand why, when I had so few moments of vivacity, I would waste them in banter, in guile.

The answer was simple, if impossible, then, to explain. I could feel her sliding away from me—to a new year, a new leaf, and new, happier friends—and I could not see how to prevent it. In the neat equation of our gleeful early friendship, what we needed from each other, what we gave and got in return, had been, it seemed, precisely balanced. But that had changed with my grief: the companionship, the sympathy, the energy and affection that I demanded were far greater in quantity than what I was able to give back. In every interaction with Heather, I felt my own insufficiency.

With the boys, though, the reckoning was elementary. "I think of you/and your eyes of a saint," the poet wrote. The lacrosse player was blond and wholesome, a good son; he planned to become a doctor. The inarticulate ache and resentment I felt around Heather vanished when I was with one of them. They didn't need me either, necessarily, but they thought they did, and that was something.

When I went home in October to be with my mother in her final weeks, Heather called me almost every day, and it seemed then that our friendship had regained its original force. For her to call that often was harder than it sounds: Swarthmore had been founded by Quakers, and due to the peculiar but egalitarian logic of the Friends, there weren't phones in dorm rooms since not all students could afford to make long-distance calls. So Heather had to find a pay phone in the library, or wait in line for one in a dorm hallway.

My mother lay in a hospital bed in what had been my brother's bedroom. She couldn't communicate anymore, but sometimes when we moved her to change her sheets, she cried out *Hail Mary, Mother of God.* The neighbors brought us soups and casseroles, and I was cruel to them: I snatched the dishes from their hands and shut the doors in their faces. I had a strange twitching in my eye.

Heather was the only person I wanted to talk to, and talking to her was pretty much the only time I didn't wish that I were dying instead, or also.

She skipped classes to fly to Ohio for my mother's service. When I couldn't seem to fix my hair that morning—the problem to which I clung to avoid the unspeakable other—she told me I looked beautiful. I wore my mother's too-large dress; it was navy blue with a white lace collar. An old family friend reached for me, weeping. "You look exactly like her," she cried.

Maybe Heather went to the florist with me to buy the funeral flowers, a giant bouquet; of freesia and delphinium. Maybe my father told her to take care of me, and maybe she had to tell me to eat. She may have stood beside me in the receiving line, greeting a church full of people she had never seen before. Who knows, in our blind grief, how much we asked of her?

Afterward, at my house, Heather and I sat together on the living room couch (my boyfriend had been kissed at the church and then banished) while my aunts and uncles and all the friends of my parents wandered from room to room, holding drinks and plates of cold cuts. There were flowers perfuming every corner; on the mantel leaned a giant photograph of my smiling mother. People came together in mournful knots, lingered, and then moved on. I knew what they were thinking: We're so young still, we barely have gray hair—how could we be dying?

Margot, my mother's cousin from Palo Alto, sat down next to us, smoothed her silky blouse, and introduced herself. Heather's social graces held; Hey, I'm from California too, she said. Margot and Heather traded West Coast moments, and then Margot told us a little about the yoga book she'd written, and the lifestyle consultant who'd advised her to wear only loose, flowing fabrics.

Then she told us that she went to an eminent palmist—$150 a reading, she said, and he's so good he'll only reveal what he knows you can bear to hear—and that in her many sessions, she had learned how to read palms too.

Margot took Heather's hand first, and then mine. She was earnest and careful. Amidst the swirl of the extended family, she ran her fingers over our palms, reading our characters. She told Heather that she was creative and strong-willed; she told me that I was ambitious, and had unreasonably high expectations of myself. She said that we ought to look at the shapes of our thumb pads—the ideal shape, she said, was full and rounded, and it signified joy and self-actualization. We didn't have thumbs like this, but Margot assured us that we could work toward them. Heather and I privately doubted, but everything else Margot said felt precisely and uncannily true, as if the secrets to our temperaments were written in script on the pink of our skin.

Then, because she had to go back to her hotel, Margot summed everything up. "You," she said to Heather, "were put on this world to use your voice."

That was perfect, I thought—with her intelligence, her drive, and her fierce dedication to social justice, Heather was going to change the world. What, then, would Margot say to me? What bright promise did my future hold?

"You," she said, her voice quieter now, and sugared with sympathy, "were put on this earth to work on relationships."

The loss of hope brings a whole new and terrible mourning. Even in those final weeks before my mother died, I could still—barely, but still—imagine a happy ending, a miracle. But back at school the following semester, there was no more pretending that my life was not forever changed. I missed my mother with a wordless and wild desperation. Like an infant, I slept, ate, cried, and slept again.

Heather tried to get me out of bed—for weeks. I don't remember this, but I have the evidence: on a Xeroxed page from a Dr. Seuss book ("Look at me, look at me, look at me NOW! It is fun to have fun BUT you have to know how"), Heather wrote: "This is a note to try and fill your mailbox and let you know that even during my most intense moments of study in the library I am thinking only of you. Love your long-lost roommate and spiritual adviser, H."

I considered how hard she worked for her classes; I counted up all her other smiling friends. Thinking only of me? Impossible, I thought. A nice thing to write—but unquestionably a lie.

Tina found out that her father had HIV that spring. Molly's relationship with her boyfriend had become complicated and unhappy, and she was also, though I didn't know it then, struggling with memories of past sexual abuse. When the four of us ate together in the dining hall, we helped ourselves to tiny portions of salad dressed only with balsamic vinegar and looked suspiciously at one another's trays. In the evenings the air in our suite crackled with tension. Throughout these weeks, nothing knocked me from my carefully guarded reign as the queen of sorrow. All of this was bad news, okay? but it wasn't like anyone else was dead yet.

And when someone did die, still I defended my position. Heather's grandmother, with whom she was close, passed away in April of that year. She had been a mystery novelist, and the *New York Times* had run an obituary. That was a big deal, Heather told me, because it was a validation of her career. I remember looking at Heather—it was sunny outside, and we were in our bedroom—and wondering why she was telling me this. My mother's death was horrible, but her grandmother's death was newsworthy—was that what she was trying to say?

"And before she died," Heather said, "she dictated the last chapter of her book to my aunt from her hospital bed."

I thought of my mother, and of how by the end, sight, movement, speech, understanding—*everything*—had been taken away from her. Dying elderly and sharp-witted? That seemed like a luxury.

One afternoon that spring Heather and I walked into town and bought a pint of Ben & Jerry's, which we took to a bench alongside the field that lay between our dorm and the main campus. The forsythia bushes had exploded into a riot of yellow blossoms, and though we were miles from water, seagulls dotted the grass, calling to one another in their shrill, hard voices. To a passerby, we would have made a lovely picture—two coeds leaning over a tub of ice cream as the girls' soccer team jogged onto the field, sending the birds wheeling away into the sky.

It had been a while since we'd spent any time alone together, and I was tense and nervous, but hopeful. We would bond, I thought—we could laugh and gossip and it would feel a little like freshman year again. At some point, after we'd sat there for a while, I noticed that I was the only one eating the ice cream. Heather made small, random stabs at it with her plastic spoon but barely took any.

"Eat more," I told her. She demurred; she wasn't hungry.

One doesn't eat ice cream because one is hungry, I thought. One eats ice cream because it is ice cream and it is delicious.

I pressed her; she shook her head and looked away. In front of us, the girls passed soccer balls back and forth, kicking them low across the field and then in high arcs through the air. But this was Heather's idea, I thought. This hour—this shared indulgence—was supposed to bring us together, or at least a few halting steps closer.

I did not then think longingly of our past—of how we used to have such an appetite for everything, be it food or talk or indignation at what we saw as an inequitable society. Nor did I think of this moment as more evidence of Heather's eating disorder, which on some level I knew she had developed. Every girl starved or gagged herself at one point or another in college, didn't she? Eating was what we controlled when we thought we couldn't control anything else—it just seemed so tiresome. All I could think about then was how angry I was at her. I just wanted to her to do this one small thing with me, eat this ice cream, and she couldn't, or wouldn't, do it.

The truth was that Heather and I hardly knew what to do with each other anymore. We had both grown snappish—though I was worse. When, in the mornings, Heather turned on public radio, I demanded to know why we couldn't have a little silence for once. When she rewound a tape in my stereo without pressing the Stop button first, I yelled that she was going to break the machine. Sometimes when she wanted to use my computer, I lied and told her that I just getting ready to use it myself.

Heather began to avoid me and started palling around with other girls in the dorm. At some point that semester, the decision was made to pull our beds apart.

As the weather got warmer, Heather was around less and less—"I'm out enjoying the spring," she would say, and it wasn't until later that I found out why. His name was Greg.

I, along with most of the other Swarthmore girls, had taken note of Greg that fall, when he returned, after a year off, to join the junior class. It was impossible not to notice him: he was an extraordinary physical specimen. He had brown, slightly unkempt hair and blue, blue eyes; it seemed possible that he might, at any moment, climb up and then rappel down something.

He was in my ecology class spring semester. I was too shy to talk to him, but sometimes, in the computer lab, we found ourselves sitting near each other, working on the same assignment. Hey, he might drawl, smiling—he always smiled—did you figure out that problem yet?

The problem was why the species of trees on one side of a small hill were so markedly different from the species on the other side. What explained it: sunlight? drainage? cultivation? I thought about it, though not very hard, and when I got a D on the paper, I called the dean and had her withdraw me from the class.

"We're both heavenly bodies," began the note Greg sent me in campus mail. What else it said I don't remember, only that it culminated in a question: Would I like to go out sometime?

I would, but it wasn't to be. When I couldn't go to the dance he'd asked me to, he went alone; there he met someone named Peggy and started dating her. I was sorely disappointed, but Heather was blasé, philosophical: Boys are stupid, she said.

Heather and Greg's first date took place a few months later, not long after Greg and Peggy's breakup. I don't remember hearing about it, or about their subsequent courtship. I only remember the night I found them together.

It was late at night, and I was alone in my room, working on a paper about the Gospel of John and drinking instant coffee brewed with Folgers crystals and warm water from the sink. At some point, I got up to go to the bathroom, which was through Tina and Molly's bedroom. I opened their door; a thin sliver of light from my desk lamp pushed feebly against the dark. I took a few steps, and then I froze; there were people in the room. I couldn't see them, but I heard the sheets rustle, caught the faint sibilance of their whispers.

The air was warm and close and humid. My body felt giant to me, immovable, and for a moment I didn't breathe. When I did, the thing that tightened my throat, the thing that buckled my knees, was the dusky, faintly rank smell of sex.

The hurt I felt then came not from the knowledge that it was Heather and Greg. It came, instead, from a sudden, flinty understanding of my own ignorance. A year ago, Heather would have told me everything about her relationship with Greg. I would have known what it felt like to kiss him, and the ways in which he professed his affections, and how much she thought about him. I would have known *this night* was going to happen—but now I was left to stumble on it, like a trespasser.

No one spoke in that room. I simply turned around, closed the door behind me, and went to the public bathrooms down the hall.

For the few weeks that remained of sophomore year, Heather and I circled each other as warily as cats. The following year we were going abroad in different semesters; we wouldn't be together at college again until we were seniors.

In deference to all we'd been through, we still called ourselves friends. But the world, for me, had shifted on its axis; I could no more be a part of Heather's active, engaged college life than she could be a part of my despair. We talked on the phone that summer, and we sent the occasional letter; we made promises to visit each other that we didn't keep. We had had that first semester—five perfect months—and then a year and a half of struggle. For a long time after that, my love for Heather was a piece of glass in my heart; it hurt every time I moved.

Against Ordinary Language: The Language of the Body

Kathy Acker

Preface Diary

I have now been bodybuilding for ten years, seriously for almost five years.

During the past few years, I have been trying to write about bodybuilding.

Having failed time and time again, upon being offered the opportunity to write this essay, I made the following plan: I would attend the gym as usual. Immediately after each workout, I would describe all I had just experienced, thought, and done. Such diary descriptions would provide the raw material.

After each workout, I forgot to write. Repeatedly. I . . . some part of me . . . the part of the "I" who bodybuilds . . . was rejecting language, any verbal description of the processes of bodybuilding.

I shall begin describing, writing about bodybuilding in the only way that I can: I shall begin by analyzing this rejection of ordinary or verbal language. What is the picture of the antagonism between bodybuilding and verbal language?

A Language Which is Speechless

Imagine that you are in a foreign country. Since you are going to be in this place for some time, you are trying to learn the language. At the point of commencing to learn the new language, just before having started to understand anything, you begin forgetting your own. Within strangeness, you find yourself without a language.

It is here, in this geography of no language, this negative space, that I can start to describe bodybuilding. For I am describing that which rejects language.

Elias Canetti, who grew up within a multitude of spoken languages, began his autobiography by recounting a memory. In this, his earliest remembrance, the loss of language is threatened: "My earliest memory is dipped in red. I come out of a door on the arm of a maid, the door in front of me is red, and to the left a staircase goes down, equally red . . ." A smiling man walks up to the child; the child, upon request, sticks out his tongue whereupon the man flips open a jackknife and holds the sharp blade against the red tongue.

"Against Ordinary Language: The Language of the Body," by Kathy Acker in *The Last Sex: feminism and outlaw bodies*, Arthur and Marilouise Kroker, editors, Palgrave Macmillan, 1993. Reprinted with permission of Palgrave Macmillan.

". . . He says: 'Now we'll cut off his tongue.'"

At the last moment, the man pulls the knife back.

According to memory, this sequence happens every day. "That's how the day starts," Canetti adds, "and it happens very often."[1]

I am in the gym every three of four days. What happens there? What does language in that place look like?

According to cliché, athletes are stupid. Meaning: they are inarticulate. The spoken language of bodybuilders makes this cliché real. The verbal language in the gym is minimal and almost senseless, reduced to numbers and a few nouns. "Sets," "squats," "reps" . . . The only verbs are "do" or "fail," adjectives and adverbs no longer exist; sentences, if they are at all, are simple.

This spoken language is kin to the "language games" Wittgenstein proposes in his *The Brown Book*.[2]

In a gym, verbal language or language whose purpose is meaning occurs, if at all, only at the edge of its becoming lost.

But when I am in the gym, my experience is that I am immersed in a complex and rich world.

What actually takes place when I bodybuild?

The crossing of the threshold from the world defined by verbal language into the gym in which the outside world is not allowed (and all of its languages) (in this sense, the gym is sacred) takes several minutes. What happens during these minutes is that I forget. Masses of swirling thought, verbalized insofar as I am conscious of them, disappear as mind or thought begins to focus.

In order to analyze this focusing, I must first describe bodybuilding in terms of intentionality.

Bodybuilding is a process, perhaps a sport, by which a person shapes her or his own body. This shaping is always related to the growth of muscular mass.

During aerobic and circuit training, the heart and lungs are exercised. But muscles will grow only if they are not exercised or moved, but actually broken down. The general law behind bodybuilding is that muscle, if broken down in a controlled fashion and then provided with the proper growth factors such as nutrients and rest, will grow back larger than before.

In order to break down specific areas of muscles, whatever areas one wants to enlarge, it is necessary to work these areas in isolation up to failure.

Bodybuilding can be seen to be about nothing but *failure*. A bodybuilder is always working around failure. Either I work an isolated muscle mass, for instance one of the tricep heads, up to failure. In order to do this, I exert the muscle group almost until the point that it can no longer move.

But if I work the same muscle group to the point that it can no longer move, I must move it through failure. I am then doing what are named "negative reps," working the muscle group beyond its power to move. Here is the second method of working with failure.

Whatever way I choose, I always want to work my muscle, muscular group, until it can no longer move: I want to fail. As soon as I can accomplish a certain task, so much weight for so many reps during a certain time span, I must always increase one aspect of this equation, weights reps or intensity, so that I can again come to failure.

I want to break muscle so that it can grow back larger, but I do not want to destroy muscle so that growth is prevented. In order to avoid injury, I first warm up the muscular group, then carefully bring it up to failure. I do this by working the muscular group through a calculated number of sets during a calculated time span. If I tried immediately to bring a muscle group up to failure by lifting the heaviest weight I could handle, I might injure myself.

I want to shock my body into growth; I do not want to hurt it.

Therefore, in bodybuilding, *failure* is always connected to counting. I calculate which weight to use; I then count off how many times I lift that weight and the seconds between each lift. This is how I control the intensity of my workout.

Intensity times movement of maximum weight equals muscular destructions (muscular growth).

Is the equation between destruction and growth also a formula for art?

Bodybuilding is about failure because bodybuilding, body growth and shaping, occurs in the face of the material, of the body's inexorable movement toward its final failure, toward death.

To break down a muscle group, I want to make that group work up to, even beyond, capacity. To do this, it helps and even is necessary to visualize the part of the body that is involved. Mind or thought, then, while bodybuilding, is always focused on number or counting and often on precise visualizations.

Certain bodybuilders have said that bodybuilding is a form of meditation.

What do I do when I bodybuild? I visualize and I count. I estimate weight; I count sets; I count repetitions; I count seconds between repetitions; I count time, seconds or minutes, between sets: From the beginning to the end of each workout, in order to maintain intensity, I must continually count.

For this reason, a bodybuilder's language is reduced to a minimal, even a closed, set of nouns and to numerical repetition, to one of the simplest of language games.

Let us name this language game, *the language of the body*.

The Richness of the Language of the Body

In order to examine such a language, a language game which resists ordinary language, through the lens of ordinary language or language whose tendency is to generate syntax or to make meanings proliferate, I must use an indirect route.

In another of his books, Elias Canetti begins talking from and about that geography that is without verbal language:

> *A marvelously luminous, viscid substance is left behind in me, defying words . . .*
> *A dream: a man who unlearns the world's languages until nowhere on earth does he understand what people are saying.*[3]

Being in Marrakesh is Canetti's dream made actual. There are languages here, he says, but I understand none of them. The closer I am moving towards foreignness, into strangeness, toward understanding foreignness and strangeness, the more I am losing my own language. The small loss of language occurs when I journey to and into my own body. Is my body a foreign land to me? What is this picture of "my body" and "I"? For years, I said in the beginning of this essay, I have wanted to describe bodybuilding; whenever I tried to do so, ordinary language fled from me.

"Man," Heidegger says, "is the strangest."[4] Why? Because everywhere he or she belongs to being or to strangeness or chaos, and yet everywhere he or she attempts to carve a path through chaos:

> *Everywhere man makes himself a path; he ventures into all realms of the essent, of the overpowering power, and in so doing he is flung out of all paths.*[5]

The physical or material, that which is, is constantly and unpredictably changing: it is chaotic. This chaos twines around death. For it is death that rejects all of our paths, all of our meanings.

Whenever anyone bodybuilds, he or she is always trying to understand and control the physical in the face of this death. No wonder bodybuilding is centered around failure.

The antithesis between meaning and essence has often been noted. Wittgenstein at the end of the *Tractatus:*

> *The sense of the world must lie outside the world. In the world everything is as it is, and everything happens as it does happen—in it no values exist, and if they did, they'd have no value. For all that happens and is the case is accidental.*[6]

If ordinary language or meanings lie outside essence, what is the position of that language game which I have named *the language of the body?* For bodybuilding (a language of the body) rejects ordinary language and yet itself constitutes a language, a method for understanding and controlling the physical which in this case is also the self.

I can now directly talk about bodybuilding. (As if speech is ever direct.)

The language game named *the language of the body* is not arbitrary. When a bodybuilder is counting, he or she is counting his or her own breath.

Canetti speaks of the beggars of Marrakesh who possess a similar and even simpler language game: they repeat the name of God.

In ordinary language, meaning is contextual. Whereas the cry of the beggar means nothing other than what it is; in the city of the beggar, the impossible (as the Wittgenstein of the *Tractatus* and Heidegger see it) occurs in that meaning and breath become one.

Here is the language of the body; here, perhaps, is the reason why bodybuilders experience bodybuilding as a form of meditation.

"I understood the seduction there is in a life that reduces everything to the simplest kind of repetition,"[7] Canetti says. A life in which meaning and essence no longer oppose each other. A life of meditation.

"I understood what those blind beggars really are: the saints of repetition . . ."[8]

The Repetition of the One: The Glimpse Into Chaos or Essence

I am in the gym. I am beginning to work out. I either say the name "bench press," then walk over to it, or simply walk over to it. Then, I might picture the number of my first weight; I probably, since I usually begin with the same warm-up weight, just place the appropriate weights on the bar. Lifting this bar off its rests, then down to my lower chest, I count "1." I am visualizing this bar, making sure it touches my chest at the right spot, placing it back on its rests. "2." I repeat the same exact motions. "3." . . . After twelve repetitions, I count off thirty seconds while increasing my weights. "1." . . . The identical process begins again only this time I finish at "10." . . . All these repetitions end only when I finish my workout.

On counting: Each number equals one inhalation and one exhalation. If I stop my counting or in any other way lose focus, I risk dropping or otherwise mishandling a weight and so damaging my body.

In this world of the continual repetition of a minimal number of elements, in this aural labyrinth, it is easy to lose one's way. When all is repetition rather than the production of meaning, every path resembles every other path.

Every day, in the gym, I repeat the same controlled gestures with the same weights, the same reps, . . . the same breath patterns. But now and then, wandering within the labyrinths of my body, I come upon something. Something I can know because knowledge depends on difference. An unexpected event. For though I am only repeating certain gestures during certain time spans, my body, being material, is never the same; my body is controlled by change and by chance.

For instance, yesterday, I worked chest. Usually I easily benchpress the bar plus sixty pounds for six reps. Yesterday, unexpectedly, I barely managed to lift this weight at the sixth rep. I looked for a reason. Sleep? Diet? Both were usual. Emotional or work stress? No more than usual. The weather? Not good enough. My unexpected failure at the sixth rep was allowing me to see, as if through a window, not to any outside, but inside my own body, to its workings. I was being permitted to glimpse the laws that control my body, those of change or chance, laws that are barely, if at all, knowable.

By trying to control, to shape, my body through the calculated tools and methods of bodybuilding, and time and again, in following these methods, failing to do so, I am able to meet that which cannot be finally controlled and known: the body.

In this meeting lies the fascination, if not the purpose, of bodybuilding. To come face to face with chaos, with my own failure or a form of death.

Canetti describes the architecture of a typical house in the geographical labyrinth of Marrakesh. The house's insides are cool, dark. Few, if any, windows look out into the street. For the entire construction of this house, windows, etc., is directed inward, to the central courtyard where only openness to the sun exists.

Such an architecture is a mirror of the body. When I reduce verbal language to minimal meaning, to repetition, I close the body's outer windows. Meaning approaches breath as I bodybuild, as I begin to move through the body's labyrinths, to meet, if only for a second, that which my consciousness ordinarily cannot see. Heidegger: "The being there of historical man means: to be posited as the breach into which the preponderant power of being bursts in its appearing, in order that this breach itself should shatter against being."[9]

In our culture, we simultaneously fetishize and disdain the athlete, a worker in the body. For we still live under the sign of Descartes. This sign is also the sign of patriarchy. As long as we continue to regard the body, that which is subject to change, chance, and death, as disgusting and inimical, so long shall we continue to regard our own selves as dangerous others.

Notes

[1]Elias Canetti, *The Tongue Set Free*, New York: The Seabury Press, 1979, p. 5.

[2]Here and throughout the rest of this article, whenever I use the phrase "language game," I am referring to Ludwig Wittgenstein's discussion of language games in *The Brown Book*, (Wittgenstein, *The Blue and Brown Books*, New York: Harper and Row, Publishers, 1960).

[3]Elias Canetti, *The Voices of Marrakesh*, New York: The Seabury Press, 1978, p. 23.

[4]Martin Heidegger, *An Introduction to Metaphysics*, New York: Anchor Books, 1961, p. 125. By "man," Heidegger means "human."

[5]Ibid., p. 127.

[6]Ludwig Wittgenstein, *Tractatus Logico Philosphicus*, London: Routledge and Kegan Paul Ltd., 1972, p. 145.

[7]Canetti, *The Voices of Marrakesh*, p. 25.

[8]Ibid., p. 26.

[9]Heidegger, *An Introduction to Metaphysics*, p. 137.

Orchids: Half Sacred, Half Profane

Faith Adiele

[Bangkok's] two most common and appealing sights . . . were its holy men, in spotless saffron robes, and its scarlet ladies. By day, the monks evoked a vision of purity . . . by night, the whole grimy city felt . . . transformed as sequined girls sang the body electric. At least, so I thought, this day-and-night division would ensure that good was good, and evil evil, and never the twain should meet.

—Pico Iyer,
Video Night in Kathmandu

Thailand has over a quarter of a million monks and twice as many prostitutes.

—Rudolph Wurlitzer,
Hard Travel to Sacred Places

Invariably every Asian advertisement serves up a graceful, gracious, smiling, pliable woman, the embodiment of the West's Orientalist desires. Often she is characterized as a flower—the delicate lotus and exotic orchid bending to your will like a green willow or bamboo reed; heady, aromatic jasmine; the slightly titillating cherry blossom you pluck. The images are nearly as powerful as a drug, and it is difficult not to drift into a fantasy of perfumed air, brilliant landscape, bouquets of hothouse flowers. As I ordain, moving out of the West and into the East, I am torn. I want the empowerment of a *maechi* without the subservience of a Thai woman. I want the privileges of Americans without the empty soul. I want beauty without danger. In this landscape, who will I be?

[photo]   Li — Shy as a flower
[photo]   Jiap — Untouched beauty
These girls are not seeking marriage or any similar relationship.

—Phuket Girls Web page

Sacred Lotus

She is lotus. *Nelumbo nucifera.* A distinctive, fragrant water lily associated with the Buddha. She is sacred yet edible (though there is truly nothing sacred about her taste). Stir her bitter rootstocks and leaves into soup, grind her stamens into tea. But her

The walk to the meal is marvelous. Cool, our feet firm, soundless, as we move along the pathway. Blind to all but the spot on the path six feet in front of me, I can feel the beauty. Far below, streams slice the vegetation—tangled greenery ranging from fragile celadon to black pine, from iced orchid to glossy crimson. Long bugs skim water. Suddenly we run into sunshine on the path, the sun still low in the hills. The path glows red-gold, warming our feet.

Our numbers increase: five lay-women in line behind me, even more new *maechi* ahead. I am still less mindful than the others, so move more quickly. This makes me appear lost and without purpose, as if dog-paddling in the air to kill time.

Also, I sleep too much, perhaps a way of avoiding mindfulness.

I notice that the *maechi's* feet in front of me are beautiful. I can just see her heels and a hint of the side when she lifts them up and places them firmly down, arched and turned slightly outward. When she leans forward, poised to take a step, her heel rises gracefully, clean white robes skimming her ankles. When she descends the steps, the robe hovers centimeters above the body, her body! Her flower inspires religious carvings and paintings, lends her name to the most important teaching in Mahayana Buddhism—*Lotus Sutra*. Upon stumbling across a pond, who could fail to be humbled at the sight of her? A cluster of glistening green pads shining atop a pond's mirrored surface, large white-and-rose blossoms unfolding like perfectly sculpted sheaves of wisdom.

She awakes. Don't touch!

When a woman wants to hand a monk something, she kneels on the ground before him and spreads a handkerchief in the space between. She then places the object on the handkerchief so that the monk may retrieve it himself without fear of touching or being touched by her.

Even as a *maechi*, I am not clear about what will happen if a man accidentally touches one of us, that is, where does impurity reside? I learn that we are not allowed to speak more than six words to a man in the absence of another *maechi*: not another monk, not another laywoman—another *maechi*. At a monthly meeting, one *maechi* tells of seeing a crazy man weaving toward her, arms outstretched, and worrying that, not understanding the significance of her robe, he would embrace her. He turned off the path before reaching her, fortunately for her but unfortunately for me, as her story ends and I never find out what would have happened had they collided.

Earlier, while preparing my research project, I had surveyed the scriptures and discourses in both Theravada and Mahayana Buddhism that deal with women, searching for historical and scriptural precedents for female transcendence. Though there was debate over whether women could become Buddhas in female form (without first being reborn as male and ordaining as monks), it was generally accepted that, upon being pressed to ordain women, the Buddha had admitted they were equally capable of living the Life of the Robe and becoming *arahants* (often translated as "saint" or "worthy one," a pure person no longer destined for rebirth).

Just before the day I met Maechi Roongdüan, I had decided that painstaking academic research was not my interest. Women as subjects of study, words on the page, the observer role of the anthropologist, were all losing their allure. To be honest, I was seeking strategies for living, for participating in life.

Prior to my ordination, I was constantly being drawn into debate—at the university, in the marketplace, in *wat*. Thai men and some women were eager to dismiss the spiritual aspirations of women. Their first strategy was to cite scriptural precedent, the Buddha's apparent disinclination to ordain women.

"After achieving enlightenment, He established the order of monks, *bhikkhus,*" my host father announced over toast and eggs sunny-side up. I grimaced at the garish yolk. "It was only after his cousin Ananda pleaded on behalf of women that he agreed—*very reluctantly*"—he stressed, emphasizing with a wave of toast—"to ordain women as *bhikkhuni.*" She Who Has Received Higher Ordination, almswoman, female monk.

I dipped the ball of rice I'd been working into *nam prik ong,* staining it red with the spiced meat, and pointed out that this supposed hesitation (if we could even believe it came from Him and not the generations of monk editors) could have been for any number of reasons. He was an Indian man, after all, living within a particular social and historical context. Perhaps He envisaged problems with the monks, who were supposed to be celibate, or with the laypeople they relied on for donations, who might now lose wives and daughters to the order.

"He also hesitated when first asked to preach." My sticky rice ball waved at his toast. "Should we now question the wisdom of the Dhamma?"

Khun Mae stepped in with a tray of dried and fried things that she'd arranged around a cup of black, pulpy chili paste. "The important thing," she trilled, "is that he *did* ordain women, giving them the exact same title as men, and that his own aunt became the first *bhikkhuni.*"

"But their status was not equal," my host sibling's favorite fried banana vendor later reminded me. "A hundred-year-old *bhikkhuni* was required to bow down before a newly ordained *bhikkhu,* and the conditions of their ordination were very strict."

With a flip of her wrist, she ran a wire ladle through her wok and dumped a mass of crispy fritters into two bags fashioned from her daughter's old homework. "Read the *Bhikkhuni-Patimokkha,* the strictures governing how *bhikkhuni* travel and live!"

I dropped six coins into her palm and handed the bags to Pōng and Nuan-wan, who grinned and crinkled their noses like hamsters. "Oh, the *Patimokkha* is simply proof of the Buddha's concern for the safety of women!" I gave an airy wave, acknowledging both the kids' *wai* of thanks and the vendor's point. "Every rule was established in response to an actual incident, such as the *bhikkhuni* who was raped by a forest-dwelling *bhikkhu.* Furthermore, it confirms women's inferior social status in ancient India—not their inferior spiritual capabilities."

moss-covered stone. This soft white pooling then quickly lifts to reveal strong ankles, the determined foot!

And the different colors and textures of white! Thick, rough, slightly wrinkled off-white. Crisp, glowing, smoothly woven white. Bluish gauzy, floating cheesecloth.

After we cross the wooden bridge we come to the gravel. The leader falters a bit and we think about the pain, crunching our way across the bits of stone.

I meditate during the serving, fascinated by the rich sounds all around me. The stately ticking of the grandfather clock. One of the owls whooping. A faint cough, muffled in white cotton. The clear call of swallows in the trees. Someone scrubbing white cloth with handfuls of soap. Another filling all of the hot water thermoses. Plastic lids being screwed on and off, picked up and put down, as if there were no hands involved.

Later I do walking in the cave. It doesn't delight me as it often does, but upon stopping I feel calm and mentally refreshed. I descend to the mid-level ledge and perch on one of the stone benches. Perfect! If I sit bolt upright with both feet on the ground, the stone railing supports my throbbing back. Fanned by cool mountain breezes, I try the "sitting in a chair" meditation posture.

Not sure if I am meditating or dreaming (how can one tell really?), I have a vision. The bottom half of a woman's torso appears: tall, slender, clothed in a billowing sarong of glowing pure white. The cloth is soaking wet, though not transparent, and thousands of water droplets sparkle in the blinding sunlight. The woman is being spun slowly in a large beam of light, as if caught in slow motion. The sarong covers her immobile feet, twisting round and round, wrapping her ankles until her torso resembles an Art Nouveau vase. It's impossible to tell front from back, but when the sarong finally stops spinning, I feel that her back is to me. The whole vision has the artificial, muffled, waiting feel of a silent movie, a scene out of Fellini.

No sooner have I noted the strangeness of the vision than another follows. This one is like a sequel—similar actors, same location, but without the fresh beauty of the original. This time the sarong is a normal bluish white. This torso is skinny and graceless, its wetness ordinary. This woman stands with her back and right side

"Well, anyway," my Thai literature professor said, moving on to the logistical part of the night's program, "the order of *bhikkhuni* has died out in Southeast Asia."

He shrugged.

"There may be *bhikkhuni* in China or Japan or even Sri Lanka, but there can be no higher ordination for women in Thailand, since only a *bhikkhuni* can ordain another *bhikkhuni.*"

Suddenly historical precedents didn't matter; it was all about current social realities. Someone misplaced the last female saffron robe, so we're stuck with something called "nuns," glorified lay-women in white. I countered that the ordination lineage for men has also died throughout Southeast Asia periodically, and that only by traveling to other countries to revive it has the tradition lasted this long.

I pressed on. "What makes Thai ordination so special, so different from ordination in east Asia or on the subcontinent?"

He pinched the Dunhill hanging from the corner of his mouth and tossed it out the window, an Asian James Dean. If it weren't rude in Thai society to stand arms akimbo, we'd be doing it.

Ajarn Boon advised me to avoid such arguments. Historical precedents were not the issue. Women have the power to change current reality. As he saw it, the Buddha was a radical, a social revolutionary who liberated women and attacked the excesses of Hinduism: "In a single gesture, He erased the entire caste system," he enthused, the shock of gray hair in the middle of his forehead bobbing up and down like a confirming second opinion.

As usual, he was motoring back dreamily from another *wat* visit, one wheel dragging the shoulder, his pale eyes contemplating the temple we'd left instead of the road.

I gripped my seat and tried not to be so attached to life.

"Buddha said, 'Out of My Mouth there are born four groups.'" Ajarn Boon held up his right hand, four fingers outstretched, and the Peugeot swerved into the right lane, narrowly missing a water-buffalo-drawn cart. He righted the car, exchanging a friendly wave with the farmer atop the cart, and the fingers descended, one at a time. "'Ordained man, householder man, ordained woman, householder woman.'"

I finally let go my breath, and mistaking my audible relief for amazement, he nodded, "Exactly!"

His eyes crinkled to nothingness. "See? Each group is equal, their worth determined simply by performance to their respective duty."

This is one of the moments I fall in love with the Buddha. There are many, in the beginning masquerading as a grudging respect for intellect. As a Unitarian Universalist and my mother's daughter, I appreciate Buddhism's tolerance toward other religions, its respect for individual intelligence, its reliance on rational, scientific inquiry: the practitioner as scientist conducting the experiment of Dhamma in the lab of her body.

Other moments in our love affair fall into the breathless, magical realm of spirituality, the unspoken hunger that's fed when I sit in meditation, when I see the Buddha's face in Ajarn Boon's amused, detached goodwill *(metta)* as he chats with abbots and children alike, in his unfaltering equanimity *(upekkha)* as he nearly kills us, in Maechi Roongdüan's fierce compassion *(karuna)* as she greets dangerous animals, in her glowing, sympathetic joy *(mudita)* at my bumbling attempts to be a lotus.

But I am certain to fall in love with a privileged prince turned revolutionary. *Each group is equal, their worth determined simply by performance to their respective duty.* From childhood I have been addicted to fairness and equality, holding them in esteem over nearly every other value. When in middle school I was caught talking in class to a known troublemaker and he was given detention while I, the top student (and a teacher's daughter to boot), was not, I rushed home hot with indignation. The next day, I insisted that my mother deliver my demand: equal sentences! Punish him less or me more.

And when our seventh-grade science teacher started letting students gamble their semester points—double or nothing—in a move clearly designed to raise the grades of star athletes, I bet and bet until I lost my straight A's.

"If the gambling counts for a single person, it counts for us all," I declared from my perch on Mount Self-righteous as poor Mr. Green puffed and blinked behind his Coke-bottle glasses like a blow-fish. "If anyone's grade improves, I expect to flunk this class."

If morality was my mother's religion, equality was mine. And if Buddhism was grounded in equality, then I would certainly give up money, my voice, and regular meals for it, yes. I was well familiar with performance and duty. Some strong (albeit unfocused) sense of it is what lifts me from my straw pallet each morning at three-thirty and propels me into the foreign landscape of spiritual sojourn.

What I can't accept in these conversations is the inherent impurity attributed to this body. I imagined that the female-body problematic was Western, stemming from Eve's loss of

exposed, legs slightly parted. She is walking in place, her legs moving back and forth, feet planted on the ground, as if she is trying to dry the soaking cloth or free her thin legs from its clinging embrace.

Unlike the first vision's slow, dreamlike pace, this one's pace is quick and realistic. Whether it is the same woman, I cannot tell. A lesson?

I meet Pranee my third day. Maechi Roongdüan finds me reading outdoors, which, while not forbidden, is a waste of daylight better spent meditating, and suggests I go meditate. I am on my way up to the caves when I see two young *maechi* gazing over the railing. The younger, only a girl, shiny and eager-faced, grins and waves me up. On the wide stone landing outside the cave, she asks if I speak Thai. At my nod, she tells me her name is Pranee and she's seventeen years old.

We beam at each other, delighted—me at having discovered my first teenage *meachi*, she at having discovered we can communicate. It feels that at any moment someone should drop in to dispense candy and bonbons.

As the elder, the other—a twenty-one-year-old with a delicate, swanlike neck—does most of the talking, asking the standard questions: *Where are you from? How do you like Thailand? Can you eat Thai food?* She then asks what "level" I am at and whether I can "practice" a lot yet. Though the literal meaning of her words is clear, I have no idea how to answer. What is "a lot"? Am I being graded, passed on or held back?

It is my first time speaking to another human being in three days, except for my daily thirty-minute lesson with Maechi Roongdüan. The Thai words feel runny and disobedient in my mouth.

The girls peer over the wall, monitoring the underbrush with obvious distraction. The newest resident, a young *upasika* in whose vow-taking I participated the previous night, stands nearby staring at the mountains surrounding us. Four mats lay at her feet, suggesting that she awaits group instruction.

All of a sudden, Pranee notices that I'm standing with one foot up on the lower rung of the bench.

"Goodness!" she cries, grabbing my leg and straightening it. "*Maechi* have to stand up straight!"

Her laughter tinkles. "Being Thai, being *maechi*—there are many rules!"

innocence and the Madonna-whore dichotomy of Christianity. Why must Buddhist female salvation be tied to purity? Why is a female devotee making an offering to the Robe a potential source of impurity? Why am I forever reminded of my own cultural dilemma—two opposing identities residing in a single body?

I fled the West precisely because of this, because of dichotomous thinking, the crushing pressure to be either-or, to exist in black or white. This pressure has led me, like any respectable American girl, to hate my body a bit. It is, after all, the site of a tiresome external identity: the blackness that will get you tossed before a subway train, the femaleness that will get you felt up or held down. The biracialness, a lack of clarity, which never fails to unsettle. The East, famously, romantically, tolerant of ambivalence, of a both-and world, is supposed to be my salvation.

I hadn't imagined that I would take it this far, that I would shave away my hair and eyebrows and hide my body. But why not? The body stood outside our house. My mother, being naturally clumsy and unnaturally bookish, abhorred physical activity. Her ideal day was camping on the sofa with a stack of history books, a box of crackers, and a paperback mystery chaser. And though I grew up with my knees perpetually skinned, once puberty hit and we moved into town, I moved into my head. Too middle-class to work the farm and not middle-class enough for the world of health clubs and varsity sports and costly uniforms and lessons, we ignored the life of the body completely. So here I am, on a year's hiatus from Western thought—a year of transcendence in the spiritual sense, of passing in the physical. Thailand reminds me that the body doesn't matter; it is just, as Maechi Roongdüan has said, a "skin sack" getting in the way of our work.

Nearly every girl had a tale to tell, and nearly always it was the same one. She grew up in a village in a family of twelve. A local man came along when she was in her early teens and promised to make her rich. He said she would make her fortune, but she ended up making his. He said she would be "a maid," then forced her to become a slave. She bore him a child, she returned alone to her village, she worked without joy or profit in the fields. Now she could support her offspring only by coming to Bangkok. Who looked after her child? "Ma-má." Did her still devoted parents know what she was doing? "No, I tell them I work in a boutique. They know I work in a bar they kill me."

—Pico Iyer,
Video Night in Kathmandu

Profane Poppy

She is poppy. Genus *Papaver somniferum,* named for sleep. With nodding buds, four crumpled petals, and milky juice. Her papery blossoms signal the beginning of opium season with white or sometimes vivid red hysteria. A Thai girlfriend and I heeded the call. We trekked a muddy road high up the side of a mountain, through narrow crevasses and mossy caves, emerging into a secret field, not a government-sanctioned and -monitored one. There she was, her brilliant bursts of red everywhere, tiny flags of blood on a green body. It was hallucinatory, and we nearly stumbled in the gaze of the thousand black-beaded eyes staring at us.

Later came the harvest, the sticky white sap oozing thick from gray-green pods. And then the smoking—a dab of brick-colored opium hissing in the pan, the sickly-sweet stench pluming the air.

"Where are all the women?" it occurred to me to ask. We were curled beneath a roofed platform with the village men.

"They're in the poppy fields," my friend muttered, "doing all the work."

We lay on our sides like babies, mouths suckling long bamboo pipes. But it was the opposite of nursing, this place of blackened teeth and no women, as life drained from our bodies. Slow death. Profane milky poppies.

Asian girls at the wildest place on earth! Bangkok girls? Thailand girls? Asian girls? Philippine girls? Oriental girls? Sexy girls! Wild girls! Beautiful girls! Here you will find real information on travel to Asia's most exotic locations in the world. You will find girls for fun, girls for sex, Asian girls to entertain you like nowhere else in the world!

—www.wildplace.com/girls

Let's be honest! Danger was partly what drew me to Thailand. I watched myself pass through the countryside, traversing towns owned by bandit kings, climbing up to drug lords lairs, jumping off trains in the middle of the night, and felt powerful. My physical body was more at risk, but my mind was infinitely more at ease. I believed I understood what was unsafe about Thailand in a way I didn't understand violence in America. Here crime followed a simple equation, its laws as causal as the Dhamma's: Obvious Wealth + Obvious Poverty = Risk of Robbery. There is solace in that. It's a hunger that can be fed, not an American-sized pain that requires an automatic weapon

Just then Maechi Roongdüan appears on the landing, as if from the sky, and with a fierce look rebukes Pranee for wasting time. Just as quickly, she joins the laywoman. As I descend the stairs, feeling sheepish, Pranee smiles sunnily, her mood undimmed. "Time's up," she whispers behind her hand, and I realize that she is the one always turning around and grinning at the swan-necked one during meals. What's this high-spirited thing doing as a *maechi*?

The young *maechi* who sits in front of me at mealtime looks a bit like Barbra Streisand. She lives somewhere else in the *wat;* her group arrives at the meal from another direction, after ours. The day before yesterday I saw her staring at me, more intently than the others do. Her eyes flickered away when I turned and caught her but returned after a beat, darting butterflies in a landscape trying to decide whether to settle on me, the strange, bedraggled *maechi.* I smiled and that clinched it; she returned a beautiful, friendly grin.

Today she takes every opportunity to catch my eye and beam. Maybe if I were staying forever, she'd even speak to me!

I'm convinced there's talking going on somewhere. Last night in my *guti*, I distinctly heard voices in the forest. Streisand probably thinks I can't speak Thai. I don't know anymore; can I? I wonder where her group goes; after the meal, they seem to disperse in all directions. Is where they go as beautiful as where we stay?

Just as I finish writing this, two *maechi* walk by, heading toward the forest and speaking out loud as if they were normal women. They're really going at it in central Thai dialect. One looks like Barbra. Both carry baskets of laundry, and as they pass by my *guti*, Not-Barbra says, "This one, with the blue sandals."

Barbra looks at my bathroom sandals on the step and laughs. "Oh-*ho*!" she exclaims. *"Rongtàuw yaayyaay!" What huge shoes!*

Since 1971 the Queen's Foundation for Thai Maechi has addressed *maechi* affairs through the Thai Institute.

A private organization affiliated with the official church hierarchy, the Institute receives no government funding and is dedicated to the stability and progress of *maechi*, increasing faith in *maechi* among the people and

and a roomful of innocent people to accompany you on your journey. Every American with a gun it seems is a potential Chinese emperor or Egyptian pharaoh, in dire need of company even in death.

We Westerners make much of Thailand's so-called contradictions. Imagine—a country with so many monks and prostitutes! We shake our heads. Raised on dichotomy, we craft tension-filled narratives that make for a fine holiday: we visit jeweled temples by day and opium dens/sex bars by night. In our narrative, it is the Thai who are delightfully hypocritical, who can't seem to reconcile themselves. Male travel writers (dedicated journalists all, who never fail to cover Thailand's flesh trade) are downright dismayed to see bar girls give alms or wear Buddhist amulets. Look at that—prostitutes with spiritual lives! In our narrative, the global economy and local pimps and johns (Think Globally, Act Locally) have nothing to do with employment; profanity resides deep within the female body.

What we don't see is the constant battle Thais wage against the profanity threatening to overtake their women. They too believe (a strain of thought traceable through Buddhist texts back to ancient India) that female sexual appetite is uncontrollable (and therefore destructive). The primary concern for girls and young women is to appear *rieb roi,* proper. *Rieb roi* girls never touch boys, not even a playful slap or poke, without an instrument, such as a rolled-up notebook, between them. *Rieb roi* girls know that dating will get them kicked out of school. *Rieb roi* girls stand with both feet flat on the ground and sit with their legs tucked beneath them. *Rieb roi* girls sleep with their brassieres on and keep a sarong around their bodies while changing, the edges held between their teeth, so that no one (they themselves included) ever sees their naked bodies. *Rieb roi* girls speak softly and *wai* beautifully and behave in a supple manner that makes Western men begin to sweat.

Before and after my ordination, I spend a great deal of my time trying to mimic this proper behavior so that stereotypes about American and black women won't put me at the kind of risk from Thai men that Asian stereotypes put Thai women at risk from Western men. It doesn't work. There is no safety for any color body. The country is filled with brown women chained to beds in exclusive beach resorts, eight-year-old girls behind glass on Patpong Road, former farmers and students who've trained their vaginas to smoke cigarettes and blow out matches and draw pictures and eat bananas. Perhaps that is the nature of the world. We lock up our own women and go out looking for theirs.

Much as I detest acting like a *rieb roi* Thai girl. it is woven into the fabric of ordination. *Maechi* are Proper Thai Girls squared. I'm not quite sure if *rieb roi* is supposed to jump-start us on the expressway to *Nibbana* or if it's simply contextual residue. The payoff, however, is clear—freedom from the emphasis on physical attributes, freedom from the gaze of men. For now I hide in white robes; later I will cloak myself in fat. Thailand teaches me that the body does matter. It teaches me the power of desire, which at times is just another word for hatred.

> *Some species of orchids are pollinated by bees that are attracted by means of deception. . . . The most exciting and unusual examples of deceit, traps, and manipulation of pollinators are to be found in those orchids that are pollinated by male euglossine bees.*
>
> —Encyclopaedia Britannia

Exotic Orchid

Thailand is where I learn to be beautiful again. After the great hoopla in the delivery room and a childhood spent receiving treats from strangers on the streets of Seattle, there was a lull in the tribute to my beauty. I was Sunnyside's only black girl, and the one boy who liked me in junior high was so ridiculed once our romance went public that he sent an emissary to break up with me the next day; the next boy—years later in high school—didn't make the same mistake. Beyond these stolen kisses, the only other encouragement I received was an anonymous request in the school newspaper to be someone's valentine, "because she's cute and smart." And though I suspected the handiwork of my longtime pal Cheryl, dispensing a Christian charity that even I couldn't fault, I glowed for a day.

In college, black tastes ran to more overtly girly types with permed hair. I did discover an exotic currency, however, in being dusky enough to spark white men's fantasies, while still behaving and speaking white enough to not scare. (It took a few parties before I got what a Liberal Education really meant.) Even better, my blackness was not American blackness; it was Special Blackness, straight from Africa! *You're half Scandinavian-American and half Nigerian?* began the eager inquiry, revving up for the inevitable refrain: *How interesting! Isn't it?*

Exotic is a tightrope to walk. If you keep moving, eyes toward the sky, you reap admiration from a distance. But if ever

training to *maechi* help lay society.

Its programs include an annual national convention, rural development training programs, a monthly magazine, and self-sufficient, all-female centers for *maechi*.

The institute also publishes a popular pamphlet with suggestions for ordination procedures and rules governing daily life and practice. The pamphlet attempts to debunk negative *maechi* stereotypes and discourage social rather than spiritual motivations for ordaining.

In addition, it regulates family ties and encourages *maechi* to transfer allegiance to the monastic community.

With Maechi Roongdüan away, the atmosphere during the meal is distinctly relaxed, except for the prissy-looking *maechi* who still sits up perfectly straight with a proper, pleased smile. She is always the last to finish eating. There's a great deal to be said for iron determination, devotion, and stamina, I'm sure, but she's too much! She makes me wanna slap her. (Lucky for her, I'm a *maechi* and we frown on that sort of thing.)

After the meal there's actual talking. A worried-looking *maechi* calls me back from the procession. She says something that sounds like, "You have a letter." I frown. Letters are forbidden me.

"Oh, can she speak Thai?" Barbra interjects, looking from Worried One to me. "She can speak Thai!"

I step back. Up close she looks like a short, creepy version of Streisand with bad teeth and no hair. The second vision.

The two exchange some words in a dialect I don't understand, and then Worried One snorts and takes my arm, pulling me to the line. The letter issue is over. If ever there were a day to talk to *maechi* today is it. Strangely, I no longer think I'm up to the task.

That new *maechi* in the *guti* next door has been here five days, each day worse than the previous. I can't meditate on the path or beneath the tree we share without her coming to her doorway and glaring at me. And I dare not go outside if she's already there. She'll stop what she's doing and stare at me, the black stubble glinting in the sunlight around her head like a demonic halo.

I think she might be crazy. She actually spits on the ground like a layperson and giggles! I heard her say that she hates it here and

you slow down, lock eyes, listen to what someone is telling you, then you tumble into the mud of the erotic. So quick the fall from sacred to profane!

After I leave the *wat,* my curls still *maechi*-short, I will wander Southeast Asia, free, oh-so-mysteriously quiet, wrapped in a colorful sarong, my bag light. One night I will find myself at a long table on a private white-sand beach seated between the drummer from one of my favorite British bands and an explorer who'd been speared in the thigh while rafting on an isolated island whose inhabitants had never before seen a white man. Bamboo torches ring the table, throwing flickering gold light on the imported proscuitto and pasta.

The men at the table will be expatriates from Australia and England, the women travelers drawn like satellites to their social systems. Each of us will be claimed during the time she is in town.

When the explorer places his hand on my thigh under the linen tablecloth, at about the same place the skin puckers, hard and shiny, on his own leg, I will stand up and walk back to my guest house and start to pack for the north. Keep moving.

She is Orchid. *Orchidales.* Inscrutable Oriental. Her thick, waxy flowers improbably shaped and spotted like sexual organs. Esoteric, exotic, erotic. She straddles the distinction between the sacred and the profane.

Chiang Mai, dubbed "the Garden of Thailand" by enterprising tour guides, was home to both us and the orchid. Scott and I visited the famed orchid gardens, which boast ten thousand species. We learned that the business of orchids is attracting "suitors" to pollinate, through deceit and traps if necessary.

We chuckled uneasily. Everything in Thailand is titillating, full of suggestion. Brochures about the zoo and local handicrafts read like pornography, everything bending like pliant willows, dripping with fruit and perfume. The glistening pseudonectaries on Thai orchids imitate the eyes of a female bee; their stigmas reflect sunlight, just like the genital orifice of the female fly. *Aren't Thai women beautiful?* Every Thai we meet chants this mantra, as if pimping around the clock.

Most tourists dive right in. Men fly halfway around the world on three-week package deals that include airfare, hotel, and a "wife"/tour guide. The deal is clinched by a staged "marriage ceremony" after which the Thai woman—invariably a dark-skinned ethnic Lao from the drought-stricken farmlands of the northeast, or a preadolescent from the factory slums of Bangkok—refers to her client as "my husband."

The "husbands" we met at the Night Market were eager to share the sheer beauty of the situation with us. "Ya see," Graphic Designer Mark from London explained, looking brightly from Scott to me (perhaps assuming we had a similar arrangement), "sex is not a sin in Buddhism!" This is a popular statement· among *farang*, almost as common as *Mai pen rai* for a Thai.

"Well, that's certainly convenient." I accepted a rose from one of my favorite child vendors. "I mean, for the prostitution and all that."

Associate professor Charles from New York knelt to adjust his Tevas. "Besides, she tells me that we treat them better than the Thai men do." His dark, earnest eyes widened. "They're actually better off!"

"Is that so?" Scott asked, with a worried glance at me.

"Well, that must be quite a relief for you." I patted my pockets for coins as the small flower girl watched, doe-eyed.

Seeing Dr. Steve from Cleveland's blank expression, I explained. "To be able to help out both the economy and the social fabric this way—while getting your rocks off."

He was just starting to shout, 'American women like you are why we have to!" when Scott dragged me away.

We ducked into a quiet bar frequented by off-duty bar girls and shared a few with pals. As we chatted, I grew intrigued by the idea of temporary marriage. The travel writer in me was tempted to make a grand sidebar statement about how any arrangement is available temporarily in Thailand—from marriage to ordination. And given the similarities between the two ceremonies, am I perhaps guilty of the same sort of disingenuous, self-serving pact with the Buddha?

But there is something more to these pseudomarriages, this desire to create a sacred space within a profane arrangement. Again two realities in the same body, but simply binary this time, not opposed. Woman as pure and impure. Like man. The john, the pimp, the monk.

Back on the ole orchid farm, Scott and I learned that night-flying moths are drawn to light-colored, strong-smelling flowers. Butterflies follow bright color. Birds choose primary colors. Flies, annoying as they are, have to be tricked.

Relegated to a separate wing of the greenhouse, far from the good flowers, these trickster orchids are the most interesting. They resemble tropical fish with their blotchy, rich colors. *Beware of smell,* a sign warned us, listing the times of day that the trickster orchids attract releasing a particular stench.

wants to go to Bangkok. Fine, go!

When she returns, Maechi Roongdüan stops by my *guti* with a magazine published by a Buddhist reform group. I've become obsessed with visiting the places described in the publications she brings me. When I leave the *wat,* I want to go to Burma, to Mahasi Sayadaw's center in Rangoon where Maechi Roongdüan studied Burmese *Satipatthana Vipassana* techniques. He's written the best handbooks on meditation I've found. Then I want to go to Ratchaburi in southern Thailand, where there's supposed to be a center solely for *maechi* and laywomen, and the National Maechi Center near Bangkok, which is rumored to have two hundred to three hundred resident *maechi*. I also want to visit Woramai Kabilsingh, the only Thai *bhikkhuni,* and her Asoke movement.

I thank Maechi Roongdüan for the magazine, and we stroll to the front of the *wat,* Maechi Roongdüan pointing out the different plants and trees in Thai and English.

"This is a *bodhi* tree, the type of tree the Buddha was sitting beneath when He became enlightened. Every temple must have one."

I remark that it's so peaceful here, and she sighs. She tells me that in Thailand, women with problems either run to the temple for a while or kill themselves. "There is no other alternative."

The evil *maechi* leaves her door open and I see inside her *guti*. It makes mine look like a frivolous palace. The sum total of her worldly belongings are: a straw mat, a thin pillow, a thermos, one cup, two blankets, a book, a pair of spectacles, a flashlight, a windup clock, and a second set of robes. The walls are bare.

This is her life. I am ashamed for harboring ill thoughts toward her.

We circled them warily, morbidly, like passersby to a car wreck, noting their underwater markings of olive and aubergine. We kept fingers near our noses, trying to identify the smell.

"Uh, that's definitely shit," Scott concluded with a brisk nod and step back "Oh yeah, that should bring in a fly boyfriend or two."

"Mine's carrion!" I complained, seeing the sign and preparing to bolt. "I don't want to smell a corpse."

"That's the price of looking," he mock-rebuked me. "Beauty has its costs, baby."

We are known for our gracious service. This includes personal attention to passenger needs, with special treats (like gift orchids for all female passengers).

THAI's distinctive livery incorporates the colours associated with Thailand: the shining gold found in its temples, the magenta of its shimmering silks and the rich purples of its orchids. Our logo has been likened to an orchid but is simply a symbol meant to convey the essence of Thailand; its soft, curving lines combined with a speed line suggest effortless flight.

Similarly, our slogan "Smooth as Silk" derives from the texture and luxurious look of Thailand's most famous creation: silk. It suggests both the way we fly our aircraft and the way we hope passengers feel when they fly with us, wrapped in comfort and pleasure.

—Thai Airways Royal Orchid Service

At times it is hard not to get caught up. When we leave the country to rejoin the ranks of Americans trawling for the most authentic Thai takeout, we will be swept into the luxury of Thai Airways. We will dazzle the flight attendants with casually dropped Thai phrases and feel honored, along with all the other travelers, to find a fresh purple orchid on our meal tray.

Far below us, the Thai woman is pale, almost white, but infinitely more touchable. Anglo women are white lilies and blushing roses who must be protected (well, at least in terms of rhetoric and literature). Snow White, Rose Red. Peach blossoms and magnolia rising high above the dark soil.

Who are the African flowers? Black women are sweet, I gather, but in a way that makes you lick your lips, rub up against her in public, take that which wasn't offered, deflower her. In a way that dispenses with the need for even the fake marriage ceremony before-hand. Brown Sugar, Mocha Delight, Chocolate Love. When do we get to be flowers? Beautiful? Untouched?

And high above the clouds, enfolded in a curve of gracious service and headed for home, we will remember how some species of orchid grow without soil, in the air—like magic!

The Homeland, Aztlán /
El otro México

Gloria Anzaldúa

El otro México que acá hemos construído
el espacio es lo que ha sido
territorio nacional.
Este es el esfuerzo de todos nuestros hermanos
y latinoamericanos que han sabido
progressar.

—Los Tigres del Norte[1]

"The *Aztecas del norte* . . . compose the largest single tribe or nation of Anishinabeg (Indians) found in the United States today. . . . Some call themselves Chicanos and see themselves as people whose true homeland is Aztlán [the U.S. Southwest]."[2]

Wind tugging at my sleeve
feet sinking into the sand
I stand at the edge where earth touches ocean
where the two overlap
a gentle coming together
at other times and places a violent clash.

Across the border in Mexico
    stark silhouette of houses gutted by waves,
        cliffs crumbling into the sea,
            silver waves marbled with spume
                gashing a hole under the border fence.
            Miro el mar atacar

---

[1]Los Tigres del Norte is a *conjunto* band.

[2]Jack D. Forbes, *Aztecas del Norte: The Chicanos of Aztlán.* (Greenwich, CT: Fawcett Publications, Premier Books, 1973), 13, 183; Eric R. Wolf, *Sons of Shaking Earth* (Chicago, IL: University of Chicago Press, Phoenix Books, 1959), 32.

la cerca en Border Field Park
con sus buchones de agua,
an Easter Sunday resurrection
of the brown blood in my veins.

Oigo el llorido del mar, el respiro del aire,
   my heart surges to the beat of the sea.
      In the gray haze of the sun
         the gulls' shrill cry of hunger,
            the tangy smell of the sea seeping into me.

         I walk through the hole in the fence
           to the other side.
      Under my fingers I feel the gritty wire
         rusted by 139 years
            of the salty breath of the sea.

Beneath the iron sky
Mexican children kick their soccer ball across,
run after it, entering the U.S.

      I press my hand to the steel curtain—
    chainlink fence crowned with rolled barbed wire—
rippling from the sea where Tijuana touches San Diego
    unrolling over mountains
         and plains
             and deserts,
this "Tortilla Curtain" turning into *el río Grande*
    flowing down to the flatlands
       of the Magic Valley of South Texas
       its mouth emptying into the Gulf.

1,950 mile-long open wound
              dividing a *pueblo,* a culture,
             running down the length of my body,
              staking fence rods in my flesh,
             splits me splits me
              me raja me raja
    This is my home
    this thin edge of
       barbwire.

    But the skin of the earth is seamless.
    The sea cannot be fenced,
el mar does not stop at borders.
To show the white man what she thought of his
              arrogance,
Yemayá blew that wire fence down.

This land was Mexican once,
was Indian always
and is.
And will be again.

Yo soy un puente tendido
del mundo gabacho al del mojado,
lo pasado me estira pa' 'trás
y lo presente pa' 'delante,
Que la Virgen de Guadalupe me cuide
Ay ay ay, soy mexicana de este lado.

The U.S.-Mexican border *es una herida abierta* where the Third World grates against the first and bleeds. And before a scab forms it hemorrhages again, the lifeblood of two worlds merging to form a third country—a border culture. Borders are set up to define the places that are safe and unsafe, to distinguish *us* from *them.* A border is a dividing line, a narrow strip along a steep edge. A borderland is a vague and undetermined place created by the emotional residue of an unnatural boundary. It is in a constant state of transition. The prohibited and forbidden are its inhabitants. *Los atravesados* live here: the squint-eyed, the perverse, the queer, the troublesome, the mongrel, the mulato, the half-breed, the half dead; in short, those who cross over, pass over, or go through the confines of the "normal." Gringos in the U.S. Southwest consider the inhabitants of the borderlands transgressors, aliens—whether they possess documents or not, whether they're Chicanos, Indians or Blacks. Do not enter, trespassers will be raped, maimed, strangled, gassed, shot. The only "legitimate" inhabitants are those in power, the whites and those who align themselves with whites. Tension grips the inhabitants of the borderlands like a virus. Ambivalence and unrest reside there and death is no stranger.

In the fields, *la migra.* My aunt saying, "*No corran,* don't run. They'll think you're *del otro lao.*" In the confusion, Pedro ran, terrified of being caught. He couldn't speak English, couldn't tell them he was fifth generation American. *Sin papeles*—he did not carry his birth certificate to work in the fields. *La migra* took him away while we watched. *Se lo llevaron.* He tried to smile when he looked back at us, to raise his fist. But I saw the shame pushing his head down, I saw the terrible weight of shame hunch his shoulders. They deported him to Guadalajara by plane. The furthest he'd ever been to Mexico was Reynosa, a small border town opposite Hidalgo, Texas, not far from McAllen. Pedro walked all the way to the Valley, *Se lo llevaron sin un centavo al pobre. Se vino andando desde Guadalajara.*

During the original peopling of the Americas, the first inhabitants migrated across the Bering Straits and walked south across the continent. The oldest evidence of humankind in the U.S.—the Chicanos' ancient Indian ancestors—was found in Texas and has been dated to 35000 B.C.[3] In the Southwest United States archeologists have found 20,000-year-old campsites of the Indians who migrated through, or

---

[3]John R. Chávez, *The Lost Land: The Chicano Images of the Southwest* (Albuquerque, NM: University of New Mexico Press, 1984), 9.

permanently occupied, the Southwest, Aztlán—land of the herons, land of whiteness, the Edenic place of origin of the Azteca.

In 1000 B.C., descendants of the original Cochise people migrated into what is now Mexico and Central America and became the direct ancestors of many of the Mexican people. (The Cochise culture of the Southwest is the parent culture of the Aztecs. The Uto-Aztecan languages stemmed from the language of the Cochise people.)[4] The Aztecs (the Nahuatl word for people of Aztlán) left the Southwest in 1168 A.D.

> Now let us go.
>> *Tihueque, tihueque,*
> *Vámonos, vámonos.*
>> *Un pájaro cantó.*
> *Con sus ocho tribus salieron*
>> *de la "cueva del origen."*
> *los aztecas siguieron al dios*
>> *Huitzilopochtli.*

Huitzilopochtli, the God of War, guided them to the place (that later became Mexico City) where an eagle with a writhing serpent in its beak perched on a cactus. The eagle symbolizes the spirit (as the sun, the father); the serpent symbolizes the soul (as the earth, the mother). Together, they symbolize the struggle between the spiritual/celestial/male and the underworld/earth/feminine. The symbolic sacrifice of the serpent to the "higher" masculine powers indicates that the patriarchal order had already vanquished the feminine and matriarchal order in pre-Columbian America.

At the beginning of the 16th century, the Spaniards and Hernán Cortés invaded Mexico and, with the help of tribes that the Aztecs had subjugated, conquered it. Before the Conquest, there were twenty-five million Indian people in Mexico and the Yucatán. Immediately after the Conquest, the Indian population had been reduced to under seven million. By 1650, only one-and-a-half-million pure-blooded Indians remained. The *mestizos* who were genetically equipped to survive small pox, measles, and typhus (Old World diseases to which the natives had no immunity), founded a new hybrid race and inherited Central and South America.[5] *En 1521 nació una nueva raza, el mestizo, el mexicano* (people of mixed Indian and Spanish blood), a race that had never existed before. Chicanos, Mexican-Americans, are the offspring of those first matings.

Our Spanish, Indian, and *mestizo* ancestors explored and settled parts of the U.S. Southwest as early as the sixteenth century. For every gold-hungry *conquistador* and soul-hungry missionary who came north from Mexico, ten to twenty Indians and

---

[4]Chávez, 9. Besides the Aztecs, the Ute, Gabrillino of California, Pima of Arizona, some Pueblo of New Mexico, Comanche of Texas, Opata of Sonora, Tarahumara of Sinaloa and Durango, and the Huichol of Jalisco speak Uto-Aztecan languages and are descended from the Cochise people.

[5]Reay Tannahill, *Sex In History* (Briarcliff Manor, NY: Stein and Day/Publishers/Scarborough House, 1980), 308.

mestizos went along as porters or in other capacities.[6] For the Indians, this constituted a return to the place of origin, Aztlán, thus making Chicanos originally and secondarily indigenous to the Southwest. Indians and *mestizos* from central Mexico intermarried with North American Indians. The continual intermarriage between Mexican and American Indians and Spaniards formed an even greater *mestizaje*.

El destierro / The Lost Land

> *Entonces corre la sangre*
> *no sabe el indio que hacer,*
> *le van a quitar su tierra,*
> *la tiene que defender,*
> *el indio se cae muerto,*
> *y el afuerino de pie.*
> *Levántate, Manquilef.*
>
> *Arauco tiene una pena*
> *más negra que su chamal,*
> *ya no son los españoles*
> *los que le hacen llorar,*
> *hoy son los propios chilenos*
> *los que le quitan su pan.*
> *Levántate, Pailahuan.*

—Violeta Parra, *"Arauco tiene una pena"*[7]

In the 1800s, Anglos migrated illegally into Texas, which was then part of Mexico, in greater and greater numbers and gradually drove the *tejanos* (native Texans of Mexican descent) from their lands, committing all manner of atrocities against them. Their illegal invasion forced Mexico to fight a war to keep its Texas territory. The Battle of the Alamo, in which the Mexican forces vanquished the whites, became, for the whites, the symbol for the cowardly and villainous character of the Mexicans. It became (and still is) a symbol that legitimized the white imperialist takeover. With the capture of Santa Anna later in 1836, Texas became a republic. *Tejanos* lost their land and, overnight, became the foreigners.

> *Ya la mitad del terreno*
> *les vendió el traidor Santa Anna,*
> *con lo que se ha hecho muy rica*
> *la nación americana.*
>
> *¿Qué acaso no se conforman*
> *con el oro de las minas?*

---

[7]Isabel Parra, *El Libro Mayor de Violeta Parra* (Madrid, España: Ediciones Michay, S.A., 1985), 156-7.

[6]Chávez, 21.

Ustedes muy elegantes
y aquí nosotros en ruinas.

—from the Mexican corrido,
"Del peligro de la Intervención"[8]

In 1846, the U.S. incited Mexico to war. U.S. troops invaded and occupied Mexico, forcing her to give up almost half of her nation, what is now Texas, New Mexico, Arizona, Colorado and California.

With the victory of the U.S. forces over the Mexican in the U.S.-Mexican War, *los norteamericanos* pushed the Texas border down 100 miles, from *el río Nueces* to *el río Grande*. South Texas ceased to be part of the Mexican state of Tamaulipas. Separated from Mexico, the Native Mexican-Texan no longer looked toward Mexico as home; the Southwest became our homeland once more. The border fence that divides the Mexican people was born on February 2, 1848 with the signing of the Treaty of Guadalupe-Hidalgo. It left 100,000 Mexican citizens on this side, annexed by conquest along with the land. The land established by the treaty as belonging to Mexicans was soon swindled away from its owners. The treaty was never honored and restitution, to this day, has never been made.

> The justice and benevolence of God
> will forbid that . . . Texas should again
> become a howling wilderness
> trod only by savages, or . . . benighted
> by the ignorance and superstition,
> the anarchy and rapine of Mexican misrule.
> The Anglo-American race are destined
> to be forever the proprietors of
> this land of promise and fulfillment.
> Their laws will govern it,
> their learning will enlighten it,
> their enterprise will improve it.
> Their flocks range its boundless pastures,
> for them its fertile lands will yield . . .
> luxuriant harvests . . .
> The wilderness of Texas has been redeemed
> by Anglo-American blood & enterprise.

—William H. Wharton[9]

---

[8] From the Mexican *corrido, "Del peligro de la Intervención"* Vicente T. Mendoza, *El Corrido Mexicano* (México. D.F.: Fondo De Cultura Económica, 1954), 42.

[9] Arnoldo De León, *They Called Them Greasers: Anglo Attitudes Toward Mexicans in Texas, 1821–1900* (Austin, TX: University of Texas Press, 1983), 2–3.

The Gringo, locked into the fiction of white superiority, seized complete political power, stripping Indians and Mexicans of their land while their feet were still rooted in it. *Con el destierro y el exilio fuimos desuñados, destroncados, destripados*—we were jerked out by the roots, truncated, disemboweled, dispossessed, and separated from our identity and our history. Many, under the threat of Anglo terrorism, abandoned homes and ranches and went to Mexico. Some stayed and protested. But as the courts, law enforcement officials, and government officials not only ignored their pleas but penalized them for their efforts, *tejanos* had no other recourse but armed retaliation.

After Mexican-American resisters robbed a train in Brownsville, Texas on October 18, 1915, Anglo vigilante groups began lynching Chicanos. Texas Rangers would take them into the brush and shoot them. One hundred Chicanos were killed in a matter of months, whole families lynched. Seven thousand fled to Mexico, leaving their small ranches and farms. The Anglos, afraid that the *mexicanos*[10] would seek independence from the U.S., brought in 20,000 army troops to put an end to the social protest movement in South Texas. Race hatred had finally fomented into an all out war.[11]

My grandmother lost all her cattle,
they stole her land.

"Drought hit South Texas," my mother tells me. "*La tierra se puso bien seca y los animales comenzaron a morirse de se'. Mi papá se murió de un* heart attack *dejando a mamá* pregnant *y con ocho huercos*, with eight kids and one on the way. *Yo fui la mayor, tenía diez años.* The next year the drought continued *y el ganado* got hoof and mouth. *Se cayeron* in droves *en las pastas y el* brushland, *panzas blancas* ballooning to the skies. *El siguiente año* still no rain. *Mi pobre madre viuda perdió* two-thirds of her *ganado.* A smart *gabacho* lawyer took the land away *mamá* hadn't paid taxes. *No hablaba inglés*, she didn't know how to ask for time to raise the money." My father's mother, Mama Locha, also lost her *terreno*. For a while we got $12.50 a year for the "mineral rights" of six acres of cemetery, all that was left of the ancestral lands. Mama Locha had asked that we bury her there beside her husband. *El cementerio estaba cercado.* But there was a fence around the cemetery, chained and padlocked by the ranch owners of the surrounding land. We couldn't even get in to visit the graves, much less bury her there. Today, it is still padlocked. The sign reads: "Keep out. Trespassers will be shot."

In the 1930s, after Anglo agribusiness corporations cheated the small Chicano landowners of their land, the corporations hired gangs of *mexicanos* to pull out the brush, chaparral and cactus and to irrigate the desert. The land they toiled over had once belonged to many of them, or had been used communally by them. Later the Anglos

---

[10]The Plan of San Diego, Texas, drawn up on January 6, 1915, called for the independence and segregation of the states bordering Mexico: Texas, New Mexico, Arizona, Colorado, and California. Indians would get their land back, Blacks would get six states from the south and form their own independent republic. Chávez, 79.

[11]Jesús Mena, "Violence in the Rio Grande Valley," *Nuestro* (Jan/Feb., 1983), 41–42.

brought in huge machines and root plows and had the Mexicans scrape the land clean of natural vegetation. In my childhood I saw the end of dryland farming. I witnessed the land cleared; saw the huge pipes connected to underwater sources sticking up in the air. As children, we'd go fishing in some of those canals when they were full and hunt for snakes in them when they were dry. In the 1950s I saw the land, cut up into thousands of neat rectangles and squares, constantly being irrigated. In the 340-day growth season, the seeds of any kind of fruit or vegetable had only to be stuck in the ground in order to grow. More big land corporations came in and bought up the remaining land.

To make a living my father became a sharecropper. Rio Farms Incorporated loaned him seed money and living expenses. At harvest time, my father repaid the loan and forked over 40% of the earnings. Sometimes we earned less than we owed, but always the corporations fared well. Some had major holdings in vegetable trucking, livestock auctions and cotton gins. Altogether we lived on three successive Rio farms; the second was adjacent to the King Ranch and included a dairy farm; the third was a chicken farm. I remember the white feathers of three thousand Leghorn chickens blanketing the land for acres around. My sister, mother and I cleaned, weighed and packaged eggs. (For years afterwards I couldn't stomach the sight of an egg.) I remember my mother attending some of the meetings sponsored by well-meaning whites from Rio Farms. They talked about good nutrition, health, and held huge barbecues. The only thing salvaged for my family from those years are modern techniques of food canning and a food-stained book they printed made up of recipes from Rio Farms' Mexican women. How proud my mother was to have her recipe for *enchiladas coloradas* in a book.

El cruzar del mojado/Illegal Crossing

"Ahora si ya tengo una tumba para llorar,"
dice Conchita, upon being reunited with
her unknown mother just before the mother dies.

—from Ismael Rodriguez' film,
Nosotros los pobres[12]

   La crisis. Los gringos had not stopped at the border. By the end of the nineteenth century, powerful landowners in Mexico, in partnership with U.S. colonizing companies, had dispossessed millions of Indians of their lands. Currently, Mexico and her eighty million citizens are almost completely dependent on the U.S. market. The Mexican government and wealthy growers are in partnership with such American conglomerates as American Motors, IT&T and Du Pont which own factories called *maquiladoras*. One-fourth of all Mexicans work at *maquiladoras*; most are young

---

[12]*Nosotros los pobres* was the first Mexican film that was truly Mexican and not an imitation European film. It stressed the devotion and love that children should have for their mother and how its lack would lead to the dissipation of their character. This film spawned a generation of mother-devotion/ungrateful-sons films.

women. Next to oil, *maquiladoras* are Mexico's second greatest source of U.S. dollars. Working eight to twelve hours a day to wire in backup lights of U.S. autos or solder minuscule wires in TV sets is not the Mexican way. While the women are in the *maquiladoras*, the children are left on their own. Many roam the street, become part of *cholo* gangs. The infusion of the values of the white culture, coupled with the exploitation by that culture, is changing the Mexican way of life.

The devaluation of the *peso* and Mexico's dependency on the U.S. have brought on what the Mexicans call *la crisis. No hay trabajo.* Half of the Mexican people are unemployed. In the U.S. a man or woman can make eight times what they can in Mexico. By March, 1987, 1,088 *pesos* were worth one U.S. dollar. I remember when I was growing up in Texas how we'd cross the border at Reynosa or Progreso to buy sugar or medicines when the dollar was worth eight *pesos* and fifty *centavos.*

<u>*La travesía.*</u> For many *mexicanos del otro lado*, the choice is to stay in Mexico and starve or move north and live. *Dicen que cada mexicano siempre sueña de la conquista en los brazos de cuatro gringas rubias, la conquista del país poderoso del norte, los Estados Unidos. En cada Chicano y mexicano vive el mito del tesoro territorial perdido.* North Americans call this return to the homeland the silent invasion.

> *"A la cueva volverán"*
>
> —El Puma *en la canción "Amalia"*

South of the border, called North America's rubbish dump by Chicanos, *mexicanos* congregate in the plazas to talk about the best way to cross. Smugglers, *coyotes, pasadores, enganchadores* approach these people or are sought out by them. *"¿Qué dicen muchachos a echársela de mojado?"*

> *"Now among the alien gods with weapons of magic am I."*
>
> —Navajo protection song, sung when going into battle.[13]

We have a tradition of migration, a tradition of long walks. Today we are witnessing *la migración de los pueblos mexicanos*, the return odyssey to the historical/ mythological Aztlán. This time, the traffic is from south to north.

El retorno to the promised land first began with the Indians from the interior of Mexico and the *mestizos* that came with the *conquistadores* in the 1500s. Immigration continued in the next three centuries, and, in this century, it continued with the *braceros* who helped to build our railroads and who picked our fruit. Today thousands of Mexicans are crossing the border legally and illegally; ten million people without documents have returned to the Southwest.

---

[13]From the Navajo "Protection Song" (to be sung upon going into battle). George W. Gronyn, ed., *American Indian Poetry: The Standard Anthology of Songs and Chants* (New York, NY: Liveright, 1934), 97.

Faceless, nameless, invisible, taunted with "Hey cucaracho" (cockroach). Trembling with fear, yet filled with courage, a courage born of desperation. Barefoot and uneducated, Mexicans with hands like boot soles gather at night by the river where two worlds merge creating what Reagan calls a frontline, a war zone. The convergence has created a shock culture, a border culture, a third country, a closed country.

Without benefit of bridges, the *"mojados"* (wetbacks) float on inflatable rafts across *el río Grande,* or wade or swim across naked, clutching their clothes over their heads. Holding onto the grass, they pull themselves along the banks with a prayer to *Virgen de Guadalupe* on their lips: *Ay virgencita morena, mi madrecita, dame tu bendición.*

The Border Patrol hides behind the local McDonalds on the outskirts of Brownsville, Texas or some other border town. They set traps around the river beds beneath the bridge.[14] Hunters in army-green uniforms stalk and track these economic refugees by the powerful nightvision of electronic sensing devices planted in the ground or mounted on Border Patrol vans. Cornered by flashlights, frisked while their arms stretch over their heads, *los mojados* are handcuffed, locked in jeeps, and then kicked back across the border.

One out of every three is caught. Some return to enact their rite of passage as many as three times a day. Some of those who make it across undetected fall prey to Mexican robbers such as those in Smugglers' Canyon on the American side of the border near Tijuana. As refugees in a homeland that does not want them, many find a welcome hand holding out only suffering, pain, and ignoble death.

Those who make it past the checking points of the Border Patrol find themselves in the midst of 150 years of racism in Chicano *barrios* in the Southwest and in big northern cities. Living in a no-man's-borderland, caught between being treated as criminals and being able to eat, between resistance and deportation, the illegal refugees are some of the poorest and the most exploited of any people in the U.S. It is illegal for Mexicans to work without green cards. But big farming combines, farm bosses and smugglers who bring them in make money off the "wetbacks'" labor—they·don't have to pay federal minimum wages, or ensure adequate housing or sanitary conditions.

The Mexican woman is especially at risk. Often the *coyote* (smuggler) doesn't feed her for days or let her go to the bathroom. Often he rapes her or sells her into prostitution. She cannot call on county or state health or economic resources because she doesn't know English and she fears deportation. American employers are quick to take advantage of her helplessness. She can't go home. She's sold her house, her furniture, borrowed from friends in order to pay the *coyote* who charges her four or five thousand dollars to smuggle her to Chicago. She may work as a live-in maid for white, Chicano or Latino households for as little as $15 a week. Or work in the garment industry, do hotel work. Isolated and worried about her family back home, afraid of getting caught and deported, living with as many as fifteen people in one room, the *mexicana* suffers serious health problems. *Se enferma de los nervios, de alta presión.*[15]

---

[14]Grace Halsell, *Los ilegales,* trans. Mayo Antonio Sánchez (Editorial Diana Mexica, 1979).

[15]Margarita B. Melville, "Mexican Women Adapt to Migration," *International Migration Review, 1978.*

La mojada, la mujer indocumentada, is doubly threatened in this country. Not only does she have to contend with sexual violence, but like all women, she is prey to a sense of physical helplessness. As a refugee, she leaves the familiar and safe home-ground to venture into unknown and possibly dangerous terrain.

> *This is her home*
> *this thin edge of*
> *barbwire.*

The Hajj
© Abbas / Magnum Photos
Published December 8, 2008, in *Slate*
http://todayspictures.slate.com/20081208/

The photo essay "The Hajj" is introduced with these words: "The last of the Five Pillars of Islam, the hajj pilgrimage to the holy city of Mecca in Saudi Arabia occurs [during Dhu al-Hijjah, the 12th month of the Islamic calender]. Muslims must complete a pilgrimage to Mecca at least once in their lifetime, if possible, and follow several sacred rituals during the journey. It is concluded with the Eid al-Adha, or Festival of Sacrifice."

The particular image above from 2003, is the eleventh in the essay. Its caption reads, "MECCA, Saudi Arabia—A prayer inside a shopping mall. During hajj, all activities are suspended during prayer time for pilgrims and merchants."

Thirteen More Ways of Looking at a Blackbird

Dorie Bargmann

1.

In one of its past lives, the Commodore building in downtown Austin had a food court and a three-story atrium. The food court attracted grackles, which scurried in through the swinging glass doors. The atrium's roof leaked, forming a mini-swamp among the large potted plants on the fourth floor landing. The combination of greenery, dripping water, and trapped birds flying to and fro created a lovely outdoor feeling, enhanced by the building's crickets and geckos. New management has wiped out the food court, which should discourage the wildlife. I do not know management's plans (if any) for evicting the ghost from the Commodore's upper floors.

2.

The Hyatt Regency sits just south of downtown, across the Colorado river. At dusk in November thousands of great-tailed grackles often roost here in the trees and shriek. "What are those birds?" an out-of-town man yells at me over cocktail chatter. "Grackles," I say. "Crackles?" he yells back. I am indoors at a noisy reception for urban administrators. I have just read research suggesting that dogs evolved to fill the ecological niche created by human garbage. Grackles often carry around bits of garbage, and I propose to this man that the birds be trained to clean up his city. He looks puzzled; possibly he can't hear me over the shrieking humans.

I am taking a proactive approach. Because it's just a matter of time before the grackles take over his city, as they have mine, and I want to nip potential hostility in the bud. Because I hear very little appreciation for grackles in Texas. "Garbage birds." "Rats with wings." "Greasy street chickens." They displace the songbirds, say my suburban friends. They eat grains and grapefruit, say the farmers. "Widely regarded as pests," say the naturalists. What can I offer in reply? That they eat grasshoppers? That they recycle hamburger buns? That, as scavengers go, they are remarkably good-looking?

3.

A neighborhood cat was chewing on a young grackle. We frightened off the cat and caught the bird, still alive. At first, he sat rigid with his eyes closed and beak pointed skywards. I fed him softened pet food, bread, and fruit. His swallowing reflex was good; he left light-green droppings in the cage. He was well-feathered, though a bit bald about the neck, with a buff chest, long tough legs, and a long tough beak. The only visible injury was at the base of one wing.

He chirped at me once, at 6:30 pm. Tsik! This sealed my affection for him, because my sister makes the exact same noise when she sneezes. I let him stand on my finger. His claws were firm, and his beak grasped my hand to adjust his stance, but he used these tools courteously, not to hurt. He lived a good twelve hours; at 10:00 p.m. I found him keeled over. He had never quite lost the expression that said, Someone's been chewing on me.

Earlier that day I had run into a lawyer who had the same puzzled, slightly cross, slightly distracted look as my grackle. We were not on intimate enough terms for me to ask who had been chewing on him.

4.

Breeding season. The winter grackle conventions break up into small groups and disperse throughout the city. The males strut their terrains and fend off challengers. They tussle and tumble beak-over-tail in the dust and chase each other up trees. Or they square off on the ground, point their beaks to the sky, and try to bend their necks back even further, in a sort of competitive grackle ballet. Finally the losers fly away, and the dominant male takes up residence on a high perch and begins a noisy come-hither call.

Male great-tails are designed for courtship and—it appears—for little else. Their black coats are uncomfortable in the Texas heat; they pant in the summer and regularly dunk themselves in water. Their long tails are a burden on windy days, when one good gust can bend the tail 90 degrees from the bird's body. Male grackles die off in larger numbers than females in winter, and it is thought that the males' greater size and poorer flying abilities make survival difficult when food is scarce.

But in courtship, the male is a star. His glossy black feathers shine blue and green and purple in different lights, and he stands on tiptoe in the tip-top of trees and sings. First a rough noise, like bad radio static; then a wavering musical note which crescendoes; then a burst of static again; then several loud, rising whistles. When the smaller, grey-brown female happens into his territory, the male flies to the ground, puffs up his feathers, fans out his tail, and flutters his wings, looking rather like an animated Elvis wig. He runs around the female, chittering. If she ignores him, the male's feather volume dies down abruptly, and the casual observer is left to wonder about the evolutionary value of Big Hair.

5.

One evening outside the (now razed) club Liberty Lunch, we passed a tree full of raucous grackles. Inside, we were bludgeoned by music. When we came out again, around 2:00 a.m., the tree still seemed to be singing. Had the amplifiers damaged my ears? Surely these birds must sleep? Naturalist Alexander Skutch set my fears to rest. "Especially at the outset of the breeding season, the [grackles] slept lightly and repeatedly awoke during the night to shatter with shrill calls the monotonous humming of insects." Or the monotonous beat of reggae.

Austin's famous Congress Avenue bridge bats are resident from March to November, but visitors in the off-season need not feel gypped. In February, simply move three blocks west of Congress Avenue, to the South First Street bridge, and you may get to witness Shrieking Hour. On some evenings, hordes of dark birds gather on the bridge rails, on the trees along the river bank, on the roofs of stores and restaurants, on the wires, on the light poles—thousands of birds perching shoulder to shoulder, shouting for all they're worth, drowning out the noise of traffic, calling cheerful hosannas to commuters crossing the bridge from downtown, welcoming them back to South Austin.

6.

Science recently settled on Quiscalus mexicanus as a name for the great-tailed grackle. Thirty years ago he was Cassidix mexicanus. Eighty years ago an Austin zoologist listed him as Megaquiscalus major macrourus, and gave him all kinds of English a.k.a.'s: Jackdaw, Big Crow Blackbird, Texas Grackle, etc.

Even the genus name Quiscalus gives scholars a case of the frets. Does it come from the Latin quis, what, and qualis, of what kind? But why? Or from quiscalis, quail? Or from the Spanish quisquilla, quibble—a reference to the noisy, chattering birds? Or from the Latin quisquiliae—refuse, dregs—the diet of the garbage bird? Linnaeus, who designated the genus, was not known to invent names, but in this instance he has left other naturalists guessing.

Mexico has separate gender terms for the grackle—clarinero or clarinete for the males; zanate or sanate for the females. Clarinero, trumpeter, is an obvious choice. Zanate comes from the Aztec tzanatl, meaning blackbird or grackle generally. The fifteenth century Aztec ruler Ahuitzotl was fond of the great-tailed grackle and had it imported from the coast to what is now Mexico City, where it became known as teotzanatl, divine or wondrous blackbird. Seventy years after Ahuitzotl's death, Fray Bernardino de Sahagun reported: "If anyone stoned them, they chided one another; the common folk said to one another, 'What are you doing over there? Do not shout at, do not stone the lord's bird!'"

7.

In 1989, a federal court in Illinois found Henry Van Fossan guilty of poisoning two mourning doves and two common grackles with strychnine. He was fined $450 and given three years' probation for violating the Migratory Species Protection Act.

In 1992, the federal government authorized the killing of 164,478 grackles nationwide. In Texas alone, in fiscal year 2000, 17,095 great-tailed grackles were poisoned under the auspices of the federal Wildlife Services program.

If you are going to kill a grackle, it's best to wait for the words, "Simon Says."

8.

In Managua at a bus stop I was sitting on a metal ring circling a thick pole. About a minute later, two things happened simultaneously: a great-tail issued its piercing, rising whistle, and an electric current traveling the metal ring jolted me to my feet. Many years later, when I first heard the grackle colonies in Austin, I felt an instant—you could say electric—affinity with them. I was passively familiar with the rest of their vocal repertoire—the squeaking and gargling resonated in memory. I must have heard them often in Central America, but I had not bothered, then, to connect the noises to a bird. Those were serious times, and I was a serious person, and the serious people I knew did not engage in bird-watching.

9.

In 1925, Austin zoologist George Finlay Simmons noted the existence of one colony of four hundred breeding great-tailed grackles in the Austin area. "Very noisy," he reported. "Possibly the noisiest of birds."

What would today's Highland Mall birds, or the South First Street bridge birds, make of these their humble origins? Four hundred birds would fit into just one large tree, and present-day colonies command whole groves. In our nation, great-tails were restricted to the Rio Grande valley in the early 1900s, but today they have been sighted in over half of the United States, as well as in Canada, and if they are not already there, they are coming soon to a town near you.

For those of you in unbesieged cities, here is how to recognize the great-tail. The adult male can grow up to seventeen inches long; his tail accounts for almost half that span. He is slender and black—a tuxedoed gentleman of a city bird, as compared with the pouchy, rumpled pigeons. The female is smaller, maybe two-thirds the size of the male; her greyish-brown coat and yellow eyes give her the coloration of a Weimaraner dog. Male and female great-tails are so different they initially seem separate species. But they have the same eyes, and the same sturdy beak, and the same savvy and irritable expression—like that of a parent who knows exactly what you've been up to and is contemplating discipline.

Juveniles all look like females until the young birds molt. A feather blanket once burst in my back yard; that is roughly what the ground looks like under a large grackle roost when the birds start molting. Except that the grackles' feathers are darker, and they fall with a certain regularity, often quill-down, spiking upwards through the lawn like grass blades themselves. As though someone had cast birdseed on the lawn, and the seed had begun to sprout literal birds.

10.

Why Austin needs the grackles #1: Austin calls itself the live music capital of the world, and grackles give many live, loud, and free performances. Why Austin needs the grackles #2: Great-tails are archetypal Texans—big, brash, and promiscuous. I use the word "promiscuous" advisedly, since the archetypal Texan now has a bit of a split personality—on the one hand, there's the five-times-married former Lieutenant Governor Bob Bullock, and on the other hand, there's the Bible Belt crew currently running Washington.

Why Austin (and the rest of us) need the grackles #3: Black birds are part of our psyche. In the 1990s a local theater company performed Charles Staggs' Tower Massacre Musical, which deals with one of the ugliest incidents in Austin's history: the gunning down of fourteen people by a sniper on the University of Texas tower in 1966. I know of the musical only through its reviews, which were favorable, and which describe, among other things, how the souls of the dead are transformed onstage into shrieking grackles. Charles Staggs, Wallace Stevens, Edgar Allen Poe, even the Beatles—black birds haunt us all.

11.

A dead grackle dropped head-first out of a tree onto the sidewalk. Another male flew down on top of him. Several females, clacking excitedly, fluttered out of the tree to surround the pair. The second male began pecking at the first, dislodging feathers. One female grabbed the corpse's tail and dragged it a few inches before the male drove her off. The females flew back to their tree; the male kept pecking at the dead bird until I came nearer, whereupon he also retreated. The dead grackle lay long and straight except for curling legs and claws. His beak was broken at the tip, and the gap between upper and lower mandibles was lined with blood. He was a sturdy, well-feathered, mature male, his back still shining blue.

I have searched the literature, but I can find no description of fatal battles between male great-tails. And the broken beak suggested violent impact, not bird wrestling. Here is my best theory: the bird hit a window or was struck by a car; it then flew, damaged, into another male's territory. The male may have attacked it, or it may have died of its injuries; in any event, after it died and fell, the females attempted to drag the corpse away, to avoid attracting predators to their nests. It is harder to understand the other male's continued aggression, unless it was simply baffled by the dead bird's behavior. The weaker male is supposed to fly away.

In 1821, John James Audubon caught a number of common grackles, as well as other birds, to send to Europe. After a few days, the grackles suddenly became violent, killing the other species as well as the weaker of their own kin. "I look upon this remarkable instance of ferocity in the Grakle with the more amazement," Audubon wrote, "as I never observed it killing any bird when in a state of freedom."

12.

Here are two stories I can neither confirm nor deny. First: a landscaper reports that grackles shadow him when he mows lawns. This, I think I believe: the birds are there to snatch the grasshoppers that flee the machinery. A power mower would frighten off most animals, but the grackles' tolerance for noise has me half-convinced they're half-deaf. In the cities, it's lawnmowers; in the countryside, tractors, no doubt; two hundred years ago, it was the plow, as Audubon also noted:

> Thus does the Grakle follow the husbandman as he turns one furrow after another, destroying a far worse enemy of the corn than itself, for every worm which it devours would else shortly cut the slender blade and thereby destroy the plant. . . . Every reflecting farmer knows this well and refrains from disturbing the Grakle at this season. . . . But man is too often forgetful of the benefit which he has received; . . . no sooner does the corn become fit for his own use, than he vows and executes vengeance on all intruders.

I am more doubtful of the second story. An acquaintance told me he once saw a parrot—presumably an escaped pet—in a local city park. While he watched, several grackles flew up to the parrot and dropped bits of food at its feet, as though they were worshiping it, bringing it offerings. Where can I find precedence for this? To date, only in 1 Kings 17:

> And the word of the Lord came to [Elijah], saying, Get thee hence, and turn thee eastward, and hide thyself by the brook Cherith, that is before Jordan. And it shall be that thou shalt drink of the brook; and I have commanded the ravens to feed thee there.

13.

I was on a green lawn at the pink state Capitol, feeding a flock of grackles half of my enormous sandwich bun. The wind was blowing. There was a whole festival of grackles at my park bench. They rushed and snatched and pushed but did not peck at one another. At last I ran out of sandwich and told them so. They blew out in the wind, broke up in patches like clouds after a rain. All but one. An old grackle, too creaky for tussling, was eyeing me. I showed him my empty hands. He drew himself up, like a scraggly, stern old prophet, and he fixed me with his yellow eyes, and he informed me that henceforth I was always to withhold a portion of bread from the rambunctious youngsters, and when they flew away, then I was to minister to him, the venerable. But I have no independent confirmation for this story, either.

Is Google Making Us Stupid?

Nicholas Carr

"Dave, stop. Stop, will you? Stop, Dave. Will you stop, Dave?" So the supercomputer HAL pleads with the implacable astronaut Dave Bowman in a famous and weirdly poignant scene toward the end of Stanley Kubrick's *2001: A Space Odyssey*. Bowman, having nearly been sent to a deep-space death by the malfunctioning machine, is calmly, coldly disconnecting the memory circuits that control its artificial "brain." "Dave, my mind is going," HAL says, forlornly. "I can feel it. I can feel it."

I can feel it, too. Over the past few years I've had an uncomfortable sense that someone, or something, has been tinkering with my brain, remapping the neural circuitry, reprogramming the memory. My mind isn't going—so far as I can tell—but it's changing. I'm not thinking the way I used to think. I can feel it most strongly when I'm reading. Immersing myself in a book or a lengthy article used to be easy. My mind would get caught up in the narrative or the turns of the argument, and I'd spend hours strolling through long stretches of prose. That's rarely the case anymore. Now my concentration often starts to drift after two or three pages. I get fidgety, lose the thread, begin looking for something else to do. I feel as if I'm always dragging my wayward brain back to the text. The deep reading that used to come naturally has become a struggle.

I think I know what's going on. For more than a decade now, I've been spending a lot of time online, searching and surfing and sometimes adding to the great databases of the Internet. The Web has been a godsend to me as a writer. Research that once required days in the stacks or periodical rooms of libraries can now be done in minutes. A few Google searches, some quick clicks on hyperlinks, and I've got the telltale fact or pithy quote I was after. Even when I'm not working, I'm as likely as not to be foraging in the Web's info-thickets' reading and writing e-mails, scanning headlines and blog posts, watching videos and listening to podcasts, or just tripping from link to link to link. (Unlike footnotes, to which they're sometimes likened, hyperlinks don't merely point to related works; they propel you toward them.)

For me, as for others, the Net is becoming a universal medium, the conduit for most of the information that flows through my eyes and ears and into my mind. The advantages of having immediate access to such an incredibly rich store of information are many, and they've been widely described and duly applauded. "The perfect recall of silicon memory," *Wired's* Clive Thompson has written, "can be an enormous boon to thinking." But that boon comes at a price. As the media theorist Marshall McLuhan pointed out in the 1960s, media are not just passive channels of information. They supply the stuff of thought, but they also shape the process of thought. And what the Net seems to be doing is chipping away my capacity for concentration and contemplation. My mind now expects to take in information the way the Net distributes it: in a swiftly moving stream of particles. Once I was a scuba diver in the sea of words. Now I zip along the surface like a guy on a Jet Ski.

I'm not the only one. When I mention my troubles with reading to friends and acquaintances—literary types, most of them—many say they're having similar experiences. The more they use the Web, the more they have to fight to stay focused on long pieces of writing. Some of the bloggers I follow have also begun mentioning the phenomenon. Scott Karp, who writes a blog about online media, recently confessed that he has stopped reading books altogether. "I was a lit major in college, and used to be [a] voracious book reader," he wrote. "What happened?" He speculates on the answer: "What if I do all my reading on the web not so much because the way I read has changed, i.e. I'm just seeking convenience, but because the way I THINK has changed?"

Bruce Friedman, who blogs regularly about the use of computers in medicine, also has described how the Internet has altered his mental habits. "I now have almost totally lost the ability to read and absorb a longish article on the web or in print," he wrote earlier this year. A pathologist who has long been on the faculty of the University of Michigan Medical School, Friedman elaborated on his comment in a telephone conversation with me. His thinking, he said, has taken on a "staccato" quality, reflecting the way he quickly scans short passages of text from many sources online. "I can't read *War and Peace* anymore," he admitted. "I've lost the ability to do that. Even a blog post of more than three or four paragraphs is too much to absorb. I skim it."

Anecdotes alone don't prove much. And we still await the long-term neurological and psychological experiments that will provide a definitive picture of how Internet use affects cognition. But a recently published study of online research habits, conducted by scholars from University College London, suggests that we may well be in the midst of a sea change in the way we read and think. As part of the five-year research program, the scholars examined computer logs documenting the behavior of visitors to two popular research sites, one operated by the British Library and one by a U.K. educational consortium, that provide access to journal articles, e-books, and other sources of written information. They found that people using the sites exhibited "a form of skimming activity," hopping from one source to another and rarely returning to any source they'd already visited. They typically read no more than one or two pages of an article or book before they would "bounce" out to another site. Sometimes they'd save a long article, but there's no evidence that they ever went back and actually read it. The authors of the study report:

> It is clear that users are not reading online in the traditional sense; indeed there are signs that new forms of "reading" are emerging as users "power browse" horizontally through titles, contents pages and abstracts going for quick wins. It almost seems that they go online to avoid reading in the traditional sense.

Thanks to the ubiquity of text on the Internet, not to mention the popularity of text-messaging on cell phones, we may well be reading more today than we did in the 1970s or 1980s, when television was our medium of choice. But it's a different kind of reading, and behind it lies a different kind of thinking—perhaps even a new sense of the self. "We are not only *what* we read," says Maryanne Wolf, a developmental psychologist at Tufts University and the author of *Proust and the Squid: The Story and Science of the Reading Brain.* "We are *how* we read." Wolf worries that the style of reading promoted by the Net, a style that puts "efficiency" and "immediacy" above all else, may be weakening our capacity for the kind of deep reading that emerged when an earlier technology, the printing press, made long and complex works of prose commonplace. When we read online, she says, we tend to become "mere decoders of information." Our ability to interpret text, to make the rich mental connections that form when we read deeply and without distraction, remains largely disengaged.

Reading, explains Wolf, is not an instinctive skill for human beings. It's not etched into our genes the way speech is. We have to teach our minds how to translate the symbolic characters we see into the language we understand. And the media or other technologies we use in learning and practicing the craft of reading play an important part in shaping the neural circuits inside our brains. Experiments demonstrate that readers of ideograms, such as the Chinese, develop a mental circuitry for reading that is very different from the circuitry found in those of us whose written language employs an alphabet. The variations extend across many regions of the brain, including those that govern such essential cognitive functions as memory and the interpretation of visual and auditory stimuli. We can expect as well that the circuits woven by our use of the Net will be different from those woven by our reading of books and other printed works.

Sometime in 1882, Friedrich Nietzsche bought a typewriter—a Malling-Hansen Writing Ball, to be precise. His vision was failing, and keeping his eyes focused on a page had become exhausting and painful, often bringing on crushing headaches. He had been forced to curtail his writing, and he feared that he would soon have to give it up. The typewriter rescued him, at least for a time. Once he had mastered touch-typing, he was able to write with his eyes closed, using only the tips of his fingers. Words could once again flow from his mind to the page.

But the machine had a subtler effect on his work. One of Nietzsche's friends, a composer, noticed a change in the style of his writing. His already terse prose had become even tighter, more telegraphic. "Perhaps you will through this instrument even take to a new idiom," the friend wrote in a letter, noting that, in his own work, his "'thoughts' in music and language often depend on the quality of pen and paper."

"You are right," Nietzsche replied, "our writing equipment takes part in the forming of our thoughts." Under the sway of the machine, writes the German media scholar Friedrich A. Kittler, Nietzsche's prose "changed from arguments to aphorisms, from thoughts to puns, from rhetoric to telegram style."

The human brain is almost infinitely malleable. People used to think that our mental meshwork, the dense connections formed among the 100 billion or so neurons inside our skulls, was largely fixed by the time we reached adulthood. But brain researchers have discovered that that's not the case. James Olds, a professor of neuroscience who directs the Krasnow Institute for Advanced Study at George Mason University, says that even the adult mind "is very plastic." Nerve cells routinely break old connections and form new ones. "The brain," according to Olds, "has the ability to reprogram itself on the fly, altering the way it functions."

As we use what the sociologist Daniel Bell has called our "intellectual technologies"—the tools that extend our mental rather than our physical capacities—we inevitably begin to take on the qualities of those technologies. The mechanical clock, which came into common use in the 14th century, provides a compelling example. In *Technics and Civilization*, the historian and cultural critic Lewis Mumford described how the clock "disassociated time from human events and helped create the belief in an independent world of mathematically measurable sequences." The "abstract framework of divided time" became "the point of reference for both action and thought."

The clock's methodical ticking helped bring into being the scientific mind and the scientific man. But it also took something way. As the late MIT computer scientist Joseph Weizenbaum observed in his 1976 book, *Computer Power and Human Reason: From Judgment to Calculation*, the conception of the world that emerged from the widespread use of timekeeping instruments "remains an impoverished version of the older one, for it rests on a rejection of those direct experiences that formed the basis for, and indeed constituted, the old reality." In deciding when to eat, to work, to sleep, to rise, we stopped listening to our senses and started obeying the clock.

The process of adapting to new intellectual technologies is reflected in the changing metaphors we use to explain ourselves to ourselves. When the mechanical clock arrived, people began thinking of their brains as operating "like clockwork." Today, in the age of software, we have come to think of them as operating "like computers." But the changes, neuroscience tells us, go much deeper than metaphor. Thanks to our brain's plasticity, the adaptation occurs also at a biological level.

The Internet promises to have particularly far-reaching effects on cognition. In a paper published in 1936, the British mathematician Alan Turing proved that a digital computer, which at the time existed only as a theoretical machine, could be programmed to perform the function of any other information-processing device. And that's what we're seeing today. The Internet, an immeasurably powerful computing system, is subsuming most of our other intellectual technologies. It's becoming our map and our clock, our printing press and our typewriter, our calculator and our telephone, and our radio and TV.

When the Net absorbs a medium, that medium is re-created in the Net's image. It injects the medium's content with hyperlinks, blinking ads, and other digital gewgaws, and it surrounds the content with the content of all the other media it has absorbed. A new e-mail message, for instance, may announce its arrival as we're glancing over the latest headlines at a newspaper's site. The result is to scatter our attention and diffuse our concentration.

The Net's influence doesn't end at the edges of a computer screen, either. As people's minds become attuned to the crazy quilt of Internet media, traditional media have to adapt to the audience's new expectations. Television programs add text crawls and pop-up ads, and magazines and newspapers shorten their articles, introduce capsule summaries, and crowd their pages with easy-to-browse info-snippets. When, in March of this year, *The New York Times* decided to devote the second and third pages of every edition to article abstracts, its design director, Tom Bodkin, explained that the "shortcuts" would give harried readers a quick "taste" of the day's news, sparing them the "less efficient" method of actually turning the pages and reading the articles. Old media have little choice but to play by the new-media rules.

Never has a communications system played so many roles in our lives—or exerted such broad influence over our thoughts—as the Internet does today. Yet, for all that's been written about the Net, there's been little consideration of how, exactly, it's reprogramming us. The Net's intellectual ethic remains obscure.

About the same time that Nietzsche started using his typewriter, an earnest young man named Frederick Winslow Taylor carried a stopwatch into the Midvale Steel plant in Philadelphia and began a historic series of experiments aimed at improving the efficiency of the plant's machinists. With the approval of Midvale's owners, he recruited a group of factory hands, set them to work on various metalworking machines, and recorded and timed their every movement as well as the operations of the machines. By breaking down every job into a sequence of small, discrete steps and then testing different ways of performing each one, Taylor created a set of precise instructions—an "algorithm," we might say today—for how each worker should work. Midvale's employees grumbled about the strict new regime, claiming that it turned them into little more than automatons, but the factory's productivity soared.

More than a hundred years after the invention of the steam engine, the Industrial Revolution had at last found its philosophy and its philosopher. Taylor's tight industrial choreography—his "system," as he liked to call it—was embraced by manufacturers throughout the country and, in time, around the world. Seeking maximum speed, maximum efficiency, and maximum output, factory owners used time-and-motion studies to organize their work and configure the jobs of their workers. The goal, as Taylor defined it in his celebrated 1911 treatise, *The Principles of Scientific Management*, was to identify and adopt, for every job, the "one best method" of work and thereby to effect "the gradual substitution of science for rule of thumb throughout the mechanic arts." Once his system was applied to all acts of manual labor, Taylor assured his followers, it would bring about a restructuring not only of industry but of society, creating a utopia of perfect efficiency. "In the past the man has been first," he declared; "in the future the system must be first."

Taylor's system is still very much with us; it remains the ethic of industrial manufacturing. And now, thanks to the growing power that computer engineers and software coders wield over our intellectual lives, Taylor's ethic is beginning to govern the realm of the mind as well. The Internet is a machine designed for the efficient and automated collection, transmission, and manipulation of information, and its legions of programmers are intent on finding the "one best method"—the perfect algorithm—to carry out every mental movement of what we've come to describe as "knowledge work."

Google's headquarters, in Mountain View, California—the Googleplex—is the Internet's high church, and the religion practiced inside its walls is Taylorism. Google, says its chief executive, Eric Schmidt, is "a company that's founded around the science of measurement," and it is striving to "systematize everything" it does. Drawing on the terabytes of behavioral data it collects through its search engine and other sites, it carries out thousands of experiments a day, according to the *Harvard Business Review*, and it uses the results to refine the algorithms that increasingly control how people find information and extract meaning from it. What Taylor did for the work of the hand, Google is doing for the work of the mind.

The company has declared that its mission is "to organize the world's information and make it universally accessible and useful." It seeks to develop "the perfect search engine," which it defines as something that "understands exactly what you mean and gives you back exactly what you want." In Google's view, information is a kind of commodity, a utilitarian resource that can be mined and processed with industrial efficiency. The more pieces of information we can "access" and the faster we can extract their gist, the more productive we become as thinkers.

Where does it end? Sergey Brin and Larry Page, the gifted young men who founded Google while pursuing doctoral degrees in computer science at Stanford, speak frequently of their desire to turn their search engine into an artificial intelligence, a HAL-like machine that might be connected directly to our brains. "The ultimate search engine is something as smart as people—or smarter," Page said in a speech a few years back. "For us, working on search is a way to work on artificial intelligence." In a 2004 interview with *Newsweek*, Brin said, "Certainly if you had all the world's information directly attached to your brain, or an artificial brain that was smarter than your brain, you'd be better off." Last year, Page told a convention of scientists that Google is "really trying to build artificial intelligence and to do it on a large scale."

Such an ambition is a natural one, even an admirable one, for a pair of math whizzes with vast quantities of cash at their disposal and a small army of computer scientists in their employ. A fundamentally scientific enterprise, Google is motivated by a desire to use technology, in Eric Schmidt's words, "to solve problems that have never been solved before," and artificial intelligence is the hardest problem out there. Why wouldn't Brin and Page want to be the ones to crack it?

Still, their easy assumption that we'd all "be better off" if our brains were supplemented, or even replaced, by an artificial intelligence is unsettling. It suggests a belief that intelligence is the output of a mechanical process, a series of discrete steps that can be isolated, measured, and optimized. In Google's world, the world we enter when we go online, there's little place for the fuzziness of contemplation. Ambiguity is not an opening for insight but a bug to be fixed. The human brain is just an outdated computer that needs a faster processor and a bigger hard drive.

The idea that our minds should operate as high-speed data-processing machines is not only built into the workings of the Internet, it is the network's reigning business model as well. The faster we surf across the Web—the more links we click and pages we view—the more opportunities Google and other companies gain to collect information about us and to feed us advertisements. Most of the proprietors of the commercial Internet have a financial stake in collecting the crumbs of data we leave behind as we flit from link to link—the more crumbs, the better. The last thing these companies want is to encourage leisurely reading or slow, concentrated thought. It's in their economic interest to drive us to distraction.

Maybe I'm just a worrywart. Just as there's a tendency to glorify technological progress, there's a countertendency to expect the worst of every new tool or machine. In Plato's *Phaedrus*, Socrates bemoaned the development of writing. He feared that, as people came to rely on the written word as a substitute for the knowledge they used to carry inside their heads, they would, in the words of one of the dialogue's characters, "cease to exercise their memory and become forgetful." And because they would be able to "receive a quantity of information without proper instruction," they would "be thought very knowledgeable when they are for the most part quite ignorant." They would be "filled with the conceit of wisdom instead of real wisdom." Socrates wasn't wrong—the new technology did often have the effects he feared—but he was shortsighted. He couldn't foresee the many ways that writing and reading would serve to spread information, spur fresh ideas, and expand human knowledge (if not wisdom).

The arrival of Gutenberg's printing press, in the 15th century, set off another round of teeth gnashing. The Italian humanist Hieronimo Squarciafico worried that the easy availability of books would lead to intellectual laziness, making men "less studious" and weakening their minds. Others argued that cheaply printed books and broadsheets would undermine religious authority, demean the work of scholars and scribes, and spread sedition and debauchery. As New York University professor Clay Shirky notes, "Most of the arguments made against the printing press were correct, even prescient." But, again, the doomsayers were unable to imagine the myriad blessings that the printed word would deliver.

So, yes, you should be skeptical of my skepticism. Perhaps those who dismiss critics of the Internet as Luddites or nostalgists will be proved correct, and from our hyperactive, data-stoked minds will spring a golden age of intellectual discovery and universal wisdom. Then again, the Net isn't the alphabet, and although it may replace the printing press, it produces something altogether different. The kind of deep reading that a sequence of printed pages promotes is valuable not just for the knowledge we acquire from the author's words but for the intellectual vibrations those words set off within our own minds. In the quiet spaces opened up by the sustained, undistracted reading of a book, or by any other act of contemplation, for that matter, we make our own associations, draw our own inferences and analogies, foster our own ideas. Deep reading, as Maryanne Wolf argues, is indistinguishable from deep thinking.

If we lose those quiet spaces, or fill them up with "content," we will sacrifice something important not only in our selves but in our culture. In a recent essay, the playwright Richard Foreman eloquently described what's at stake:

> I come from a tradition of Western culture, in which the ideal (my ideal) was the complex, dense and "cathedral-like" structure of the highly educated and articulate personality—a man or woman who carried inside themselves a personally constructed and unique

version of the entire heritage of the West. [But now] I see within us all (myself included) the replacement of complex inner density with a new kind of self—evolving under the pressure of information overload and the technology of the "instantly available."

As we are drained of our "inner repertory of dense cultural inheritance," Foreman concluded, we risk turning into "'pancake people'—spread wide and thin as we connect with that vast network of information accessed by the mere touch of a button."

I'm haunted by that scene in *2001*. What makes it so poignant, and so weird, is the computer's emotional response to the disassembly of its mind: its despair as one circuit after another goes dark, its childlike pleading with the astronaut—"I can feel it. I can feel it. I'm afraid"—and its final reversion to what can only be called a state of innocence. HAL's outpouring of feeling contrasts with the emotionlessness that characterizes the human figures in the film, who go about their business with an almost robotic efficiency. Their thoughts and actions feel scripted, as if they're following the steps of an algorithm. In the world of *2001*, people have become so machinelike that the most human character turns out to be a machine. That's the essence of Kubrick's dark prophecy: as we come to rely on computers to mediate our understanding of the world, it is our own intelligence that flattens into artificial intelligence.

Brick Wall

Charles D'Ambrosio

Now what remains of the place is an anonymous wall of brick, but not so long ago my uncle ran a bar at 112 1/2 Clinton Street, the half being our family's share in the City of Big Shoulders, Chicago. If the Sears Tower were considered the gnomon of a sundial, and you were inclined to tell time by organizing shadows, then the bar was located at roughly ten o'clock in the morning. By midmorning the shadows swept in, the air darkened, and the streets turned silty, creating sunken rivers of early night, murky and unpromising to most people but suiting just fine the shady temper of the hardcore drinkers and gamblers the bar catered to. In fact they came precisely for that halfness, that demimonde aspect of the address. The building itself occupied an alley that had formerly served as a cattle run from the trains to the stockyards and packing plants on the South Side. Soon after the butchering ended, the bar opened for business. It must have been a big improvement not to taste blood in the wind, blown over the city from the slaughterhouses. When I lived in Chicago, those old abattoirs, long ago lost to history, had become inviolate and fixed in legend, but the city was changing again.

It was destroying itself, or sloughing off its old industrial self, and many of the brick warehouses and factory buildings in the neighborhood, gutted and windowless, deserted, were no better than caves hollowed from rock, with doors gaping open blackly, home to the homeless, the vast vacant interiors lit only by the light of fires burning in oil drums. In seeking the future a city like Chicago wrecks itself and returns to stone, at least briefly. There were piles of rubble such as you imagine in war, but the absence of declared enemies, and the lethargic unfolding of time, its leisurely pace, kept people from seeing the scale of the shift as catastrophic. Factories and warehouses and hotels, these old muscular hopes came down in heaps of brick and mortar, of pulverized concrete and cracked limestone, and then those cairns of rock, in turn, were cleared off to become barren lots as flat and featureless as the prairie they'd supplanted. Now brand-new buildings staunchly occupy those spaces, but for the duration, for the brief winter, spring, and summer I lived and worked next door to the bar, there was the constant gray taste of mortar on my tongue, my lips burning from the lime it was laced with, as clouds of dust were set adrift by each new day's demolition.

Brick is relocated earth, and the streets of a city like Chicago re-create a riverbank, in this case the clay banks of both the Mississippi and Ohio Rivers, where a good portion of Chicago's brick originally came from. The mining of clay is often referred to as "winning," a curious kind of victory, considering the clay used in brickmaking comes from the Carboniferous period, a subcategory of the Paleozoic, some 340 million years ago. Such a vast span of time would seem to temper any man's sense of triumph. It was during the Carboniferous that amniote eggs allowed ancestral birds, mammals, and reptiles to reproduce on land; flight was first achieved, too, as insects evolved wings. And then something happened, something happened to the birds and mammals and reptiles, to the nascent flying insects, to the whole ambition and direction of that geologic age. Everything died off and disappeared in that silent way only an eon can absorb and keep secret.

And yet with death the seedless vascular plants that existed in tropical swamp forests provided the organic material that became coal. These dead plants didn't completely decay and instead turned to peat bogs. When the sea covered the swamps, marine sediments covered the peat, and eventually intense pressure and heat transformed these organic remains into coal and shale. Curiously, burning brick in kilns only extends and completes the process epochal time itself used to form the source clay initially. Brick manufacturers use coal to fire and harden the clay, removing moisture and the last memory, the last vestiges of fluidity from the brick. (In fact there's a taxonomy of bricks based on how burnt they are: clinker brick, nearest the fire, becomes vitrified, glassy and brittle; red brick is the hardest and most desirable product of the kiln; and salmon brick, sitting farthest from the fire, is underburned and soft, unsuitable for exposed surfaces.) The obvious advantage of brick as a building material is that it's already burned, which accounts for its presence in Chicago after the fire of 1871. Brick transformed the city, ushering in an era of industrial greatness, completing— no, not completing, but extending—extending a process that began with a mysterious extinction, a vast unimagined loss.

During my time in Chicago my day job was to load cars and trucks with reproduction furniture, the historical imperative of which had vanished, vaguely, around the turn of the century. Nonetheless, shoppers from the suburbs drove to the city to browse the warehouse, its four floors and forty thousand square feet of fake antiques. They bought oxblood leather wingbacks, banker's lamps, baker's racks, oak iceboxes, old phones with a crank on the side that would, with a turn or two, summon the operator. The furniture was hokey, farmy, Depressiony. Of course none of the people who shopped the warehouse were cutting blocks of winter ice to haul by horse and wagon and then pack and preserve in layers of straw for the long hot summer. They lived in the suburbs; they had appliances. It was curious and teleologically baffling. Why buy a phone you have to crank by hand when you can punch buttons to place your call? Why a wrought-iron baker's rack for men and women whose cookies and bread did their cooling at the factory? Why buy an antique that was hardly two weeks old?

The chaotic layout of the warehouse led many customers to believe they might, in some obscure corner, find a rare treasure, overlooked by others. But all this old stuff was absolutely brand-new; we carried special crayons in our pockets to keep it that way, coloring in the scratches before we showed people their purchases. These people wanted old furniture but perfect, they wanted antiques without time (the main ingredient and, you'd think, the very source of value in anything vintage). Still, the animating urge, the desire for the real, wasn't dead; the day I started the job I noticed nobody bought from the top, no one purchased the front item. Looking behind, for these people, equaled searching for the past, the authentic. Picky, savvy shoppers always made their selections by searching deep into the stacks and piles, mistrusting the surface, the present appearance of things.

Maybe nostalgia is a species of the ideal, a dream of a last interior, where all the commotion of a life is finally rewarded with rest, drained of history. We were selling the memory of something, of hard work and industry, of necessity, of craft and artisanship—the mendacious idea that life was gathered with greater force and organized in superior ways in the past. These faux antiques replaced the real past with an emblematic one. Or something. I could never quite untwist the riddle completely. When you stood in the warehouse the eye was pleasantly bombarded by a vastness filled. But the inspiration for most of the furniture we sold came originally from hardscrabble times, times of scarcity and unrest and an economy based on need, not surplus, and certainly not this absurd superfluity, this crazy proliferation, where two hundred oak iceboxes, stacked to the ceiling on layers of cardboard, would easily sell out on a Saturday afternoon. Why were people so avid and enthusiastic for the emblems of hardship? For what idealized interior could this possibly serve as honest décor?

After closing I'd slip a padlock in the loading-dock door, then stay inside: the furniture warehouse was also my home, I lived in there, vaguely employed as a nightwatchman. Every night I slept on one of, I'm guessing, two hundred sofas. I ate take-out dinners on tables that would be sold the next day. I read books by the greenish light of an ugly banker's lamp, set on a fake oak icebox. My boss was a man of great good fortune who liked to squire his mistress around town in a restored Model T Ford. He hired me to deter theft, set out glue traps, and hose down the dumpsters so bums wouldn't light the cardboard on fire, trying to keep warm. I simplified my job by rigging a cheap alarm system out of magnetic triggers and a hundred yards of lamp wire and a couple Radio Shack sirens perched on the windowsills. In the evenings I'd arm the thing by twisting together the exposed copper strands and head next door to my uncle's bar.

You entered the bar through a black door with a diamond peephole. There were nine stools covered in red leatherette. My uncle did book and collected numbers. Among the patrons you found a deep well of faith, a certain gut feel for what Catholic theologians would call analogical thinking, whereby you come to know the reality of God through signs. Gambling was how you negotiated the tricky path between situation and symbol. Winning was always an answer to a question. Most of the men were spooky about the stool they sat on and would rather stand all night than take a seat that had somehow been hoodooed by past bad luck. Many of these gamblers were afraid of the past, haunted by it, and this tilted their faith in the direction of fate, a less ample, less accommodating idea. On any given night thousands of bloated dollars would sit on the bar in wet frowning stacks. I'd never seen such sums. I drank

Old Style and peppermint schnapps and lived off pork rinds and pickled eggs. The eggs floated in a gallon jar of green amniotic pond-water like specimens of some kind of nascent life-form.

Gambling and dim light and slow-rising smoke and the forgottenness of the place made it seem like everybody in the bar had strange and compelling mysteries behind them. They were dense with background, or so you inferred, or romanticized, because the present, the very surface of life, was so meager, so without evidence or account. In this sense my take on these men wasn't all that different from the way the warehouse customers saw our fake antiques. Any "background" I granted them was just another kind of décor, the décor of history, of image—in particular, history and image in their arrested or hardened forms, as nostalgia and cliché. The bar was the kind of place where people were "characters" and were known, to the extent that they were known at all, by some fragment of personality, a piece of self broken off and magnified until it was more recognizable than the original man behind it, overshadowing him. Character, in the bar, really was fate.

And so a character named Red Devil seemed a proxy voice, speaking for everybody, when he would cackle hysterically and yell out, "Mantina, 1963. I'm history!" Mantina was the state prison, but nothing beyond that was elaborated. To be history in America doesn't mean to be recorded, noted, added to the narrative, but precisely the opposite, to be gone, banished, left behind. To be history is to be cut from the story.

Other characters? Here are two. They even have character names, names I'd avoid if I were writing fiction: Al and George.

Al tended the bar at night. He'd been in the merchant marine and ate with a fat clunky thumb holding down his plate as if he were afraid the whole place might pitch and yaw and send his dinner flying. He was dwarfish and looked like an abandoned sculpture, a forgotten intention. His upper body was a slablike mass, a plinth upon which his head rested; he had a chiseled nose and jaw, a hack-job scar of a mouth; his hands were thick and stubby, more like paws than anything prehensile. Sitting back behind the bar, smoking Pall Malls, he seemed petrified, the current shape of his body achieved by erosion, his face cut by clumsy strokes and blows. His eyes, though, were soft and blue, always wet and weepy with rheum, and when you looked at Al, you had the disorienting sense of something trapped, something fluid and human caught inside the gray stone vessel of his gargoyle body, gazing out through those eyes. He was my only real neighbor. At closing he'd collect the glasses, wipe down the bottles, shut the blinds, and go to sleep on the bar. In the morning he'd fold his blankets and stow them away in a cardboard box.

George was another fixture in the bar, a salesman working, like me, in the furniture warehouse. He drank beer all day, chased with shots of peppermint schnapps so that his breath would smell fresh, as though he'd just brushed his teeth. Like most drunks he had the baffling notion he was getting away with it, fooling everybody. I felt sorry for George because he wasn't fooling anybody and couldn't see the truth, that he was being tolerated and temporarily ignored. With his insulin shots, instant coffee, his shabby dress, his elaborate comb-over, he led an obscure life, irregular and unobserved, except at the bar. There he gambled with a nervousness torqued up tight by a belief in the quick tidy fate of accidents, of moments that decide everything. Sometime in the past, he believed, things had gone wrong, gone fatally so. The present was his evidence. Divorce. Bankruptcy. Alcoholism. He had a gimpy leg, he was diabetic. He gambled the games, the horses, the numbers, the state lottery, everything. Sometime in the future there was a wager that would be won, a score that would redress everything, and perhaps this injection of faith, more than, say, a visit to the doctor, eased the pain for him.

"When I have money," he told me, "I can't sleep, I can't hardly eat. I don't feel good until it's gone."

In the bar a small bet was called "an interest bet," a wager that attached you fiercely, with greater vividness, to the flow of an otherwise monotonous day. It offered you a way into time, via the wide and democratic avenue of chance; even the smallest gamble instantly gave you a stake in the outcome of time itself. With a bet on, time had something to show you, held the promise of a revelation. When George was betting he had the sensibility of a psychotic, or a poet. There were nuances to assay, meanings to consider. Accidents became auguries. The odds on unrelated matters changed. Emotions rose to the surface, the buried inner life became relevant, and he grew sensitive, tender, his instinctual self, now resuscitated, engaged in the world's new density. Nothing out in the actual world demanded quite the same concentration of being, the same focused energy. With money on the line, he became aware of time, of his place in it, and planned ahead. On payday he broke half his check into quarters, dimes, and nickels, storing the coins in a coffee can at home; it was the only way he could keep himself from gambling all his money and make sure he'd have enough saved aside for food at the end of the month.

Most people in the area around the bar were passing through, transient. They were commuters who caught the trains and left behind an acute emptiness, a hollow around seven o'clock every night. Of course some people came in search of precisely this lacuna, this moment when the day lapsed into nothingness. Richard Speck sought it, holing up at the Star Hotel a few blocks away, paying ninety cents a night for his furnished room, in the weeks after he'd murdered eight student nurses. This was 1966 and Speck planned to hop a freight train west but never managed to leave the Loop until he was sentenced to death. The single nurse who survived that attack, hidden flat beneath a bed, figured in my dreams for years. She squeezed herself beneath that bed and for hours listened to the sounds of sex followed by the sounds of death. I was a very young boy when this protohorrific crime happened but for some reason I know Speck tenderly asked the last woman he was raping if she'd wrap her legs around him. That winter they tore down the Star Hotel and I watched from a distance, watched the swing of a wrecking ball as it arced through the air, collided soundlessly, then came through, a couple seconds later, with a laggard explosion of crumbling brick.

At night black men in jalopy flatbeds scavenged through mounds of debris to save the bricks. In a book about brick, D. Knickerbacker Boyd writes: "When two bricks are struck together, they should emit a metallic ring." That's true. Bricks clink together with a satisfying ring akin to fine crystal. The sound has a clarity, a rightness. Bricks also improve with age and highly valued skids of cured Chicago brick were sold to people as far away as Phoenix and San Francisco, people who made walkways, garden walls, and barbecues from remnants of old factories. At night the air cleared of dust. To the west was Greek Town, across the freeway, with a row of restaurants concentrated enough so that some nights I'd pick up the arid scent of oregano; north was the Haymarket with its rotting fruit; and from somewhere, on certain nights, in a building I searched for but could never locate, a candymaker spread the smell of chocolate and cinnamon in the air. From my window in the warehouse I'd hear the black men knocking away like moonlighting archaeologists, knocking until the old soft mortar was chipped loose and the clean red brick rang out as resonantly as a bell.

In the bar people kept drinking and betting right up to the very end. One night a stranger appeared and took George by the arm and led him gently, like a church usher, out to the sidewalk. Words were exchanged in pantomime. After a minute the stranger crushed George in the head with a length of pipe. George had raised his arms in supplication, beseeching, and when the pipe crashed down, his head bowed penitentially before he slumped to his knees, then fell forward on his face. You hardly ever see adults on the ground, they don't spin or twirl, they don't flop over and fall for the fun of it, not like kids. In my experience adults only went to the ground in death. George owed the man money. It was a confusing sight, seeing him like that, a grown man sprawled out on the sidewalk, small and broken, with no more control over himself than a child.

Now when I think of it, I understand it was never so much the potential for gain that animated gamblers like George, these men who had nothing, but being reawakened to a world where loss was once again possible. That's really what gave them life and drove them again and again to the game. Loss was their métier and to have that taken away, to be, finally, lost, was the worst thing imaginable. As long as you could fall farther you distinguished yourself from the fallen. Loss reinstated possibility, but possibility without hope. And perhaps this explains how all of us blithely imagined that the general wreckage would pass over the bar, that it was somehow exempt. Gambling offered a refuge from the outside world, its advances, its mysterious evolution. No one believed the bar would end, not because we didn't believe in progress, but instead, more precisely, because our kind of gambling, the wish of it, was an attempt to salvage the past. We weren't so much hoping to change the future as we were trying to amend history. We wanted the past completely restored and made livable. We believed that was the only kind of winning that counted.

My Memory and Witness

Lis Goldschmidt & Dean Spade

Dean—

Hey. How's things in NYC? Tired here. Just home from hanging out with every-one. Feeling really tired of the class stuff we were talking about the other day. Tired of people fronting like they're poor or grew up poor or whatever—like it's cool to be poor. You know the deal. They put it on like an accessory. You know? Just like co-opting any culture. Do you know what I mean? It's like people who wear "native garb" from wherever they're exoticizing at the moment—but the thing is, they take it off when it gets old to them.

I guess I'm just feeling pretty pissed. Like I can't take it off. Like it *is* old. It's always been old. And makes me feel old and fucking tired. And small.

I don't mean to rant.

The main reason I'm writing is 'cause you carry the facts and I feel like I need them. You know the details that I think can help me not feel erased by these kinds of nights. You know how much Mom made. You know the welfare info. It sounds dumb—I know what it was like, but I've spent my whole life pretending it was something else, my whole life trying to pass as something else—and I need the numbers to feel justified or some shit. I need those numbers to prove me wrong or call me out or something. Does that sound weird? It's like I've even convinced myself . . . also like I want some fact to separate me from those people.

I mean I remember it. I remember what it was like. I remember the shame and all that. I remember that greedy excited fucked-up feeling I got when she'd bring home the groceries. I remember swallowing myself one zillion times. I remember being an invisible eyesore. I remember knowing this couldn't be right. When I think of it now I get that same empty, gagging thing. I remember that heavy fucking cloud that hung around our tiny house. That fog that made it so hard to breathe. That stress that kept us all quiet and angry and sad. Remember?

I'm scrambling to think of something good and light, but it goes back as far as I can remember. It only got darker and heavier.

The end was the worst, right? I guess for me it was the worst because I felt like I was the mom when she was sick. You know? Not that we didn't both have to pick up what she couldn't carry anymore. But I remember doing the grocery shopping by myself. You know, I think it's really only the last maybe five years that I don't have some crazy fear while in line at the grocery store. I think this is actually the first time I've really thought about it. There's the shame of shopping at the discount store. Scared someone from school would see us or something—and scared that if anyone ever came to our house (not that they ever did), they'd see the bags from there. (Not to mention just seeing the house!) But then there were all the times we had to put stuff back—do you remember that? I cringe thinking about it now. It was terrible. Embarrassing. I remember being scared to look at Mom in that moment. How she'd look it all over and have to decide what to put back. How did she do that? How can you decide what food your three kids *don't* need? Can you imagine how stressful that must have been for her? *Ugh.* It fucking makes me want to puke. Then there was the shame of using food stamps. It's funny how kids I know now use food stamps with so much pride.

Dean, this sucks. I hate thinking about this stuff. I'm trying to reclaim it or something but sometimes it just feels like Mom trained us so well that passing is easier and the shame is too thick. Sometimes I think I'd make the world's greatest spy because I can pretend so well. Time to sleep.

I hope you're well—

I'm glad we have each other in this.

—xo, Lis

Dear Lis,

I took this letter with me to Montreal where I was showing the film Tara and I are making about trans people and bathrooms. While I was there, friends of friends had a "white trash"–themed barbecue. The people I was staying with called the hosts to voice our protest to this theme, and heard that others were also upset, so we went anyway, thinking people wouldn't participate in the theme and that the message had gotten across. Of course, we were too optimistic. Many people came fake-pregnant, with giant Budweiser cans, fake southern accents, and severe blue eye shadow. What to do? I thought about how "trashy" it is for poor people to have children, how differently poor people's substance abuse is surveyed and punished, how easily these white people employed a term that suggests that all nonwhite people are trash while only some white people require such labeling. I thought about the time you were invited to a white-trash event where people were encouraged to black out their teeth, and I thought of how Mom lived her whole life hiding that she had dentures—like everyone in her family—from a time when "dental care for the poor" was pulling out all their teeth in adolescence. When she died I learned she had hidden this from me (you too?) my whole life—sleeping in uncomfortable dentures all those nights during our thirteen years together when I was too scared to sleep alone—all to hide from even me her poverty and shame. (Meanwhile I dreamt of the braces the other kids at school could afford.) I thought of my own consciousness, starting in elementary school, of the need to separate myself from the term "white trash." Be careful how you smell, who sees your house. Try to get Mom not to curse or smoke in front of other people's parents.

But at this party I bit my tongue and turned my head when they arrived in costumes. Couldn't bring myself to speak on this rooftop full of people I had just met. I spend sixty to eighty hours a week exclusively talking about poverty and advocating for poor people, but I could not advocate for myself, could not give up the small amount of passing, of blending in. We left fast and Pascal, Brianna, and I ranted on the street, wondering how we should have handled it, talking about how girl-social conditioning still operates in our trans bodies, convincing us we shouldn't confront. With every passing hour I've become more irate. No place to put it. More anger to add to the churning crushing pile that lives behind my sternum.

Tired. I hear you about being tired. I'm tired of being diplomatic about poverty. Tired of trying to convince rich people at nonprofits, rich people at foundations, and rich gay people especially to care about and support the lives of low-income intersex and trans people. I'm tired of helping them notice that we exist, trying not to make them too uncomfortable to give money to the struggle that (when we win, which we will) will end wealth and poverty for everyone. Tired of being gentle and nonthreatening and helping them appease the guilt about their hoarding lifestyles so they can act a little. And I'm tired of hearing that you're getting paid less than the private-college educated man who sits next to you doing the same job, and tired of seeing all my trans friends without jobs or adequate housing and trapped in the criminal-injustice system. I'm tired of other poverty lawyers (from upper-class backgrounds) telling me I don't pay myself enough when I make twice what Mom supported four people on in the years she had jobs, and when our clients are fighting like hell for a couple hundred bucks a month from welfare or ten bucks to make a call from jail. I have to figure out how to not get too tired. Sometimes I think that's what killed our mom. Somehow, you and I got out of there, out of that dirty house, off those gravel roads, out of Virginia, but she didn't make it. I think all the time of what it would be like if she could see us now—if I could make her a fancy dinner in my apartment (artichokes) and take her to see something city-beautiful; if, for her birthday, we could fly her to San Francisco and all three of us could have tea in your kitchen and walk around Golden Gate Park and she'd tell us the names of all the flowers. It's almost Mother's Day.

You asked for the facts. I carry them around like the chip on my shoulder. The most she ever made was $18,000 one year. Our welfare was less than $400 a month. We got a total of $50 when we three spent Saturdays cleaning the glass and mirror store, less when we cleaned houses. The social security survivors benefits our foster parents got for us were about $500 a month each until we turned eighteen. (It's sick that she could support us better by dying but there was not money to help keep her alive.) The jacket she always wanted when she was in middle and high school, that all the other kids had but she never got, cost $7.02 Canadian. The most important fact, maybe, is that if we'd been in the same situation after the 1996 welfare cuts, we wouldn't have been entitled to the same benefits because of her immigration status, and, in my estimation, we would have had a much harder time keeping a place to live or staying together as a family as long as we did.

I love you, Lis. You're my memory and my witness, and my only connection to all that we've lost. I love that you keep the sweatpants Mom got in rehab and that I slept in when you were caring for me after my chest surgery. When I'm not biting my tongue, it's because I'm thinking of how quickly you call people on their shit, how vicious your wit can be, and how you always have my back.

Love, Dean

To Sleep, Perchance to Dream
© Carl De Keyzer/Magnum Photos
Published March 2, 2009, in *Slate*
http://todayspictures.slate.com/20090302/

The image above, from 1987, is the first in the photo essay "To Sleep, Perchance to Dream," which includes photographs of rest and slumber from around the world. Its caption reads, "ALLEPPEY, India—Kerala waters."

Leaving Babylon: A Walk Through the Jewish Divorce Ceremony

Judyth Har-Even

Two years after Cyrus, King of Persia, conquered the Babylonian Empire, he allowed the Children of Israel to return to their land. The year was 537 BCE. Two thousand five hundred and thirty-six years later, I walk down his street in Jerusalem, on my way to get divorced at the district rabbinic court. The travel agencies on Cyrus Street are not advertising group tours to Iraq, not yet. Nonetheless, Babylon is on my mind. By its rivers we sat down and wept when we remembered Zion and wondered how we could sing the Lord's song in a strange land. I wept and wondered, too, for twenty-seven years of married life. Now, just as the Children of Israel walked back to their homeland, their freedom, I am walking to mine.

If all goes well at the courthouse this morning, I will receive my *get*, a Jewish writ of divorce. I already have a civil-divorce document, signed and stamped by an Israeli judge from the district family court. But to remarry in Israel, where I live, and to have "Divorced" rather than "Married" written on my identity card, I need the *get*. Only this document states categorically that I am divorced according to the Law of Moses and Israel.

The civil divorce derives from the decree of a civil court. The Jewish divorce derives from a ceremony steeped in tradition, played out by husband and wife in a rabbinic court. Friends have told me that the *get* ceremony, to which I am walking, is demeaning, primitive, and meaningless.

Demons flitter and play along the narrow hallways of Jerusalem's rabbinic court. They are waiting to snatch a soul. Rabbinic legend claims that when people—women, especially—are in transition from one stage of life to another, demons get restless. Since the rabbinic court is the venue for changing one's personal status, the building is a playground for demons. Watch out, the Talmudic sages warned. Break a glass at weddings; walk around the groom seven times; read Psalms; wear amulets—anything to keep away the evil spirits.

I weave my way through the hallways and arrive intact at the waiting room of Hall A. Other than Psalms, there are no instructions for the soon-to-be-divorced, save

"Leaving Babylon: A Walk Through the Jewish Divorce Ceremony," by Judyth Har-Even as appeared in *Creative Non-Fiction*. Reprinted by permission of Judy Labensohn, www.WriteInIsrael.com.

for two signs on the door to the courtroom: TURN OFF YOUR CELLULAR PHONE, and DRESS MODESTLY. I pick up Psalms, open it randomly to number 13, and read:

> *How long will I have cares on my mind, grief in my heart all day?*
> *How long will my enemy be exalted over me?*
> *Look and hear me, O Lord my God:*
> *Restore the luster to my eyes, lest I sleep the sleep of death . . .*

I am wearing a long black skirt, a white blouse with sleeves that cover my lascivious elbows, and a black sun hat. When my husband enters the room and sees me dressed in uncharacteristically ultramodest garb, reading Psalms, he chides, "Who the fuck are you kidding?"

I am sitting at home by myself, reading the newspaper by the light of one lamp. There is a knock at the door. It is snowing outside, but I can't see the snow because black paper is still taped to the windows. The Yom Kippur War has been over for two months. My husband, a paratrooper, is still stationed in Goshen. Before the war we were trying to make a baby, but now with him being mobilized, there is no chance. My eggs escape unnoticed, untouched. The snow has closed all the roads to Jerusalem.

The knocking persists.

All day I work with bereaved families. As a volunteer social worker for the Ministry of Defense, I help mothers mourn their sons, widows their husbands, children their fathers. I am afraid to open the door, because I know it could be a team of soldiers saying to me, "Your husband is dead."

The knocking persists. I walk to the door. I open it. A man stands there in a green uniform covered with mud and snow. He holds an M16 in one hand and ten red roses in the other.

"Ovulate yet?" he asks.

An usher calls out our last name and escorts us into the chamber. Opposite the door, towering above us, is a long Formica desk. Behind it, three rabbinic judges sit ensconced on cushioned chairs. They wear costumes—black jackets, white shirts, gray beards, and black hats with flat rims. The rabbi on the left is immersed in reading a tome and does not look up when we enter the courtroom. The rabbi on the right is sucking his thumb. He avoids my incredulous stare, which he would have to interpret as lecherous, versed as he must be in rabbinic wisdom. The judge in the middle looks at my husband and me as if our whole sad history is incised on our foreheads.

To the left of the long desk is a small green Formica desk with a computer. Here sits the court secretary. He is a kindly-looking man, bald, with a skullcap.

"Has your w-w-witness arrived?" the attentive rabbi asks.

"Yes," I respond.

"Tell her to come in and then be seated."

I do as I'm told. Nechama, my witness, is an observant Jew from my hometown in the United States. She has played this role for other divorcing friends.

Act One: The Name

"Do you know this woman's f-f-father?" the rabbi asks Nechama.

"Yes. I knew him."

The rabbi listens as if this is the most important information he has heard since his political party became the second largest in Israel.

"Was he a C-C-Cohen?"

"I don't know."

Now the rabbi leans over his desk to question me.

"Did your father ever tell you he was a C-C-Cohen?"

My thoughts race to Moses, the prophet who stuttered. I repress a smile. My father didn't even know what a Cohen was.

"Never," I say.

We are both surprised at the discrepancy in the religious documents. Apparently my name on the *ketubah*, the marriage contract, says I am the daughter of a Cohen. The marriage certificate, however, issued by the Ministry of Religious Affairs after the wedding, says I am a daughter of Israel.

For the purposes of personal status, Jews are divided into two categories: Cohen, the priestly class, and Israel, the rest. I always thought I was one of the rest, but now it appears I may belong to the priestly class.

"What name was used when your father was called up to the T-T-Torah?" the rabbi demands.

A Jewish name, for purposes of marriage and divorce, consists of a given name, the given names of one's mother and father, and the father's religious class, that is, Cohen or Israel. This is why we are spending twenty minutes trying to figure out who I am. Judyth? Judy? Yehudit? Cohen? Israel?

My precise name and lineage is of the utmost importance because the writ of divorce has to be written specifically for me. The legal principle that the *get* be written for a specific wife on a particular day derives from interpretations of the first two verses in chapter 24, Deuteronomy:

> *When a man has taken a wife and married (possesses) her and it comes to pass that she no longer finds favor in his eyes, because he has found some unseemly thing in her, then let him write her a bill of divorce and give it in her hand and send her out of his house. And when she is departed out of his house, she may go and be another man's wife.*

This passage offered fertile soil for reams of rabbinic free associations and legalities, which were ultimately woven together in Tractate Gittin of the Babylonian Talmud, compiled in 500 CE. Talmudic sages deduced at least nine legal principles from the passage in Deuteronomy:

1. *A man must divorce his wife of his own free will.*
2. *A woman must be divorced in writing.*
3. *The* get *must be a document that states clearly that it severs all ties between husband and wife.*

4. *The husband must give the* get *to the wife. She cannot take it.*
5. *He must put it in her hand. The woman is not divorced until the* get *comes into her possession.*
6. *The document must state that he sends her out.*
7. *The* get *must be given in the presence of two or three witnesses. (This is based on a common word—*davar*—"thing," which appears in Deuteronomy 24:1–2 and 19:15 where it refers to witnesses.)*
8. *The* get *must be given immediately after it is written. (For instance, if a husband goes bowling after he writes the* get *or obtains it from a scribe, and then delivers it, the* get *is invalid, unkosher.)*
9. *The* get *must be given only for the purpose of divorce; it cannot be used as a threat.*

"Was her father a C-C-Cohen?" the rabbi pleads again.

It is one hour before the wedding. The men are sitting around a table with the officiating Orthodox rabbi filling in the details of the ketubah. *The rabbi turns to my father.*
"What was the name you gave your daughter at birth?"
"She was christened Judy."
The other men, including my husband-to-be, cannot believe their ears. They motion my father to shut up.
"Christened?" the rabbi repeats, eyebrows raised.
"Yes. At birth we called her Judy."
"But . . . was she christened?"
"Oh, I don't know. That's what we called her."
"Was she christened?"
"What the hell difference does it make? You think every word is important? Let's just get her married, for Christ's sake."

"Who was the rabbi who officiated at your w-w-wedding?" This rabbi is desperate for details, where, some believe, God dwells.

"Rabbi Natan," I reply, "an Orthodox rabbi from Jerusalem." I emphasize this last point so he will understand that someone in his own Orthodox establishment screwed up in 1972.

The talking rabbi looks at the reading rabbi, who points at his watch and urges him to proceed.

The rabbi decides that I am an Israel, thanks my witness, and dismisses her. Then he calls my husband's witness. The man is a jerk. He makes light of my husband's many nicknames. The rabbi reminds him this is serious business, chooses two names among the many, and sends him away after a ten-minute interrogation.

At this juncture a cellular phone in my husband's briefcase rings. The judges and court secretary take cover, as if a knife-wielding terrorist has burst into the room.

"Didn't you read the sign?" the rabbi yells. "Turn that thing off. A little respect for the court, please."

I wonder if Moses lost his stutter when he reprimanded the Children of Israel.

Act Two: The Players

The rabbi calls in two *shlubs*. Their shirttails hang over their black trousers, and their black skullcaps dangle from the sides of their heads. Tweedledee and Tweedledum are full-time employees of the Ministry of Religious Affairs, two of six men who play the role of witness at divorce proceedings. They enter from a side door like extras on a movie set, their only task to stand up, pay attention, and say "Yes" or "No" when asked. My taxes pay their salaries.

The two witnesses stand between the court secretary and the rabbis. Then the talking rabbi calls in my husband's emissary. Enter the Torah scribe. He is a short man wearing a white shirt with a frayed collar and a black skullcap placed on his bald head like a dot over an *i*. He takes up his position opposite my husband. His props are a piece of parchment made from the skin of a kosher animal, a *kulmus*, or reed pen, and a small bottle of ink. The ink is made of crushed sap, pomegranate skin, gallnut, and soot from burnt grapevines, all brewed in water for twelve hours. The exact recipe has been passed down from generation to generation for the past sixteen hundred years, give or take.

The drama begins when the rabbi tells the scribe to give his writing instruments to my husband.

"These are now y-y-yours," says the rabbi, looking at my husband. "Repeat after me: 'These are my writing implements.'"

My husband swallows his pride and intelligence to get out the sentence. "These are my writing implements."

"Speak up and take the gum out of your mouth."

My husband takes the gum out of his mouth and holds it in his right hand. Then he repeats, "These are my writing implements."

The rabbi swivels toward the witnesses and asks if they heard.

"Yes," they chirp.

Then he swivels back.

"Now give your writing implements to the Torah scribe and say, 'I am giving you my implements, and you will write the *get* for me.'"

"I am giving you my implements, and you will write the *get* for me," my husband whispers as he hands the writing materials to the scribe.

The rabbi turns to the scribe and asks, "Did he just give you these writing m-m-materials?"

Well versed, the scribe produces a clear "Yes." Then the rabbi instructs the scribe, my husband, and the two witnesses to retire to a separate room to write the *get*, the writ of divorce. I am dismissed for intermission.

A scribe writes the *get* on a parchment marked with a stylus. The text consists of twelve lines of Hebrew and Aramaic, 12 being the numerical value of the Hebrew letters *gimmel* and *tet*, which spell *get*. The exact wording was finalized by the Babylonian sages of the fourth century CE, who also laid down strict details for its calligraphy. The *get* could only be written in a city or town with a source of water.

This is the standard Jerusalem text, which my husband and the two witnesses watched the scribe write with his reed pen:

On the _____ day of the week, the _____ day of the month _____, in the year _____
of the creation of the world, according to the number of years we count here in Jerusalem, on
the waters of the Siloam Spring and by cistern waters, I, called _____, son of _____, called
_____, standing today in Jerusalem, the city which has cisterns for water, do hereby consent
with my own free will, without any duress, to free and release and divorce you, my wife, called
_____, daughter of _____, called _____, standing today in Jerusalem, who has previ-
ously been my wife, and now I release and send away and divorce you so that you will be free
to go and govern yourself and be married to any man you desire and let no person oppose you
from this day and forever and behold you are permitted to every man. And this shall be for you
from me a bill of divorce and an epistle of sending away and a bill of release according to the
Law of Moses and Israel.
_____, son of _____, witness
_____, son of _____, witness

The Mishna, the code of Jewish law edited by Judah the Prince in Zippori, Lower Galilee, around 2000 CE, says that a husband can write the writ of divorce on the horn of a bull, but then the husband must hand his wife the whole bull. A husband or his scribe can write the prescribed lines on the hand of a slave, but then the wife gets the living, full-bodied slave. The rabbis argued over whether the writ of divorce could be written on an olive leaf. I think about these disputes as I wait for the final act of my *get* ceremony. My tradition often seems bizarre, ludicrous, and surreal. These are the qualities that my friends warned me about, interpreting the ceremony as demeaning, primitive, and mean-ingless. But this strangeness stems from the ceremony being rooted in a time when Jews owned slaves and scribes wrote on horns. Though part of me chuckles at the antics of the three rabbis this morning, another part acknowledges that the tradition is larger and richer than those rabbis who claim to be its guardians. Standing in front of the politically appointed rabbinic judges, I look beyond them and see the Israelites who walked out of Babylon and those who left Egypt. The Israelites came home from the north and from the south at different periods in my history. They came from the east and from the west throughout the centuries, all yearning to create a new life in a promised land.

We are all players in the same story. It is an ancient tale, told and retold, and though the ceremony this morning in 1999 seems absurd, I love it for the continuity it affords. Each jot and tittle holds me in place against torrents of upheaval. When pieces of my life shatter like shards, the tradition binds. Moreover, the same sages and texts that prescribe my Jewish divorce determined the ceremony in which I was wed, that in which my sons entered the Covenant and those that I enact every Sabbath and on holidays. It is that tradition, that Jewish sanctification of time, that provided the scaffolding for holding my family together for twenty-seven years. Ironically it is that same tradition that allows me an out.

Jewish tradition accepts divorce as a necessary evil, evil because ideally a marriage parallels the eternal covenant between God and Israel. The prophet Malachi admonishes, "Let no one break faith with the wife of his youth. For I detest divorce, said the Lord, the God of Israel." Being human, however, the Talmudic sages recognized the difference between the ideal and the real. They understood that divorce was sometimes necessary, but they did not want to make it an easy procedure.

A kosher divorce cannot be derived by a simple public statement of "You are no longer my wife." A valid divorce cannot be derived from one action—a husband sending out his wife from their home. The sages determined that a divorce, according to the Law of Moses and Israel, is valid only if a specific document is written in the presence of two witnesses and given to the wife in the presence of those same witnesses. The Talmudic sages hoped that the husband, while going through the involved process, would reconsider and not divorce.

Whereas God was present in my wedding ceremony, He is absent from the divorce proceedings. His name is neither mentioned nor invoked. I imagine Him off in a corner, sulking, and for good reason. What, after all, has God been doing every day since the creation of the world? According to the Babylonian Talmud, He has been running a dating service, matchmaking, a task more difficult, the sages claim, than splitting the waters during the Exodus.

My tradition is the palace in which I play out universal themes. Encountering it here in the rabbinic court on a summer morning at the end of the second millennium, I feel as if I have been catapulted back to my roots. The penchant for detail springs from these rock-bottom roots.

I am fortunate that my husband is cooperating in granting me a *get*. Thousands of Jewish women are not so lucky. Called *agunot*, they are locked in unwanted, often violent marriages because their husbands refuse to grant them a *get*. For them the tradition is a prison. For me it is an ancient palace, rising out of a chaotic sea, a palace I visit at the most meaningful transitions of my life.

Act Three: The Walk

After twenty minutes my husband returns with the scribe and the witnesses. They are not smiling. The five of us walk back into the chambers.

The rabbi asks my husband if he is giving me this divorce of his own free will or if somebody is forcing him to do so. In Jewish tradition only the man can grant the woman a divorce. Even if the woman initiates the divorce, the man must say that he is willingly granting it. I hesitate. My husband could balk. He could scream, "It's all *her* idea. *She's* the one who left *me*. *She's* the one who's always taking the initiative. *I* didn't want to get married in the first place. It was *her* idea. It's all *her* fault."

The ambivalence in my heart would like him not to cooperate, at least for a minute. I would like to hear a refusal because it would be an acknowledgment that he cares. But he acquiesces, albeit softly.

"I can't hear you," the rabbi bellows.

"Yes, my own free will. Nobody is forcing me." He barely opens his lips.

We are standing under the wedding canopy in 1972. It is a warm May evening—Lag B'Omer, the thirty-third day of the counting of the barley offering in Jerusalem two thousand years ago, and the only date between Passover and the Feast of Weeks when Orthodox Jewish weddings can take place. Two witnesses and my mother stand with us under the canopy. Tears squat in the corners of my mother's eyes. I see them when I walk around my fiancé seven times. After the seventh circle, I stop next to my man. He looks like a child who has been praised by his kindergarten teacher. He lifts my veil to give me a sip of wine. It is sweet and sanctified. Then he opens his lips slightly, just slightly, and takes a sip. God is crossing His fingers.

The rabbi turns to the witnesses. "Did you hear him?"

"Yes," they chant.

The scribe hands the parchment to my husband, who hands it to the rabbi, who folds it into sixths and hands it back to my husband. The parchment is like a hot potato. Nobody wants to hold it because it is human evidence that God failed. And if His matchmaking is faulty, what about His other interventions?

The rabbi tells my husband to say the following words to me: "Behold, this is your *get*. Accept it, for with it you will be divorced from me from this moment and be permitted to all men." My husband follows the rabbi's orders. He looks straight into my eyes.

"Behold, this is your *get*. Accept it, for with it you will be divorced from me from this moment and be permitted to all men."

The words freeze in the hot July air. I cannot believe he is letting me go, sending me out to copulate with other men. We were enmeshed for so many years. How can he do this to me?

It is the first year of our marriage. Every night, I lie on top of my husband, who lies on the living room couch and watches television. We are one flesh. Eventually I want to sit up. I even want to go into the other room to read a book. I go.

For weeks he does not respond when I talk to him. Over the years we try five marriage counselors. Nothing works. One night after twenty-four years of marriage, he throws a damp towel onto my desk.

"This was out of place," he shouts.

I ask him to leave.

"If you don't like it, lady, you know where the fuck you can go."

Now the rabbi tells me to hold my arms out toward my husband and cup my hands together, with my thumbs slightly inside the cups. I do as I am told.

"No, do not move your thumbs. Do not grab," he admonishes. "You are a vessel. Let the parchment fall into your hands. He must give it to y-y-you."

Now he directs my husband. "Hold the folded parchment about half a meter above her h-h-hands." My husband obeys.

"As soon as he drops it," the rabbi instructs me, "I want you to grasp it with two hands, like this." He holds his hands in the position of Christian prayer.

We both do as we're told. My husband drops the writ of divorce into my hands. I clutch the folded parchment.

"Did you see that?" the rabbi turns to ask the witnesses, who are still awake.

"Yes," they yawn.

"Now hold your hands in front of you, grasping the writ, and walk over th-th-there," he tells me, pointing to the far side of the room.

I am a good walker.

It is a Friday night, the Sabbath. We are seated at either end of the dining room table, flanked by our three children. I have blessed the Sabbath candles; my husband has blessed the wine; our youngest son has blessed the bread. This is the only time during the week we sit together as a family. I want it to be pleasant, so I make conversation and encourage the children to speak. My husband watches the TV weekly news roundup. I hope he won't explode this week, when the wine spills on the tablecloth. I want it to be pleasant, a blessing.

As my fourteen-year-old daughter and I clear the soup plates—homemade vegetable barley—she says to me, "Don't you see he doesn't love you?"

I control the tears through the homemade apple strudel and then run out the door, down the sixty-four stairs, up seven blocks, down two hills, over three neighborhoods, halfway to Bethlehem. I walk fast, tears streaming down my cheeks, arms swinging violently.

By the time I return to the living room an hour later, everyone is sitting in silence in front of the TV, watching the latest terrorist attack.

In the courtroom I take large, powerful strides, but the room, being small and crowded, is big enough only for three. I would crash through the wall if the rabbi told me to, but when I come up against the corner, he says to turn around and come back. I walk. I stand below the three rabbis, the folded parchment between my palms. The rabbi looks at me and says, "You are now a divorced woman. You are permitted to any m-m-man, and you can get married in ninety-two days. Please give me the parchment."

I hand the rabbi the document. He tears it slightly to assure that another couple with our exact names will not use this *get* today.

I say "Thank you" and "Goodbye." The reading rabbi closes his book; the sucking rabbi extracts his thumb; and Moses wishes us good luck in our new lives.

When I say "Thank you" and "Goodbye" to my ex-husband, his silent armor glistens.

Downstairs, outside, a smile breaks forth. It stretches from Cyrus Street to King Solomon Road. I walk over to King David Street and think what a pity these kings are dead, now that I am available and my self-esteem can handle royalty. Marriage, however, is not on my mind, despite the rabbi's mention of those ninety-two days. According to the calculations of the Talmudic sages, that is how long it will take to determine if I am pregnant. This is important, in order to determine the hypothetical fatherhood of the hypothetical fetus.

The King David Hotel on King David Street is bustling with activity. U.S. envoy Dennis Ross is in town trying to help Israelis and Palestinians piece together a separation agreement. Tourist buses block the road. I am glad I am not a tourist. The only place I want to go to is the land of self-respect, the land of my freedom. My feet will take me there. I turn onto Hebron Way. Cars, buses, and ambulances race by as I walk out of bondage, leaving Babylon.

For our first anniversary, I want to buy him something special. He doesn't like jewelry. In fact he doesn't even wear a wedding ring. I choose the Encyclopedia Judaica and buy it on installments. I imagine my husband will be proud to own this rich compendium of Jewish knowledge.

On the eve of our anniversary, he opens the carton, looks, hesitates, and then closes it. He turns to me with disappointment.

"You really don't know who I am, do you?"

I turn onto Ein Gedi Street, where I live with solitude in a garden apartment. Suddenly, the earth whimpers; a soft hiss rises from the ground. From the north an unnatural dampness saturates the street. Sniffles and staccato breaths ride the hot July air. I stop. I wipe tears from my cheeks and rub my fingers on the amulet around my neck.

I will miss Babylon, where I stayed too long. Even in a strange land, one learns to sing.

Like shards, the final words from Tractate Gittin scatter before me on the damp pavement. I pick them up and reconstruct the ancient truth, "When a man divorces the wife of his youth, even the altar sheds tears."

Judy Har-Even on *"Leaving Babylon"*

I wrote "Leaving Babylon" during my first year in the low-residency MFA program in creative nonfiction at Goucher College. Lisa Knopp, one of the program's excellent mentors, had given a presentation about libraries and research techniques for personal essays. The idea of researching anything for a personal essay astounded me, because for years I had written personal essays simply because they demanded, or so I thought, no research. Lisa's ideas were challenging and, ultimately, liberating.

At the time, I was reading the anthropologist Victor Turner on pilgrimage and I thought the *get* ceremony, which I had recently experienced, offered a wealth of research possibilities. But as much as I wanted to explore the ancient ceremony, I also wanted to express the personal pain, for which I needed no library.

I read books on Jewish divorce, all of which referred to the Talmud, of course. I knew I would have to overcome my fear of opening this humbling compendium of Jewish law and lore which until recently only Jewish men studied. In less than a week, I leafed through an English translation of the Aramaic/Hebrew text of Tractate Gittin, over which others spend years. I constantly had to tell myself, *It's okay to superficially leaf through the Talmud. You're not a Torah scholar. Just a divorcée looking for enlightenment.*

The next guilt barrier to overcome was that toward my ex. *How dare you take our marriage and make it public?* my conscience battered. I overcame this barrier by using a pseudonym, which respects the family's right to privacy. I also restrained myself from telling all. Instead, I chose a few scenes to be emblematic of the relationship.

In the first draft, my ex-husband turned out one-dimensional. Phil Gerard and Diana Hume George, my mentors at Goucher that year, reminded me that there must have been good reasons why I married this man. Show them. Their pushing forced me to confront the pain, and thereafter I was able to put it on the page. I like the fact that the last line of a complicated Talmudic text expresses that personal pain in an impersonal way, so I appropriated the line for my ending. The image of these words being written on shards scattered on the tear-soaked pavement came to me when I sat still and imagined.

Once I realized there were three elements in the essay that I had to juggle, or balance, I was on my way: the description of the ceremony; the story of the couple; and the biblical and Talmudic background. Each element demanded its own development and voice. For the description of the ceremony, I tried to let the facts speak for themselves, but editorializing did creep in. Flashback scenes of the couple's marriage, placed associatively in the text, proved a fruitful way to describe the deteriorating relationship. The most difficult element was the researched background. How to make that interesting and not boring? I tried to simplify and use clear language, relevancy always my compass. I did not want to sound like a teacher; more like a participant in the discovery of material, which I found fascinating.

I write poetry, fiction, journalism, and nonfiction because the world is too rich for only one genre and the human soul has multifarious needs. Poetry, with its strict attention to word choice and rhythm, has been the strongest influence on my creative nonfiction.

When I finished "Leaving Babylon," I started to follow my passions in a less solipsistic way, for which I am grateful. When the writer probes history, others, and texts, in addition to her own heart, she can shed light in a deeper, richer, more meaningful way. And that, I feel, is the purpose of writing: to light up the darkness.

"What About the Boys?" What the Current Debates Tell Us— and Don't Tell Us—About Boys in School[1]

Michael S. Kimmel

I've placed the question contained in my title—"what about the boys?"—in quota-tion marks. In that way, I can pose two different questions to frame the discussion of boys in school. First, the question within the quotation marks is the empirical one: What *about* the boys? What's going on with them? The second question, expressed by the question *and* the quotation marks, is cultural and political: Why is the ques-tion "what about the boys?" such a pressing question on the cultural agenda? Why is the question popping up increasingly in the cultural conversation about gender? Why has it become one of the litany of questions that compose the backlash against feminism?

I believe that the answers to both questions are linked. But first let's look at each separately.

What About the Boys?

Are boys in trouble in school? At first glance, the statistics would suggest that they are. Boys drop out of school, are diagnosed as emotionally disturbed, and commit suicide

[1]This paper began as the keynote address at the 6th annual K-12 Gender Equity in Schools Conference, Wellesley College Center for Research on Women, Wellesley College, January, 2000. A revised version was also presented at The Graduate School of Education, Harvard University, May, 2000. Although modified and revised, I have tried to retain the language and feeling of the original oral presentation. I am grateful to Susan McGee Bailey and Carol Gilligan for inviting me, and to Amy Aronson, Peggy McIntosh, Martin Mills, and Nan Stein, for their comments and support, and to the editors at *Michigan Feminist Studies,* and especially Laura Citrin, for their patience and editorial precision.

four times more often than girls; they get into fights twice as often; they murder ten times more frequently and are 15 times more likely to be the victims of a violent crime. Boys are six times more likely to be diagnosed with Attention Deficit Disorder (see, for example, Knickerbocker).

If they can manage to sit still and not get themselves killed, the argument seems to go, boys get lower grades on standardized tests of reading and writing, and have lower class rank and fewer honors than girls (Kleinfeld).

Finally, if they succeed in dodging the Scylla of elementary and high school, they're likely to dash themselves against the Charybdis of collegiate male bashing. We read that women now constitute the majority of students on college campuses, passing men in 1982, so that in eight years women will earn 58 percent of bachelor's degrees in U.S. colleges. One reporter tells us that if present trends continue, "the graduation line in 2068 will be all females." (That's like saying that if the enrollment of black students at Ol' Miss was 1 in 1964, 24 in 1968 and 400 in 1988, that by 1994 there should have been no more white students there.) Doomsayers lament that women now outnumber men in the social and behavioral sciences by about three to one, and that they've invaded such traditionally male bastions as engineering, where they now make up about 20 percent of all students, and biology and business, where the genders are virtually on par (see Lewin; Koerner).

So, the data might seem to suggest that there are fewer and fewer boys, getting poorer grades, with increasing numbers of behavioral problems. Three phenomena—numbers, achievement and behavior—compose the current empirical discussion about where the boys are and what they are doing.

"What About the Boys?"

These three themes—numbers, grades, behavior—frame the political debate about boys as well. (Now I'm going to include the quotation marks.) Given these gender differences, it's not surprising that we're having a national debate. After all, boys seem not only to be doing badly, but they are also doing worse than girls. What may be surprising, though, is the way the debate is being framed.

To hear some tell it, there's a virtual war against boys in America. Best-sellers' subtitles counsel us to "protect" boys, to "rescue" them. Inside these books, we read how boys are failing at school, where their behavior is increasingly seen as a problem. We read that boys are depressed, suicidal, emotionally shut down. Therapists advise anguished parents about boys' fragility, their hidden despondence and depression, and issue stem warnings about the dire consequences if we don't watch our collective cultural step.

But if there is a "war against boys" who has declared it? What are the sides of the conflict? Who is to blame for boys' failures? What appears to be a concern about the plight of boys actually masks a deeper agenda—a critique of feminism. And I believe that in the current climate, boys need defending against precisely those who claim to defend them; they need rescuing from precisely those who would rescue them.

The arguments of these jeremiads go something like this: First, we hear, feminism has already succeeded in developing programs for girls, enabling and encouraging girls to go into the sciences, to continue education, to imagine careers outside the home. But, in so doing, feminists have over-emphasized the problems of girls, and distorted the facts. Particularly objectionable are the findings of the American Association of University Women (AAUW) reports on the "chilly classroom climate." According to these critics, the salutary effects of paying attention to girls have been offset by the increasing problematization of boys. It was feminists, we hear, who pitted girls against boys, and in their efforts to help girls, they've "pathologized" boyhood.

Elementary schools, we hear, are "anti-boy," emphasizing reading and restricting the movements of young boys. They "feminize" boys, forcing active, healthy and naturally rambunctious boys to conform to a regime of obedience, "pathologizing what is simply normal for boys," as psychologist Michael Gurian put it (qtd. in Zachary 1). In *The Wonder of Boys,* Gurian argues that with testosterone surging through their little limbs, we demand that they sit still, raise their hands, and take naps. We're giving them the message, he says, that "boyhood is defective" (qtd. in Zachary 1).

In many ways, these discussions rehearse debates we've had several times before in our history. At the turn of the century, for example, cultural critics were concerned that the rise of white collar businesses meant increasing indolence for men and the separation of spheres meant that women—as mothers, teachers, and Sunday school teachers—had taken primary responsibility for the socialization of children, both boys and girls. With women teaching boys to become men, a generation of effeminate dandies were being produced. Then, as now, the solutions were to find arenas in which boys could simply be boys, and where men could be men as well. At the turn of the century, fraternal lodges offered men a homosocial sanctuary, and dude ranches and sports provided a place where these sedentary men could experience what Theodore Roosevelt called "the strenuous life." Boys, in danger of feminization by female teachers, Sunday school teachers and mothers could troop off with the Boy Scouts, designed as a fin-de-siecle "boys' liberation movement." Modern society, was turning hardy robust boys into, as the Boy Scouts' founder Ernest Thompson Seton put it, "a lot of flat chested cigarette smokers with shaky nerves and doubtful vitality" (qtd. in Kimmel, *Manhood in America* 170).

Today, women teachers are still to blame for boys' feminization. "It's teachers' job to create a classroom environment that accommodates both male and female energy, not just mainly female energy," explains the energetic therapist Michael Gurian (qtd. in Knickerbocker 2). Since women also may run those boy scout troops and may actually run circles around the boys on the soccer field, men may be feeling a tad defensive these days. Not to worry—we can always retreat into our den to watch "The Man Show" and read *Men's Health* magazine.

In this way, the problem of boys is a problem caused entirely by women who both feminize the boys and pathologize them in their rush to help girls succeed. I'll return to these issues later, but for now, let me turn to what I see are the chief problems with the current "what about the boys?" debate.

What's Wrong with the "What About the Boys?" Debate

First, it creates a false opposition between girls and boys, pretending that the educational reforms undertaken to enable girls to perform better actually hindered boys' educational development. But these reforms—new initiatives, classroom configurations, teacher training, increased attentiveness to students' processes and individual learning styles—actually enable larger numbers of boys to get a better education.

And since, as Susan McGee Bailey and Patricia Campbell point out in their comment on "The Gender Wars in Education" in the January, 2000 issue of the *WCW Research Report,* "gender stereotypes, particularly those related to education, hurt both girls and boys," the challenging of those stereotypes, decreased tolerance for school violence and bullying, and increased attention to violence at home actually enables *both* girls *and* boys to feel safer at school (13).

Second, the critics all seem to be driven to distraction by numbers—the increasing percentages of women in high education and the growing gender gap in test scores. But here's a number they don't seem to factor in: zero—as in zero dollars of *any* new public funding for school programs for the past twenty years, the utter dearth of school bond issues that have passed, money from which might have developed remedial programs, intervention strategies, and teacher training. Money that might have prevented cutting school sports programs and after-school extra-curricular activities. Money that might have enabled teachers and administrators to do more than "store" problem students in separate classes.

Nor do the critics mention managed care health insurance, which virtually demands that school psychologists diagnose problem behavior as a treatable medical condition so that drugs may be substituted for costly, "unnecessary" therapy. These numbers—numbers of dollars—don't seem to enter the discussion about boys, and yet they provide the foundation for everything else. But even the numbers they *do* discuss—numbers and test scores—don't add up. For one thing, more *people* are going to college than ever before. In 1960, 54 percent of boys and 38 percent of girls went directly to college; today the numbers are 64 percent of boys and 70 percent of girls (Mortenson).

And while some college presidents fret that to increase male enrollments they'll be forced to lower standards (which is, incidentally, exactly the opposite of what they worried about 25 years ago when they all went coeducational) no one seems to find gender disparities going the other way all that upsetting. Of the top colleges and universities in the nation, only Stanford sports a 50-50 gender balance. Harvard and Amherst enroll 56 percent men, Princeton and Chicago 54 percent men, Duke and Berkeley 52 percent and Yale 51 percent. And that doesn't even begin to approach the gender disparities at Cal Tech (65 percent male, 35 percent female) or MIT (62 percent male, 38 percent female) (Gose "Liberal Arts Colleges Ask"). Nor does anyone seem driven to distraction about the gender disparities in nursing, social work, or education. Did somebody say "what about the girls?" Should we lower standards to make sure they're gender balanced?

In fact, much of the great gender difference we hear touted is actually what sociologist Cynthia Fuchs Epstein calls a "deceptive distinction," a difference that appears to be about gender but is actually about something else—in this case, class or race (see Epstein *Deceptive Distinctions*). Girls' vocational opportunities are far more restricted than boys' are. Their opportunities are from the service sector, with limited openings in manufacturing or construction. A college-educated woman earns about the same as a high-school educated man, $35,000 to $31,000 (Gose "Colleges Look for Ways").

The shortage of male college students is also actually a shortage of *non-white* males. The gender gap between college-age white males and white females is rather small, 51 percent women to 49 percent men. But only 37 percent of black college students are male, and 63 percent female, and 45 percent of Hispanic students are male, compared with 55 percent female (Lewin). (If this is a problem largely of class and race, why do the books that warn of this growing crisis have cute little white boys on their covers?)

These differences among boys—by race, or class, for example—do not typically fall within the radar of the cultural critics who would rescue boys. These differences are incidental because, in their eyes, all boys are the same: aggressive, competitive, rambunctious little devils. And this is perhaps the central problem and contradiction in the work of those who would save boys. They argue that it's testosterone that makes boys into boys, and a society that paid attention to boys would have to acknowledge testosterone. We're making it impossible for boys to be boys.

This facile biologism mars the apologists' often insightful observations about the sorry state of boyhood. "Testosterone equals vitality," writes Australian men's movement guru Steve Biddulph, "and it's our job to honor it and steer it into healthy directions" (54). Feminists, Gurian argues, only make the problem worse, with an unyielding critique of the very masculinity that young boys are trying so desperately to prove *(A Fine Young Man)*.

This over-reliance on biology leads to a celebration of all things masculine as the simple product of that pubescent chemical elixir. Gurian, for example, celebrates all masculine rites of passage, "like military boot camp, fraternity hazings, graduation day, and bar mitzvah" as "essential parts of every boy's life" *(A Fine Young Man* 151). Excuse me? Hazing and bar mitzvahs in the same breath? I've read of no reports of boys dying at the hands of other boys on their bar mitzvahs.

Feminist emphases on gender discrimination, sexual harassment, or date rape only humiliate boys and distract us from intervening constructively. These misdiagnoses lead to some rather chilling remedies. Gurian suggests reviving corporal punishment, both at home and at school—but only when administered privately with cool indifference and never in the heat of adult anger. He calls it "spanking responsibly" *(A Fine Young Man* 175), though school boards and child welfare agencies might call it child abuse.

Permit me a brief digression about testosterone. On the surface, the experiments on testosterone and aggression appear convincing. Males have higher levels of testosterone and higher rates of aggressive behavior. What's more, if you increase the level of testosterone in a normal male, his level of aggression will increase. Castrate him—or at least a rodent proxy of him—and his aggressive behavior will cease. Though this might lead one to think that testosterone is the cause of the aggression, Stanford neurobiologist Robert Sapolsky warns against such leaps of logic. He explains that if you take a group of five male monkeys arranged in a dominance hierarchy from 1-5, then you can pretty much predict how everyone will behave toward everyone else. (The top monkey's testosterone level will be higher than the ones below him and levels will decrease down the line.) Number 3, for example, will pick fights with numbers 4 and 5, but will avoid and run away from numbers 1 and 2. If you give number 3 a massive infusion of testosterone, he will likely become more aggressive—but only toward numbers 4 and 5, with whom he has now become an absolute violent torment. He will still avoid numbers 1 and 2, demonstrating that the "testosterone isn't causing aggression, it's exaggerating the aggression that's already there" (155).

It turns out that testosterone has what scientists call a "permissive effect" on aggression: It doesn't cause it, but it does facilitate and enable the aggression that is already there. What's more, testosterone is produced *by* aggression. In studies of tennis players, medical students, wrestlers, nautical competitors, parachutists, and officer candidates, winning and losing determined levels of testosterone, so that the levels of the winners rose dramatically, while those of the losers dropped or remained the same. This was true of women's testosterone levels as well (Kemper; Kling).

What these experiments tell us, I think, is that the presence or absence of testosterone is not the critical issue—but rather the presence or absence of social permission for aggression. Thus, arguments to let boys be boys are likely to exacerbate precisely the problems they attempt to alleviate.

If the cause of the problem is not feminists' deliberately ignoring or raging against male hormones, then it must be the result of that other current social calamity—fatherlessness. It must be, we hear, that boys today lack adequate role models because their fathers are either at work all the time or divorced with limited custody and visitation privileges. Discussions of boys' problems almost invariably circle back to fathers, or rather, the lack of them.

Contemporary jeremiads about fatherlessness remind us how central fathers are to family life, and how fatherlessness is the single cause of innumerable social problems, from crime, delinquency, to drug taking, sexual irresponsibility, poverty and the like. Fathers bring something irreplaceable to the family, something, "inherently masculine" notes Wade Horn, director of the National Fatherhood Initiative (qtd. in Knickerbocker 18).

Unfortunately, we never hear exactly what the cause of all this fatherlessness is. To be sure, we hear about unwed mothers, single-parent families, babies having babies, and punitive and vindictive ex-wives (and their equally punitive and wealthy lawyers) who prevent men from being more present in the lives of their children. They *would* be there, if only women would let them.

"Fortunately," writes Australian Steve Biddulph, "fathers are fighting their way back into family life" (74). Fighting against whom exactly? Women? Feminist women have been pleading with men to come home and share housework and child care—let alone to help raise their sons—for what, 150 years?!

As role models, fathers would provide a model of decisiveness, discipline, and ability to control one's emotions—which would be useful for their naturally aggressive, testosterone-juiced sons at school. But how do these same biologically driven, rambunctious, boys magically grow up to be strong, silent, decisive and controlled fathers?

Easy—by women doing what they are biologically programmed to do: stay home and raise boys (but not for too long) and constrain the natural predatory, aggressive and lustful impulses of their men. In leaving the home and going to work, women abandoned their naturally prescribed role of sexual constraint. Presto: a debate about fatherhood and boyhood, becomes a debate not about masculinity, but about feminism.

What's Missing from the Debate about Boys

I believe that it is *masculinity* that is missing in the discussions of both fathers and sons. Though we hear an awful lot about *males,* we hear very little about *masculinity,* about the cultural meanings of the biological fact of maleness. Raising the issue of masculinity, I believe, will enable us to resolve many of these debates.

When I say that masculinity is invisible in the discussion, what could I possibly mean? How is masculinity invisible? Well, let me ask you this: when I say the word "gender," what gender do you think of? In our courses and our discourses, we act as if women alone "had" gender. This is political; this is central.

Let me tell you a story about that invisibility, one that will also reveal the ways that invisibility is political. (I take this from Kimmel *Manhood in America*). In the early 1980s, I participated in a small discussion group on feminism. In one meeting, in a discussion between two women, I first confronted this invisibility of gender to men. A white woman and a black woman were discussing whether all women were, by definition, "sisters," because they all had essentially the same experiences and because all women faced a common oppression by men. The white woman asserted that the fact that they were both women bonded them, in spite of racial differences. The black woman disagreed.

"When you wake up in the morning and look in the mirror, what do you see?" she asked.

"I see a woman," replied the white woman.

"That's precisely the problem," responded the black woman. "I see a *black* woman. To me, race is visible every day, because race is how I am *not* privileged in our culture. Race is invisible to you, because it's how you are privileged. It's why there will always be differences in our experience."

As I witnessed this exchange, I was startled, and groaned—more audibly, perhaps, than I had intended. Being the only man in the room, someone asked what my response had meant.

"Well," I said, "when I look in the mirror, I see a human being. I'm universally generalizable. As a middle-class white man, I have no class, no race, no gender. I'm the generic person!"

Sometimes, I like to think that it was on that day that I *became* a middle-class, white man. Sure, I had been all that before, but these identities had not meant much to me. Since then, I've begun to understand that race, class, and gender don't refer only to other people, who were marginalized by race, class or gender privilege. Those terms also described me. I enjoyed the privilege of invisibility. The very processes that confer privilege to one group and not another group are often invisible to those upon whom that privilege is conferred. What makes us marginal or powerless are the processes we see, partly because others keep reminding us of them. Invisibility is a privilege in a double sense—describing both the power relations that are kept in place by the very dynamics of invisibility, and in the sense of privilege as luxury. It is a luxury that only white people have in our society not to think about race every minute of their lives. It is a luxury that only men have in our society to pretend that gender does not matter.

Let me give you another example of how power is so often invisible to those who have it. Many of you have email addresses, and you write email messages to people all over the world. You've probably noticed that there is one big difference between email addresses in the United States and email addresses of people in other countries: their addresses have "country codes" at the end of the address. So, for example, if you were writing to someone in South Africa, you'd put "za" at the end, or "jp" for Japan, or "uk" for England or "de" for Germany. But when you write to people in the United States, the email address ends with "edu" for an educational institution, "org" for an organization, "gov" for a federal government office, or "com" or "net" for commercial internet providers. Why is it that the United States doesn't have a country code? It is because when you are the dominant power in the world, everyone else needs to be named. When you are "in power," you needn't draw attention to yourself as a specific entity, but, rather, you can pretend to be the generic, the universal, the generalizable. From the point of view of the United States, all other countries are "other" and thus need to be named, marked, noted. Once again, privilege is invisible. Only an American could write a song titled "We are the World."

There are consequences to this invisibility: privilege, as well as gender, remains invisible. And it is hard to generate a politics of inclusion from invisibility. The invisibility of privilege means that many men, like many white people, become defensive and angry when confronted with the statistical realities or the human consequences of racism or sexism. Since our privilege is invisible, we may become defensive. Hey, we may even feel like victims ourselves.

Let me give you two more illustrations of this that are quite a bit closer to our topic. In a recent article about the brutal homophobic murder of Mathew Shepard, the reporter for the *New York Times* writes that "[y]oung men account for 80 percent to 90 percent of people arrested for 'gay bashing' crimes, says Valerie Jenness, a sociology professor who teaches a course on hate crimes" at U. C. Irvine. Then the reporter quotes Professor Jenness directly: "'This youth variable tells us they are working out identity issues, making the transition away from home into adulthood'" (Brooke A16). Did you hear it disappear? The *Times* reporter says "young men" account for . . .," the sociologist, the expert, is quoted as saying, "this youth variable." That is what invisibility looks like.[2]

And finally, here's one more illustration of the invisibility of masculinity in the discussion of young boys, and how that invisibility almost always plays out as a critique of feminism. Asked to comment on the school shootings at Columbine and other high schools, House Majority Leader Tom DeLay said that guns "have little or nothing to do with juvenile violence" but rather, that the causes were daycare, the teaching of evolution, and "working mothers who take birth control pills" (qtd. in *The Nation* 5).

Some of the recent boy books do get it; they get that masculinity—not feminism, not testosterone, not fatherlessness, and not the teaching of evolution—is the key to understanding boyhood and its current crisis. For example, in *Raising Cain,* Dan Kindlon and Michael Thompson write that male peers present a young boy with a "culture of cruelty" in which they force him to deny emotional neediness, "routinely disguise his feelings," and end up feeling emotionally isolated (89). And in *Real Boys,* therapist William Pollack calls it the "boy code" and the "mask of masculinity"—a kind of swaggering posture that boys embrace to hide their fears, suppress dependency and vulnerability, and present a stoic, impervious front.

What exactly is that "boy code?" Twenty-five years ago, psychologist Robert Brannon described the four basic rules of manhood

1. "No Sissy Stuff"—one can never do anything that even remotely hints of femininity; masculinity is the relentless repudiation of the feminine.
2. "Be a Big Wheel"—Wealth, power, status are markers of masculinity. We measure masculinity by the size of one's paycheck. In the words of that felicitous Reagan-era phrase, "He who has the most toys when he dies, wins."
3. "Be a Sturdy Oak"—what makes a man a man is that he is reliable in a crisis, and what makes a man reliable in a crisis is that he resembles an inanimate object. Rocks, pillars, trees are curious masculine icons.
4. "Give em Hell!"—exude an aura of daring and aggression. Live life on the edge. Take risks (Brannon and David).

Of course, these four rules are elaborated by different groups of men and boys in different circumstances. There are as sizable differences among different groups of men as there are differences between women and men. Greater in fact. Just because we make masculinity visible doesn't mean that we make other categories of experience—race, class, ethnicity, sexuality, age—invisible. What it means to be a 71 year-old, black, gay man in Cleveland is probably radically different from what it means to a 19 year-old, white, heterosexual farm boy in Iowa.

Forget that biology and testosterone stuff: there's plenty of evidence that boys are not just boys everywhere and in the same way. Few European nations would boast of

---

[2]In fairness to Professor Jenness, whose work on gay bashing crimes I admire, it is possible that her quotation was only part of what she said, and that it was the newspaper, not the expert, who again rendered masculinity invisible.

such violent, homophobic, and misogynist adolescent males. If it's all so biological, why are Norwegian or French or Swiss boys so different? Are they not boys?

One cannot speak of masculinity in the singular, but of *masculinities,* in recognition of the different definitions of manhood that we construct. By pluralizing the term, we acknowledge that masculinity means different things to different groups of men at different times. But, at the same time, we can't forget that all masculinities are not created equal. All American men must also contend with a singular vision of masculinity, a particular definition that is held up as the model against which we all measure ourselves. We thus come to know what it means to be a man in our culture by setting our definitions in opposition to a set of "others"—racial minorities, sexual minorities, and, above all, women. As the sociologist Erving Goffman once wrote:

> In an important sense there is only one complete unblushing male in America: a young, married, white, urban, northern, heterosexual, Protestant, father, of college education, fully employed, of good complexion, weight, and height, and a recent record in sports. . . . Any male who fails to qualify in any one of these ways is likely to view himself—during moments at least—as unworthy, incomplete, and inferior. (128)

I think it's crucial to listen carefully to those last few words. When men feel that they do not measure up, Goffman argues, they are likely to feel "unworthy, incomplete and inferior." It is, I believe, from this place of unworthiness, incompleteness and inferiority that boys begin their efforts to prove themselves as men. And the ways they do it—based on misinformation and disinformation—is what is causing the problems for girls and boys in school.

How Does the Perspective on Masculinity Transform the Debate?

Introducing masculinities into the discussion alleviates several of the problems with the "what about the boys?" debate. It enables us to explore the ways in which class and race complicate the picture of boys' achievement and behaviors, for one thing. For another, it reveals that boys and girls are on the same side in this struggle, not pitted against each other.

For example, when Kindlon and Thompson describe the things that *boys* need, they are really describing what *children* need. Adolescent boys, Kindlon and Thompson inform us, want to be loved, get sex, and not be hurt (195-6). And girls don't? Parents are counseled to: allow boys to have their emotions (241); accept a high level of activity (245); speak their language and treat them with respect (247); teach that empathy is courage (249); use discipline to guide and build (253); model manhood as emotionally attached (255); and teach the many ways a boy can be a man (256). Aside from the obvious tautologies, what they advocate is exactly what feminist women have been advocating for girls for some time.

Secondly, a focus on masculinity explains what is happening to those boys in school. Consider again the parallel for girls. Carol Gilligan's astonishing and often moving work on adolescent girls describes how these assertive, confident and proud young girls "lose their voices" when they hit adolescence (see, for example, Brown and Gilligan). At the same moment, William Pollack notes, boys become *more* confident, even beyond their abilities. You might even say that boys *find* their voices, but it is the inauthentic voice of bravado, of constant posturing, of foolish risk-taking and gratuitous violence. The "boy code" teaches them that they are supposed to be in power, and thus begin to act like it. They "ruffle in a manly pose," as William Butler Yeats once put it, "for all their timid heart."

What's the cause of all this posturing and posing? It's not testosterone, but privilege. In adolescence, both boys and girls get their first real dose of gender inequality: girls suppress ambition, boys inflate it.

Recent research on the gender gap in school achievement bears this out. Girls are more likely to undervalue their abilities, especially in the more traditionally "masculine" educational arenas such as math and science. Only the most able and most secure girls take such courses. Thus, their numbers tend to be few, and their grades high. Boys, however, possessed of this false voice of bravado (and many facing strong family pressure) are likely to *over-value* their abilities, to remain in programs though they are less qualified and capable of succeeding. This difference, and not some putative discrimination against boys, is the reason that girls' mean test scores in math and science are now, on average, approaching that of boys. Too many boys who over-value their abilities remain in difficult math and science courses longer than they should; they pull the boys' mean scores down. By contrast, few girls, whose abilities and self-esteem are sufficient to enable them to "trespass" into a male domain, skew female data upwards.

A parallel process is at work in the humanities and social sciences. Girls' mean test scores in English and foreign languages, for example, also outpace boys. But this is not the result of "reverse discrimination"; rather, it is because the boys bump up against the norms of masculinity. Boys regard English as a "feminine" subject. Pioneering research in Australia by Wayne Martino found that boys are uninterested in English because of what it might say about their (inauthentic) masculine pose (see, for example, Martino "Gendered Learning Practices," "'Cool Boys'"; see also Yates "Gender Equity", "The 'What About the Boys' Debate"; Lesko). "Reading is lame, sitting down and looking at words is pathetic," commented one boy. "Most guys who like English are faggots" (Martino "Gendered Learning Practices" 132). The traditional liberal arts curriculum is seen as feminizing: as Catharine Stimpson recently put it sarcastically, "real men don't speak French" (qtd. in Lewin A26).

Boys tend to hate English and foreign languages for the same reasons that girls love it. In English, they observe, there are no hard and fast rules, but rather one expresses one's opinion about the topic and everyone's opinion is equally valued. "The answer can be a variety of things, you're never really wrong," observed one boy.

"It's not like math and science where there is one set answer to everything." Another boy noted:

> I find English hard. It's because there are no set rules for reading texts . . . English isn't like math where you have rules on how to do things and where there are right and wrong answers. In English you have to write down how you feel and that's what I don't like. (Martino "Gendered Learning Practices" 133)

Compare this to the comments of girls in the same study:

> I feel motivated to study English because . . . you have freedom in English—unlike subjects such as math and science—and your view isn't necessarily wrong. There is no definite right or wrong answer and you have the freedom to say what you feel is right without it being rejected as a wrong answer. (Martino "Gendered Learning Practices" 134)

It is not the school experience that "feminizes" boys, but rather the ideology of traditional masculinity that keeps boys from wanting to succeed. "The work you do here is girls' work," one boy commented to a researcher. "It's not real work" (Mac an Ghaill 59; for additional research on this, see Lesko).

Are Single Sex Schools the Answer?

So, are single-sex schools the answer? There are many people who think so. It's true that there is some evidence that single-sex schools are beneficial to women. There has even been some evidence that men's achievement was improved by attending a single-sex college. Empirically, however, these findings are not persuasive, since the effects typically vanish when social class and boys' secondary school experiences were added to the equation.

In their landmark book, *The Academic Revolution,* sociologists Christopher Jencks and David Riesman write:

> The all male-college would be relatively easy to defend if it emerged from a world in which women were established as fully equal to men. But it does not. It is therefore likely to be a witting or unwitting device for preserving tacit assumptions of male superiority . . . Thus while we are not against segregation of the sexes under all circumstances, we are against it when it helps preserve sexual arrogance.[3] (300, 298)

In short, what women often learn at all-women's colleges is that they can do anything that men can do. By contrast, what men learn at all-men's colleges is that they (women) cannot do what they (the men) do. In this way, women's colleges may constitute a challenge to gender inequality, while men's colleges reproduce that inequality.

---

[3]Despite his own findings, Riesman supported the continuation of VMI and Citadel's single sex policy and testified on their behalf. See David Riesman.

Consider an analogy with race here. One might justify the continued existence of historically all-black colleges on the grounds that such schools challenge racist ideas that black students could not achieve academically and provide a place where black students are free of everyday racism and thus free to become serious students. But one would have a more difficult time justifying maintaining an all-white college, which would, by its very existence, reproduce racist inequality. Returning to gender, as psychologist Carol Tavris concludes, "there is a legitimate place for all-women's schools if they give young women a stronger shot at achieving self-confidence, intellectual security, and professional competence in the workplace." On the other hand, since coeducation is based "on the premise that there are few genuine differences between men and women, and that people should be educated as individuals, rather than as members of a gender," the question is "not whether to become coeducational, but rather when and how to undertake the process" (Tavris 127; see also Priest, Vitters and Prince, 1978 590).

Single-sex education for women often perpetuates detrimental attitudes and stereotypes about women, that "by nature or situation girls and young women cannot become successful or learn well in coeducational institutions" (Epstein "Myths and Justifications" 191). Even when supported by feminist women, the idea that women cannot compete equally with men in the same arena, that they need "special" treatment, signals an abandonment of hope, the inability or unwillingness to make the creation of equal and safe schools a national priority. "Since we cannot do that," we seem to be telling girls, "we'll do the next best thing—separate you from those nasty boys who will only make your lives a living hell."

Such proposals also seem to be based on faulty understandings of the differences between women and men, the belief in an unbridgeable chasm between "them" and "us" based on different styles of learning, qualities of mind, structures of brains, and ways of knowing, talking, or caring. John Dewey, perhaps America's greatest theorist of education, and a fierce supporter of women's equal rights, was infuriated at the contempt for women suggested by such programs. In 1911, Dewey scoffed at "'female botany,' 'female algebra,' and for all I know a 'female multiplication table,'" (59). "Upon no subject has there been so much dogmatic assertion based on so little scientific evidence, as upon male and female types of mind." Coeducation, Dewey argued, was beneficial to women, opening up opportunities previously unattainable. Girls, he suggested, became less manipulative, and acquired "greater self-reliance and a desire to win approval by deserving it instead of by 'working' others. Their narrowness of judgment, depending on the enforced narrowness of outlook, is overcome; their ultra-feminine weaknesses are toned up" (60).

What's more, Dewey claimed, coeducation was beneficial to men. "Boys learn gentleness, unselfishness, courtesy; their natural vigor finds helpful channels of expression instead of wasting itself in lawless boisterousness," he wrote (60). Another social and educational reformer, Thomas Wentworth Higginson, also opposed single-sex schools: "Sooner or later, I am persuaded, the human race will look upon all these separate collegiate institutions as most American travelers now look at the vast monastic establishments of Southern Europe; with respect for the pious motives of their founders, but with wonder that such a mistake should ever have been made" (1).

Ultimately, I believe that we're going to have to do this together. Single-sex schools for women may challenge male domination, but single-sex schools for men tend to perpetuate it. Single-sex schools for women also perpetuate the idea that women can't do well without extra assistance and that masculinity is so impervious to change that it would be impossible to claim an education with men around. I believe this insults both women and men.

The Real Boy Crisis is a Crisis of Masculinity

Making masculinity visible enables us to understand what I regard as the *real* boy crisis in America. The real boy crisis usually goes by another name. We call it "teen violence," "youth violence," "gang violence," "suburban violence," "violence in the schools." Just who do we think are doing it—girls?

Imagine if all the killers in the schools in Littleton, Pearl, Paducah, Springfield, and Jonesboro were all black girls from poor families who lived instead in New Haven, Newark, or Providence. We'd be having a national debate about inner-city, poor, black girls. The entire focus would be on race, class, and gender. The media would invent a new term for their behavior, as with "wilding" a decade ago. We'd hear about the culture of poverty, about how living in the city breeds crime and violence, about some putative natural tendency among blacks towards violence. Someone would even blame feminism for causing girls to become violent in a vain imitation of boys. Yet the obvious fact that these school killers were all middle-class, white boys seems to have escaped everyone's notice.

Let's face facts: Men and boys are responsible for 95 percent of all violent crimes in this country. Every day 12 boys and young men commit suicide—seven times the number of girls. Every day 18 boys and young men die from homicide—ten times the number of girls (see Kimmel *The Gendered Society*). From an early age, boys learn that violence is not only an acceptable form of conflict resolution, but one that is admired. Four times more teenage boys than teenage girls think fighting is appropriate when someone cuts into the front of a line. Half of all teenage boys get into a physical fight each year.

And it's been that way for many years. No other culture developed such a violent "boy culture," as historian E. Anthony Rotundo calls it in his book, *American Manhood.* Where else did young boys, as late as the 1940s, actually carry little chips of wood on their shoulders daring others to knock it off so that they might have a fight? It may be astonishing to readers that "carrying a chip on your shoulder" is literally true—a test of manhood for adolescent boys.

In what other culture did some of the reigning experts of the day actually *prescribe* fighting for young boys' healthy masculine development? The celebrated psychologist, G. Stanley Hall, who invented the term "adolescence," believed that a non-fighting boy was a "nonentity," and that it was "better even an occasional nose dented by a fist . . . than stagnation, general cynicism and censoriousness, bodily and psychic cowardice" (154).

And his disciples vigorously took up the cause. Here, for example is J. Adams Puffer in 1912, from his successful parental advice book, *The Boy and His Gang:*

> There are times when every boy must defend his own rights if he is not to become a coward, and lose the road to independence and true manhood . . . The strong willed boy needs no inspiration to combat, but often a good deal of guidance and restraint. If he fights more than, let us say, a half-dozen times a week—except of course, during his first week at a new school—he is probably over-quarrelsome and needs to curb. (91)

Boys are to fight an average of once a day, except during the first week at a new school, during which, presumably they would have to fight more often!

From the turn of the century to the present day, violence has been part of the meaning of manhood, part of the way men have traditionally tested, demonstrated and proved their manhood. Without another cultural mechanism by which young boys can come to think of themselves as men, they've eagerly embraced violence as a way to become men.

I remember one little childhood game called "Flinch" that we played in the school yard. One boy would come up to another and pretend to throw a punch at his face. If the second boy flinched—as any *reasonable* person would have done—the first boy shouted "you flinched" and proceeded to punch him hard on the arm. It was his right; after all, the other boy had failed the test of masculinity. Being a man meant never flinching.

In the recent study of youthful violent offenders, psychologist James Garbarino locates the origins of men's violence in the ways boys swallow anger and hurt. Among the youthful offenders he studied, "[d]eadly petulance usually hides some deep emotional wounds, a way of compensating through an exaggerated sense of grandeur for an inner sense of violation, victimization, and injustice" (128). In other words, as that famous Reagan-era bumper-sticker put it, "I don't just get mad, I get even." Or, as one prisoner said, "I'd rather be wanted for murder than not wanted at all" (132).

James Gilligan is even more specific. In his book *Violence,* one of the most insightful studies of violence I've ever read, he argues that violence has its origins in "the fear of shame and ridicule, and the overbearing need to prevent others from laughing at oneself by making them weep instead" (77).

Recall those words by Goffman again—"unworthy, incomplete, inferior." Now listen to these voices: First, here is Evan Todd, a 255-pound defensive lineman on the Columbine football team, an exemplar of the jock culture that Dylan Klebold and Eric Harris—the gunmen at Columbine High School—found to be such an interminable torment: "Columbine is a clean, good place, except for those rejects," Todd says. "Sure we teased them. But what do you expect with kids who come to school with weird hairdos and horns on their hats? It's not just jocks; the whole school's disgusted with them. They're a bunch of homos, grabbing each others' private parts. If you want to get rid of someone, usually you tease 'em. So the whole school would call them homos" (*qtd. in* Gibbs and Roche 50-51). Harris says people constantly made fun of "my face, my hair, my shirts" (44). Klebold adds, "I'm going to kill you all. You've been giving us s____ for years" (44).

Our Challenge

If we really want to rescue boys, protect boys, promote boyhood, then our task must be to find ways to reveal and challenge this ideology of masculinity, to disrupt the facile "boys will be boys" model, and to erode boys' sense of entitlement. Because the reality is that it is this ideology of masculinity that is the problem for *both* girls *and* boys. And seen this way, our strongest ally, it seems to me, is the women's movement.

To be sure, feminism opened the doors of opportunity to women and girls. And it's changed the rules of conduct: in the workplace, where sexual harassment is no longer business as usual; on dates, where attempted date rape is no longer "dating etiquette"; and in schools, where both subtle and overt forms of discrimination against girls—from being shuffled off to Home Economics when they want to take physics, excluded from military schools and gym classes, to anatomy lectures using pornographic slides—have been successfully challenged. And let's not forget the legal cases that have confronted bullying, and sexual harassment by teachers and peers.

More than that, feminism has offered a blueprint for a new boyhood and masculinity based on a passion for justice, a love of equality, and expression of a fuller emotional palette. So naturally, feminists will be blamed for male bashing—feminists imagine that men (and boys) can do better (see, for example, Miedzian; Silverstein and Rashbaum).

And to think feminists are accused of male bashing! Actually, I think the anti-feminist right wing are the real male bashers. Underneath the anti-feminism may be perhaps the most insulting image of masculinity around. Males, you see, are savage, predatory, sexually omnivorous, violent creatures, who will rape, murder and pillage unless women perform their civilizing mission and act to constrain us. "Every society must be wary of the unattached male, for he is universally the cause of numerous social ills," writes David Popenoe (12). When they say that boys will be boys, they mean boys will be uncaged, uncivilized animals. Young males, conservative critic Charles Murray wrote recently, are "essentially barbarians for whom marriage . . . is an indispensible civilizing force" (23). And what of evolutionary psychologist Robert Wright, who recently "explained" that women and men are hard-wired by evolutionary imperatives to be so different as to come from different planets. "Human males," he wrote, "are by nature oppressive, possessive, flesh-obsessed pigs" (22). Had any radical feminist said these words, anti-feminist critics would howl with derision about how feminists hated men!

And here's that doyenne of talk radio, Dr. Laura Schlesinger: "Men would not do half of what they do if women didn't let them," she told an interviewer for *Modern Maturity* magazine recently. "That a man is going to do bad things is a fact. That you keep a man who does bad things in your life is your fault" (qtd. in Goodman 68).

Now it seems to me that the only rational response to these insulting images of an unchangeable, hard-wired, violent manhood is, of course, to assume they're true. Typically when we say that boys will be boys, we assume that propensity for violence is innate, the inevitable fruition of that prenatal testosterone cocktail. So what? That only begs the question. We still must decide whether to organize society so as to maximize boy's "natural" predisposition toward violence, or to minimize it. Biology alone cannot answer that question, and claiming that boys will be boys, helplessly shrugging our national shoulders, abandons our political responsibility.

Besides, one wants to ask, which biology are we talking about? Therapist Michael Gurian demands that we accept boy's "hard wiring." This "hard wiring," he informs us, is competitive and aggressive. "Aggression and physical risk taking are hard wired into a boy," he writes. Gurian claims that he likes the kind of feminism that "is not anti-male, accepts that boys are who they are, and chooses to love them rather than change their hard wiring" (*A Fine Young Man* 53-4).

That's too impoverished a view of feminism—and of boys—for my taste. I think it asks far too little of us, to simply accept boys and this highly selective definition of their hard-wiring. Feminism asks more of us—that we *not* accept those behaviors that are hurtful to boys, girls, and their environment—because we can do better than what this *part* of our hard wiring might dictate. We are also, after all, hard-wired towards compassion, nurturing and love, aren't we?

Surely we wouldn't insult men the way the right-wing insults men, by arguing that only women are hard-wired for love, care-giving, nurturing, and love, would we? (I am sure that those legions of men's rights types, demanding custody wouldn't dare do so!) I'm reminded of a line from Kate Millett's path-breaking book, *Sexual Politics,* more than thirty years ago:

> Perhaps nothing is so depressing an index of the inhumanity of the male supremacist mentality as the fact that the more genial human traits are assigned to the underclass: affection, response to sympathy, kindness, cheerfulness. (324-6)

The question, to my mind, is not whether or not we're hard wired, but rather which hard wiring elements we choose to honor and which we choose to challenge.

I remember one pithy definition that feminism was the radical idea that women are people. Feminists also seem to believe the outrageous proposition that, if given enough love, compassion and support, boys—as well as men—can also be people. That's a vision of boyhood I believe is worth fighting for.

Works Cited

Adams, Lorraine, and Dale Russakoff. "Dissecting Columbine's Cult of the Athlete." *The Washington Post,* 15 July 1999.

American Association of University Women. *How Schools Shortchange Girls: The AAUW Report, A Study of Major Findings on Girls and Education.* Washington, DC: American Association of University Women Educational Foundation, 1992.

——. *Gender Gaps: Where Schools Still Fail Our Children.* New York: Marlowe and Co., 1999.

Bailey, Susan McGee, and Patricia B. Campbell, "The Gender Wars in Education." *WCW Research Report.* Wellesley, MA: Wellesley Center for Research on Women, 1999/2000.

Biddulph, Steve. *Raising Boys.* Berkeley: Ten Speed P, 1999.

Brannon, Robert, and Deborah David. "Introduction" to *The Forty-Nine Per Cent Majority*. Reading, MA: Addison, Wesley, 1976.

Brooke, James. "Men Held in Beating Lived on the Fringes." *The New York Times*. 16 October 1998: A16.

Brown, Lyn Mikeal, and Carol Gilligan. *Meeting at the Crossroads*. New York: Ballantine, 1992.

Connell, R. W. "Teaching the Boys: New Research on Masculinity and Gender Strategies for Schools." *Teachers College Record*, 98 (2), Winter 1996.

Dewey, John. "Is Coeducation Injurious to Girls?" *Ladies Home Journal*. 11 June 1911.

Epstein, Cynthia Fuchs. *Deceptive Distinctions*. New Haven: Yale UP, 1988.

——. "The Myths and Justifications of Sex Segregation in Higher Education: VMI and the Citadel." *Duke Journal of Gender Law and Policy* 4, 1997.

Garbarino, James. *Lost Boys: Why Our Sons Turn Violent and How We Can Save Them*. New York: The Free P, 1999.

Gibbs, Nancy and Timothy Roche. "The Columbine Tapes." *Time* 154 (25), 20 December 1999: 40-51.

Gilbert, Rob, and Pam Gilbert. *Masculinity Goes to School*. London: Routledge, 1998.

Gilligan, Carol. *In a Different Voice*. Cambridge: Harvard UP, 1982.

Gilligan, James. *Violence*. New York: Vintage, 1997.

Goffman, Erving. *Stigma: Notes on the Management of Spoiled Identity*. Englewood Cliffs, NJ: Prentice-Hall, 1963.

Goodman, Susan. "Dr. No." *Modern Maturity*, September–October, 1999.

Gose, Ben. "Liberal Arts Colleges Ask: Where Have the Men Gone?" *Chronicle of Higher Education*. 6 June 1997: A35-6.

Gose, Ben. "Colleges Look for Ways to Reverse a Decline in Enrollment of Men." *Chronicle of Higher Education*. 26 November 1999: A73.

Gurian, Michael. *A Fine Young Man: What parents, mentors, and educators can do to shape adolescent boys into exceptional men*. New York: Jeremy P. Tarcher/Putnam, 1998.

——. *The Wonder of Boys: What parents, mentors, and educators can do to shape boys into exceptional men*. New York: Jeremy P. Tarcher/Putnam, 1996.

Hall, G. Stanley. "The Awkward Age." *Appleton's Magazine*, August 1900.

Higginson, Thomas Wentworth. "Sex and Education." *The Woman's Journal*, 1874. Reprinted in *History of Woman Suffrage*, Vol. 3, S. B. Anthony, E. C. Stanton, and M. J. Gage, Eds. New York: Woman Suffrage Association Press, n.d.

Jencks, Christopher, and David Riesman. *The Academic Revolution*. Chicago: U of Chicago P, 1977.

Kemper, Theodore. *Testosterone and Social Structure*. New Brunswick, NJ: Rutgers UP, 1990.

Kimmel, Michael. *The Gendered Society*. New York: Oxford UP, 2000.

——. *Manhood in America: A Cultural History*. New York: The Free P, 1996.

Kindlon, Dan, and Michael Thompson. *Raising Cain: Protecting the Emotional Life of Boys*. New York: Ballantine, 1999.

Kleinfeld, Judith. "Student Performance: Males Versus Females." *The Public Interest*. Winter 1999.

Kling, Arthur. "Testosterone and Aggressive Behavior in Man and Non-human Primates." Eds. B. Eleftheriou and R. Sprott. *Hormonal Correlates of Behavior.* New York: Plenum, 1975.

Knickerbocker, Brad. "Young and Male in America: It's Hard Being a Boy." *Christian Science Monitor.* 29 April 1999.

Koerner, Brendan. "Where the Boys Aren't." *U. S. News and World Report.* 8 February 1999.

Lesko, Nancy, ed. *Masculinities and Schools.* Newbury Park, CA: Sage Publications, 2000.

Lewin, Tamar. "American Colleges Begin to Ask, Where Have All the Men Gone?" *The New York Times.* 6 December 1998.

Lingard, Bob. "Masculinity Politics, Myths and Boys' Schooling: A Review Essay." *British Journal of Educational Studies,* 45 (3), September 1997.

Mac an Ghaill, Mairtin. *The Making of Men: Masculinities, Sexualities and Schooling.* London: Open UP, 1994.

——. "'What About the Boys?': Schooling, Class and Crisis Masculinity." *Sociological Review,* 44 (3), 1996.

Martino, Wayne. "Gendered Learning Practices: Exploring the Costs of Hegemonic Masculinity for Girls and Boys in Schools." *Gender Equity: A Framework for Australian Schools.* Canberra: np, 1997.

——. "'Cool Boys,' 'Party Animals', 'Squids,' and 'Poofters': Interrogating the Dynamics and Politics of Adolescent Masculinities in School." *British Journal of Sociology of Education,* 20 (2), 1999.

Miedzian, Myriam. *Boys will be Boys: Breaking the Link Between Masculinity and Violence.* New York: Doubleday, 1991.

Millett, Kate. *Sexual Politics.* New York: Random House, 1969.

Mills, Martin. "Disrupting the 'What About the Boys?' Discourse: Stories from Australia" paper presented at the Men's Studies Conference, SUNY at Stony Brook, 6 August 1998.

Mortenson, Thomas. "Where are the Boys? The Growing Gender Gap in Higher Education." *The College Board Review,* 188, August 1999.

Murray, Charles. "The Emerging British Underclass." London: IEA Health and Welfare Unit, 1990.

The Nation. "News of the Week in Review." 15 November 1999.

Pollack, William. *Real Boys: Rescuing Our Sons from the Myths of Boyhood.* New York: Henry Holt, 1998.

Popenoe, David. *Life Without Father.* New York: The Free P, 1996.

Priest, R., A. Vitters, and H. Prince, "Coeducation at West Point." *Armed Forces and Society,* 4 (4), 1978.

Puffer, J. Adams. *The Boy and His Gang.* Boston: Houghton, Mifflin, 1912.

Riesman, David. "A Margin of Difference: The Case for Single-Sex Education." Eds. J. R. Blau and N. Goodman. *Social Roles and Social Institutions: Essays in Honor of Rose Laub Coser.* Boulder: Westview P, 1991.

Rotundo, E. Anthony. *American Manhood: Transformations of Masculinity from the Revolution to the Present Era.* New York: BasicBooks, 1993.

Salisbury, Jonathan, and David Jackson. *Challenging Macho Values: Practical Ways of Working with Adolescent Boys.* London: The Falmer P, 1996.

Sapolsky, Robert. *The Trouble with Testosterone.* New York: Simon and Schuster, 1997.

Silverstein, Olga, and Beth Rashbaum. *The Courage to Raise Good Men.* New York: Penguin, 1995.

Tavris, Carol. *The Mismeasure of Woman.* New York: Simon and Schuster, 1992.

Wright, Robert. "The Dissent of Woman: What Feminists can Learn from Darwinism." *Matters of Life and Death: Demos Quarterly,* 10, 1996.

Yates, Lyn. "Gender Equity and the Boys Debate: What Sort of Challenge is it?" *British Journal of Sociology of Education,* 18 (3), 1997.

——. "The 'What About the Boys?' Debate as a Public Policy Issue." Ed. Nancy Lesko. *Masculinities and Schools.* Newbury Park, CA: Sage Publications, 2000.

Zachary, G. Pascal. "Boys Used to be Boys, But Do Some Now See Boyhood as a Malady." *The Wall Street Journal,* 2 May 1997.

A Small Place

Jamaica Kincaid

If you go to Antigua as a tourist, this is what you will see. If you come by aeroplane, you will land at the V. C. Bird International Airport. Vere Cornwall (V. C.) Bird is the Prime Minister of Antigua. You may be the sort of tourist who would wonder why a Prime Minister would want an airport named after him—why not a school, why not a hospital, why not some great public monument? You are a tourist and you have not yet seen a school in Antigua, you have not yet seen the hospital in Antigua, you have not yet seen a public monument in Antigua. As your plane descends to land, you might say, What a beautiful island Antigua is—more beautiful than any of the other islands you have seen, and they were very beautiful, in their way, but they were much too green, much too lush with vegetation, which indicated to you, the tourist, that they got quite a bit of rainfall, and rain is the very thing that you, just now, do not want, for you are thinking of the hard and cold and dark and long days you spent working in North America (or, worse, Europe), earning some money so that you could stay in this place (Antigua) where the sun always shines and where the climate is deliciously hot and dry for the four to ten days you are going to be staying there; and since you are on your holiday, since you are a tourist, the thought of what it might be like for someone who had to live day in, day out in a place that suffers constantly from drought, and so has to watch carefully every drop of fresh water used (while at the same time surrounded by a sea and an ocean—the Caribbean Sea on one side, the Atlantic Ocean on the other), must never cross your mind.

You disembark your plane. You go through customs. Since you are a tourist, a North American or European—to be frank, white—and not an Antiguan black returning to Antigua from Europe or North America with cardboard boxes of much needed cheap clothes and food for relatives, you move through customs swiftly, you move through customs with ease. Your bags are not searched. You emerge from customs into the hot, clean air: immediately you feel cleansed, immediately you feel blessed (which is to say special); you feel free. You see a man, a taxi driver; you ask him to take you to your destination; he quotes you a price. You immediately think that the price is in the local currency, for you are a tourist and you are familiar with these things (rates of exchange) and you feel even more free, for things seem so cheap, but then your driver ends by saying, "In US currency." You may say, "Hmmmm, do you have a formal sheet that lists official prices and destinations?" Your driver obeys the law and shows you the sheet, and he apologises for the incredible mistake he has made in quoting you a price off the top of his head which is so vastly different (favouring him) from the one listed. You are driven to your hotel by this taxi driver in his taxi, a brand-new Japanese-made vehicle. The road on which you are travelling is a very bad road, very much in need of repair. You are feeling wonderful, so you say, "Oh, what a marvellous change these bad roads are from the splendid highways I am used to in North America." (Or, worse, Europe.) Your driver is reckless; he is a dangerous man who drives in the middle of the road when he thinks no other cars are coming in the opposite direction, passes other cars on blind curves that run uphill, drives at sixty miles an hour on narrow, curving roads when the road sign, a rusting, beat-up thing left over from colonial days, says 40 MPH. This might frighten you (you are on your holiday; you are a tourist); this might excite you (you are on your holiday; you are a tourist), though if you are from New York and take taxis you are used to this style of driving: most of the taxi drivers in New York are from places in the world like this. You are looking out the window (because you want to get your money's worth); you notice that all the cars you see are brand-new, or almost brand-new, and that they are all Japanese-made. There are no American cars in Antigua—no new ones, at any rate; none that were manufactured in the last ten years. You continue to look at the cars and you say to yourself, Why, they look brand-new, but they have an awful sound, like an old car—a very old, dilapidated car. How to account for that? Well, possibly it's because they use leaded gasoline in these brand-new cars whose engines were built to use non-leaded gasoline, but you musn't ask the person driving the car if this is so, because he or she has never heard of unleaded gasoline. You look closely at the car; you see that it's a model of a Japanese car that you might hesitate to buy; it's a model that's very expensive; it's a model that's quite impractical for a person who has to work as hard as you do and who watches every penny you earn so that you can afford this holiday you are on. How do they afford such a car? And do they live in a luxurious house to match such a car? Well, no. You will be surprised, then, to see that most likely the person driving this brand-new car filled with the wrong gas lives in a house that, in comparison, is far beneath the status of the car; and if you were to ask why you would be told that the banks are encouraged by the government to make loans available for cars, but loans for houses not so easily available; and if you ask again why, you will be told that the two main car dealerships in Antigua are owned in part or outright by ministers in government. Oh, but you are on holiday and the sight of these brand-new cars driven by people who may or may not have really passed their driving test (there was once a scandal about driving licenses for sale) would not really stir up these thoughts in you. You pass a building sitting in a sea of dust and you think, It's some latrines for people just passing by, but when you look again you see the building has written on it PIGOTT'S SCHOOL. You pass the hospital, the Holberton Hospital, and how wrong you are not to think about this, for though you are a tourist on your holiday, what if your heart should miss a few beats? What if a blood vessel in your neck should break? What if one of those people driving those brand-new cars filled with the wrong gas fails to pass safely while going uphill on a curve and you are in the car going in the opposite direction? Will you be comforted to know that the hospital is staffed with doctors that no actual Antiguan trusts; that Antiguans always say about the doctors, "I don't want them near me"; that Antiguans refer to them not as doctors but as "the three men" (there are three of them); that when the Minister of Health himself doesn't feel well he takes the first plane to New York to see a real doctor; that if any one of the ministers in government needs medical care he flies to New York to get it?

It's a good thing that you brought your own books with you, for you couldn't just go to the library and borrow some. Antigua used to have a splendid library, but in The Earthquake (everyone talks about it that way—The Earthquake; we Antiguans, for I am one, have a great sense of things, and the more meaningful the thing, the more meaningless we make it) the library building was damaged. This was in 1974, and soon after that a sign was placed on the front of the building saying, THIS BUILD-ING WAS DAMAGED IN THE EARTHQUAKE OF 1974. REPAIRS ARE PENDING. The sign hangs there, and hangs there more than a decade later, with its unfulfilled promise of repair, and you might see this as a sort of quaintness on the part of these islanders, these people descended from slaves—what a strange, unusual per-ception of time they have. REPAIRS ARE PENDING, and here it is many years later, but perhaps in a world that is twelve miles long and nine miles wide (the size of Antigua) twelve years and twelve minutes and twelve days are all the same. The library is one of those splendid old buildings from colonial times, and the sign telling of the repairs is a splendid old sign from colonial times. Not very long after The Earthquake Antigua got its independence from Britain, making Antigua a state in its own right, and Antiguans are so proud of this that each year, to mark the day, they go to church and thank God, a British God, for this. But you should not think of the confusion that must lie in all that and you must not think of the damaged library. You have brought your own books with you, and among them is one of those new books about economic history, one of those books explaining how the West (meaning Europe and North America after its conquest and settlement by Europeans) got rich: the West got rich not from the free (free—in this case meaning got-for-nothing) and then under-valued labour, for generations, of the people like me you see walking around you in Antigua but from the ingenuity of small shopkeepers in Sheffield and Yorkshire and Lancashire, or wherever; and what a great part the invention of the wristwatch played in it, for there was nothing noble-minded men could not do when they discovered they could slap time on their wrists just like that (isn't that the last straw; for not only did we have to suffer the unspeakableness of slavery, but the satisfaction to be had from "We made you bastards rich" is taken away, too), and so you needn't let that slightly funny feeling you have from time to time about exploitation, oppression, domination develop into full-fledged unease, discomfort; you could ruin your holi-day. They are not responsible for what you have; you owe them nothing; in fact, you did them a big favour, and you can provide one hundred examples. For here you are now, passing by Government House. And here you are now, passing by the Prime Minister's Office and the Parliament Building, and overlooking these, with a splen-did view of St. John's Harbour, the American Embassy. If it were not for you, they would not have Government House, and Prime Minister's Office, and Parliament Building and embassy of powerful country. Now you are passing a mansion, an extraordinary house painted the colour of old cow dung, with more aerials and antennas attached to it than you will see even at the American Embassy. The people who live in this house are a merchant family who came to Antigua from the Middle East less than twenty years ago. When this family first came to Antigua, they sold dry goods door to door from suitcases they carried on their backs. Now they own a lot of Antigua; they regularly lend money to the government, they build enormous (for Antigua), ugly (for Antigua), concrete buildings in Antigua's capital, St. John's, which the government then rents for huge sums of money; a member of their family is the Antiguan Ambassador to Syria; Antiguans hate them. Not far from this mansion is another mansion, the home of a drug smuggler. Everybody knows he's a drug smuggler, and if just as you were driving by he stepped out of his door your driver might point him out to you as the notorious person that he is, for this drug smuggler is so rich people say he buys cars in tens—ten of this one, ten of that one—and that he bought a house (another mansion) near Five Islands, contents included, with cash he carried in a suitcase: three hundred and fifty thousand American dollars, and, to the surprise of the seller of the house, lots of American dollars were left over. Overlooking the drug smuggler's mansion is yet another mansion, and leading up to it is the best paved road in all of Antigua—even better than the road that was paved for the Queen's visit in 1985 (when the Queen came, all the roads that she would travel on were paved anew, so that the Queen might have been left with the impression that riding in a car in Antigua was a pleasant experience). In this mansion lives a woman sophisticated people in Antigua call Evita. She is a notorious woman. She's young and beautiful and the girlfriend of somebody very high up in the government. Evita is notorious because her relationship with this high government official has made her the owner of boutiques and property and given her a say in cabinet meetings, and all sorts of other privileges such a relationship would bring a beautiful young woman.

Oh, but by now you are tired of all this looking, and you want to reach your destination—your hotel, your room. You long to refresh yourself; you long to eat some nice lobster, some nice local food. You take a bath, you brush your teeth. You get dressed again; as you get dressed, you look out the window. That water—have you ever seen anything like it? Far out, to the horizon, the colour of the water is navy-blue; nearer, the water is the colour of the North American sky. From there to the shore, the water is pale, silvery, clear, so clear that you can see its pinkish-white sand bottom. Oh, what beauty! Oh, what beauty! You have never seen anything like this. You are so excited. You breathe shallow. You breathe deep. You see a beautiful boy skimming the water, godlike, on a Windsurfer. You see an incredibly unattractive, fat, pastry like-fleshed woman enjoying a walk on the beautiful sand, with a man, an incredibly unattractive, fat, pastrylike-fleshed man; you see the pleasure they're taking in their surroundings. Still standing, looking out the window, you see yourself lying on the beach, enjoying the amazing sun (a sun so powerful and yet so beautiful, the way it is always overhead as if on permanent guard, ready to stamp out any cloud that dares to darken and so empty rain on you and ruin your holiday; a sun that is your personal friend). You see yourself taking a walk on that beach, you see yourself meeting new people (only they are new in a very limited way, for they are people just like you). You see yourself eating some delicious, locally grown food. You see yourself, you see yourself . . . You must not wonder what exactly happened to the contents of your lavatory when you flushed it. You must not wonder where your bathwater went when you pulled out the stopper. You must not wonder what happened when you brushed your teeth. Oh, it might all end up in the water you are thinking of taking a swim in; the contents of your lavatory might, just might, graze gently against your ankle as you wade carefree in the water, for you see, in Antigua, there is no proper sewage-disposal system. But the Caribbean Sea is very big and the Atlantic Ocean is even bigger; it would amaze even you to know the number of black slaves this ocean has swallowed up. When you sit down to eat your delicious meal, it's better that you don't know that most of what you are eating came off a plane from Miami. And before it got on a plane in Miami, who knows where it came from? A good guess is that it came from a place like Antigua first, where it was grown dirt-cheap, went to Miami, and came back. There is a world of something in this, but I can't go into it right now.

The thing you have always suspected about yourself the minute you become a tourist is true: A tourist is an ugly human being. You are not an ugly person all the time; you are not an ugly person ordinarily; you are not an ugly person day to day. From day to day, you are a nice person. From day to day, all the people who are supposed to love you on the whole do. From day to day, as you walk down a busy street in the large and modern and prosperous city in which you work and live, dismayed, puzzled (a cliché, but only a cliché can explain you) at how alone you feel in this crowd, how awful it is to go unnoticed, how awful it is to go unloved, even as you are surrounded by more people than you could possibly get to know in a lifetime that lasted for millennia, and then out of the corner of your eye you see someone looking at you and absolute pleasure is written all over that person's face, and then you realise that you are not as revolting a presence as you think you are (for that look just told you so). And so, ordinarily, you are a nice person, an attractive person, a person capable of drawing to yourself the affection of other people (people just like you), a person at home in your own skin (sort of; I mean, in a way; I mean, your dismay and puzzlement are natural to you, because people like you just seem to be like that, and so many of the things people like you find admirable about yourselves—the things you think about, the things you think really define you—seem rooted in these feelings): a person at home in your own house (and all its nice house things), with its nice back yard (and its nice back-yard things), at home on your street, your church, in community activities, your job, at home with your family, your relatives, your friends—you are a whole person. But one day, when you are sitting somewhere, alone in that crowd, and that awful feeling of displacedness comes over you, and really, as an ordinary person you are not well equipped to look too far inward and set yourself aright, because being ordinary is already so taxing, and being ordinary takes all you have out of you, and though the words "I must get away" do not actually pass across your lips, you make a leap from being that nice blob just sitting like a boob in your amniotic sac of the modern experience to being a person visiting heaps of death and ruin and feeling alive and inspired at the sight of it; to being a person lying on some faraway beach, your stilled body stinking and glistening in the sand, looking like something first forgotten, then remembered, then not important enough to go back for; to being a person marvelling at the harmony (ordinarily, what you would say is the backwardness) and the union these other people (and they are other people) have with nature. And you look at the things they can do with a piece of ordinary cloth, the things they fashion out of cheap, vulgarly colored (to you) twine, the way they squat down over a hole they have made in the ground, the hole itself is something to marvel at, and since you are being an ugly person this ugly but joyful thought will swell inside you: their ancestors were not clever in the way yours were and not ruthless in the way yours were, for then would it not be you who would be in harmony with nature and backwards in that charming way? An ugly thing, that is what you are when you become a tourist, an ugly, empty thing, a stupid thing, a piece of rubbish pausing here and there to gaze at this and taste that, and it will never occur to you that the people who inhabit the place in which you have just paused cannot stand you, that behind their closed doors they laugh at your strangeness (you do not look the way they look); the physical sight of you does not please them; you have bad manners (it is their custom to eat their food with their hands; you try eating their way, you look silly; you try eating the way you always eat, you look silly); they do not like the way you speak (you have an accent); they collapse helpless from laughter, mimicking the way they imagine you must look as you carry out some everyday bodily function. They do not like you. They do not like me! That thought never actually occur to you. Still, you feel a little uneasy. Still, you feel a little foolish. Still, you feel a little out of place. But the banality of your own life is very real to you; it drove you to this extreme, spending your days and your nights in the company of people who despise you, people you do not like really, people you would not want to have as your actual neighbour. And so you must devote yourself to puzzling out how much of what you are told is really, really true (Is ground-up bottle glass in peanut sauce really a delicacy around here, or will it do just what you think ground-up bottle glass will do? Is this rare, multicoloured, snout-mouthed fish really an aphrodisiac, or will it cause you to fall asleep permanently?). Oh, the hard work all of this is, and is it any wonder, then, that on your return home you feel the need of a long rest, so that you can recover from your life as a tourist?

That the native does not like the tourist is not hard to explain. For every native of every place is a potential tourist, and every tourist is a native of somewhere. Every native everywhere lives a life of overwhelming and crushing banality and boredom and desperation and depression, and every deed, good and bad, is an attempt to forget this. Every native would like to find a way out, every native would like a rest, every native would like a tour. But some natives—most natives in the world—cannot go anywhere. They are too poor. They are too poor to go anywhere. They are too poor to escape the reality of their lives; and they are too poor to live properly in the place where they live, which is the very place you, the tourist, want to go—so when the natives see you, the tourist, they envy you, they envy your ability to leave your own banality and boredom, they envy your ability to turn their own banality and boredom into a source of pleasure for yourself.

My Metaphor Weighs Tons

William Davies King

On a hot summer day in 1998, I pulled up at the house I still owned with the woman who was soon to become my ex-wife to find that she had delivered every item connected with me to the garage. My surprise was not that she had divvied up our goods, though I would rather have done the work myself, but the spectacle of what an immense and unattractive volume of me there was.

I was forty-three, wearing shorts and an old T-shirt already heavy with sweat, in the dusty glare of desert suburbia, Ryder truck still hissing and ticking at my back as the great panel door swung open with a shriek. The door shuddered, and I shuddered too. There were the usual black plastic bags of shoes and canted piles of shirts on hangers, portable radios and razors and power tools, but also the singular multiplicity of diverse collections of nothing, stuff of no clear value to anyone but someone like me. I did not like what I saw under the bare bulb in that shadowy garage. Mixed in with my necessaries there shone forth what had doomed me to a life of collecting—that super-superfluity of sub-substance. During twenty years of living with my wife, decades of relentless acquisition, I had found ways of weaving my collections into the lattice of our life. Now, brought out from concealment, arranged in heaps, not carelessly but also not artfully, these things looked like signs of hoarding, which is a diagnosis, not a hobby.

Middle-class life is itself a collection: a spouse, a house, a brace of children, a suitable car, a respectable career, cuddly pets, toys for all ages and hours, coffee and coffeepots, coffee cups and spoons, coffee tables and coffee-table books. I had the set, and then I had another set, which included: fifty-three Cheez-It boxes, empty; thirty-four old dictionaries; three dozen rusted skeleton keys; a mound of used airmail envelopes, most culled from mailroom trash; a pipe-tobacco tin chock-full of smooth pebbles; many plastic cauliflower bags, all mimicking the sphericity of a cauliflower head; business cards of business-card printers, though I had no business card; cigar ribbons, though I do not smoke. If you looked at each item for just two seconds, you'd be bored for a long time, if not for eternity.

I left behind just one collection, of naturally sculpted beach boulders. I had gathered them on countless long drives from Claremont to my job in Santa Barbara,

"My Metaphor Weighs Tons," from *Collections of Nothing* by William Davies King, Chicago: University of Chicago Press, 2008. Reprinted by permission of University of Chicago Press and William Davies King.

130 miles away. I would often stop at a beach on the drive home, hoping the night air might stave off drowsiness. It was there that I fell in love with these Brancusi boulders. They looked like naked bodies in the moonlight, wrapped warm and tight to one another. Soon I was rolling the larger rocks up a board into the trunk of my car. The next day, like a curator of antiquities home from Rome, I would place them in the yard or gardens. I collected a thousand or so, five or six at a time. To set these boulders off, I practiced a sort of topiary mowing, sculpting patches of alligator grass with my Murray mower to accent their sea-worn contours. In the spring, lush green would arabesque salty gray. By late summer, the grass would turn sharp and sallow amid the seemingly liquid rocks, and huge wolf spiders would finish the brutal composition with no-nonsense webs. Many people commented on them, and perhaps they still do, though the lawn now has the conventionally trimmed look of bimonthly mow-and-blow yardmen. The stones remain, never moving, monumental. So I have left behind the heaviest of all that I was, and it looks good.

It has been said that virtually all children have the urge to collect, though many accumulate no more than a few pebbles, shells, or bottle caps. Some four million American adults declare that they too collect, and typically something more than pebbles. Do you have a closet or wall or cabinet that is dedicated to a multiplicity of objects explainable only by the fact that in relation to one another they define a unity? If so, then you are a collector of something. I am the collector of nothing. Nothing. It sounds like a metaphor, but my metaphor weighs tons.

The first collection of my adult life began when I started to save the labels of all the food products I consumed—cereal, soup, candy, beer. I did not keep the cans or jars, only the paper or cellophane or plastic labels. Boxes and cartons I cut or dismantled. Everything had to lie flat, like a leaf in a book. Initially, I glued each item to a sheet of paper, most of it reclaimed from some other use. Eventually, I decided to keep the boxes unbound, flattened but not cut or glued, so they could be reassembled if the need ever arose. I did not keep duplicates, but the smallest variations—new graphics, a new incentive deal or coupon, even a change in the quality or color of the printing—seemed interesting enough for me to preserve. At first, I kept the labels in my file cabinet, but soon I began to punch holes and place the leaves in a binder. That way I was creating a "book," and I would soon have a lot of these books.

At this point, I estimate there are seventeen to eighteen thousand labels of all sorts in the collection, and it continues to grow daily. There are also about five hundred crown bottle caps (the metal kind with crinkly edges), also kept in binders, in plastic pages meant to hold photographic slides. It took me several years to find the bottle opener that does the least damage to a bottle cap. It's a double-pronged, curved-flange lifter, and it was for me a vital piece of equipment before the era of twist-tops, though in fact I get most of my bottle caps from the sidewalk, because I rarely drink beer. Again, the nothingness I cherish dovetails with the valuable goods discarded by others. I love it all. I love you for what you do not love, what you throw away. There's a paradox in that. I love you for your lack of love for what I love.

My pride in this label collection, and my determination to keep it up, are balanced by my annoyance with it and my sporadic resolve to give it up, even to throw it out. By now it has swollen to such proportions that no one would ever have the time or interest to explore it all. The bigger the collection gets, the harder it is to keep. The bigger the collection gets, the more completely it represents me and my history, and the more I feel oppressed by it. The bigger the collection gets, the more extraordinary and "valuable" it is, and the more I mourn the thousands of hours spent assembling it. It is a burgeoning collection full of emptiness. It is a collection of nothing. That is my title, and I am its lord, its consumer and author and subject and victim.

Is Whole Foods Wholesome?

Field Maloney

It's hard to find fault with Whole Foods, the haute-crunchy supermarket chain that has made a fortune by transforming grocery shopping into a bright and shiny, progressive experience. Indeed, the road to wild profits and cultural cachet has been surprisingly smooth for the supermarket chain. It gets mostly sympathetic coverage in the local and national media and red-carpet treatment from the communities it enters. But does Whole Foods have an Achilles' heel? And more important, does the organic movement itself, whose coattails Whole Foods has ridden to such success, have dark secrets of its own?

Granted, there's plenty that's praiseworthy about Whole Foods. John Mackey, the company's chairman, likes to say, "There's no inherent reason why business cannot be ethical, socially responsible, and profitable." And under the umbrella creed of "sustainability," Whole Foods pays its workers a solid living wage—its lowest earners average $13.15 an hour—with excellent benefits and health care. No executive makes more than 14 times the employee average. (Mackey's salary last year was $342,000.) In January, Whole Foods announced that it had committed to buy a year's supply of power from a wind-power utility in Wyoming.

But even if Whole Foods has a happy staff and nice windmills, is it really as virtuous as it appears to be? Take the produce section, usually located in the geographic center of the shopping floor and the spiritual heart of a Whole Foods outlet. (Every media profile of the company invariably contains a paragraph of fawning produce porn, near-sonnets about "gleaming melons" and "glistening kumquats.") In the produce section of Whole Foods' flagship New York City store at the Time Warner Center, shoppers browse under a big banner that lists "Reasons To Buy Organic." On the banner, the first heading is "Save Energy." The accompanying text explains how organic farmers, who use natural fertilizers like manure and compost, avoid the energy waste involved in the manufacture of synthetic fertilizers. It's a technical point that probably barely registers with most shoppers but contributes to a vague sense of virtue.

Fair enough. But here's another technical point that Whole Foods fails to mention and that highlights what has gone wrong with the organic-food movement in the last couple of decades. Let's say you live in New York City and want to buy a pound of tomatoes in season. Say you can choose between conventionally grown New Jersey tomatoes or organic ones grown in Chile. Of course, the New Jersey tomatoes will be cheaper. They will also almost certainly be fresher, having traveled a fraction of the distance. But which is the more eco-conscious choice? In terms of energy savings, there's no contest: Just think of the fossil fuels expended getting those organic tomatoes from Chile. Which brings us to the question: Setting aside freshness, price, and energy conservation, should a New Yorker just instinctively choose organic, even if the produce comes from Chile? A tough decision, but you can make a self-interested case for the social and economic benefit of going Jersey, especially if you prefer passing fields of tomatoes to fields of condominiums when you tour the Garden State.

Another heading on the Whole Foods banner says "Help the Small Farmer." "Buying organic," it states, "supports the small, family farmers that make up a large percentage of organic food producers." This is semantic sleight of hand. As one small family farmer in Connecticut told me recently, "Almost all the organic food in this country comes out of California. And five or six big California farms dominate the whole industry." There's a widespread misperception in this country—one that organic growers, no matter how giant, happily encourage—that "organic" means "small family farmer." That hasn't been the case for years, certainly not since 1990, when the Department of Agriculture drew up its official guidelines for organic food. Whole Foods knows this well, and so the line about the "small family farmers that make up a large percentage of organic food producers" is sneaky. There are a lot of small, family-run organic farmers, but their share of the organic crop in this country, and of the produce sold at Whole Foods, is minuscule.

A nearby banner at the Time Warner Center Whole Foods proclaims "Our Commitment to the Local Farmer," but this also doesn't hold up to scrutiny. More likely, the burgeoning local-food movement is making Whole Foods uneasy. After all, a multinational chain can't promote a "buy local" philosophy without being self-defeating. When I visited the Time Warner Whole Foods last fall—high season for native fruits and vegetables on the East Coast—only a token amount of local produce was on display. What Whole Foods does do for local farmers is hang glossy pinups throughout the store, what they call "grower profiles," which depict tousled, friendly looking organic farmers standing in front of their crops. This winter, when I dropped by the store, the only local produce for sale was a shelf of upstate apples, but the grower profiles were still up. There was a picture of a sandy-haired organic leek farmer named Dave, from Whately, Mass., above a shelf of conventionally grown yellow onions from Oregon. Another profile showed a guy named Ray Rex munching on an ear of sweet corn he grew on his generations-old, picturesque organic acres. The photograph was pinned above a display of conventionally grown white onions from Mexico.

These profiles may be heartwarming, but they also artfully mislead customers about what they're paying premium prices for. If Whole Foods marketing didn't revolve so much around explicit (as well as subtly suggestive) appeals to food ethics, it'd be easier to forgive some exaggerations and distortions.

Of course, above and beyond social and environmental ethics, and even taste, people buy organic food because they believe that it's better for them. All things being equal, food grown without pesticides is healthier for you. But American populism chafes against the notion of good health for those who can afford it. Charges of elitism—media wags, in otherwise flattering profiles, have called Whole Foods "Whole Paycheck" and "wholesome, healthy for the wholesome, wealthy"—are the only criticism of Whole Foods that seems to have stuck. Which brings us to the newest kid in the organic-food sandbox: Wal-Mart, the world's biggest grocery retailer, has just begun a major program to expand into organic foods. If buying food grown without chemical pesticides and synthetic fertilizers has been elevated to a status-conscious lifestyle choice, it could also be transformed into a bare-bones commodity purchase.

When the Department of Agriculture established the guidelines for organic food in 1990, it blew a huge opportunity. The USDA—under heavy agribusiness lobbying—adopted an abstract set of restrictions for organic agriculture and left "local" out of the formula. What passes for organic farming today has strayed far from what the shaggy utopians who got the movement going back in the '60s and '70s had in mind. But if these pioneers dreamed of revolutionizing the nation's food supply, they surely didn't intend for organic to become a luxury item, a high-end lifestyle choice.

It's likely that neither Wal-Mart nor Whole Foods will do much to encourage local agriculture or small farming, but in an odd twist, Wal-Mart, with its simple "More for Less" credo, might do far more to democratize the nation's food supply than Whole Foods. The organic-food movement is in danger of exacerbating the growing gap between rich and poor in this country by contributing to a two-tiered national food supply, with healthy food for the rich. Could Wal-Mart's populist strategy prove to be more "sustainable" than Whole Foods? Stranger things have happened.

Out of Iowa

From a photo essay by Danny Wilcox Frazier, text by Ted Genoways, book
published by Duke University Press. Reprinted in *Mother Jones*, February 22, 2008.
http://motherjones.com/photoessays/2008/02/out-iowa

The photo essay "Out of Iowa: An Inside Look at the Real American Heartland" is introduced with these words: "On either side of old Highway 218 in far southeastern Iowa, rows of corn are broken to stubble and furrows are filled with ice. It's late December, just days to the caucuses, and the wind knifes across the prairie, so bitter cold that even red-tailed hawks, feathers fluffed for warmth, hunker atop speed limit signs. Granted, much of what you see here is what you'd expect: each town with its water tower and circumscribed cemetery, each small farm with its Harvestore silos and propane tanks huddled under leaf-bare oaks. These are the cliches of the Midwest and the Great Plains – what folks on the coasts call 'the heartland' when they're feeling generous, 'flyover country' when they're not – and like all cliches, there's some truth to them."

The particular image above, from 2006, is the seventh in the essay. It is titled "Getting to Know Each Other, Johnson County, Iowa." Its caption reads, "The places Frazier has photographed – small towns that straddle either side of 218, like Coppock, Conesville, Kalona, Riverside, Hills, and North Liberty – are daily disappearing, casualities of a generational and economic divide that separates rural and urban classes."

The Vocabulary of Comics

Scott McCloud

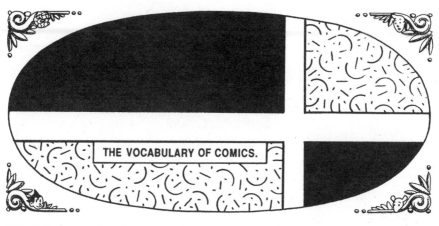

THE VOCABULARY OF COMICS.

THIS IS NOT A MAN.

THESE ARE NOT IDEAS.

THIS IS NOT
A LEAF

THESE ARE NOT PEOPLE

THIS IS NOT A COUNTRY.

THIS IS NOT MUSIC.

THIS IS NOT A COW.

THIS IS NOT / MY VOICE.

THIS IS NOT SOUND.

THESE ARE NOT FLOWERS.

STOP

THIS IS NOT LAW.

THIS IS NOT A PLANET.

THIS IS NOT ME.

THIS IS NOT A CAR.

THIS IS NOT FOOD.

THIS IS NOT A
COMPANY.

THIS IS NOT A
FACE.

THESE ARE NOT SEPARATE
MOMENTS.

NOW, THE WORD *ICON* MEANS MANY THINGS.

THIS IS PAPER

THIS IS INK ON PAPER

FOR THE PURPOSES OF THIS CHAPTER, I'M USING THE WORD *"ICON"* TO MEAN ANY IMAGE USED TO REPRESENT A A PERSON, PLACE, THING OR *IDEA.*

ICON

THAT'S A BIT BROADER THAN THE DEFINITION IN MY DICTIONARY, BUT IT'S THE CLOSEST THING TO WHAT I NEED HERE.

"SYMBOL" IS A BIT TOO *LOADED* FOR ME.

THE SORTS OF IMAGES WE USUALLY *CALL* SYMBOLS ARE ONE *CATEGORY* OF ICON, HOWEVER.

THESE ARE THE IMAGES WE USE TO REPRESENT *CONCEPTS, IDEAS* AND *PHILOSOPHIES.*

THEN THERE ARE THE ICONS OF *LANGUAGE, SCIENCE* AND *COMMUNICATION.*

ICONS OF THE *PRACTICAL* REALM.

AND FINALLY, THE ICONS WE CALL *PICTURES:* IMAGES DESIGNED TO ACTUALLY *RESEMBLE* THEIR SUBJECTS.

BUT AS RESEMBLANCE VARIES, SO DOES THE LEVEL OF ICONIC CONTENT.

OR TO PUT IT SOMEWHAT *CLUMSILY,* SOME PICTURES ARE JUST MORE ICONIC THAN OTHERS.

IN THE *NON-*PICTORIAL ICONS, MEANING IS *FIXED* AND *ABSOLUTE.* THEIR APPEARANCE DOESN'T AFFECT THEIR MEANING BECAUSE THEY REPRESENT *INVISIBLE* IDEAS.

IN *PICTURES,* HOWEVER, MEANING IS *FLUID* AND *VARIABLE* ACCORDING TO APPEARANCE. THEY DIFFER FROM *"REAL-LIFE"* APPEARANCE TO VARYING *DEGREES.*

WORDS ARE TOTALLY *ABSTRACT* ICONS. THAT IS, THEY BEAR NO RESEMBLANCE AT ALL TO THE *REAL McCOY.*

EYE

BUT IN PICTURES THE *LEVEL* OF ABSTRACTION *VARIES.* SOME, LIKE THE FACE IN THE *PREVIOUS* PANEL, SO CLOSELY RESEMBLE THEIR *REAL-LIFE COUNTERPARTS* AS TO ALMOST *TRICK THE EYE!*

OTHERS, LIKE YOURS TRULY, ARE QUITE A BIT *MORE* ABSTRACT AND, IN FACT, ARE VERY MUCH *UNLIKE* ANY HUMAN FACE YOU'VE EVER SEEN!

LET'S SEE IF WE CAN PUT THESE *PICTORIAL ICONS* IN SOME SORT OF ORDER.

COMMON WISDOM HOLDS THAT THE *PHOTOGRAPH* AND THE *REALISTIC* PICTURE ARE THE ICONS THAT MOST RESEMBLE THEIR REAL-LIFE COUNTERPARTS.

THERE ARE MANY THINGS THAT SET THESE APART FROM ACTUAL *FACES*--THEY'RE SMALLER, FLATTER, LESS *DETAILED,* THEY DON'T MOVE, THEY LACK COLOR-- BUT AS PICTORIAL ICONS GO, THEY ARE PRETTY *"REALISTIC."*

REALITY THIS WAY.

WHY-- --ARE-- --WE-- --SO-- --INVOLVED?

WHY WOULD *ANYONE*, YOUNG OR OLD, RESPOND TO A CARTOON AS MUCH OR MORE THAN A *REALISTIC IMAGE?*

WHY IS OUR CULTURE *SO IN THRALL* TO THE *SIMPLIFIED REALITY* OF THE *CARTOON?*

DEFINING THE CARTOON WOULD TAKE UP AS MUCH SPACE AS DEFINING *COMICS*, BUT FOR *NOW*, I'M GOING TO EXAMINE CARTOONING AS A FORM OF *AMPLIFICATION THROUGH SIMPLIFICATION.*

WHEN WE *ABSTRACT* AN IMAGE THROUGH *CARTOONING*, WE'RE NOT SO MUCH *ELIMINATING* DETAILS AS WE ARE *FOCUSING* ON *SPECIFIC DETAILS.*

BY *STRIPPING DOWN* AN IMAGE TO ITS ESSENTIAL *"MEANING,"* AN ARTIST CAN *AMPLIFY* THAT MEANING IN A WAY THAT REALISTIC ART *CAN'T.*

FILM CRITICS WILL SOMETIMES DESCRIBE A *LIVE-ACTION* FILM AS A "CARTOON" TO ACKNOWLEDGE THE STRIPPED-DOWN *INTENSITY* OF A SIMPLE STORY OR VISUAL STYLE.

THOUGH THE TERM IS OFTEN USED *DISPARAGINGLY*, IT CAN BE EQUALLY WELL APPLIED TO MANY *TIME-TESTED CLASSICS*. SIMPLIFYING CHARACTERS AND IMAGES TOWARD A *PURPOSE* CAN BE AN EFFECTIVE TOOL FOR STORYTELLING IN *ANY* MEDIUM.

CARTOONING ISN'T JUST A WAY OF *DRAWING*, IT'S A WAY OF *SEEING!*

FOLLOW! FOLLOW!

THE ABILITY OF CARTOONS TO *FOCUS* OUR ATTENTION ON AN IDEA IS, I THINK, AN IMPORTANT PART OF THEIR SPECIAL POWER, BOTH IN COMICS AND IN DRAWING GENERALLY.

ONE   A FEW   THOUSANDS   MILLIONS   (NEARLY) ALL

ANOTHER IS THE *UNIVERSALITY* OF CARTOON IMAGERY. THE MORE CARTOONY A FACE IS, FOR INSTANCE, THE MORE PEOPLE IT COULD BE SAID TO *DESCRIBE*.

BUT I BELIEVE THERE'S SOMETHING *MORE* AT WORK IN OUR MINDS WHEN WE VIEW A CARTOON--ESPECIALLY OF A HUMAN FACE-- WHICH WARRANTS FURTHER INVESTIGATION.

WHAT   ARE YOU

REALLY   SEEING?

THE FACT THAT YOUR MIND IS *CAPABLE* OF TAKING A *CIRCLE, TWO DOTS* AND A *LINE* AND TURNING THEM INTO A *FACE* IS NOTHING SHORT OF *INCREDIBLE!*

BUT STILL *MORE* INCREDIBLE IS THE FACT THAT YOU CANNOT *AVOID* SEEING A FACE HERE. YOUR MIND WON'T *LET* YOU!

ASK A FRIEND TO DRAW YOU SOME SHAPES ON A PIECE OF PAPER. THEY SHOULD BE *CLOSED CURVES*, BUT *OTHERWISE* CAN BE AS *WEIRD* AND *IRREGULAR* AS HE OR SHE *WANTS*.

LET'S SAY THE RESULTS LOOK SOMETHING LIKE *THIS*.

NOW-- YOU'LL FIND THAT NO MATTER WHAT THEY *LOOK* LIKE, EVERY SINGLE *ONE* OF THOSE SHAPES *CAN* BE MADE INTO A FACE WITH ONE SIMPLE ADDITION.

YOUR MIND HAS NO TROUBLE AT ALL CONVERTING SUCH SHAPES INTO FACES, YET WOULD IT EVER MISTAKE *THIS*--

--FOR *THIS?*

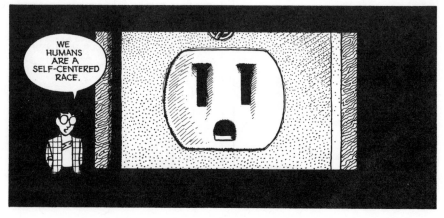

WE HUMANS ARE A SELF-CENTERED RACE.

ALL SET?

GOOD.

NOW, *SMILE.*

C'MON, NOBODY'S LOOKING.

GOOD. NOW, WHAT *CHANGED* WHEN YOU SMILED? WHAT DID YOU SEE?

NOTHING, RIGHT.

YET, YOU *KNOW* YOU SMILED! NOT JUST BECAUSE YOU FELT YOUR CHEEKS COMPRESS OR THE CRINKLING AROUND YOUR EYES!

YOU *KNOW* YOU SMILED BECAUSE YOU TRUSTED THIS MASK CALLED YOUR FACE TO *RESPOND!*

BUT THE FACE YOU SEE IN YOUR *MIND* IS NOT THE SAME AS *OTHERS* SEE!

WHEN TWO PEOPLE INTERRACT, THEY USUALLY LOOK DIRECTLY *AT* ONE ANOTHER, SEEING THEIR PARTNER'S FEATURES IN *VIVID DETAIL.*

EACH ONE *ALSO* SUSTAINS A CONSTANT AWARENESS OF HIS OR HER *OWN* FACE, BUT *THIS* MIND-PICTURE IS NOT NEARLY SO VIVID; JUST A SKETCHY ARRANGEMENT...A SENSE OF SHAPE... A SENSE OF *GENERAL PLACEMENT*.

SOMETHING AS *SIMPLE* AND AS *BASIC*--

--AS A *CARTOON*.

THUS, WHEN YOU LOOK AT A PHOTO OR REALISTIC DRAWING OF A FACE--

--YOU SEE IT AS THE FACE OF *ANOTHER*.

BUT WHEN YOU ENTER THE WORLD OF THE *CARTOON*--

-- YOU SEE *YOURSELF.*

I BELIEVE THIS IS THE *PRIMARY CAUSE* OF OUR CHILDHOOD FASCINATION WITH *CARTOONS,* THOUGH OTHER FACTORS SUCH AS *UNIVERSAL IDENTIFICATION, SIMPLICITY* AND THE *CHILDLIKE FEATURES* OF MANY CARTOON CHARACTERS ALSO PLAY A PART.

THE CARTOON IS A *VACUUM* INTO WHICH OUR *IDENTITY* AND *AWARENESS* ARE PULLED...

...AN *EMPTY SHELL* THAT WE INHABIT WHICH *ENABLES* US TO TRAVEL IN *ANOTHER REALM.*

WE DON'T JUST *OBSERVE* THE CARTOON, WE *BECOME* IT!

THAT'S WHY I DECIDED TO *DRAW* MYSELF IN SUCH A SIMPLE *STYLE.*

WOULD YOU HAVE *LISTENED* TO ME IF I LOOKED LIKE *THIS??*

I *DOUBT* IT! YOU WOULD HAVE BEEN FAR TOO AWARE OF THE *MESSENGER* TO FULLY RECEIVE THE *MESSAGE!*

APART FROM WHAT LITTLE I TOLD YOU ABOUT MYSELF IN *CHAPTER ONE,* I'M PRACTICALLY A *BLANK SLATE!*

IT WOULD NEVER EVEN *OCCUR* TO YOU TO WONDER WHAT MY *POLITICS* ARE, OR WHAT I HAD FOR *LUNCH* OR WHERE I GOT THIS *SILLY OUTFIT!*

I'M JUST A LITTLE VOICE INSIDE YOUR *HEAD.*

A *CONCEPT.*

YOU GIVE ME LIFE BY READING THIS BOOK AND BY "*FILLING UP*" THIS VERY *ICONIC* (CARTOONY) *FORM.*

WHO I AM IS IRRELEVANT. I'M JUST A LITTLE PIECE OF *YOU.*

BUT IF WHO I AM MATTERS *LESS,* MAYBE WHAT I *SAY* WILL MATTER *MORE.*

THAT'S THE *THEORY,* ANYWAY.

SO FAR, WE'VE ONLY DISCUSSED *FACES,* BUT THE PHENOMENON OF *NON-VISUAL SELF-AWARENESS* CAN, TO A *LESSER DEGREE,* STILL APPLY TO OUR *WHOLE BODIES.* AFTER ALL, DO WE NEED TO *SEE* OUR HANDS TO KNOW WHAT THEY'RE DOING?

THERE'S *MORE,* TOO!

THE LATE GREAT *MARSHALL MCLUHAN* OBSERVED A *SIMILAR* FORM OF *NON-VISUAL AWARENESS* WHEN PEOPLE INTERACT WITH *INANIMATE OBJECTS.*

WHEN *DRIVING*, FOR EXAMPLE, WE EXPERIENCE MUCH MORE THAN OUR *FIVE SENSES* REPORT.

THE *WHOLE CAR*--NOT JUST THE PARTS WE CAN SEE, FEEL AND HEAR--IS VERY MUCH ON OUR MINDS AT ALL TIMES.

THE VEHICLE BECOMES AN *EXTENSION* OF OUR BODY. IT *ABSORBS* OUR SENSE OF *IDENTITY.* WE *BECOME* THE CAR.

IF ONE CAR *HITS* ANOTHER, THE DRIVER OF THE VEHICLE BEING *STRUCK* IS MUCH MORE LIKELY TO SAY:

KLUNK!

HEY! HE *HIT* ME!!

THAN "HE HIT MY *CAR!*"

OR "HIS *CAR* HIT MY CAR", FOR THAT MATTER.

OUR *IDENTITIES* AND *AWARENESS* ARE INVESTED IN MANY *INANIMATE OBJECTS* EVERY DAY. OUR *CLOTHES*, FOR EXAMPLE, CAN TRIGGER *NUMEROUS TRANSFORMATIONS* IN THE WAY OTHERS SEE US AND IN THE WAY WE SEE *OURSELVES.*

OUR ABILITY TO *EXTEND* OUR IDENTITIES INTO INANIMATE OBJECTS CAN CAUSE PIECES OF WOOD TO BECOME *LEGS...*

PIECES OF METAL TO BECOME *HANDS...*

PIECES OF PLASTIC TO BECOME *EARS...*

PIECES OF GLASS TO BECOME *EYES.*

AND IN *EVERY CASE,* OUR CONSTANT AWARENESS OF *SELF--*

--FLOWS *OUTWARD* TO INCLUDE THE OBJECT OF OUR *EXTENDED IDENTITY.*

AND JUST AS OUR AWARENESS OF OUR *BIOLOGICAL* SELVES ARE *SIMPLIFIED CONCEPTUALIZED IMAGES--*

--SO TOO IS OUR AWARENESS OF *THESE* EXTENSIONS GREATLY *SIMPLIFIED.*

ALL THE THINGS WE *EXPERIENCE* IN LIFE CAN BE SEPARATED INTO *TWO REALMS,* THE *REALM OF THE CONCEPT--*

--AND THE REALM OF THE *SENSES.*

OUR IDENTITIES BELONG *PERMANENTLY* TO THE *CONCEPTUAL* WORLD. THEY CAN'T BE *SEEN, HEARD, SMELLED, TOUCHED* OR *TASTED.* THEY'RE MERELY *IDEAS.* AND *EVERYTHING ELSE*--AT THE START--BELONGS TO THE *SENSUAL WORLD,* THE WORLD *OUTSIDE* OF US.

GRADUALLY WE REACH *BEYOND* OURSELVES.

WE ENCOUNTER THE *SIGHT, SMELL, TOUCH, TASTE* AND *SOUND* OF OUR OWN BODIES.

AND OF THE WORLD *AROUND* US.

AND SOON WE DISCOVER THAT OBJECTS OF THE *PHYSICAL WORLD* CAN *ALSO* CROSS OVER--

--AND POSSESS IDENTITIES OF THEIR OWN.

OR, AS OUR *EXTENSIONS*--

--BEGIN TO GLOW--

--WITH THE LIFE--

--WE *LEND* TO THEM.

BY DE-EMPHASIZING THE *APPEARANCE* OF THE *PHYSICAL* WORLD IN FAVOR OF THE *IDEA* OF FORM, THE CARTOON PLACES ITSELF IN THE WORLD OF *CONCEPTS.*

THROUGH TRADITIONAL *REALISM,* THE COMICS ARTIST CAN PORTRAY THE WORLD *WITHOUT--*

--AND THROUGH THE *CARTOON,* THE WORLD *WITHIN.*

WHEN CARTOONS ARE USED *THROUGHOUT* A STORY, THE *WORLD* OF THAT STORY MAY SEEM TO *PULSE WITH LIFE.*

INANIMATE OBJECTS MAY SEEM TO POSSESS *SEPARATE IDENTITIES* SO THAT IF ONE *JUMPED UP* AND STARTED *SINGING* IT WOULDN'T FEEL OUT OF PLACE.

BUT IN EMPHASIZING THE *CONCEPTS* OF OBJECTS OVER THEIR *PHYSICAL APPEARANCE,* MUCH HAS TO BE *OMITTED.*

IF AN ARTIST WANTS TO PORTRAY THE BEAUTY AND COMPLEXITY OF THE *PHYSICAL WORLD--*

--REALISM OF *SOME* SORT IS GOING TO PLAY A PART.

WHEN DRAWING THE FACE AND FIGURE, NEARLY *ALL* COMICS ARTISTS APPLY AT LEAST *SOME* SMALL MEASURE OF CARTOONING. EVEN THE MORE REALISTIC *ADVENTURE* ARTISTS--

--ARE A *FAR CRY* FROM *PHOTO-REALISTS!*

STORYTELLERS IN *ALL* MEDIA KNOW THAT A SURE INDICATOR OF *AUDIENCE INVOLVEMENT*--

--IS THE DEGREE TO WHICH THE AUDIENCE *IDENTIFIES* WITH A STORY'S *CHARACTERS.*

AND SINCE *VIEWER-IDENTIFICATION* IS A *SPECIALTY* OF CARTOONING, CARTOONS HAVE HISTORICALLY HELD AN *ADVANTAGE* IN *BREAKING INTO WORLD POPULAR CULTURE.*

ON THE OTHER HAND, NO ONE EXPECTS AUDIENCES TO IDENTIFY WITH *BRICK WALLS* OR *LANDSCAPES* AND INDEED, BACKGROUNDS TEND TO BE SLIGHTLY MORE *REALISTIC.*

IN *SOME* COMICS, THIS SPLIT IS FAR MORE *PRONOUNCED.* THE BELGIAN *"CLEAR-LINE"* STYLE OF HERGÉ'S *TINTIN* COMBINES VERY ICONIC CHARACTERS WITH UNUSUALLY *REALISTIC* BACKGROUNDS.

THIS COMBINATION ALLOWS READERS TO *MASK* THEMSELVES IN A CHARACTER AND SAFELY ENTER A SENSUALLY STIMULATING WORLD.

ONE SET OF LINES TO *SEE.* ANOTHER SET OF LINES TO *BE.*

IN THE WORLD OF *ANIMATION,* WHERE THE EFFECT HAPPENS TO BE A PRACTICAL *NECESSITY,* DISNEY HAS USED IT WITH IMPRESSIVE RESULTS FOR OVER *50 YEARS!*

IN *EUROPE* IT CAN BE FOUND IN MANY POPULAR COMICS, FROM *ASTERIX* TO *TINTIN* TO WORKS OF *JACQUES TARDI.*

IN *AMERICAN* COMICS, THE EFFECT IS USED FAR LESS *OFTEN,* ALTHOUGH IT HAS CREPT UP IN THE WORKS OF ARTISTS AS DIVERSE AS *CARL BARKS, JAIME HERNANDEZ* AND IN THE TEAM OF *DAVE SIM* AND *GERHARD.*

CEREBUS © DAVE SIM.

IN *JAPAN,* ON THE OTHER HAND, THE MASKING EFFECT WAS, FOR A TIME, VIRTUALLY A *NATIONAL STYLE!*

ART © HAYASI AND OSIMA.

THANKS TO THE *SEMINAL INFLUENCE* OF COMICS CREATOR *OSAMU TEZUKA,* JAPANESE COMICS HAVE A LONG, RICH HISTORY OF ICONIC CHARACTERS.

BUT, IN RECENT DECADES JAPANESE FANS ALSO DEVELOPED A TASTE FOR *FLASHY, PHOTO-REALISTIC ART.*

CLIK!

THE RESULTANT HYBRID STYLES HAD TREMENDOUS ICONIC *RANGE,* FROM EXTREMELY CARTOONY CHARACTERS TO *NEAR-PHOTOGRAPHIC BACKGROUNDS.*

"MONA GOES TOKYO"

BUT JAPANESE COMICS ARTISTS TOOK THE IDEA A STEP FURTHER.

SOON, SOME OF THEM REALIZED THAT THE *OBJECTIFYING POWER* OF REALISTIC ARTS COULD BE PUT TO *OTHER* USES.

FOR EXAMPLE, WHILE *MOST* CHARACTERS WERE DESIGNED *SIMPLY,* TO ASSIST IN *READER-IDENTIFICATION--*

--*OTHER* CHARACTERS WERE DRAWN MORE *REALISTICALLY* IN ORDER TO *OBJECTIFY* THEM, EMPHASIZING THEIR *"OTHERNESS"* FROM THE READER.

A PROP LIKE THIS *SWORD* MIGHT BE VERY *CARTOONY* IN *ONE* SEQUENCE--

--DUE TO THE *"LIFE"* IT POSSESSES AS AN EXTENSION OF MY CARTOON IDENTITY!

BUT SUPPOSE I NOTICE SOME *MYSTERIOUS WRITING* CARVED ON THE SWORD'S *HILT.*

IN JAPANESE COMICS, THE SWORD MIGHT *NOW* BECOME VERY *REALISTIC,* NOT ONLY TO SHOW US THE DETAILS, BUT TO MAKE US AWARE OF THE SWORD AS AN *OBJECT,* SOMETHING WITH *WEIGHT, TEXTURE* AND *PHYSICAL COMPLEXITY.*

IN THIS AND IN *OTHER WAYS,* COMICS IN JAPAN HAVE EVOLVED VERY *DIFFERENTLY* FROM THOSE IN THE WEST.

WE'LL RETURN TO THESE DIFFERENCES SEVERAL TIMES DURING THIS BOOK.

I *LIKE* THE MASKING EFFECT, PERSONALLY, BUT IT'S JUST ONE OF *MANY* POSSIBLE APPROACHES TO COMICS ART.

MANY OF MY *FAVORITE ARTISTS* USE IT VERY *RARELY.*

STILL, I HOPE THE JAPANESE PERSPECTIVE ON CARTOONING HELPS DEMONSTRATE THAT ONE'S CHOICE OF STYLES CAN HAVE CONSEQUENCES FAR BEYOND THE MERE *"LOOK"* OF A STORY.

AS I WRITE THIS, IN 1992, AMERICAN AUDIENCES ARE JUST BEGINNING TO REALIZE THAT A SIMPLE *STYLE* DOESN'T NECESSITATE SIMPLE *STORY.*

THE PLATONIC IDEAL OF THE CARTOON MAY SEEM TO OMIT MUCH OF THE *AMBIGUITY* AND *COMPLEX CHARACTERIZATION* WHICH ARE THE HALLMARKS OF *MODERN LITERATURE,* LEAVING THEM SUITABLE ONLY FOR *CHILDREN.*

BUT SIMPLE ELEMENTS CAN COMBINE IN COMPLEX WAYS, AS ATOMS BECOME MOLECULES AND MOLECULES BECOME LIFE.

AND *LIKE* THE ATOM, GREAT POWER IS LOCKED IN THESE FEW SIMPLE LINES.

RELEASEABLE ONLY BY THE READER'S MIND.

THERE'S A LOT MORE TO *CARTOONS* THAN MEETS THE EYE!

MEANING RETAINED.

RESEMBLANCE *GONE.*

WORDS--

--ARE THE ULTIMATE ABSTRACTION.

MOST AMERICAN COMICS, NOTABLY COMIC *BOOKS,* HAVE LONG EMPHASIZED THE *DIFFERENCES* BETWEEN WORDS AND PICTURES.

WRITING AND DRAWING ARE SEEN AS *SEPARATE DISCIPLINES,* WRITERS AND ARTISTS AS *SEPARATE BREEDS--*

-- AND "GOOD" COMICS AS THOSE IN WHICH THE *COMBINATION* OF THESE VERY *DIFFERENT* FORMS OF EXPRESSION IS THOUGHT TO BE *HARMONIOUS.*

BUT JUST HOW "DIFFERENT" *ARE* THEY?

WORDS, PICTURES AND OTHER ICONS ARE THE *VOCABULARY* OF THE LANGUAGE CALLED **COMICS.**

A SINGLE UNIFIED *LANGUAGE* DESERVES A SINGLE, UNIFIED *VOCABULARY.*

WITHOUT IT, COMICS WILL CONTINUE TO *LIMP ALONG* AS THE *"BASTARD CHILD"* OF WORDS AND PICTURES.

SEVERAL FACTORS HAVE CONSPIRED *AGAINST* COMICS RECEIVING THE *UNIFIED IDENTITY* IT *NEEDS.*

AND AMONG THEM LIE SOME OF OUR VERY *BEST* INSTINCTS.

BOTH ARTIST AND WRITER BEGIN, HANDS JOINED ACROSS THE GAP, WITH A COMMON PURPOSE: TO MAKE COMICS OF *"QUALITY"*

"ARTIE"   "RITA"

THE ARTIST KNOWS THAT THIS MEANS MORE THAN JUST *STICK-FIGURES* AND *CRUDE CARTOONS.* HE SETS OFF IN SEARCH OF A *HIGHER* ART.

THE WRITER KNOWS THAT THIS MEANS MORE THAN JUST *OOF! POW! BLAM!* AND *ONE-A-DAY GAGS.* SHE SETS OFF IN SEARCH OF SOMETHING *DEEPER.*

IN MUSEUMS AND IN LIBRARIES, THE ARTIST FINDS WHAT HE'S LOOKING FOR. HE STUDIES THE TECHNIQUES OF THE *GREAT MASTERS* OF *WESTERN ART.* HE PRACTICES *NIGHT AND DAY.*

SHE *TOO* FINDS WHAT SHE'S LOOKING FOR, IN THE GREAT MASTERS OF *WESTERN LITERATURE.* SHE READS AND WRITES *CONSTANTLY.* SHE SEARCHES FOR A VOICE *UNIQUELY HERS.*

FINALLY, THEY'RE READY. BOTH HAVE *MASTERED THEIR ARTS.* HIS BRUSHSTROKE IS NEARLY *INVISIBLE* IN ITS SUBTLETY, THE FIGURES PURE *MICHAELANGELO.* HER DESCRIPTIONS ARE *DAZZLING.* THE WORDS FLOW TOGETHER LIKE A *SHAKESPEAREAN SONNET.*

THEY'RE READY TO *JOIN HANDS* ONCE MORE AND CREATE A *COMICS MASTERPIECE.*

TWO EYES, ONE NOSE, ONE MOUTH.

PICTURES ARE **RECEIVED** INFORMATION. WE NEED NO FORMAL EDUCATION TO *"GET THE MESSAGE."* THE MESSAGE IS *INSTANTANEOUS.*

WRITING IS **PERCEIVED** INFORMATION. IT TAKES TIME AND SPECIALIZED KNOWLEDGE TO DECODE THE ABSTRACT SYMBOLS OF LANGUAGE.

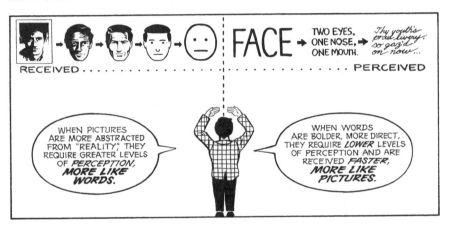

FACE → TWO EYES, ONE NOSE, ONE MOUTH. → *Thy youth's proud livery, so gaz'd on now...*

RECEIVED · PERCEIVED

WHEN PICTURES ARE MORE ABSTRACTED FROM "REALITY," THEY REQUIRE GREATER LEVELS OF *PERCEPTION, MORE LIKE WORDS.*

WHEN WORDS ARE BOLDER, MORE DIRECT, THEY REQUIRE *LOWER* LEVELS OF PERCEPTION AND ARE RECEIVED *FASTER, MORE LIKE PICTURES.*

OUR NEED FOR A UNIFIED **LANGUAGE** OF COMICS SENDS US TOWARD THE CENTER WHERE WORDS AND PICTURES ARE LIKE TWO SIDES OF *ONE COIN!*

BUT OUR NEED FOR **SOPHISTICATION** IN COMICS SEEMS TO LEAD US *OUTWARD,* WHERE WORDS AND PICTURES ARE MOST *SEPARATE.*

BOTH ARE **WORTHY ASPIRATIONS.** BOTH STEM FROM A LOVE OF COMICS AND A DEVOTION TO ITS FUTURE.

CAN THEY BE *RECONCILED?*

I SAY THE ANSWER IS *YES,* BUT SINCE THE REASONS BELONG IN A *DIFFERENT CHAPTER,* WE'LL HAVE TO COME BACK TO THIS *LATER.*

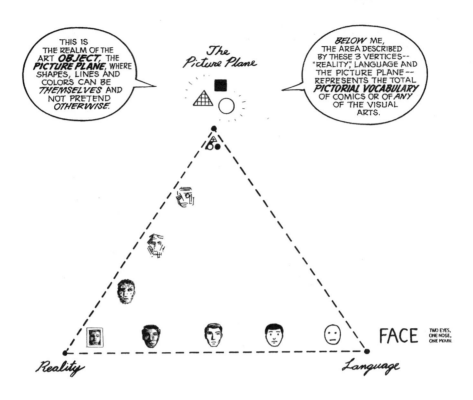

THIS IS THE REALM OF THE ART *OBJECT*, THE *PICTURE PLANE*, WHERE SHAPES, LINES AND COLORS CAN BE *THEMSELVES* AND NOT PRETEND *OTHERWISE*.

The Picture Plane

BELOW ME, THE AREA DESCRIBED BY THESE 3 VERTICES-- "REALITY", LANGUAGE AND THE PICTURE PLANE-- REPRESENTS THE TOTAL *PICTORIAL VOCABULARY* OF COMICS OR OF *ANY* OF THE VISUAL ARTS.

FACE — TWO EYES, ONE NOSE, ONE MOUTH.

Reality

Language

MOST COMICS ART LIES NEAR THE *BOTTOM*-- THAT IS, ALONG THE *ICONIC ABSTRACTION* SIDE WHERE EVERY LINE HAS A *MEANING*.

NEAR THE LINE, BUT NOT NECESSARILY *ON* IT! FOR EVEN THE MOST *STRAIGHT-FORWARD* LITTLE CARTOON CHARACTER HAS A *"MEANINGLESS"* LINE OR TWO!

WATCH THAT *NOSE!*

IF WE INCORPORATE LANGUAGE AND OTHER ICONS *INTO* THE CHART, WE CAN BEGIN TO BUILD A COMPREHENSIVE *MAP*--

--OF THE *UNIVERSE* CALLED *COMICS.*

1. **MARY FLEENER** at her most abstract. 2. **MARISCAL**'s Piker. 3. **DAVE McKEAN** employing one of the many styles found in his series CAGES. 4. **MARC HEMPEL**'s GREGORY. 5. **MARK BEYER**. 6. **LARRY MARDER**'s Beanish from TALES OF THE BEANWORLD. "Resembling" nothing ever seen (hence all the way to the right), Marder's beans walk the line from design to meaning. 7. **SAUL STIENBERG**. 8. **PENNY MORAN VAN-HORN** from THE LIBRARIAN. 9. **LORENZO MATTOTI** in FIRES (© Editions Albin Michel S.A.) combines deeply impressionistic lighting with iconic forms and strong, design-oriented compositions. In other words, he's a hard one to place. 10. **ALINE KOMINSKY-CRUMB**. 11. **PETER BAGGE**'s Chuckie-Boy from NEAT STUFF. Compare to 39. 12. **KRISTINE KRYTTRE**. 13. **REA IRVIN**. THE SMYTHES © Field Newspaper Syndicate. 14. **STEVE WILLIS**'s Morty. 15. **PHIL YEH**'s FRANK THE UNICORN. 16. **JERRY MORIARTY**'s "Jack Survives". Based closely on real world light and shadow, but decomposed into rough shapes. Similar effects are found in no.s 8,18,19,20 and 34. 17. **JEFF WONG**'s art for Scott Russo's JIZZ. 18. **ROLF STARK**'s expressionistic RAIN. 19. **SPAIN**'s TRASHMAN. 20. **FRANK MILLER**'s THE DARK KNIGHT RETURNS. Batman © D.C. Comics. Batman created by Bob Kane. 21. **WILLIAM MESSNER-LOEBS**'s Wolverine MacAlistair from JOURNEY. 22. **DON SIMPSON**'s MEGATON MAN. Beginning from a realistic anatomical base, Simpson distorts and exaggerates M.M.'s features to the brink of abstraction. 23. **MICHAEL CHERKAS** from SILENT INVASION, © Cherkas and Hancock. 24. **RICK GEARY**. 25. **PETER KUPER**. 26. **GARRY TRUDEAU**'s DOONESBURY. 27. **LYNDA BARRY**. 28. **SAMPEI SHIRATO**. 29. **CHARLES BURNS**'s BIG BABY. 29 1/2. (Whoops) **CLIFF STERRETT**. The character pictured here (from POLLY AND HER PALS) might belong a bit lower, but Sterrett's art, like Fleener's often heads upward toward the wildly abstract. P.A.H.P. is © Newspaper Features Syndicate, Inc. 30. **SERGIO ARAGONES**'s GROO THE WANDERER. Simple, straightforward, but with a strong gestural quality that always reminds us of the hand that holds the pen (also true of 14,28,31,41). 31. **ROBERTA GREGORY**'s Bitchy Bitch from NAUGHTY BITS. 32. **DAVID MAZZUCCHELLI** from BATMAN: YEAR ONE. Commissioner Gordon © D.C. Comics. 33. **JOSE MUNOZ** from "Mister Conrad, Mister Wilcox". © Munoz and Sampayo. 34. **CAROL**

Keep in mind that these are my copies of the original drawings.

The Picture Plane

"Reality"

THE   REPRESENTAT

PLEASE NOTE: ARTISTS IN THIS CHART ARE NOT NECESSARILY CHOSEN FOR ARTISTIC MERIT. SOME VERY IMPORTANT CREATORS ARE NOT INCLUDED.

SWAIN. **35. CHESTER GOULD's DICK TRACY** © Chicago Tribune-New York Syndicate, Inc. **36. JACK KIRBY's** Darkseid, © D.C. Comics. **37. BOB BURDEN. 38. DANIEL TORRES's** Rocco Vargas from TRITON. **39. PETER BAGGE's** Buddy Bradley from HATE. Compare to 11. **40. SETH. 41. MARK MARTIN. 42. JULIE DOUCET. 43. EDWARD GOREY. 44. CRAIG RUSSELL's** Mowgli from Kipling's THE JUNGLE BOOKS. Russell's characters are as finely observed and realistically based as Hal Foster's or Dave Stevens' but with an unparalleled sense of design that draws them toward the upper vertex. Lately, Russell has been moving a bit higher and toward the right in some cases. **45. GOSEKI KOJIMA** from KOZURE OKAMI

("Wolf and Cub") © Koike and Kojima. **46. EDDIE CAMPBELL's ALEC.** Realistic in tone, but also gestural and spontaneous. The *process* of drawing isn't hidden from view. **47. ALEX TOTH.** Zorro © ZorroProductions, Inc. Art © Walt Disney Productions. (Zorro created by Johnston McCulley). **48. HUGO PRATT's** CORTO MALTESE © Casterman, Paris-Tourmai. **49. WILL EISNER's** from TO THE HEART OF THE STORM. **50. DORI SEDA. 51. R. CRUMB** swings between realistic and cartoony characters, usually staying about this high but occasionally venturing upward. **52. STEVE DITKO. 53. NORMAN DOG. 54. VALENTINO's NORMALMAN** sits a bit to the right and up from his current SHADOWHAWK (whose iconic mask made him a bit harder to place). **55. ROZ CHAST. 56. JOOST SWARTE's** Anton Makassar. **57. ELZIE SEGAR's** POPEYE © King features Syndicate, Inc. **58. GEORGE HERRIMAN's** "Offissa Pupp" from KRAZY KAT. © International feature Service, Inc. **59. JIM WOODRING's FRANK. 60. NEAL ADAMS.** from X-MEN © Marvel Entertainment Group, Inc. (X-Men created by Lee and Kirby). **61. GIL KANE** from ACTION COMICS © D.C. Comics, Inc. **62. MILTON CANIFF's STEVE CANYON.** Nick Fury appearing in X-MEN © Marvel Entertainment Group, Inc. **54. JOHN BYRNE.** Superman © D.C. Comics, Inc. (Superman created by Jerry Siegel and Joe Schuster). **65. JACQUES TARDI** from LE DEMON DES GLACES © Dargaud Editeur. **66. JEAN-CLAUDE MEZIERES.** Laureline from the VALERIAN series. © Dargaud Editeur. **67. BILL GRIFFITH's** ZIPPY THE PINHEAD. **68. JOE MATT. 69. KYLE BAKER** from WHY I HATE SATURN. **70. TRINA ROBBINS's**

MISTY. © Marvel Entertainment Group, Inc. **71. RIYOKO IKEDA's** Oscar from THE ROSE OF VERSAILLES. **72. GEORGE McMANUS.** BRINGING UP FATHER © International Feature Service, Inc. **73. CHARLES SCHULZ's** Charlie Brown from PEANUTS © United Features Syndicate, Inc. **74. ART SPIEGELMAN** from MAUS. **75. MATT FEAZELL's** CYNICALMAN. **76.** The company Logo. The picture as symbol. **77.** Title Logo. The word as object. **78.** Sound Effect. The word as sound. **79. TOM KING's** SNOOKUMS, THAT LOVABLE TRANSVESTITE, a photo-comic. **80. DREW FRIEDMAN. 81. DAVE STEVENS. 82. HAL FOSTER.** TARZAN created by Edgar Rice Burroughs. **83. ALEX RAYMOND.** Flash Gordon © King Features Syndicate, Inc. **84. MILO MANARA.** The Vision © Marvel Entertainment Group. **86. CAROL LAY's** Irene Van de Kamp from GOOD GIRLS. A bizarre character, but drawn in a very straightforward style. **87. GILBERT HERNANDEZ. 88. JAIME HERNANDEZ. 89. COLIN UPTON. 90. KURT SCHAFFENBERGER.** Superboy © D.C. Comics. **91. JACK COLE's PLASTIC MAN,** © D.C. Comics. **92. REED WALLER's OMAHA THE CAT DANCER** © Waller and Worley. **93. WENDY PINI's** Skywise from ELFQUEST. © WaRP Graphics. **94. DAN DE CARLO.** Veronica © Archie Comics. **95. HAROLD GRAY's** LITTLE ORPHAN ANNIE. © Chicago Tribune- New York News Syndicate. **96. HERGE's** TINTIN © Editions Casterman. **97. FLOYD GOTTFREDSON.** Mickey Mouse © Walt Disney Productions. **98. JEFF SMITH's** BONE. **99.** Smile Dammit. **100. COLLEEN DORAN's** A DISTANT SOIL. **101. ROY CRANE's CAPTAIN EASY** © NEA Service, Inc. **102. DAN CLOWES. 103. WAYNO. 104. V.T. HAMLIN's** ALLEY OOP © NEA Service, Inc. **105. CHESTER BROWN. 106. STAN SAKAI's** USAGI YOJIMBO. **107. DAVE SIM's** CEREBUS THE AARDVARK. **108. WALT KELLY's** POGO © Selby Kelly. **109. RUDOLPH DIRKS's** HANS AND FRITZ © King Features Syndicate, Inc. **110. H.C. "BUD" FISHER's** Jeff from MUTT AND JEFF © McNaught Syndicate, Inc. **111. MORT WALKER's** HI AND LOIS © King Features Syndicate, Inc. **112. OSAMU TEZUKA's** ASTROBOY. **113. CARL BARKS.** Scrooge McDuck © Walt Disney Productions. **114. CROCKETT JOHNSON's** Mister O'Malley from BARNABY © Field Newspaper Syndicate, Inc. **115. PAT SULLIVAN's** FELIX THE CAT © Newspaper Feature Service. **116. UDERZO.** ASTERIX by Goscinny and Uderzo © Dargaud Editeur.

MOST OF THE PRECEDING EXAMPLES WERE PLACED ON OUR CHART BASED ON THE DRAWING STYLES USED ON *SPECIFIC CHARACTERS*.

EACH CREATOR EMPLOYS A *RANGE* OF STYLES, THOUGH, AND MANY OCCUPY *SEVERAL* PLACES ON THE CHART DURING A GIVEN PROJECT.

SOME, LIKE MATT FEAZELL'S *CYNICALMAN*, KEEP TO ONE AREA CONSISTENTLY

THE COMBINATION OF *EXTREMELY ICONIC CHARACTERS* AND *ENVIRONMENTS*, MIXED WITH *SIMPLE, DIRECT LANGUAGE* AND A *SOUND EFFECT* OR TWO WOULD GIVE US A SHAPE SOMETHING LIKE *THIS*:·

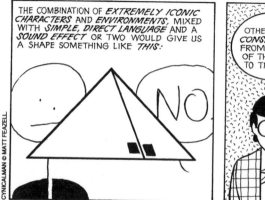

CYNICALMAN © MATT FEAZELL

BUT OTHERS *RANGE CONSIDERABLY* FROM ONE END OF THE CHART TO THE OTHER.

WE'VE ALREADY DISCUSSED THE RANGE OF HERGÉ AND OTHERS WHO CONTRAST *ICONIC CHARACTERS* WITH *REALISTIC BACKGROUNDS*.

HERGÉ STRETCHES NEARLY FROM *LEFT TO RIGHT*-- FROM *REALISM* TO *CARTOONING*-- BUT VENTURES VERY *LITTLE* INTO THE *UPPER* WORLD OF *NON-ICONIC* ABSTRACTION.

ART © EDITIONS CASTERMAN.

MARY FLEENER, ON THE OTHER HAND, VARIES ONLY SLIGHTLY IN HER LEVEL OF ICONIC CONTENT, WHILE THE LEVEL OF NON-ICONIC ABSTRACTION GOES NEARLY FROM TOP TO BOTTOM!

ART © MARY FLEENER.

HEY!! COME TA THINK OF IT... WHAT ABOUT THAT WALKIN' TIME BOMB??

THAT'S RIGHT!! IF HE'S STILL LOOSE... THERE'S NO TELLING WHAT'LL HAPPEN!!

IN THE MID-SIXTIES, JACK KIRBY, ALONG WITH STAN LEE, STAKED OUT A MIDDLE GROUND OF ICONIC FORMS WITH A SENSE OF THE REAL ABOUT THEM, BOLSTERED BY A POWERFUL DESIGN SENSE.

ART: JACK KIRBY AND JOE SINNOTT (MY FACSIMILE) SCRIPT: STAN LEE.

TODAY, MANY AMERICAN MAINSTREAM COMICS STILL FOLLOW KIRBY'S LEAD FOR STORYTELLING, BUT THE DESIRE FOR MORE REALISTIC ART AND MORE ELABORATE SCRIPTS HAS PUSHED ART AND STORY FURTHER APART IN MANY CASES.

A FIGHT STARTED ON HIS DOORSTEP, HE PUT A STOP TO IT. FAR AS ANYONE KNOWS, ALL THE SURVIVORS ARE PRETTY MUCH OKAY.

WAY YOU TALK, NICHOLAS, FOLKS EXPECT HIM TO START NUKIN' MAMA RUSSIA ANY MOMENT.

ART FROM COLOR PANELS TRACED FOR REPRODUCTION.
© MARVEL ENTERTAINMENT GROUP, INC.

ART: JIM LEE AND SCOTT WILLIAMS (FACSIMILE) SCRIPT: CHRIS CLAREMONT.

IN THE EIGHTIES AND NINETIES, MOST OF THE COUNTERCULTURE OF INDEPENDENT CREATORS, WORKING MOSTLY IN BLACK AND WHITE, STAYED TO THE *RIGHT* OF MAINSTREAM COMICS ART WHILE COVERING A BROAD RANGE OF WRITING STYLES.

THIS FOLLOWS THE LEAD OF THE POST-KURTZMAN GENERATION OF *UNDERGROUND* CARTOONISTS WHO USED CARTOONY STYLES TO PORTRAY ADULT THEMES AND SUBJECT MATTER.

IRONIC THAT THE TWO BASTIONS OF *CARTOONY* ART ARE *UNDERGROUND* AND *CHILDREN'S* COMICS!

PRETTY *FAR APART* AS GENRES GO!

SOME ARTISTS, SUCH AS THE IRREPRESSIBLE *SERGIO ARAGONES*, STAKED THEIR CLAIM ON A PARTICULAR AREA *LONG AGO* AND HAVE BEEN QUITE HAPPY SINCE.

OTHERS, SUCH AS *DAVE McKEAN*, ARE FOREVER *ON THE MOVE*, EXPERIMENTING, TAKING CHANCES, NEVER SATISFIED.

WHEN AN ARTIST IS DRAWN TO ONE END OF THE CHART OR ANOTHER, THAT ARTIST MAY BE *REVEALING* SOMETHING ABOUT HIS OR HER STRONGEST *VALUES* AND *LOYALTIES* IN ART.

THOSE WHO APPROACH THE *LOWER LEFT*, FOR EXAMPLE, ARE PROBABLY ATTRACTED BY A SENSE OF THE BEAUTY OF *NATURE.*

THOSE AT THE *TOP* BY THE BEAUTY OF *ART.*

AND THOSE ON THE RIGHT BY THE BEAUTY OF *IDEAS.*

FOR COMICS TO *MATURE* AS A *MEDIUM,* IT MUST BE CAPABLE OF EXPRESSING EACH ARTIST'S *INNERMOST NEEDS* AND IDEAS.

BUT EACH ARTIST HAS *DIFFERENT* INNER NEEDS, DIFFERENT POINTS OF VIEW, DIFFERENT *PASSIONS,* AND SO NEEDS TO FIND DIFFERENT *FORMS OF EXPRESSION.* *

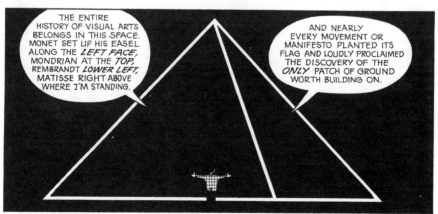

THE ENTIRE HISTORY OF VISUAL ARTS BELONGS IN THIS SPACE. MONET SET UP HIS EASEL ALONG THE *LEFT FACE,* MONDRIAN AT THE *TOP,* REMBRANDT *LOWER LEFT,* MATISSE RIGHT ABOVE WHERE I'M STANDING.

AND NEARLY EVERY MOVEMENT OR MANIFESTO PLANTED ITS FLAG AND LOUDLY PROCLAIMED THE DISCOVERY OF THE *ONLY* PATCH OF GROUND WORTH BUILDING ON.

* CHECK OUT WASSILY KANDINSKY'S TERRIFIC 1912 ESSAY, " ON THE PROBLEM OF FORM."

ICONS DEMAND OUR PARTICIPATION TO MAKE THEM WORK.

THERE IS NO LIFE HERE EXCEPT THAT WHICH YOU GIVE TO IT.

IT'S *YOUR* JOB TO CREATE AND *RECREATE* ME MOMENT BY MOMENT, NOT JUST THE CARTOONIST'S.

IT'S BEEN OVER *TWENTY YEARS* SINCE McLUHAN FIRST OBSERVED THAT THOSE PEOPLE GROWING UP IN THE LATE TWENTIETH CENTURY DIDN'T WANT *GOALS* SO MUCH AS THEY WANTED *ROLES,/* AND THAT'S WHAT VISUAL ICONOGRAPHY IS ALL ABOUT.

SMILE!

PAF!

AS IT HAPPENS, ONLY *TWO* POPULAR MEDIA WERE IDENTIFIED BY McLUHAN AS "COOL" MEDIA-- THAT IS, MEDIA WHICH COMMAND AUDIENCE INVOLVEMENT THROUGH *ICONIC FORMS.*

ONE OF THEM, *TELEVISION,* HAS REACHED INTO THE LIVES OF EVERY HUMAN BEING ON EARTH--

--AND FOR BETTER OR WORSE, ALTERED THE COURSE OF HUMAN AFFAIRS FROM HERE 'TIL *DOOMSDAY.*

THE FATE OF THE *OTHER* ONE, *COMICS--*

SEQUENTIAL ART

-- IS ANYONE'S GUESS.

Human Restoration

Bill McKibben

The Hilton Hotel on the slope below the state capitol in Albany, New York, houses an endless rotation of people who would like the Empire State to behave in some particular way. One day it's the snack food dealers demanding lower taxes on potato chips, the next it's landlords fulminating against rent control, the next it's paving contractors with lists of new roads to build. They pass through in groups, distinguishable by name tag, feeding on buffets and open bars and trays of shrimp; when they meet a legislator they either shyly flatter or browbeat him depending on his seniority or vulnerability. They press the flesh, rub shoulders, build new relationships or re-establish old ones, elect leaders, and then they migrate on, back to the daily grind of selling Fritos or bitumen.

I've seen timber wolves exactly once in my life—a pair of them, in the downstairs ballroom of this very Hilton in the fall of 1996. An environmental group called Defenders of Wildlife was sponsoring a wolf conference at the hotel, with experts from all over the nation. "We chose Albany as our conference site in order to draw attention to our proposal to restore the eastern timber wolf to the Great Woods of the Northeast," wrote the president of Defenders. In other words, they wanted something from the government too: permission to stick wolves back into, say, the Adirondack Park in northern New York, where I live, or the Maine Woods, or the White Mountain National Forest, or Vermont's Northeast Kingdom. Even though they were more earnest than the snack dealers, the Defenders came with the same sorts of apparatus—charts, polling surveys, the implicit promise that there might be a political payoff for those who supported such works. And they came with props—a pair of captive-born wolves from a wolf center somewhere out West. The conference organizers were savvy enough to know that two or three reporters might cover a conference full of papers on topics like "Evaluating Vasectomy as a Means of Wolf Control," and "Tracing the Life History of a Dispersing Female Wolf in Northern Wisconsin," but that every TV station in the neighborhood could be counted on to send a camera if there were living wolves to shoot.

Some functionary ushered all the reporters and camera crews into the subterranean ballroom; everyone plugged in their mikes; speeches were heard and literature

"Human Restoration," Bill McKibben from *The Return of the Wolf: Reflections on the Future of Wolves in the Northeast,* John Elder, editor. © University Press of New England, Hanover, NH. Reprinted with permission.

distributed. And then, finally, a pair of handlers ushered in the wolves themselves. And suddenly everything changed. A cold front blew in, cutting the damp human-flavored air. The wolves showed next to no interest in the dais full of whirring motordrives and humming videocams; though they were on leashes, the room was theirs by right and they explored it thoroughly. One saw a thermostat high on a wall, and lifted up on his hind legs to look at it, stretching his long body till his muzzle reached the dial. The other stretched out on the carpet a moment. Those deep unselfconscious stretches, almost more feline than canine, declared them masters of the terrain—none of the tense jostling of photographers eager for a tighter shot, none of the favor-begging of the environmentalists. They were simply there. Not larger than life. It's just that human life seemed a bit smaller in their presence. They were life-size. They fit their skins. They didn't charge the air. They relaxed the air.

Since I've now exhausted my firsthand knowledge of wolves, let me move on to a topic I know something more about: a forest without wolves. I've spent some time in the New England forests, but my real experience is confined to the Adirondacks, a range of mountains that bulges out in a great dome from northern New York. Bordered roughly by Lake George and Lake Champlain on the east, Lake Ontario on the west, the St. Lawrence on the north; and the Mohawk valley on the south, the Adirondack Park covers a swath of land larger than Glacier, Grand Canyon, Yellowstone, and Yosemite national parks combined. On a map of the eastern U.S., it's the large patch of green in the upper right hand corner; if you fly over it in a light plane, that green patch on the map becomes a green patch of ground—unbroken trees as far as the eye can see, none of the clearcuts that checkerboard Oregon or Washington or Maine. It's just trees and mountains and lakes and rivers, interspersed with small towns scattered every ten or twenty miles.

What makes it interesting, however, is less its current beauty than its scarred past. Remember these two dates: 1899 and 1907. In 1899, St. Lawrence County paid the last bounty in northern New York on a dead wolf; as far as anyone knows, that was the last *Canis lupus* to lope through these mountains. Her death marked the symbolic end of an era of spasmodic destruction that had begun in the early nineteenth century, a space of six or seven decades that saw a nearly primeval forest cut over, burned, plowed, and polluted with great ferocity. People had come late to the central Adirondacks—the Indians used the mountains only as a seasonal hunting ground, and the first European didn't climb the range's highest peak until 1837, a generation after Lewis and Clark had returned from the Pacific. But when they came, they came with a vengeance. The first images of environmental destruction chiseled into the national imagination were lithographs and early photos of bare Adirondack hillsides sliding into creeks, of moonscape vistas from high peaks.

The epic destruction coincided with the birth of what we'd now call adventure tourism, as city dwellers rode the rails to escape the Industrial Revolution for a few weeks and enjoy this accessible paradise. (The first public building on Earth with electric light was the big hotel on Blue Mountain Lake; that should give you some sense of it.) These tourists helped spur the efforts to protect the forest, which also gained support from downstate tycoons worrying that deforestation would silt in the economically all-important Hudson River, which rises in these mountains (an insight they gained at least in part by reading best-selling proto-ecologist George Perkins Marsh, the Vermont polymath who was then midwifing environmental science). Together they passed landmark laws creating the forest preserve, and began the slow task of buying land within that six-million acre park. It's murky work trying to fix the right date for the end of the park's decline—while the state constitution was amended to draw a "blue line" around the Airondacks in the 1890, the most destructive logging may not have taken place until the early years of this century. But 1899 will do—the last wolf howl strangled, the wildness of the place seemingly gone. No bears were left, or almost none; no mountain lions, elk, or lynx. The Adirondacks had been subdued.

And then, eight years later, in 1907, something happened that seemed unimportant at the time. State officials released a few pairs of beavers from Yellowstone Park in a couple of drainages in the southernmost part of the Adirondack Mountains. The beaver had been extirpated too—trapped out for its pelt, its habitat cut down, dried up, dammed for mills. But now a few people were interested in bringing the beaver back. And it took. With protection from game wardens, the animals started to spread north, back into forests that were slowly recovering—many of them forests the state had bought, or taken over for nonpayment of taxes, forests protected as "forever wild" under the state constitution, where no human could cut a tree. The law did not apply to beaver, of course, and before long the early succession white birch were lying on the ground beside one pond after another, before long the dams were backing up trickles into wetlands on a thousand watersheds, before long the tailslaps of nighttime warning were cracking out across three thousand ponds.

This was the beginning of Adirondack restoration, one of the earliest such efforts anywhere. From 1907 on, people were trying not just to protect what was left of the Adirondacks, but to recover some of their original character. A great experiment was underway: could you unscramble an egg? Bruce Babbitt, Bill Clinton's gregarious Secretary of the Interior, has insisted in recent years that restoration must be the hallmark of twenty-first-century conservation; he's already helped take out a few big dams. But for the Adirondacks (and in a subtler way for much of the eastern forest), the twentieth century has already been a restoration epoch. So what news do we have to share?

When I think about restoration, as I said, I begin by thinking about beavers. I try to imagine what these woods would be like if someone had not trucked the beavers out from Wyoming and let them go in a couple of streams. It would be much quieter, I think—the noisiest places I know in the woods are murky small sunlit ponds backed up by some intricate dam or another, algal places filled all summer with every kind of buzzing and droning and croaking. The beaver waddled back into the Adirondacks trailing life of infinite variety behind him. That's the first thing, obviously; restoring animals means restoring processes.

Other creatures wandered back too. I know old men in my town who can remember the first bear they ever saw, sometime in the 1930s. Now there are trees enough to hide them by the thousands: they hoot from the ridges by night, they leave great piles of berry-colored scat on the trail and wide clawtracks on the smooth-skinned beech. Every once in a while they get so lost in their eating that they don't hear you coming and then they finally do and crash off through the undergrowth, making your heart beat hard. I can't imagine this landscape without bears; it would seem *lean,* austere. Restoring animals means restoring the spirit of a place.

As the animals have returned, the forest has returned; ghost flora conjuring up ghost fauna and vice versa. About half the Adirondacks now belongs to the state as inviolate wilderness; the other half is in private hands, used mostly for timbering, but under fairly tight forestry laws that prevent the abuses common elsewhere. There is enough land that the moose wandered back about a decade ago, somehow crossing the highways and lakes that separate us from New England.

People reacted to the return of the moose in an interesting way. When big environmental groups, with tacit support from the state, proposed reintroducing the huge animals, many local residents hated the idea. In public meetings they worried aloud that the moose might spread disease to the deer herd, and that Adirondackers would surely die in collisions with the beasts (the haunch of a moose is just about windshield-high). And so the state backed off. But just about the same time, the moose began reestablishing themselves, and no one complained at all about that. In fact, people loved it—when a moose is spotted in our town, the phones begin to ring as everyone shares the news. Nature was simply taking its course, and that didn't seem to bother anyone.

If the wolf would simply walk back in—if a pack from Algonquin Park in Ontario would simply decide to wander south a few hundred miles—then I suspect they too would be greeted with open arms. But that isn't going to happen, because big highways, broad stretches of open farm valley, and the St. Lawrence River all stand in the way. The wolf, killed off by people a century ago, needs people to bring it back. Which is a problem.

Even two decades ago, the idea of reintroducing wolves here would have been a non-starter, ludicrous. But it's easy to underestimate how successfully environmentalists have shifted people's thinking, at least about animals. The Red Riding Hood crowd is smaller now, and mostly older. At least as many people have some Farley Mowat story stashed away in their hearts. When Defenders of Wildlife commissioned a poll in 1996, a huge majority of New Yorkers, and a substantial majority of Adirondackers, favored bringing back the wolf.

That doesn't mean a restoration would happen easily, though. Among the park's political powers, there is little support for reintroduction. County governments have passed symbolic resolutions prohibiting the release of "dangerous predators" within their borders; various barroom heroes have boasted to the newspapers that they would kill the creatures if they ever appeared. Some of their arguments have been pretty tenuous; a great deal of concern is expressed for the almost nonexistent livestock of these forested mountains, for example. The visceral opposition comes mostly from people who don't want to be pushed around from outside, who don't want someone else telling them what to do. In the words of a leader of the Adirondack Association of Towns and Villages, approached by a reporter on the day that Defenders first suggested a reintroduction: "I don't know much about it, but I'm sure we're against it." Against some outside notion of what constitutes the proper forest.

No one even knows if a reintroduction would be successful—the first reports from biologists cast doubt on the ability of the Adirondacks to support a pack, in part because they fear too many would be shot. But the deeper debate goes on outside the facts. What constitutes a wilderness restored? Is the process begun in 1907 still underway, or has it reached its limit? How far can restoration go in a place where human beings live? Because, of course, what makes the Adirondacks interesting, besides its scarred past, is its peopled present. This is not like Yellowstone, where you need to worry about the surrounding ranchers; here, wilderness and human settlement are completely intertwined.

We know that human beings can wipe out most other large creatures; we know that if humans set aside a large enough wilderness they can save most creatures (though we're only beginning to appreciate how large, and how intact, that land must sometimes be). What we don't know—and it's a fairly important question for a world of six billion people headed for ten—is whether in the modern age you can have small but complete human settlements amidst intact wilderness. That's the experiment the Adirondacks, without exactly knowing it, undertook a century ago; that's the experiment that environmentalists have begun in many tropical regions within the last decade. It's still a new experiment. The results are only starting to trickle in.

Often, in the winter, I'll be out skiing on some backcountry lake and come across the stomach, the head, the hooves, and some of the skin of a deer. That's all that's left a day after the coyotes have chased it out on the ice, the whitetail's skinny legs windmilling till they snap. When the coyotes eat their fill, the ravens descend, and so on down a long cafeteria line.

One way of asking if a place has been restored is to ask if its biology works, if something is missing that causes something else to be out of balance, and so on. If you visit my in-laws' house in suburban Connecticut, the answer couldn't be clearer. They have no rosebushes left. Pie plates dangle from their shrubberies in an effort to keep the deer at bay. Does and fawns browse with utter unconcern in the backyard; if you run out to chase them away, they look at you with unconcealed contempt. Since you can't hunt very well in this land of cul-de-sacs, and since there are no predators, and since people have created a smorgasbord of browse with their lawns and gardens, it is deer heaven. As Richard Nelson makes clear in his classic book *Heart and Blood: Living with Deer in America,* most of America is now deer heaven for just such reasons: "By 1991 an estimated 1,500 whitetails lived within the city limits of Philadelphia. That is more than the total number of deer inhabiting the state of Pennsylvania in 1900."

But in the Adirondacks you don't see so many deer. They are there—on many lakes you can see a good browse line, where they've nibbled the lower branches of the shoreline hemlocks to the same height as they stood on the ice—but three things have kept their numbers in some kind of check. First, there's not a lot of opening in the forest; without clearcuts, and with three million acres of the park off limits to any logging at all, sunlight doesn't reach the forest floor in sufficient quantity to grow great pastures of browse. Second, humans hunt them. And third, in these mountains the coyote has grown into something like a wolf.

Coyotes are supposed to be lone scroungers, loping through the world looking for an easy meal. They are superbly adaptable (a biologist I knew once said, "when the last man dies there will be a coyote howling over his grave"), but we don't think of them as a top predator. In the absence of the wolf, however, that may be how they have evolved in parts of the American East. Our coyotes are big, they have learned to hunt in packs, and they eat a lot of whitetail—the 1,200 coyotes now living in the Adirondack may consume 12,000 deer annually. So if you have a wolf substitute, why do you need a wolf, especially if it might mean Government Restrictions of some kind?

The biological answer is not completely clear. Wolves and coyotes aren't identical; coyotes haven't learned how to kill beaver as efficiently as wolves do, for instance, and so beaver numbers are booming (just ask the road crews who spend half the year draining flooded roads). And despite the fears of the sportsmen, wolves might actually benefit human hunters; if the biologists are right, they will chase off lots of coyotes, perhaps enough to actually diminish the wild deer kill. But it's not an overpowering argument. The mountains like wolves, as Aldo Leopold pointed out so memorably, but they have probably come to appreciate the coyote as well.

There's a kind of theological argument too, of course. Wolves were here, and we chased them out, so we should invite them back. Amen, hallelujah, thanks be to Noah.

I've felt the power of this kind of reasoning. A few years back I spent some time on the Alligator River National Wildlife Refuge on the Atlantic shore of North Carolina, an aggressively nasty place. Old pine plantation, absolutely flat, gridded with dirt roads that ran at right angles, microwaved by the Sun, guarded by nine kinds of things that fly and bite, and two or three that slither and bite. I'm sure that if you grew up there you might develop some slight affection for the place, but every tourist I saw was heading swiftly for the Barrier Islands. Yet something incredible hung in the air, for it was in this place that *Canis rufus,* the red wolf, had been resurrected.

Red wolves once ran across much of the continent; they may have made it up into the Adirondacks. But by the 1980s, just a few were left in the United States, hanging out in Texas. They weren't going to hang on many years more, so federal officials hauled the last ones into zoos. This strand of DNA, this voice on the land, this particular fancy of creation, seemed to have run its course, and not just in one place, like the Adirondack beaver, but every place. Forever. But the environmentalists and the feds hadn't quite given up, and they found a piece of land in eastern North Carolina, in the former range of the red wolf, to reintroduce them into the world.

In 1987, the Fish and Wildlife Service opened some cages and released four pairs of captive-born adult red wolves. By the mid-1990s, ninety-four pups had been born in the wild. These were fourth- and fifth-generation wild wolves.

I didn't see them—I only see the wolves in hotel ballrooms. A Fish and Wildlife worker drove me around the refuge for long hot hours, sticking rank bait in traps as he tried to catch some study animals that needed new batteries in their radio collars. I didn't hear them howl or bark; I just heard their beeping transmitters as I held the antenna out the window and we tried to home in on them. But that didn't much matter—it was the simple fact that these wolves existed that mattered. For a while the red wolf had not existed; it was alive in a zoo somewhere, but that was nothing more than keeping its DNA on ice. It hadn't existed as part of the sweet battle and concert of life bumping up against other life, and now it did again. God smiled.

For the timber wolf in the North Woods, though, the case is not so clear. Wolves live other places—lots of them in Alaska and Canada, healthy and well-established populations in Minnesota and Wisconsin, the new packs roaming Yellowstone. They have become accepted in most of those places, just as the red wolf has become accepted in North Carolina. Long caravans of cars go out on nighttime wolf-howling expeditions. In Minnesota, they named their damn basketball team for them, and tens of thousands of people visit the International Wolf Center in Ely, a hard-to-get-to little town hard by the Canadian border that now boasts daily plane service from the Twin Cities. At least on this continent, wolves seem safe as a species.

So if the wolf doesn't need to be here, and the deer don't need them here, who needs them? Might it be the same species that needs cable TV, high-speed modems, hair transplants, twenty-one-speed mountain bikes, frappucinos, frappucino grandes, frappucino tres grandes? Could it be the same species that needs two-thousand-square-foot houses and monster trucks and 17-gigabyte hard drives? Could be.

The world as we now know it is shaped by human desire, especially by the incredible needs developed by the affluent West in a single century. Those needs shaped the landcape in obvious ways—the suburbs with their endless circling roads are desire poured from the back of a cement mixer, the desire for convenience, comfort, privacy, individuality. And now those needs shape the landscape in more insidious and permanent ways. You can read our desires, our needs, in every cubic meter of the air, and in every upward inching of the thermometer. Our needs for mobility, for elbow room, for never getting too hot or cold or bored, all require the consumption of gas and oil and coal, and that endless combustion fills the atmosphere with carbon dioxide. Spring comes to the northern hemisphere a week earlier now than it did two decades ago, because of our needs. The warmer air holds more water vapor, and hence severe storms are twenty percent more common—that's our appetite at work. The warmer oceans expand, and glacier melt pours more water into the sea; the scientists say that the Atlantic and the Pacific will be a couple of feet higher before this century is out, thanks to our needs. We are machines for generating needs and then generating technologies to fill those needs (and sometimes the other way around). So what might it mean to say we need the wolf?

We need something new to consume. We need wolf howl, we need the little frisson that comes with thinking: there's a wolf pack out here in these woods where I'm spending the summer. This kind of symbolic consumption is old news, of course. Folks buy Durangos or Blazers or Pathfinders or Dakotas or Tahoes or Expeditions or the other behemoths of the sport utility tribe knowing full well they'll never take them off road. The extra fifty horsepower and thousand pounds of steel and eight inches of clearance give them rights to a certain image. You can buy it for two bucks in a pack of Marlboros. In the same way, I'd like wolves in my backyard because I'd like to think of my backyard as wonderfully rugged. The more rugged my backyard, the more rugged I can claim to be. I live with wolves, or I vacation with wolves, hence I am close kin to Kevin Costner. It rubs off. That's how consumerism works in an age when we're light-years past food and clothes and shelter.

In Abruzzo, Italy, where an active recovery plan brought the wolf back from the edge of extirpation (in a park one-sixtieth the size of the Adirondacks), 2,500 tourists a year used to visit Civitella Alfredena; now they've opened a wolf museum and 100,000 come annually. Wolf tourism is one of the big advantages cited by the environmentalists who want to reintroduce the animals, but there's something a bit creepy about it. The biologists at Algonquin say it doesn't damage the wolves to have organized howling parties out night after night in the summer, but who knows? It might damage the howlers—it's only an inch away from paying some sleazeball aquarium owner for the chance to swim with their dolphins and caress their blowholes. It's consuming, literally, the time and the attention and the wildness of another creature for some little jolt in return. For a story to tell when you get back from your trip. It's *about you.* The wolf becomes one more thing to experience, to own in some way or another. We live in a culture capable of taking a Civil War battlefield and transforming it into a theme park. We live in a culture fully capable of taking a wolf howl and turning into a commodity.

But maybe we still live in a culture capable of more than that.

Most Civil War battlefields haven't been handed over to the theme-park developers, thank heaven. Many of them, in the custody of the Park Service, lie in that fast-suburbanizing corner of Maryland and Virginia and Pennsylvania, curious eddies of open space in a tide of pavement that has swept by on all sides. They have very little to do with that culture—the battlefields speak not to convenience or comfort, but to honor, obedience, glory, to that whole compound of older martial virtues now mostly mysterious to us. When we stroll Bloody Angle or the Sunken Road, when we climb Seminary Ridge, we visit powerfully different ideas of what we might be. Men gave their lives here for the Union? For Virginia? It's not that these were necessarily wise ideas—it may be far better to think of Virginia as an interchangeable place with San Jose or Tampa, a place to live until it's time to move. Glory and honor and obedience have caused their share of pain over the years. But the mere existence of these spots helps keep these alternate conceptions of human life alive and real.

I grew up in Lexington, Massachusetts, and I spent my summers in a tricorne hat, giving tours of the Battle Green. Some part of my political restlessness comes from endlessly reciting the story of the eight men killed on that common, men who inhabited a moral universe profoundly different from the moral universe of the twentieth-century Boston suburb that was otherwise shaping my soul. I remember the night in 1973 when I was twelve and I saw my father and five hundred other good suburbanites arrested because they refused to leave that Green during a protest of the war in Vietnam. They might have behaved the same way on some anonymous patch of ground, but they might not have, too; for an evening, two centuries of time collapsed, and Captain Parker's admonition to his troops ("If they mean to have a war let it begin here") nerved up another militia. We journey to Rome, to Mecca, to Benares, to Antietam, to Birmingham, and to the shiny black wall of the Vietnam Memorial with the sense that something there might change us. A pilgrimage, by definition.

So if we should be wary of how our endless neediness might shape our encounter with the wolf, we should be equally open to the idea that the wolf might be one force able to help us to reshape our endless neediness. The encounter with history at a battlefield or a shrine might be like the encounter with real wildness in a forest or a mountain or a seacoast; each might hold the power to break us out of the enchantment under which we now labor, the enchantment of things, an enchantment that is quite literally wrecking the world.

In fact, I would go further than that. Contact with the natural world is one of the two forces potentially powerful enough to break through the endless jamming static of our culture and open us to other, wider possibilities. (The other force is contact with the non-possessive forms of love, be they found at Fredericksburg or in Mother Teresa's hospice). I have seen this effect in enough people, myself sometimes included, to be confident of its truth. Show me an environmentalist who did not start with an encounter with the more-than-human world, and I will show you an exception to the rule. And try to find someone who has had such an encounter without it changing her politics, her priorities, her very sense of self.

This encounter need not be wild in the traditional sense—it need not involve Gore-Tex. Consider E. O. Wilson and his ants, or Rachel Carson wandering her short stretch of the Maine coast. Consider the birdwatchers of Central Park, necks eternally stiff from their involvement in the modest life above them. For those of us with thicker shells, however, some starker wildness, some drama, helps kick the message home. John Muir, on his Thousand Mile Walk to the Gulf, found himself fixated on the notion of alligators; later, in his exuberant first summer in the Sierra, a season that defined forever our grammar of wildness, it was earthquakes and windstorms as well as sunny afternoons and butterflies that helped him understand that "we are now in the mountains and they are now in us, making every nerve quiet, filling every pore and cell of us."

I've had some of the same sense of dissolving into the world on days when I've stood staring at grizzly tracks in Alaskan mud. But I felt it much more one day in the woods behind my house. I was wandering along, happy for the exercise but lost as usual in some plan, lost as usual in my own grandness. Suddenly, the fiercest pain I've ever felt boiled up my torso toward my face. I whirled, staggered downslope, cracked into a tree, fell; by now I could see the yellowjackets coating my t-shirt. I ran, flicked, ran; eventually they were gone. But I could tell I was reacting to their venom. Hives popped out across my upper body. All I could think of for a minute were all the risks I'd heard dismissed by comparing them with bee stings: "you're less likely to die by tornado/plane crash/shark attack." But as I jogged back through the woods the few trailless miles to my house, I found those thoughts replaced by another almost overpowering urge. The urge to pray, and not a prayer of supplication but a prayer of thanksgiving. The trees had never looked more treelike, the rocky ridges more solid and rich, the world more real. The drama had somehow taken me out of myself, and though the sensation faded as the weeks passed, it has never disappeared altogether.

As I tried to describe the experience to others, I would say it was the first time I had felt a part of the food chain. But that was glib. In some way it was the first time I'd felt a part of any chain other than the human one. The first time I glimpsed the sheer overpowering realness of the world around me, the first time I'd realized fully that it was something more than a stage set for my life.

A healthy wolf has never attacked and killed a person in this country—yellow-jackets are several orders of magnitude more dangerous, and let's not even discuss the Durangos and the Blazers and the Pathfinders. In a way, though, it's almost too bad that news is spreading of their benign image, almost too bad that people are starting to think of them as cuddly. Too bad because it's not true (on the basis of my hotel ball-room encounter, I will say I have rarely seen a being more aloof), and too bad because some of their power to shake us from our enchantment comes from their dramatic image.

Beavers just happened to be extirpated from the East; it was their poor luck that fashion found a use for the skin with which evolution had equipped them. But wolves were extirpated systematically, based on our understanding of their wolf nature. No creature save perhaps the snake has been more unremittingly vil-ified—the little pigs cowering in their shoddy homes, Little Red Riding Hood deceived by the granny-killer, werewolves snarling from page and screen, the very language making them the image of poverty ("the wolf at the door") and of the predatory male.

As much as anything else, that's the reason we need to invite them back in. Not to make it up to them—wolves roam outside the culture of victimhood—but because it is hard for us to do so. It would be a meaningful gesture.

You must remember that the Adirondacks, the Whites, the Greens, the North Woods of Maine are four or five or six hours drive from Madison Avenue, from the epicenter of the idea that everything should be easy. They are four or five or six hours north of the first suburbs on the planet, those ever-expanding monuments to the god-dess convenience. They are due north of the megalopolis, of the notion that humans might survive in an entirely human corridor. They are, in other words, within range of the problem that needs solving.

I've been circling the exact nature of that problem, for it is daunting to search out the central point of a culture, but to state it as clearly as I can: we believe too firmly that we, each of us as individuals, are the most important things on Earth. This belief is so strong in us that we begin to imagine that things we have not created are not quite real. Thus, we can fret with real worry about dangers to the economy (the chance, say that the Y2K computer bug might damage it) but we cannot muster the same concern for the natural world, which seems to us more abstract. Certainly we cannot muster enough concern to actually change the ways in which we live so as to protect that natural world. Only the largest jolts break through that shell, allow us to feel small in any way. Look at the few books about the natural world popular at the moment; invariably they concern climbs up Mt. Everest (and only deadly climbs at that), or storms producing hundred-foot boat-eating waves; consider the vogue for adventure travel. How much has changed even in the course of a hundred years, since the time that gentle John Burroughs, with his stories about woodchucks and chickadees, reigned as the most popular writer of any sort in the nation.

Which in turn reminds us of how new this particular problem is, at least in certain ways. Humans have always tended toward selfishness, always thought too much of themselves—that's the message from the Buddha, from the Christ. But for most of human history, we had other problems too. No one living in the Adirondacks a century ago, or in any part of America fifty years before that, was in any danger of forgetting that the world was real, any more than someone inhabiting the delta of Bangladesh at the moment is likely to forget. Our forebears faced the very real problem of individual survival—of getting food on the table—and so, even with the benefit of hindsight, it seems wrong to condemn them for chasing the wolf away. Theirs was still the age-old problem that humans are slow and hairless and dull-sensed.

But that's not *our* problem. In this country, at this moment, our problem is somehow reining ourselves in, figuring out that each one of us does not reside at the exact center of the universe. Some years ago I wrote an odd book that required me to watch everything that came across the nation's biggest cable TV system in the course of a single day: 2,400 hours of videotape. If you condensed all those quiz shows and sitcoms and commercials and newscasts down to a single idea, it was that each viewer is the most important entity imaginable. That is an idea that would have at least been questioned in most cultures in most places in most periods (cultures that paid more attention to gods or to tribes), but it is the very bulwark of the consumerist society we've built. We marinate in that idea—the idea that there should be no limits placed on us. And we have the technology to annihilate those limits at least temporarily. That is a dangerous combination. Many of the dangers of our moment—environmental, societal, psychological—flow from that sense that we're all that counts.

So it comes as a piece of great irony—and maybe great luck—that the part of the planet most committed to the idea that ease and comfort and convenience are all that matters is also the place where nature has returned most visibly in the last hundred years. The eastern United States, birthplace of suburb and highway and car culture, co-creator with Hollywood of the mirror we gaze into so fixedly, is also the only large region of the planet that has gone from brown to green in the twentieth century. Once topsoil was discovered in Midwest, the attraction of farming in New England, not to mention its economic viability, all but disappeared. Farms were abandoned and trees returned. You could no more have reintroduced the wolf to Civil War-era New Hampshire than to the moon; but now its landscape is so much less manipulated, its forest so much denser, that the real possibility exists. We live in a biologically fortunate region, with enough humidity to erase some of the excesses of our past; if this isn't primeval forest, it's pretty prime nonetheless.

Here, then, we can contemplate reversing time a little, having a second chance, this time not driven by sheer survival needs. We can contemplate putting ourselves in the background enough to allow, and even encourage, the return of a difficult example of the more-than-human, a creature that won't attack and kill us but might possibly take a lamb here or there, might even take a pet dog or cat, might force certain restrictions about land use or road closure on us, might provide some competition for our deer-hunt. And a creature that, even more, might excite us in certain new ways, open us more fully to the beauty and intrinsic meaning of the more-than-human world. If the wolf was not a difficult animal, then we could simply consume it, as we too often consume, say, loons. If the wolf was not in many ways a thrilling animal, then it would not offer as much promise for opening us to the real. But the wolf is both; when it howls, the hair stands up on the back of your neck for a variety of reasons.

To most effectively nudge our culture off balance, we should reintroduce the timber wolf to White Plains, not the White Mountains; to Scarsdale and not Saranac. But that's asking rather a lot of a shy animal. In any event, it's not as if we who live in the mountains have escaped the general drift of our times. Adirondackers often live in the world that pulses through the satellite dish more fully than the world that surrounds them; most kids make it through high school without spending much time in the outdoors. Our life is increasingly unreal too. And if we would pay most of the price for this experiment—our pet dogs at risk—we would reap most of the benefit too. We'd hear the wolf howls year-round, not just in August.

By now the conceit of this essay should be apparent. It's not wolves that stand in need of restoration; wolves, though chased to the fringes of the continent, have managed to retain their essence. Even tied on leashes in the windowless basement ballroom of a slightly shabby hotel they were what they were.

People, on the other hand, especially the subspecies that inhabits the Western world, and especially the troop of them that has grown up on the eastern edge of North America, find themselves badly out of balance, operating under the influence of a spell. An intoxication, with ourselves. It's an intoxication that will likely grow deeper as the next few decades progress. Our unthinking consumption of resources has now reached the point where we are changing the global temperature, and with it the speed of the wind, the size of storms, the pace of the seasons. When we see the formerly natural world, we see ourselves. Our morally casual manipulation of genes may mean that within a very short time most of the organisms that we see around us will reflect our desires—will reflect us. We may be entering a period of overwhelming and unavoidable loss, of species extinction so profound that it may leave us with a planet almost empty of other meanings. The enchantment that prevents us from recognizing our peril as a peril, spiritual as well as pragmatic, and from making the changes necessary to correct it—that enchantment is our problem.

Happily, any child's bookshelf provides a series of recipes for dealing with dangerous enchantments. It's not the kisses of princes that will wake us up in time; our culture is one long wet kiss. But maybe the howl of a wolf might help, the howl of a wolf echoing out over the hills of the East.

One Sentence

John Medeiros

I learned it all from first grade to fifth when I learned the components of a sentence, when I learned that the beauty of language is that we are all part of that language, that as we study what it means to be a noun, or a verb, or an adjective—all things I will reveal later—we also, simultaneously, as if the universes of emotion and alphabet were suddenly fused into one, we also *feel* what it means to be a noun, or a verb, or an adjective, and at that moment of fusion, when life becomes the word on paper, I finally come to terms with my life: a sentence, a line of words strung together sometimes with meaning, sometimes without meaning, always containing those things a sentence always seems to contain, like a noun, a common noun at that, like *faggot* (as in *God hates a faggot*, but not as in *God hates your faggot ways* because then I am no longer a noun, but an adjective, and that, you will find, comes much later in life), so instead my life, at this moment, is a noun—sometimes a common noun but then sometimes a proper noun (as in *Tommy*), or a compound noun (as in *twinship*), or a collective noun (as in *the genes that made us this way*), or a possessive noun (as in *I am and I will always be my brother's keeper*); and only once when I am a noun, whether it be a common noun or a proper noun or a collective noun or a possessive noun—something inside me yearns to be, something inside yearns to give the nouns in my life meaning, and it is only when the desire to be burns inside like an ember struggling to stay lit that I suddenly unfold and become a verb—an inactive verb today (*to be*, as in *I am gay*), an active verb tomorrow, as in *replicate* (like carbon copies, or identical twins, or infectious viral particles); and as a verb I will be a variety of tenses, sometimes more than one simultaneously, sometimes just present (*I have AIDS*), sometimes present continuous (*I am trying to tell you I have AIDS*), sometimes just past (*I tried to tell you I have AIDS*), and sometimes future (*I will die with this disease*); regardless of which, I can be one or I can be all, but I will always be tense, and once I've seen myself as noun and verb, I will slowly grow into adjective to describe myself and make myself more interesting to you, my audience, so that you will no longer see me as *your twin* but instead will come to know me as *your gay HIV-positive twin*, and to the parents who once knew me as *their son*, I will be remembered as *their sick son*, sick from too much language and too much love, adjectives can do that to a person, and sometimes the adjective I become is multiple in meaning, and so I am split (as in *zygote*) and split (as in *personality*)—the adjectives I become can be confusing to a person; the adverb, on the other hand, disassociates itself from the subject and marries itself instead to its action; so, whereas I love, I can now love *too deeply*, and whereas I cry, I now cry *passionately*, and when it comes to loving, and when it comes to crying, the sentence of my life takes on objects, and when those objects are direct I no longer love too deeply, instead I love *you* too deeply, and when those objects are indirect I no longer cry passionately, I cry passionately only *for you*, and so it is, as is the case with most twins, that the components of my life take on meaning and structure, and my life becomes the very sentence I use to describe it; yet like a sentence, as in the string of words full of subject and predicate, my life, too, is another sentence, a prison sentence, as in removed from the outside world, a sentence as in a final verdict, a judgment, a lack of freedom, or a loss of freedom once owned, a life once held in the palm of my hand and then taken away, forever, leaving me with only a series of words never without a verb to follow; otherwise, if I could, I'd be *individual* or *asexual* or *undetectable*: words all by themselves—words, ironically, only befitting a prisoner.

Gender and Videogames:
The Political Valency of Lara Croft

Maja Mikula

The Face: Is Lara a feminist icon or a sexist fantasy?
Toby Gard: Neither and a bit of both. Lara was designed to be a tough, self-reliant, intelligent woman. She confounds all the sexist cliches apart from the fact that she's got an unbelievable figure. Strong, independent women are the perfect fantasy girls—the untouchable is always the most desirable (Interview with Lara's creator Toby Gard in *The Face* magazine, June 1997).

Lara Croft is a fictional character: a widely popular videogame[1] superwoman and recently also the protagonist of the blockbuster film *Lara Croft: Tomb Raider* (2001). Her body is excessively feminine—her breasts are massive and very pert, her waist is tiny, her hips are rounded and she wears extremely tight clothing. She is also physically strong, can fight and shoot, has incredible gymnastic abilities and is a best-selling writer.

Germaine Greer does not like Lara Croft. In her latest book, *The Whole Woman* (1999), Greer has unequivocally condemned the enforcement of artificial and oppressive ideals of femininity through pop icons such as the Barbie Doll. Lara Croft, whose 'femaleness' is clearly shaped by a desire to embody male sexual fantasies, is the antithesis of Greer's 'whole woman'; Greer calls her a 'sergeant-major with balloons stuffed up his shirt [. . .] She's a distorted, sexually ambiguous, male fantasy. Whatever these characters are, they're not real women' (Jones, 2001).

She may not be a 'real woman', but on the other hand Lara is clearly a 'positive image' for women, as Linda Artel and Susan Wengraf defined the term in 1976:

The primary aim of [annotated guide] *Positive Images* was to evaluate media materials from a feminist perspective. We looked for materials that had at least one of the following characteristics: presents girls and women, boys and men with non-stereotyped behaviour and attitudes: independent, intelligent women: adventurous, resourceful girls . . . presents both sexes in non-traditional work or leisure activities . . . women flying planes, etc. (Artel and Wengraf, 1976 [1990], p. 9).

As the sole survivor of a plane crash, who used her wilderness skills to stay alive for two weeks—as well as being a trained rock climber, expert shooter, motorcyclist and world famous archaeologist—there is little doubt that Lara qualifies for this category. It is for this reason that a (female) participant in the WomenGamers Discussion Forum can lionize Lara as a role model: 'I like the fact that she's a loner. She doesn't rely upon any male character to lead her around, or to rescue her if she were to break a nail.'

Lara is everything that is bad about representations of women in culture, and everything good—and thus analysing the circulation and discussion of Lara in Western culture allows us to explore the current predicament of feminist identity politics, epitomizing the range of contemporary feminist stances in relation to the body and the consumer culture of late capitalism. In particular, changes in the way that texts circulate—which have been enabled by changes in communication technologies—make it more difficult to generalize about the function of media texts. The fact that Lara Croft has no obviously attributable author, is so easily taken up by fan-producers, and is readily detached from the circumstances of her initial production makes it difficult to make any convincing claims about what such a text 'really' means.

Identification/Objectification

As feminist debates have begun to explore the degree to which it is possible to under-stand a sexualized performance of traditional femininity as a form of empowerment (see Wolf, 1993; Roiphe, 1993; Denfeld, 1995; Lumby, 1997, p. 8), many commen-tators have pointed to a recent tendency to allow female characters to be physically and emotionally powerful and independent—so long as they're young, pretty and have large breasts (see Inness, 1999). In a way, the debates which take place about Lara are familiar ones: accepting that her character is everything that an earlier generation of feminists wished for, does this become irrelevant when she still has to win her place in popular culture by having large breasts?

It is useful to begin thinking about such a question by addressing the ways in which players of Tomb Raider—the game in which Lara was introduced to the world—are invited to relate to this character. The concept of 'identification' with characters is often employed to discuss the function of films and television pro-grammes in offering gender roles to audiences. But this term isn't obviously useful for making sense of the ways in which the texts of videogames work. Are players invited to 'identify' with Lara? Or, to complete the familiar binary, to 'objectify' her (see Mulvey, 1975 [1990])?

Until recently there were few female characters in videogames. Women were largely represented by 'damsels in distress'—vulnerable victims of violence, to be res-cued by muscular male heroes. It was the first Tomb Raider game (1996) that broke away from the familiar pattern. Instead of being the 'object' of rescue, Lara Croft is the protagonist and the driving force of the game plot. Since Lara's groundbreaking entry into this traditionally male world, the number of female characters in action videogames has been on a steady increase, but it is still considerably lower than the number of males (Mayfield, 2000).

Following the established videogame-industry marketing trends, developers of Tomb Raider, Derby-based company Core Design, identified the target audience for the first Tomb Raider game as 'males between 15 and 26 years of age' (Pretzsch, 2000). In the early stages of development, two possible protagonists were considered—one male and one female. The female character, initially called Laura Cruise, finally prevailed, despite fears in the marketing department that such an unheard-of choice would undermine the sales of the product. But is this target audience—the young men who take on the character of Lara in order to play—primarily being invited to take sexual pleasure from *looking* at her? Or to enjoy the pleasures of *being* her? We know that there are certainly masculine pleasures to 'being' Lara, even with her unprecedentedly feminine body. The violence in Tomb Raider is understood to be desirable for men. A study undertaken two years ago by the American Association of University Women (AAUW) Educational Foundation indicates that girls 'often dislike violent video games and prefer personalized, interactive, role-playing games' (Mayfield, 2000); and the 'girl games' which multiplied on the market since the mid-1990s almost exclusively focused on shopping, fashion, dating and appearance. So Lara's behaviour is understood to be 'masculine', and to appeal to men. The idea that violence could appeal to women is unthinkable in the logic of computer game marketing.

But can men 'identify' with Lara as they perform her violence? The binary logic of 'identification/objectification', so well developed in film theory, doesn't seem very useful for thinking about the ways in which Lara Croft functions. To complicate things even further, research suggests that the very idea of 'identifying' with a character is a gendered one. According to one study, the process of identification is more important for female gamers, who tend to become 'irritated' when they cannot identify with their female character (Wright, 2000). Men are not so keen to 'identify' with videogame characters at all; and it is not obvious that the game encourages them to do so. Despite the first-person format of the game-play, Tomb Raider enables the gamer to 'impersonate' Lara while having her body in full view. For the player, Lara can be both 'self' and 'other'—at the same time. An enthusiastic male reviewer of the first Tomb Raider game has declared that 'having a *person* in the game' [my emphasis] made him 'more cautious and protective'. Ironically, he found himself not 'just controlling Lara', but 'looking after her as well' (Olafson, 1997, p. 100). His experience of the game thus encapsulates the patriarchal rhetoric of 'control' and 'care', by a male subject of a female object. Ironically, even when offered empowerment through a possibility of conflating the subject-object distinction, male players seem to view themselves in the position of the subject and see Lara as the object of their 'control' and 'care', with her exaggerated sexuality subjected to their disciplining gaze. When the latest Tomb Raider game title, *The Angel of Darkness*, introduced a new male character, Kurtis Trent, who is controlled by players just like Lara, Lara's aficionados expressed hostility to (jealousy of?) the new male character: 'he better not take over too much of the game, 'cause I need to spend some quality time with Lara, as I haven't talked with her in ages'; or 'I hate to control a male in Tomb Raider. Tomb Raider is the world of Lara!'[2] For these male players, it is obvious that at least part of the pleasure of playing this game involved 'controlling' a female character as feisty and attractive as Lara; while 'controlling' a male character is perceived to be somehow wrong.

All of this seems straightforward enough: for these male players, even as they 'are' Lara, they are distanced from, controlling—perhaps 'objectifying' the character. But the ambivalence of Lara's function is emphasized when we notice that contributions by female participants to an Internet forum on Tomb Raider[3] indicate that women's experiences of the game are quite different from men's; and that the empowerment activated by game-play is strongly influenced by different gamers' experience and enactment of gender codes. It involves experimentation with and testing of these codes, reminiscent of the widespread gender-swapping practices in the virtual worlds of Multi-user Dungeons (MUDs).[4] By and large, women enjoy 'being' Lara, rather than controlling her. According to one female gamer, Lara is 'everything a bloke wants and everything a girl wants to be'; for others, she is a role model, symbolizing 'adventure, independence, possibility and strength'. One enthusiastic woman gamer admits: 'Heck, I imagine I AM [*sic*] Lara when I'm playing, I know some might say "come on, it's only pixels" but what Lara and her environment is made of is irrelevant in my eyes.' The game makes it possible to be excited about identifying with this strong and capable archaeologist; or to enjoy looking after an excessively feminine character.

The Death of the Author?

Lara was originally conceived by Englishman Toby Gard: another female 'creation' by a male 'creator' in a long series of patriarchal representations of women, epitomized in the Western tradition by the story of Pygmalion in Ovid's *Metamorphoses* (X, pp. 243–298). Gard's original description of his creation included elements of an intentionally ironic masculinist imaginary, such as 'Lara likes to work with underprivileged children and the mentally disabled. She has a degree in needlework [. . .]' (Pretzsch, 2000). A twenty-something-year-old familiar with products of a globalized popular culture, Gard went on to imbue his vision with elements of such iconic creations as Indiana Jones and James Bond. According to media reports, Gard had consciously resisted fitting his heroine out with 'spangly thongs and metal bras so popular with digital women', because he felt that she 'had more dignity' (Jones, 2001).

Soon after the release of Tomb Raider I, Toby Gard left Core to found his own company, Confounding Factor, purportedly because he wanted to 'have greater control over the new characters and games [he] wanted to design' (Gibbon, 2001). He described his distancing from his mind-child as 'similar to losing a love', since 'you're not really allowed to go near her' (Snider, 2001). Since then, Core and Eidos have avoided naming a single person as Lara's creator and have consistently emphasized a collective authorship of the game, reinforced by Eidos/Core franchise ownership.

After Gard's departure from Core, in the sequels to the original game, both Lara's aggression and sex appeal steadily increased, effectively blending a death wish with the pleasure principle and thus digging deeply into the essence of the Freudian Id. In an editorial review at WomenGamers.Com, we read that:

> [in] Tomb Raider II and III, Lara became an obnoxious sex object, more intent on steal-ing the hearts of men than relating to her female following. Her physique became more and more unrealistic as the series progressed. Her attitude became more deliberately sex-ual as well (Lara Croft Tomb Raider Series 2001).

Lara's transformation is emblematic of the impossibility of 'ownership' of products of popular culture in our media-saturated world. Her estrangement from her original creator(s)/owner(s) can be observed at two levels: at one level, the embryonic Lara 'betrays' Toby Gard by developing into a consumer product 'owned' by Core and Eidos; at the other, Lara is reconceptualized through media manipulations which by nature cannot be controlled by either of her creator(s)/owner(s). The first 'betrayal' involves moulding of the character by the Core design team, to simultaneously antic-ipate and reproduce the demands of the market.

This type of 'betrayal' has been common in cultural production for centuries, but with the advent of new technologies it has assumed a new dimension. In the past, products of the so-called 'high culture' were likely to be consciously shaped by their authors with reference to the tastes and desires of influential patrons instrumental in supporting the production stage and/or facilitating the circulation of the final prod-uct. By contrast, works pertaining to popular culture often cannot be attributed to a single author and their ever-changing individual re-enactments reflect the artist/performer's expectations of her/his temporary audience (Lord, 1960). The new tech-nologies of computer-mediated communication have refashioned the circulation of popular culture mainly by undermining the possibility of 'fixing' the audience and thus anticipating their likes and dislikes, as well as their cultural knowledge, experi-ence or skills which would equip them to fully appreciate a given product.

To appeal to an essentially unpredictable global market, Lara had to be conceived as an 'empty sign', which would allow diverse, often contradictory inscriptions and interpretations. To quote Lara's cinematic avatar Angelina Jolie, Lara is 'a bit of every-thing. She's like every kind of sexy Italian actress I've ever watched, and yet she's also that guy in Crocodile Hunter in Australia—completely in love with danger' (Kolmos, 2001, p. 105). In fact, the only 'inscription' undertaken and proliferated by Core Design and Eidos Interactive is the one understood unmistakably to signify power. The heroine's constructed identity is no more than an amalgam of values represent-ing all the different faces of empowerment in advanced capitalist societies: class, wealth, appearance, physical fitness, strong will, intelligence and independence.

Lara is comfortable with ambiguities and contradictions—they are in fact the very 'material' she is made of.[5] The values of an idealized world of security and tradi-tion are brought in by means of Lara's constructed biography, well known to the faith-ful, which was conspicuously created in response to public demand only after the first game was finished. Lara Croft is a member of British aristocracy, a graduate of Gor-donstoun, Prince Charles's alma mater, with a mission to '[prepare] students for a full and active role as international citizens in a changing world'.[6] Following a plane crash in the Himalayas, where she is the only survivor and struggles for two weeks to stay alive in the wilderness, Lara renounces the safety of her former modus vivendi in favour of a life of uncertainty and adventure. Despite this rupture, she remains branded by the world she originates from, through her polished British accent, tea-drinking habit and—when considered appropriate—through her complete mastery of what may be considered a 'refined' social behaviour.

Lara thus brings together the aspirations of modernism—the imperialist pursuit of power and global prestige—and their postmodern problematization and fragmentation. Paradoxically, she critiques neo-imperialism by enacting her own complicity with it. The element of 'critique', however, may be promoted or indeed entirely overlooked in individual readings. Lara's appeal, as well as that of other virtual characters created for a global market, rests on this multivocality, parodic potential and a capacity for endless contextualization. In fact, each contextualization by definition reduces the multivocality and jeopardizes the characters' universal, i.e. globally marketable appeal. This is particularly evident when the characters are contextualized in environments and the media other than the virtual environment of the videogame medium they originated from. Lara's appearance in advertising[7] and film[8] has by necessity 'betrayed' some of the heroine's virtual possibilities by fixing her according to the imperatives of the medium and the genre. The same is true for her trans-contextualizations in comic strip,[9] music[10] and narrative fiction.[11]

In the mythology surrounding Lara Croft, there is hardly a hint of the notion of moral responsibility, but while the earlier game titles focused on violence in the service of adventure and self-defence, the latest release, 'The Angel of Darkness', aims at bringing forth Lara's true 'dark side'. The rejection of moral responsibility goes hand in hand with the overall abandonment of faith in a 'universal truth' motivating moral choices, characteristic of postmodernism.

The principle of multivocality also underlies the visual/graphic representation of Lara Croft. Her facial features and skin colour are fairly non-descript and invite diverse readings; her exaggerated body ironically 'compensates' for her non-corporeality. Overstated muscles for males and Barbie-like proportions for females are a commonplace in the videogame genre. With Lara's extravagant curves in full view, gamers can indulge in sexual fantasies, manipulating camera angles to focus on the most prominent bodily parts.

Making Sense of Lara

There is no single author to whom we can appeal to guarantee Lara's political intent. Unlike those forms of high culture which maintain a strong connection with an authorial figure—Salman Rushdie can still be interviewed to ask what he 'really' meant—if we want to talk about Lara's political function, we have to find out from her consumers.

Again, the technical specificity of Lara's existence is relevant here: because in the world of computer-generated characters it is not unusual for consumers also to be producers. And when we examine the ways in which Lara functions for gamers we find no simple consensus on her political nature, just an ever-increasing variety of Laras, whose characters, natures—and even bodies—are in a state of flux. To reduce Lara to a single image—a 'sergeant-major with balloons stuffed up his shirt'—and then condemn that image, as Greer does, shows little understanding of how such computer images function.

Patch distribution is a widespread activity in the gaming community, which offers alternative versions of game plots and characters, engendering transformations at the borders of official game genres. Hackers alter the original source code from a game engine to modify game structure, characters' appearance and game play itself. By far the most popular unofficial interventions in the Tomb Raider source code are related to the heroine's sexuality and enactment of gender. The fact that this aspect of Lara's virtual identity is also left ambiguous—i.e. there have been no clear 'hints' in the games pointing to the heroine's hetero- or homosexuality—has intrigued the participants in Tomb Raider fan forums, who speculate on her 'gayness', 'straightness', relationships, attitudes to marriage, maternal instincts: 'She's a good het girl who wants a husband and babies'; or, 'there is much about her that is consistent with a sapphic orientation, and nothing that rules it out'; or, 'when Lara retires, I think she'll be an incredible wife, sitting near a fireplace telling her children about her adventures— while her husband is washing the dishes'.[12] Similar speculations often inform Tomb Raider fan fiction and artworks, where fans reproduce their own ideas on sexuality and gender.

The most widespread patches exploiting Lara's ambiguous sexuality are the so-called 'Nude Raider' patches, which replace Lara's already scanty clothes with nude skin textures.[13] The more straitlaced among Lara's aficionados oppose this disrobing trend and display 'Nude Raider Free' banners on their Internet sites. Other interventions, such as Robert Nideffer's Duchampian[14] manipulations of the original Nude Raider patches, represent Lara as transsexual or butch lesbian. As an empty sign, Lara is the ideal gender-bender for the hacking community, and cyberspace critics interpret this as her primary subversive potential:

> From Lara as female automaton, Lara as drag queen, Lara as dominatrix, Lara as girl power role model, to Lara as queer babe with a shotgun, and from the gaps in between, a new range of subject positions will emerge in online game hacking culture that challenge given gender categories and adapt them to the diverse gender sensibilities of men, women and others (Schleiner, 2001).

Feminist Lara

Lara's appeal for her fans is the open nature of the character: attempts to employ the traditional language of feminist cultural theory to pin down her political effects simply don't work in this terrain. She is drag queen and female automaton, dominatrix and queer babe, at the same time, in different ways, for different audiences. We cannot simply answer the questions: 'is she a feminist icon or a sexist fantasy?'; a 'male fantasy' or a 'positive image'? But we can state, with some certainty, that she has certainly been taken up by feminists, and used for feminist ends.

A subversive manipulation of Lara Croft with a specifically feminist bent was staged by a group of participants in the International Women's University (ifu) in Hannover in August 2000, within the project entitled 'Reconstructing Gender'. They chose Lara for their performance, because they were attracted by her virtuality and multivocality:

> Since she is virtual she could be anything—but she is limited to heroine and sex-symbol; she could be fluid and challenge existing borders—instead she reinforces them; she could subvert traditional meanings and meaning-making—instead she is represented to us in the most traditional contexts; she could be used to explore the implications of postmodernism, of new technologies, of changes in society—both the chances and the threats—instead she is used to try and convince us that in spite of all the changes things will essentially remain the same.[15]

For these feminists, Lara herself has potential and possibilities: but they don't think they have been well enough exploited. Like the creators of patches, they remake Lara for themselves. The group involved in this project kidnapped a cardboard Lara Croft figure out of a MacShop in Hamburg. The women then dressed the cardboard Lara in traditional costumes from different cultures and staged her in contexts she is not normally associated with—for example, as pregnant, or, in the toilet. Finally, they decorated the effigy with 250 URLs related to feminism and returned her to her original 'abode', the MacShop.

In one way nothing more than a familiar genre of performance art project that seeks to claim a superior feminist sensibility to the bad mass culture it plays with, this feminist work is more interesting in its very ordinariness. The group were not, in fact, doing anything special. They were wrong to state that 'she is limited to heroine and sex-symbol'. Their act of provocation is important precisely for the fact that it is neither radical, nor shocking. It is not unusual to imagine Lara in a range of different circumstances: the consumer-producers do so all the time. New Laras are always being produced. Lara shocks feminist writers; Lara excites feminist writers. There are many Laras, and many positions that can be taken on her politics. She is indeed a sex object; she is indeed a positive image and a role model; and many things in between.

Correspondence: maja.mikula@uts.edu.au

Notes

[1]Since Tomb Raider is both a 'computer game' and a 'videogame' (PlayStation, Sega Saturn and Game Boy), the two terms will be used interchangeably in this paper.

[2]http://www.eidosgames.com/ubb/Forum22/HTML/034613.html (May 2002).

[3]Eidos's official Website, http://www.eidosgames.com/ubb/Forum22/HTML/034058.html

[4]According to Turkle, people use gender swapping as a 'first-hand experience through which to form ideas about the role of gender in human interactions' (Turkle, 1996, p. 362). Players

become conscious of social practices related to gender that they tend not to notice in real life: as female characters, male MUDers are sometimes surprised to find themselves 'besieged with attention, sexual advances, and unrequested offers of assistance which imply that women can't do things by themselves' (Turkle, 1996, pp. 362–363).

[5]Even her date of birth—14 February 1968—brings together the numbers commonly associated with such mutually 'irreconcilable' concepts as 'love' (14 February—Valentine's Day) and 'dissent' (1968, the year of revolts).

[6]Gordonstoun Mission Statement from http://www.gordonstoun.org.uk

[7]In an aggressive marketing campaign, Lara's debut on the computer screen was soon followed by mass production of a wide variety of merchandise for the ever-growing hordes of her aficionados: from action figures to paint-it-yourself resin statues, from screen savers to clothing. It has been noted that the images of Lara featuring on a majority of these products depict the heroine as a sex object and that the products themselves—for example T shirts, which are only available in sizes XL and XXL—are obviously aimed at male consumers: 'There is no imagery inviting a woman's gaze or trying to establish a bond between Lara and a female viewer. Most representations seem to completely ignore women as potential viewers' (Pretzsch, 2000). The same study also identifies this bias towards male viewers in advertisements for Tomb Raider games, as well as some other unrelated products—such as Seat cars and Lucozade soft drinks—where Lara is used in the advertising campaign. Moreover, the tensions between seemingly contradictory aspects of Lara's personality—aggression, sex appeal, speed, loneliness, intelligence, etc.—tend to be resolved in favour of the features considered compatible with the advertised product. Advertisements for Seat cars thus capitalize on the concept of speed. We are also reminded that the car industry has in the past made extensive use of images of sexy women to promote the concept of success 'promised' to potential buyers.

[8]Tomb Raider is not the first videogame to cross the boundary from the computer to the cinematic screen—suffice it to mention Super Mario Bros, with Bob Hoskins and Dennis Hopper—and it becomes clear that the crossing is not an easy one. Reviews of *Lara Croft: Tomb Raider* (2001) have been largely negative, focusing mainly on the unconvincing and contrived plot, as well as a rather superficial portrayal of main characters. The film's shortcomings can also be interpreted in terms of the argument outlined above: for the film version, the unresolved tensions and contradictions cohabiting in the virtual medium had to be resolved in favour of 'privileged' interpretations. As a consequence, Lara's exploratory spirit, her intelligence, panache and a certain humour are hardly noticeable in the film.

[9]Lara's entry into the comic medium dates back to 1997, when Michael Turner included her for the first time in an episode of his widely popular *Witchblade* series. Rather than as a mere subordinate to the heroine, New York policewoman and Sandra Bullock lookalike Sara Pezzini, Lara featured as her equal partner in stopping a bloody vendetta. Other episodes followed, with the two sexy women joining forces to exhibit their formidable bodies and fighting power. Since late 1999, Eidos has published a series of comics, written by Dan Jurgens (Jurgens, 1999–2000), in which Lara appears as the main character. The comic genre abounds in strong self-reliant females—from Modesty Blaise, Superwoman, Wonderwoman and Darkchylde, to Catwoman, Elektra, Glory and Tank Girl.

[10]Lara's ironic and ultimately subversive aspects have to date been discerned and put to good use only in the music scene, by the German punk rock band Die Ärzte and the Irish pop band U2. The former use Lara in a video-clip for a song satirizing the macho stereotype, entitled

Ein Schwein namens Männer. Lara is shown in a gunfight with the three members of the band—a fight she herself initiated and which she leaves victorious. The three men seem unimpressed by Lara's body and engage in a serious fight with her, but they cannot match her wits and dexterity. The latter, U2, featured Lara on a large video screen during their PopMart tour in 1997/1998, to accompany the song 'Hold Me, Kill Me, Kiss Me, Thrill Me' from the soundtrack of the film Batman Forever. Lara's screen appearance reinforces the theme of the song: shown in the beginning as loving and shy, she then quickly disappears on her motorbike, only to return with a gun and aim it at Bono, the lead singer.

[11]David Stern's novel *Lara Croft: Tomb Raider* (2001), based on the screenplay for the film, suffers from very much the same maladies as the film itself: the ambiguities of the heroine are resolved in an unconvincing, dull way; the potential for ironic critique is left unexplored and even the action itself is paralysed through uninspired narration.

[12]http://www.eidosgames.com/ubb/Forum22/HTML/032935.html (May 2001).

[13]There have been rumours that these patches were originally launched by Eidos itself, in an attempt to boost the publicity of Tomb Raider Games. Whatever the origin of the patches, it is true that—despite a clear increase in sexual overtones with each new title in the Tomb Raider series and a decidedly suggestive marketing campaign—Core and Eidos have characteristically avoided nudity and pornographic innuendoes, and thus managed to keep the game's rating at PG-13.

[14]Nideffer's patches are reminiscent of Marcel Duchamp's well known parodic addition of a moustache and a goatee on a reproduction of Leonardo's *Mona Lisa*, entitled L.H.O.O.Q. ('Elle a chaud au cul', or 'She has a hot ass').

[15]http://www.vifu.de/students/(May 2002).

References

Artel, Linda and Susan Wengraf (1976 [1990]) Positive images: screening women's films, in Patricia Erens (ed.), *Issues in Feminist Film Criticism*. Bloomington and Indianapolis: Indiana University Press, pp. 9–12.

Denfeld, Rene (1995) *The New Victorians: a Young Woman's Challenge to the Old Feminist Order*. New York: Warner Books.

Gard, Toby (1997) Interview for *The Face* magazine, http://www.cubeit.com/ctimes/news0007a.html

Gibbon, Dave (2001) The man who made Lara, *BBC News Online*, 28 June, http://news.bbc.co.uk/hi/english/entertainment/new_media/newsid_1410000/1410480.stm

Greer, Germaine (1999) *The Whole Woman*. New York: Doubleday.

Inness, Shirley (1999) *Tough Girls: Women Warriors and Wonder Women in Popular Culture*. Philadelphia: University of Pennsylvania Press.

Jones, Chris (2001) Lara Croft: fantasy games mistress, *BBC News Online*, 6 July, http://news.bbc.co.uk/hi/english/uk/newsid_1425000/1425762.stm

Jurgens, Dan (1999–2000) *Tomb Raider the Series*. Los Angeles: Top Cow Comics and Eidos Interactive.

Kolmos, Keith M. (2001) *Tomb Raider the Book: Prima's Official Strategy Guide*. Roseville, CA: Prima Games.

Lara Croft Tomb Raider Series (2001) WomenGamers.Com, http://www.women gamers.com/dw/lara.html

Lord, Albert B. (1960) *The Singer of Tales*. Cambridge, MA: Harvard University Press.

Lumby, Catharine (1997) *Bad Girls: the Media, Sex and Feminism in the '90s*. Sydney: Allen & Unwin.

Mayfield, Kendra (2000) A pretty face is not enough, *Wired News*, 18 December, http://wired.com/news/print/0,1294,40478,00.html

Mulvey, Laura (1975 [1990]) Visual pleasure and narrative cinema, in Patricia Erens (ed.), *Issues in Feminist Film Criticism*, Bloomington and Indianapolis: Indiana University Press, pp. 28–40.

Olafson, Peter (1997) Dance to this tomb: Tomb Raider is novel and gorgeous, *Computer Gaming World* 152 (March), pp. 100–101.

Ovid (1980) *Metamorphoses*, A. E. Watts (trans.). San Francisco: North Point Press.

Pretzsch, Birgit (2000) *A Postmodern Analysis of Lara Croft: Body, Identity, Reality*, http://www.frauenuni.de/stndents/gendering/lara/LaraCompleteTextWOPics.html

Roiphe, Katie (1993) *The Morning After: Sex, Fear, and Feminism*. Boston: Little, Brown.

Schleiner, Anne-Marie (2001) Does Lara Croft wear fake polygons?, *Leonardo* 34 (3), pp. 221–226.

Snider, Mike (2001) Tomb creator saw no profits, but has new game, *USA Today*, 18 June, http://www.usatoday.com/life/enter/movies/2001-06-18-tomb-raider-creator.htm

Stern, Dave (2001) *Lara Croft: Tomb Raider*. New York and London: Simon & Schuster.

Turkle, Sherry (1996) Constructions and reconstructions of the self in virtual reality, in Timothy Druckrey (ed.), *Electronic Culture: Technology and Visual Representation*. New York: Aperture, pp. 354–365.

Turner, Michael (1997/8) *Witchblade/Tomb Raider Special 1*. Los Angeles: Top Cow Comics and Eidos Interactive.

Turner, Michael (1999) *Witchblade/Tomb Raider 1–2*. Top Cow Comics and Eidos Interactive.

Wolf, Naomi (1993) *Fire with Fire: the New Female Power and How it Will Change the Twenty-first Century*. New York: Random House.

WomenGamers.Com Discussion Forum (1999) http://forums.womengamers.com

Wright, Kathryn (2000) GDC 2000: race and gender in games, WomenGamers.Com, http://www.womengamere.com/articles/racegender.html

Life in the Dorms

Rebekah Nathan

Walking down the dorm corridor to find my room for the first time, I was struck most by the sheer amount of "stuff." Rooms and corridors were piled high with clothes, appliances, bedding, furniture, and countless boxes. As the clutter cleared during the day and rooms assumed their final appearance, it was hard to believe how many things had been squeezed into a ten-by-twenty-foot space.

I had personally made several shopping trips to stock my dorm room, and had moved in a few carloads of items, but my room—with its computer, lamp, night table, ten-inch TV, microwave oven, wok, books, comforter, and two posters—was bare compared with those of my younger compatriots. In addition to articles like mine, they had joysticks, couches, mountain bikes, ski and sports equipment, guitars and keyboards, large and elaborate sound systems, multiple-layered electronics shelves holding TVs, VCRs, DVD players, refrigerators, tables, cabinets, floor and pole lamps, overstuffed throw pillows, as well as coffeemakers, slow cookers, and illegal sandwich grills. What's more, many rooms had duplicates of every appliance—dueling computers, TV sets, microwave ovens, stereo systems.

Each room contained two single beds, a small sink and mirror, a large built-in armoire, and a double desk running the width of the room with multiple drawers and bookshelves, but almost all residents added creatively to the available storage space. There were hooks to hold bicycles that couldn't be left outside and under-the-bed containers for extra clothing. Some students bunked their beds to create space for their couches, bean-bag chairs, electronics, and appliances; others placed their desk chairs on top of their desks to create floor space (I saw some do their homework up there as well). The rooms, built in the 1940s, literally could not hold all the items brought, and many residents built storage structures upward from floor to ceiling. Among the biggest differences in dorm room arrangement from my youth were lofts—elaborate wood frames that held a sec-ond-story platform over one's bed, creating another level of living and storage space.

Two people shared most rooms, with a few singles thrown in here and there. The geography, like the community, began with one's immediate wing, and then extended to one's corridor, floor, and finally dorm. The largest public spaces were on the ground floor and were communal for the entire dorm. A large lobby area with fireplace, lounge furniture, and television set greeted residents, with student newspapers, coupons, pizza delivery flyers, and activity calendars spread on a table for the taking. Depending on the day and the hour, student workers or resident assistants (RAs) staffed the front desk and were available from 8 AM to 10 PM for questions, problems, emergencies, and lending requests from the small video library. On this floor, too, there was a small communal kitchen, with a single stove, which served the entire building, as well as a computer lab open only at night and an exercise room, each the size of two dorm rooms.

My floor consisted of two contiguous male and female halls with a shared coed lounge area in between that housed a TV with VCR (but no DVD), two round tables with chairs, and a few overstuffed couches and chairs. The two female wings on each floor shared a same-sex bathroom, and the two male wings shared a second common bathroom. The female wings were slightly more populous, so approximately seventy women used four toilet stalls, four showers, and one bathtub. Most mornings, before the start of popular 9–10 AM classes, there would be a line of women in bathrobes carrying plastic shower caddies with soap and shampoo, waiting for an open shower.

Resident assistants' rooms or suites were positioned strategically in high-traffic areas. There were three on my floor. You could tell their rooms by the animated decorations on their doors and wall spaces around their rooms. You might see a giant brightly colored name tag, a "Good luck with classes!" banner, or a door wrapped like a package, with a "Come on In" sign. The RA usually provided some way of knowing where he or she was at all times, with pointers indicating "eating out," "in class," "out and about," "studying—only emergencies," or "I'm there—knock." RA spaces, always busy with displays and messages, conveyed a kind of big brother or big sister authority, a mixture of law enforcement and availability, concern, and counsel.

Are We Having Fun Yet?

As I would do if I had moved into a village, I started my research by recording my immediate surroundings and taking a census of who lived where. There was a lot to record. Dorm doors, hallways, and bathrooms were filled with messages in the form of flyers, jokes, bulletin board displays, photos, and collages, all in their own way telling me something about the culture of the dorm.

Bulletin boards provided the official imagery of dorm life. There were several on each floor, and creating the displays was an important part of the RA's job. They were usually changed each month, so in a year's time one could see a healthy sample of topics and presentations. I typically wandered the halls on weekend mornings when they were reliably deserted because students were either sleeping or had left on Friday for a weekend adventure. By April of my second semester, I had recorded fifty-seven different formal bulletin board displays in my residence hall.[1]

It was clear that the bulletin boards were coordinated efforts, influenced by directives from the RHD (residence hall director); they rotated in a discernible pattern relating to the time of year and desired theme, although RAs had considerable leeway in deciding how a message appeared. At the beginning of the year the corridors all sported "get involved" messages as well as rape and sexual assault warnings. Mid-semester messages contained more academic advice but also focused on conflict resolution, roommate, and relationship problems. Around the December holidays, health and body image messages were more frequent, while around Valentine's Day was a profusion of boards relating to love, sex, and relationships. "Diversity" issues seemed relegated to the weeks surrounding the Martin Luther King Jr. holiday. I saw one board on voting preceding November elections.

Approximately one in five bulletin boards throughout the year concerned academics, and most of these offered tips and tools, including items such as "dealing with test anxiety" or "ten steps to academic success." The biggest category of displays—more than one-quarter—dealt with psychological and physical health, as well as threats to health. This category included four displays on sexual assault and sexually transmitted diseases, three on drugs and alcohol, and four on body image (for example, "Love your Lumps," urging us to accept our bodily imperfections).

Scattered comic relief boards that drew on college culture themes ("Fifty Things Admissions Never Told You about College," "Crazy Things to Do for under $10," "Fifty Fun Things to Do at Wal-Mart") appeared throughout the year. Almost 20 percent of all messages had danger motifs, warning students about the consequences (suspension/expulsion, AIDS, jail, STDs, pregnancy, sickness, even death) that given actions would reap. In visiting the dorm the following year, I found that many of the boards were recycled, suggesting that this formal culture—touting health, educational and academic advice, information, and warnings—had some consistency over time.

Resident doors, by contrast, belonged to the informal student culture. Although RAs had affixed a handmade name tag and welcome materials to each of our doors, I quickly learned that cool students added things and, boys in particular, took RA items down. Within three weeks of moving in, 60 percent of the boys' doors had been stripped of their RA materials. It was women, though, at about a 3 to 1 ratio to men, who had designed new, often elaborate door displays.

Although not all students of either gender decorated their doors, expressive door art was a regular feature of college life. A variety of objects, text, drawings, photos, collages, pictures, quotes, comic strips, and symbols—often ten to twenty or more on a single door—appeared as public yet personal door displays. If you were to ask students directly about the rules and meaning of door decoration, they would likely say that there are no rules (except for avoiding racial and ethnic slurs) and that door displays don't "mean" anything beyond the interests of the occupant. An anthropologist, though, would say that there are very particular rules and patterns that define the expressive culture of undergraduates, and the way students choose to represent themselves to others is very telling.

If the formal culture stressed advice, academics, and warnings, informal culture stressed sociability, fun, and humor. "Friendly fun," as Michael Moffatt found at Rutgers University, was "the bread and butter of college life."[2] In 2003, "fun" continued to be one of the most ubiquitous words in college discourse, a way to describe a good evening, a good person, or a good class. "Fun," as a concept, is associated with spontaneity, sociability, laughter, and behavior (including sexuality) that is unconstrained.

The value placed on fun was evident in many forms on student doors, in the images and words that were selected for public viewing.

Probably the most common door display included strings of phrases and words cut from magazines, usually interspersed with cutout images. Although some doors posted discrete messages such as "Saying of the Week" or "Quotable Quotes," most used a collage-like genre to create a carefully constructed impression of freethinking spontaneity and individuality. On one representative door on my hall were the following phrases:

> Friends don't let friends party naked; Bitch; 24 hours in a day. 24 bottles of beer in a case. Coincidence? I think Not; Z-Man!! We Test Animals; Crazy Wild; Where the Stars Go; How Long Should you Wait?

While this reads on one level like a highly individualized, almost stream-of-consciousness expression, it is actually highly stylized. Its cutout words and phrases, set at different angles and using different sizes and fonts of type, were in the same visual style that appeared on most doors. Its content references to booze, nakedness, craziness, youth, celebrity, and sexuality were also common themes, which conveyed even larger themes of freedom and fun. Thus, down the hall on a neighboring door, one could see different phrases, also in pasted cutouts, that were manifestations of the same themes: "Bare your butt," "Young and Royal," "Las Vegas," "A Colorful Character," "Once Upon a Mattress," "The Next Best Thing to Naked," or on the next one "Welcome to CrazyWorld" and "Naked on Roller Skates."

Nudity, sexuality, drinking, craziness. These are certainly part of the college scene, but concentrating on the literal content alone misses the underlying values—fun, expressiveness, individuality, freedom, spontaneity—which are really the point. Images, like words, convey the same few themes. On one door it will be "nakedness" phrases that impart the impression of individuality, fun, a lack of limits; on another the same message is communicated with outdoor sport photos, showing a mountain biker or a skier in mid-air or a surfer riding a giant curling wave.

Acceptable alternative images or text include antiestablishment themes, in which the same core values of individuality and freedom are directed toward critique and rebellion. These door displays use dark, ghoulish, or frightening images: faces or bodies dripping with blood, Dracula-type/punk/goth images, skull and crossbones, a figure holding an automatic weapon. One such door with "dark" images displayed these verbal messages:

> Swaying to the Rhythm of the New World Order; The Boogymen are Coming; Every time you Masturbate, God Kills a Kitten; Sort of; Korn Untouchables; Quit Smoking Later; The Rocky Horror Picture Show; Pay No Mind What Other Voices Say, they don't care about you.

Other acceptable messages are funny, cryptic, or eccentric, like this string of phrases on a single door: "Fight Club," "The Only Good Clown is a Dead Clown," and "Dream, Do you?" Although women and men share most of the expressive themes, friendship and love are, on the average, overrepresented on women's doors, while men's doors more frequently show images of violence, political critique, and humor, particularly in the form of cartoons.

Many of the implicit messages of dorm doors directly contradict those of the formal sector. Whereas careful forethought and the consideration of consequences are primary messages in the formal sector, informal student culture emphasizes spontaneity. Drinking, smoking, drugs, and sexuality, while commonly featured in warnings on bulletin boards and official postings, appear as objects of admiration on student doors. And while official messages wholeheartedly urge students to accept their bodies, the images on student doors are unambiguously young, lean, attractive, buff, and/or voluptuous. When fat, old, or unattractive people appear, they are almost always associated with ridicule and humor, thus reinforcing the inverse message.

Some of the most common images on student doors involve leisure and the "good life"—including martini glasses, palm trees, cowboys, guitars, flowers, bikinis, hearts, Hawaii, belly dancers, beaches. They offer an alternative to the "buckle down" vision of college in the formal sector, which implores students to apply themselves, to balance their social lives with study and seriousness of purpose. Among the diverse images I observed on student doors, none depicted books, studying, or academic honors—not even to critique them.

At least half of all pictures of people on student doors came from magazines or commercial posters, an indication that pop culture is a primary well from which students draw to construct their public identities. The range of "people images" typically included music, sports, and TV or film celebrities as well as anonymous sexy young men and women, models from ads who were either just "looking good" or engaged in an intense but "fun" activity: snowboarding, skiing, surfing, rock climbing, and cycling to name a few. Men, particularly but not exclusively, posted pictures depicting naked women, beauty queens, lesbian sexuality, and other sexualized women's images that were the objects of both comic and lustful gazes.

The images of "real" people—that is, photographs of the resident and people the resident knew—appeared on several doors, though less frequently than media images. With one exception, in hundreds of images there were no pictures of family members. Images that students chose for their doors were a particular genre of photograph that I can best describe with some examples (I cannot *show* them because of confidentiality requirements):

- The resident on a trip with a group of his friends. They all face the camera with arms outstretched in an "end-of-show" gesture, some on half-bended knees.
- A collage of photos taken during what clearly is a party. In one there are people wall-to-wall, as the resident holds up a glass in a toast.
- The two residents of the room, both making faces at the camera.
- A resident sticking her tongue out at the camera.
- Two residents of the room bending over and sticking out their rear ends (clad in jeans) at the camera.
- A mixed-gender group of friends on the ground, each person's head resting on the next person's stomach. The shot is taken from above, and everyone is laughing.

- The female resident and two girlfriends outdoors, facing the camera, with arms around one another's waist. The girl in the middle opens her mouth in mock surprise as the girls on either side point to her.

The images typically are not serious; they are often posed, but in poses that contrast with the family album picture. Instead of smiling naturally, people are often making faces, or purposely "over"-smiling, or sticking out their tongues. They appear in unusual positions (on the ground; with their butts sticking out) and/or off-balance, with legs and arms akimbo, as if caught in some spontaneous and "fun" activity. The photos almost exclusively feature the resident with others of the same age group.

Many of the photos—just as the words, phrases, and images included—are calculated to say something like: "Here I am doing crazy/spontaneous/'fun' things"; "Here I am having a good time with my friends"; or sometimes, "I'm a unique and eccentric individual." What makes door art, from phrases to images to photos, similar is the spirit and the values it conveys: friendliness, youth, freedom, sexiness, sociability, irreverence, fun, humor, intensity, eccentricity, lack of limits, spontaneity. These are the values of undergraduate life, and although there are many students who do not individually advance or emulate these values, they nonetheless serve as the cultural standard.[3]

The Absolutely Positively Mandatory First Hall Meeting

My first formal introductions to others on the corridor came in the form of a required corridor meeting, the first of the season. A few days before, I happened on a group of hall mates in the lounge making signs for the meeting. In addition to advertising, as usual, that "pizza will be provided," the posters included urgent phrases such as "You MUST be there!" "Yes, we mean YOU!" "ABSOLUTELY MANDATORY MEETING."

"See you there," I said in passing, as one of the sign makers glanced up, but he responded that he wasn't looking forward to the meeting and might not go himself. He mocked: "Don't pee on the toilets, don't leave trash in the halls . . . I know what they're going to say. I don't need to hear it again."

"Yeah," said another sign maker to both of us, "but we wanna show support for our RA for the first meeting, so we probably *will* be there."

Not all corridor residents did show up, but the lounge still could not hold the fifty-plus men and women who arrived for the first meeting; the overflow sat in the doorways, draped themselves over the arms of couches, and squeezed into tiny open spots on the floor. As an icebreaker the RAs asked us to tell two things about ourselves that others would probably not know from meeting us. I was one of the first to go and mentioned that I had lived overseas in a remote place for a few years; others mentioned musical talents or double-jointedness, but most people reverted to departmental major, name, and hometown. No one ever asked me about the place where I'd lived or why I'd lived there.

After introductions we moved on to rules, such as "Don't take the screens out of your windows" and "Don't prop the outside doors open." Those of us with no room-mate were directed to move all our things to one side of the room unless we had paid for a single room. This portion of the meeting was not terribly different from that envisioned by the sign makers. We were then asked what dorm activities we'd like to have this year, to a lackluster response.

Finally, the meeting turned to the subject of alcohol. Although I didn't openly take notes, the discussion went something like this. "If you're not twenty-one, you can't buy alcohol," the RA began.

"Hey, who on the floor is over twenty-one?" a resident asked to laughter as the "over twenty-ones" enthusiastically raised their hands to show the underage students who could buy liquor for them.

"Listen," said the male RA, "the RHD [residence hall director] is really serious about that—he'll turn you in to the police if it comes out that you bought liquor for anyone underage. But, hey, we're not here to bust your butt. We're not here to catch you at anything. So don't give us reason to. Like I said, if you're underage, it is illegal to drink, but if you're in your own room, and you've got your door shut, and you're not loud, and no one's getting sick—well, we have no reason to go in there. Get the message?"

We certainly did. This dual message was, I found, the primary way that student authority was expressed within college culture, and perhaps with the exception of those living in freshmen-only dorms, this speech was consistent with the experiences of most students. I also found the same pattern mentioned in literature about other universities.[4] "Bad" RAs enforced the letter of the law; "good" ones enforced what we students believed to be its spirit.

Besides RAs, the only authority figure ever mentioned in dorm meetings was the residence hall director, and a student saw the RHD only if there was a problem or an issue that needed handling. Unless one did something outrageous or unluckily pub-lic, most of student life flew under the radar of university-level authorities, whom, as in Moffatt's day, few students could even name. The deans, provosts, and vice presi-dents, so important to faculty, remained part of an amorphous university structure that had little to do with students unless they really bungled their lives. In college cul-ture the rules are perceived to come from "outside," and it was the job of an astute college student to keep his or her real life private and "inside," certainly behind closed doors.

That first all-hall meeting would be the last dorm meeting that more than a handful of people attended—even the absolutely positively mandatory ones.

School Days

My first week of college, before classes began, fit my idealized sense of college life. There was a buzz of activity as we all unpacked and began putting our rooms and door displays together. I watched carefully, realizing that most students were hanging message boards outside their doors that could record greetings, questions, and invitations from others who came by to visit when they were out. I bought and hung my own message board, realizing that, like dorm doors generally, it too served as a symbol—of friendliness and perhaps, when filled with messages, one's popularity.

During the day, dorm room doors were left wide open, as people unpacked and rearranged, and there was an animated life to the halls. The sights and sounds on my corridor were most vibrant in the evenings: one girl rolling another in a laundry basket down the hall to accompanying peals of laughter; someone drunk and sick throwing up in the girls' bathroom; two guys skateboarding illegally in the corridor; a bass thumping from one of the boys' rooms that shook the entire corridor; and the continual beeps from the boys' hall of XBX video game players who had shot one of the enemy.

There was a stream of social activities—a movie; a game night; an ice cream social; a bonfire and concert on the square, which most of the RAs attended and actively solicited us to join. One night I was the official spinner for the lobby game of Twister, which we played until we couldn't determine a winner. On another night I joined a group watching a video in the RA's room, contributing my plate of oozing microwaved eggrolls to the bags of microwaved popcorn already popped for the occasion. Together, propped on floor pillows, we watched a video about a man who loses his wife, a doctor, in an accident and finds another, a waitress, who received his wife's heart in a transplant. Although I had never encountered this film anywhere, it was apparently a cherished standby for most in attendance, who had seen it multiple times.

I spent one fascinating evening that I didn't fully understand. For more than two hours I watched five students set up a scenario for a role-playing game, an exceedingly complex contemporary iteration of Dungeons and Dragons. Among the activities laid down by the game leader was a random name generator that, on one of its runs, put together "academic title" words into new combinations, generating results such as "theoretical psychological anthropologist," "applied philosophical mathematician," and "critical historical sociologist." While I was chuckling to myself that these weren't far from the jargon that academics invent, one of the students commented that "these titles are as bogus as what we are actually doing here," to murmurs of agreement.

Then classes started. The planned daily activities ended and RA attentiveness waned. People retreated to their own lives and insular social groups, and real dorm life, as I would come to know it, began.

The start of classes brought a whole new slate of contacts and relationships, and it also ushered in a new set of daily responsibilities and realities. To get a sense of the rhythms of people's lives, I did my best to observe carefully the comings and goings on my own hall. As schedules became more regularized, I had hoped to perceive the shape of undergraduate days and nights.

This proved an elusive task because of the nature of our lives as students. Bombarded with lists of books to get (or return) and first assignments, I found it hard enough to keep track of my own life, let alone the activities of numerous others. I began to feel as harried as my fellow students as I located my rescheduled classrooms, met my professors, and began feeling the pressing demands of homework. My daily journal included entries that reminded me of my high school diary, filled with anxieties about deadlines and frustrations over mundane events: "Had to return to the bookstore four times (!) because professors subtracted or added books!"; "Bought my day planner but no time to fill it in"; "Went to three different buildings before I found my freshman seminar class."

My hall mates were like ships that passed in the night, greeting one another cursorily as we came back and forth from classes. Dorm life continued to be friendly, and I regularly inquired, as did my fellow students, about hall mates' days and classes. "How was your first week of college?" one boyfriend of a neighbor asked in amusement as I walked down the hall.

"Overwhelming," I responded.

"It gets better," he assured me.

"Did anybody make it to all their classes?" someone else asked a group of four. Only one person admitted she did.

Somehow, though, I had expected students' lives to be more public, more like my first week in the dorms, and for students to be involved with dorm mates in a number of joint events. I found that much more of student life than I had initially thought occurred behind closed doors and was not amenable to my participation or observation. As I would realize later on, these initial experiences reflected more than methodological problems; they pointed, as will become clear in this chapter, to some central themes in contemporary college life.

It wasn't until my own life as a student had settled more, and I began to do interviews and collect time diaries from other students, that I would begin to notice the patterns and patterned variations in student life.[5] It took even longer still to understand the forces behind the patterns.

Some things about college life had probably not changed that much since the 1970s, when Moffatt initially collected data about students at Rutgers University. His student sample, like mine, slept about eight hours a day and attended classes or dealt with university bureaucracy about four hours per day during the week. In his data, two-thirds studied about two hours a day, 10 to 15 percent worked harder than that, and 25 percent studied hardly at all, usually cramming at exam time.[6]

National samples of students suggest that class preparation time in 2003 was about the same, or, if anything, had slightly eroded. Forty-five percent of seniors in the United States (and 43 percent of freshmen) reported spending between one and ten hours per seven-day week preparing for class—well under two hours a day—while 20 percent worked more than twenty hours (with 11 percent reporting more than twenty-five hours per week), and the rest somewhere in between.[7]

These statistics roughly jibe with my own student reports. In the twenty days of student diaries I collected, the median daily class preparation time was about an hour and forty-five minutes (two hours if you use the average), or twelve and a quarter hours per week, a figure that included studying, reading, doing research, and writing papers, as well as watching class videos and meeting with project groups. The variation from day to day, though, was notable. While one-third of the time, students put in one hour or less of daily course preparation, they put in four or more hours on one out of every five days.

So if students are studying a little less, are they relaxing and partying more? The answer, despite the rhetoric of student culture, is no. Moffatt's students relaxed and socialized an estimated four hours per day. Only 12 percent of seniors and 17 percent of freshmen in the 2003 National Survey of Student Engagement (NSSE) reported relaxing or socializing even *three* or more hours a day. Sixty percent of seniors nationwide, and 53 percent of freshmen, said that they relaxed or socialized between one and ten hours per week, decidedly less than two hours per day. Even if one assumes, as I do, that these national surveys—which ask students to reflect on an entire week and self-report—are flawed, I also saw a relative dearth of "down time" when I totaled the minutes spent in various activities from the more reliable daily diary logs. In my own hall sample, the median number of hours spent socializing or relaxing was 2.88 hours a day,[8] down considerably from Moffatt's observations in the 1970s and 1980s.

The data suggested then that, compared to students a couple of decades ago, today's public college students are both studying a little less and socializing less. What, then, are they doing with their "extra" time?

According to my local sample, students were first and foremost working jobs, both inside and outside the university. Whereas Moffatt reported that one of eight of his sampled students was working, more than half of my sample had a wage-paying job, working from six to over twenty-five hours, with a median of fifteen hours, every week. The NSSE survey for 2003 confirmed the huge upswing in students at work nationwide, finding that 31 percent of freshmen and a whopping 56 percent of seniors held some kind of *off-campus* paying job. And many more students worked on campus. In total, two-thirds of all students were working, including 54 percent of first-year students and 88 percent of seniors. Nationally, full-time students worked an average of ten hours per week.

My AnyU sample called attention to some other changes in time use as well. Although extracurricular clubs and organizations were not a central focus of student activity in either Moffatt's study or my own,[9] my interviews with students about their extracurricular participation showed that about half of those in my sample were involved in professional clubs and in volunteer work. I mention these in the same breath because I learned from interviews that joining professional clubs and volunteering are related. As one junior, Kate, explained to me:

> As a freshman I joined the pre-vet club and then last year I joined my professional Honor Society, which meets every other Thursday. Both of them require community service hours—which it's really important to have for vet school. That's why we [the organization's membership] do volunteer hours and fundraisers for community causes—the group helps us to beef up our résumés, and this helps us professionally when we apply to schools.

Many students who spoke with me viewed clubs and community work with this same eye for career. In a group of thirteen students whom I had interviewed about club participation, six were currently members of a professional group, most requiring community service, while only two participated in, sports groups, two at some level of student government or politics, and one in a religious group. Personal interest clubs were noticeably lacking. Although sports and fitness interest ran high, many in the sample had declined to join a group and instead worked out at the gym either individually or with a friend. Kyle had participated in a poetry slam group, Deb had joined a campus booster/guide program, and Kate had attended a karate club, but all had grown too busy to continue. It was these groups that were sacrificed in students' participation histories, with only one student maintaining a multiyear membership in a group focused on her personal interests.

For half of the six ethnic minorities in my interview sample, an ethnic-based club or professional organization was important in their lives, and although their degree of participation waned and waxed in some semesters, these groups were an enduring presence over their college career.

By listing and aggregating the activities named in students' daily diaries, one could see that only about fifty types of activities—which included eating, socializing, napping, walking to class, going on-line, watching TV and videos, working out, studying or doing homework, listening to music, playing video games, and attending meetings—accounted for most of what students do in a given week. Students typically "multitasked": many went on-line while they ate or chatted on the cell phone while walking to class or did homework while watching TV.

It might surprise parents to learn that on a typical weeknight, more than half of dorm residents were in bed by 11:30 PM, and most were up the next morning by 9 AM.[10] The real experience of "college life," though, was in the variation—the sense that it was also considered normal to stay up past 2 AM or to awaken after noon. One-quarter of the time, sampled hall mates stayed up after 1 AM (several after 3 AM), and 15 percent of the time, students slept past noon, even on a weekday. Thus, college culture included the comical and ubiquitous ringing of alarm clocks at 2:00 in the afternoon, just as it did an abiding tolerance for those whose schedules are the inverse of one's own.

A typical week was thus very different for different students. Whereas the ROTC students were up before 6 AM to fit in their training commitments, and kept their evening outings to a minimum, the sorority pledge was out late both nights recorded in her diary log and confided that because of sorority commitments, there were many weeks when she had four late nights of obligations. She slept in past noon when she could. The varsity runner on the floor could almost never attend an outside dorm or university event in the evening; between his classes, daily morning and evening workouts, and weekend track meets, the only time he could study was weekday evenings.

All ten of the students I followed closely had constructed lives so distinct that their paths would cross only with great effort. It is no wonder that I had difficulty discerning the rhythm of the typical student day, as you can see in just these brief portraits of four students on my hall.

Casey is up at 5 AM most days because of ROTC training, which she admits is the biggest part of her life. Despite this daily commitment, she also remains active in a professional club and a demanding multicultural leadership program. Casey dropped her meal plan because she no longer had time to eat, and adds that she thought about joining a sorority but felt that "if I added that to my plate, I couldn't finish it." What social life she has centers on other ROTC students, including her roommate, whose schedules have more in common with her own. She typically eats alone in her dorm room whenever there's a break—mostly ramen noodles and microwave food— and finds that she has to extend her day past the bedtime she'd like in order to finish studying.

Ossie's days are longer, too, but for different reasons. An ethnic minority like Casey, Ossie, by his own admission, has become a terrible procrastinator—more lax and relaxed than in high school days. "One of the reasons is that I'm not sure what I want to do," he says. "I've changed my major seven times." Because of this he has had to go to school in the summer to stay on track, and his biggest challenge in college is keeping up with classes. "I stay at the university because of my friends—if it wasn't for them I'd be at a different school." Ossie likes to get out and socialize at least three nights a week. As he describes it, "I also like to keep busy," so in addition to his school and social life, Ossie works over twenty-five hours a week, which provides money for food and his nights out. Ossie's schedule leaves no time for clubs or interest groups.

Cynthia shared a class with me which she regularly "ditched." It is a matter, she explains, of priorities. She is an art major, and very serious about her art, which takes up most of her time. In addition to her heavy studio schedule, Cynthia works—both on campus, at an office, and off campus, at a local bar. Between her classes, her art, and her jobs, there is little time for much else. She stopped her regular attendance at two student groups she had joined and admits, "I don't see friends a lot. My social life is my [bar] job." Aside from a close roommate from high school, the only other friends she sees are people in her art classes. She eats irregularly, by her admission, whenever she can fit it in, and so she passed on a meal ticket: "I have to remind myself, 'Don't forget to eat!'" She estimates that she gets only five or six hours of sleep because she doesn't start studying until 10 PM when she's not working in the bar.

As a committed Christian, Kyle has a well-rounded life that centers on a small but close set of friends who are deeply involved in his church. A good student, Kyle apportions part of every week day for studying. He has learned to treat school like a nine-to-five job, and between those hours he attends class and tries to fit in all his reading, papers, and preparation. This is purposeful so that nights and weekends are free for Kyle's social, church, and volunteer activities. With others in his circle, he volunteers at a food bank and visits the elderly two nights a week; he spends two out of every three weekends away at religious retreats or outreach programs. He has chosen to live with and close to other members of the Christian community, and they try to have an evening meal or tea with one another at least twice a week. Kyle has a meal ticket, as do some others of his group, and they often buy meals for those in their circle without a ticket so that they can all eat together.

On one level, the diverse student lifestyles described here are simply attributable to choices emanating from differences in individual agendas and personality. From a cultural standpoint, though, it is clear that while people everywhere are different, the social structures in which they live do not always give free rein to those differences.

Daily college routines, and the huge variation in the shape of days from student to student, was really a manifestation of something deeper about the nature of the university. Beneath differences in daily routine was a set of decisions that students made, and underlying their decisions was a set of options built in to AnyU and in to the structure of the American university. Would the students major in A or B or Z? Go to Spanish class, section 1 or section 10? Would they live on campus or off? In dorm X or dorm Y? Would they sign up for a meal plan or eat in their room? Would they spend most weekends away? Would they get a job while they went to school? Do volunteer work? Join ROTC? Would they pledge a fraternity or sorority?

In many ways, the microcosm of my corridor explained much about my experience of college life, and about why the national cries for "community" in the American college go unanswered.[11] It is hard to create community when the sheer number of options in college life generate a system in which no one is in the same place at the same time.

This is less a feature of intentional academic policy than it is of the premium Americans place on individuality and choice coupled with basic mathematics. If one hundred people make one choice, such as dorm A or dorm B, then, assuming the options are equally attractive, fifty people will be dorm A mates while fifty will live together in dorm B. But say, then, that the same fifty people in each dorm choose from one of five majors and one of three meal plans. How many have made the same choices and are likely to be in the same dining area, dorm, and major classes? Just three of the original one hundred, and that takes into account only this limited range of options. If we allow people to choose from one hundred majors, and add in decisions like being in a fraternity, going out for a sport, or living off campus, we can see that even with the thousands of students at a state university, very few students will have created college paths that cross frequently. Even good friends who have chosen to live together will have different majors, different courses, different clubs, and jobs that define divergent paths in their day-to-day lives.

Two implications follow from what can be called our "over-optioned" public university system. The first is that there is little that is automatically shared among people by virtue of attending the same university. On a practical level, what this means is that friends won't normally take the same classes; classmates won't usually go home to the same dorm; and hall mates won't often eat together, because some have meal plans while others buy their own food. It thus takes forethought and effort to overlap with others or to build a social circle, and the people who "naturally" meet (i.e., by virtue of having the same commitments) are most likely to be those who are glaringly alike.

The second implication is that, despite the emphasis on community, one can easily opt to move out of the dorm, drop the class, change majors, or quit the club, resulting in a social world that always seems to be in flux. The university "community" becomes both elusive and unreliable. When I came back to visit my dorm the semester after I finished my project, I could not find one person on my old corridor whom I recognized. "What happened?" I asked incredulously when I found one familiar RA face on a different floor. "Everyone moved. I think there's only one person from last year still on your corridor." I had seen 10 percent of my dorm population change by the time my first semester ended and 25 percent by the third week of my second semester.[12] One year later it was clear that, at least in university housing, one could never "go home." I shouldn't have been so surprised, really, because in a system in which one can choose from a number of living arrangements at any time, people do choose, and choose again.

The same is true of most aspects of university life. Thus, in my very small sample, the majority of students I interviewed had had at least two different majors, switching from one to seven times. Most also had joined and left at least one organization or club, quitting because the organization no longer appealed to them or the meeting bumped heads with another, more important activity.

In this light, the university becomes, for individual students, an optional set of activities and a fluid set of people whose paths are ever-shifting. Seen from the level of the institution, "community" is a lofty ideal but with few common activities, rituals, or even symbols to bind together its diverse inhabitants. What little one might share with some other students—a major, a residence hall, an interest—is always in flux.

Notes

[1]In a given year there are probably almost double this amount. Some boards, however—such as birthday boards—appear each month; others are recycled, moved from one floor to another. I counted these only once.

[2]Moffatt 1989, 33.

[3]It is important to understand that the connection between culture and individual behavior is not always a direct one. As in the larger world, so it is in the dorms. The frequent images of and references to drinking, for instance, are both real and symbolic. Students certainly drink, but most reserve drinking for appropriate times, even though its imagery is everywhere. In interviews it was commonplace to hear upperclassmen explain that they're not "into the bar and drinking scene" or how they've learned to moderate their drinking, unlike freshmen, who are still young and foolish.

[4]See, for instance, Rubington 1990.

[5]I conducted one-hour interviews with fourteen hall mates, ten of whom completed time diaries of their activities for a two-day period during selected weeks. In all, I sampled twenty days of diary information—a small sample, but one in which I knew the people, and thus the context of the information I was receiving.

[6]Moffatt 1989, 32–33.

[7]National Survey of Student Engagement (NSSE) 2003.

[8]Not all "downtime" was included. I excluded eating alone and running errands either alone or with others but included napping and telephone and Internet exchanges with friends as relaxing or socializing.

[9]Moffatt (1989) reported that approximately one-quarter of students spent one to two hours a day in extracurricular activities. The NSSE 2003 survey found that 42 percent of seniors and 36 percent of freshmen didn't participate in any "co-curricular" activities, and 31 percent of students participated only one to five hours in an entire week.

[10]In my small sample, students were in bed by 11:30 PM 55 percent of the time and up by 9 PM 70 percent of the time.

[11]Carnegie Foundation for the Advancement of Teaching, 1990.

[12]According to the AnyU Office of Residence Life, of the 3,564 upperclassmen living in the dorms (I exclude family living and freshman dorms) on August 31, 2002, 405 people had moved by December 1, 2003, and by January 31, 2003, 938 people had moved.

Works Cited

Carnegie Foundation for the Advancement of Teaching. 1990. *Campus Life: In Search of Community.* Princeton: Carnegie Foundation for the Advancement of Teaching.

Moffatt, Michael. 1989. *Coming of Age in New Jersey: College and American Culture.* New Brunswick: Rutgers University Press.

National Survey of Student Engagement. 2003. *2003 Overview.* Bloomington, IN: Center for Postsecondary Research, Policy, and Planning. http://nsse.iub.edu/2003 annual report/.

Rubington, Earl. 1990. "Drinking in the Dorms: A Study of the Etiquette of RA-Resident Relations." *Journal of Drug Issues* 20, no. 3 (summer): 451–62.

Opposites Attract
CONEY ISLAND, N.Y. – An old man and a muscle man on the beach.
(c) Bruce Gilden/Magnum Photos
Published July 9, 2008, in *Slate*.
http:/todayspictures.slate.com/20080709

The image above, from 1976, is the first in the photo essay, "Opposites Attract," which includes photographs of opposites, produced in recognition of physicist Nikola Tesla's birthday.

The man who once conquered Everest now faces an even greater challenge. He, in his old, withered form, must defend his honor and family from this monster of muscle. Its towering and formidable build are intimidating, but the old man's resolve is unwavering.

Why Bother?

Michael Pollan

Why bother? That really is the big question facing us as individuals hoping to do something about climate change, and it's not an easy one to answer. I don't know about you, but for me the most upsetting moment in "An Inconvenient Truth" came long after Al Gore scared the hell out of me, constructing an utterly convincing case that the very survival of life on earth as we know it is threatened by climate change. No, the really dark moment came during the closing credits, when we are asked to . . . change our light bulbs. That's when it got really depressing. The immense disproportion between the magnitude of the problem Gore had described and the puniness of what he was asking us to do about it was enough to sink your heart.

But the drop-in-the-bucket issue is not the only problem lurking behind the "why bother" question. Let's say I do bother, big time. I turn my life upside-down, start biking to work, plant a big garden, turn down the thermostat so low I need the Jimmy Carter signature cardigan, forsake the clothes dryer for a laundry line across the yard, trade in the station wagon for a hybrid, get off the beef, go completely local. I could theoretically do all that, but what would be the point when I know full well that halfway around the world there lives my evil twin, some carbon-footprint doppel-gänger in Shanghai or Chongqing who has just bought his first car (Chinese car owner-ship is where ours was back in 1918), is eager to swallow every bite of meat I forswear and who's positively itching to replace every last pound of CO_2 I'm struggling no longer to emit. So what exactly would I have to show for all my trouble?

A sense of personal virtue, you might suggest, somewhat sheepishly. But what good is that when virtue itself is quickly becoming a term of derision? And not just on the editorial pages of The Wall Street Journal or on the lips of the vice president, who famously dismissed energy conservation as a "sign of personal virtue." No, even in the pages of The New York Times and The New Yorker, it seems the epithet "virtuous," when applied to an act of personal environmental responsibility, may be used only iron-ically. Tell me: How did it come to pass that virtue—a quality that for most of history has generally been deemed, well, a virtue—became a mark of liberal softheadedness?

How peculiar, that doing the right thing by the environment—buying the hybrid, eating like a locavore—should now set you up for the Ed Begley Jr. treatment.

And even if in the face of this derision I decide I am going to bother, there arises the whole vexed question of getting it right. Is eating local or walking to work really going to reduce my carbon footprint? According to one analysis, if walking to work increases your appetite and you consume more meat or milk as a result, walking might actually emit more carbon than driving. A handful of studies have recently suggested that in certain cases under certain conditions, produce from places as far away as New Zealand might account for less carbon than comparable domestic products. True, at least one of these studies was co-written by a representative of agribusiness interests in (surprise!) New Zealand, but even so, they make you wonder. If determining the carbon footprint of food is really this complicated, and I've got to consider not only "food miles" but also whether the food came by ship or truck and how lushly the grass grows in New Zealand, then maybe on second thought I'll just buy the imported chops at Costco, at least until the experts get their footprints sorted out.

There are so many stories we can tell ourselves to justify doing nothing, but perhaps the most insidious is that, whatever we do manage to do, it will be too little too late. Climate change is upon us, and it has arrived well ahead of schedule. Scientists' projections that seemed dire a decade ago turn out to have been unduly optimistic: the warming and the melting is occurring much faster than the models predicted. Now truly terrifying feedback loops threaten to boost the rate of change exponentially, as the shift from white ice to blue water in the Arctic absorbs more sunlight and warming soils everywhere become more biologically active, causing them to release their vast stores of carbon into the air. Have you looked into the eyes of a climate scientist recently? They look really scared.

So do you still want to talk about planting gardens?

I do.

Whatever we can do as individuals to change the way we live at this suddenly very late date does seem utterly inadequate to the challenge. It's hard to argue with Michael Specter, in a recent New Yorker piece on carbon footprints, when he says: "Personal choices, no matter how virtuous [N.B.!], cannot do enough. It will also take laws and money." So it will. Yet it is no less accurate or hardheaded to say that laws and money cannot do enough, either; that it will also take profound changes in the way we live. Why? Because the climate-change crisis is at its very bottom a crisis of lifestyle—of character, even. The Big Problem is nothing more or less than the sum total of countless little everyday choices, most of them made by us (consumer spending represents 70 percent of our economy), and most of the rest of them made in the name of our needs and desires and preferences.

For us to wait for legislation or technology to solve the problem of how we're living our lives suggests we're not really serious about changing—something our politicians cannot fail to notice. They will not move until we do. Indeed, to look to leaders and experts, to laws and money and grand schemes, to save us from our predicament represents precisely the sort of thinking—passive, delegated, dependent for solutions on specialists—that helped get us into this mess in the first place. It's hard to believe that the same sort of thinking could now get us out of it.

Thirty years ago, Wendell Berry, the Kentucky farmer and writer, put forward a blunt analysis of precisely this mentality. He argued that the environmental crisis of the 1970s—an era innocent of climate change; what we would give to have back that environmental crisis!—was at its heart a crisis of character and would have to be addressed first at that level: at home, as it were. He was impatient with people who wrote checks to environmental organizations while thoughtlessly squandering fossil fuel in their everyday lives—the 1970s equivalent of people buying carbon offsets to atone for their Tahoes and Durangos. Nothing was likely to change until we healed the "split between what we think and what we do." For Berry, the "why bother" question came down to a moral imperative: "Once our personal connection to what is wrong becomes clear, then we have to choose: we can go on as before, recognizing our dishonesty and living with it the best we can, or we can begin the effort to change the way we think and live."

For Berry, the deep problem standing behind all the other problems of industrial civilization is "specialization," which he regards as the "disease of the modern character." Our society assigns us a tiny number of roles: we're producers (of one thing) at work, consumers of a great many other things the rest of the time, and then once a year or so we vote as citizens. Virtually all of our needs and desires we delegate to specialists of one kind or another—our meals to agribusiness, health to the doctor, education to the teacher, entertainment to the media, care for the environment to the environmentalist, political action to the politician.

As Adam Smith and many others have pointed out, this division of labor has given us many of the blessings of civilization. Specialization is what allows me to sit at a computer thinking about climate change. Yet this same division of labor obscures the lines of connection—and responsibility—linking our everyday acts to their real-world consequences, making it easy for me to overlook the coal-fired power plant that is lighting my screen, or the mountaintop in Kentucky that had to be destroyed to provide the coal to that plant, or the streams running crimson with heavy metals as a result.

Of course, what made this sort of specialization possible in the first place was cheap energy. Cheap fossil fuel allows us to pay distant others to process our food for us, to entertain us and to (try to) solve our problems, with the result that there is very little we know how to accomplish for ourselves. Think for a moment of all the things you suddenly need to do for yourself when the power goes out—up to and including entertaining yourself. Think, too, about how a power failure causes your neighbors—your community—to suddenly loom so much larger in your life. Cheap energy allowed us to leapfrog community by making it possible to sell our specialty over great distances as well as summon into our lives the specialties of countless distant others.

Here's the point: Cheap energy, which gives us climate change, fosters precisely the mentality that makes dealing with climate change in our own lives seem impossibly difficult. Specialists ourselves, we can no longer imagine anyone but an expert, or anything but a new technology or law, solving our problems. Al Gore asks us to change the light bulbs because he probably can't imagine us doing anything much more challenging, like, say, growing some portion of our own food. We can't imagine it, either, which is probably why we prefer to cross our fingers and talk about the promise of ethanol and nuclear power—new liquids and electrons to power the same old cars and houses and lives.

The "cheap-energy mind," as Wendell Berry called it, is the mind that asks, "Why bother?" because it is helpless to imagine—much less attempt—a different sort of life, one less divided, less reliant. Since the cheap-energy mind translates everything into money, its proxy, it prefers to put its faith in market-based solutions—carbon taxes and pollution-trading schemes. If we could just get the incentives right, it believes, the economy will properly value everything that matters and nudge our self-interest down the proper channels. The best we can hope for is a greener version of the old invisible hand. Visible hands it has no use for.

But while some such grand scheme may well be necessary, it's doubtful that it will be sufficient or that it will be politically sustainable before we've demonstrated to ourselves that change is possible. Merely to give, to spend, even to vote, is not to do, and there is so much that needs to be done—without further delay. In the judgment of James Hansen, the NASA climate scientist who began sounding the alarm on global warming 20 years ago, we have only 10 years left to start cutting—not just slowing—the amount of carbon we're emitting or face a "different planet." Hansen said this more than two years ago, however; two years have gone by, and nothing of consequence has been done. So: eight years left to go and a great deal left to do.

Which brings us back to the "why bother" question and how we might better answer it. The reasons not to bother are many and compelling, at least to the cheap-energy mind. But let me offer a few admittedly tentative reasons that we might put on the other side of the scale:

If you do bother, you will set an example for other people. If enough other people bother, each one influencing yet another in a chain reaction of behavioral change, markets for all manner of green products and alternative technologies will prosper and expand. (Just look at the market for hybrid cars.) Consciousness will be raised, perhaps even changed: new moral imperatives and new taboos might take root in the culture. Driving an S.U.V. or eating a 24-ounce steak or illuminating your McMansion like an airport runway at night might come to be regarded as outrages to human conscience. Not having things might become cooler than having them. And those who did change the way they live would acquire the moral standing to demand changes in behavior from others—from other people, other corporations, even other countries.

All of this could, theoretically, happen. What I'm describing (imagining would probably be more accurate) is a process of viral social change, and change of this kind, which is nonlinear, is never something anyone can plan or predict or count on. Who knows, maybe the virus will reach all the way to Chongqing and infect my Chinese evil twin. Or not. Maybe going green will prove a passing fad and will lose steam after a few years, just as it did in the 1980s, when Ronald Reagan took down Jimmy Carter's solar panels from the roof of the White House.

Going personally green is a bet, nothing more or less, though it's one we probably all should make, even if the odds of it paying off aren't great. Sometimes you have to act as if acting will make a difference, even when you can't prove that it will. That, after all, was precisely what happened in Communist Czechoslovakia and Poland, when a handful of individuals like Vaclav Havel and Adam Michnik resolved that they would simply conduct their lives "as if" they lived in a free society. That improbable bet created a tiny space of liberty that, in time, expanded to take in, and then help take down, the whole of the Eastern bloc.

So what would be a comparable bet that the individual might make in the case of the environmental crisis? Havel himself has suggested that people begin to "conduct themselves as if they were to live on this earth forever and be answerable for its condition one day." Fair enough, but let me propose a slightly less abstract and daunting wager. The idea is to find one thing to do in your life that doesn't involve spending or voting, that may or may not virally rock the world but is real and particular (as well as symbolic) and that, come what may, will offer its own rewards. Maybe you decide to give up meat, an act that would reduce your carbon footprint by as much as a quarter. Or you could try this: determine to observe the Sabbath. For one day a week, abstain completely from economic activity: no shopping, no driving, no electronics.

But the act I want to talk about is growing some—even just a little—of your own food. Rip out your lawn, if you have one, and if you don't—if you live in a high-rise, or have a yard shrouded in shade—look into getting a plot in a community garden. Measured against the Problem We Face, planting a garden sounds pretty benign, I know, but in fact it's one of the most powerful things an individual can do—to reduce your carbon footprint, sure, but more important, to reduce your sense of dependence and dividedness: to change the cheap-energy mind.

A great many things happen when you plant a vegetable garden, some of them directly related to climate change, others indirect but related nevertheless. Growing food, we forget, comprises the original solar technology: calories produced by means of photosynthesis. Years ago the cheap-energy mind discovered that more food could be produced with less effort by replacing sunlight with fossil-fuel fertilizers and pesticides, with a result that the typical calorie of food energy in your diet now requires about 10 calories of fossil-fuel energy to produce. It's estimated that the way we feed ourselves (or rather, allow ourselves to be fed) accounts for about a fifth of the greenhouse gas for which each of us is responsible.

Yet the sun still shines down on your yard, and photosynthesis still works so abundantly that in a thoughtfully organized vegetable garden (one planted from seed, nourished by compost from the kitchen and involving not too many drives to the garden center), you can grow the proverbial free lunch—CO_2-free and dollar-free. This is the most-local food you can possibly eat (not to mention the freshest, tastiest and most nutritious), with a carbon footprint so faint that even the New Zealand lamb council dares not challenge it. And while we're counting carbon, consider too your compost pile, which shrinks the heap of garbage your household needs trucked away even as it feeds your vegetables and sequesters carbon in your soil. What else? Well, you will probably notice that you're getting a pretty good workout there in your garden, burning calories without having to get into the car to drive to the gym. (It is one of the absurdities of the modern division of labor that, having replaced physical labor with fossil fuel, we now have to burn even more fossil fuel to keep our unemployed bodies in shape.) Also, by engaging both body and mind, time spent in the garden is time (and energy) subtracted from electronic forms of entertainment.

You begin to see that growing even a little of your own food is, as Wendell Berry pointed out 30 years ago, one of those solutions that, instead of begetting a new set of problems—the way "solutions" like ethanol or nuclear power inevitably do—actually beget other solutions, and not only of the kind that save carbon. Still more valuable are the habits of mind that growing a little of your own food can yield. You quickly learn that you need not be dependent on specialists to provide for yourself—that your body is still good for something and may actually be enlisted in its own support. If the experts are right, if both oil and time are running out, these are skills and habits of mind we're all very soon going to need. We may also need the food. Could gardens provide it? Well, during World War II, victory gardens supplied as much as 40 percent of the produce Americans ate.

But there are sweeter reasons to plant that garden, to bother. At least in this one corner of your yard and life, you will have begun to heal the split between what you think and what you do, to commingle your identities as consumer and producer and citizen. Chances are, your garden will re-engage you with your neighbors, for you will have produce to give away and the need to borrow their tools. You will have reduced the power of the cheap-energy mind by personally overcoming its most debilitating weakness: its helplessness and the fact that it can't do much of anything that doesn't involve division or subtraction. The garden's season-long transit from seed to ripe fruit—will you get a load of that zucchini?!—suggests that the operations of addition and multiplication still obtain, that the abundance of nature is not exhausted. The single greatest lesson the garden teaches is that our relationship to the planet need not be zero-sum, and that as long as the sun still shines and people still can plan and plant, think and do, we can, if we bother to try, find ways to provide for ourselves without diminishing the world.

The Last Bus Home

Miranda Purves & Jason Logan

I take my 3-year-old son, Woolf, to preschool in the morning on the B75 bus, in Brooklyn—the 8:48 if we are firing on all cylinders, the 9:28 when the chaos wins out. Initially, I resented this routine: crabby bus drivers; occasionally menacing-seeming passengers; the excessive lurching. But slowly, I became familiar with the other regulars: the old woman with the bad knees en route to her quilting class, the drunk in a wheelchair who still maintains a cheerful independence.

Woolfie and I made our "doughnut friends," a single mom and her son, who get on with a different doughnut every day, and now always sit behind us. The two boys both speak public transit. "What's your favorite train?" Woolfie asks, running his toy N express train along the back of the seats. "The G!" his friend says, referring to the one train that doesn't dip through Manhattan on its way from Queens to Brooklyn.

Ridership on our rat-gnawed, dingy and highly efficient mass transportation system may be at its highest in decades—but because of pre-existing debt coupled with plummeting real estate tax revenue, the Metropolitan Transportation Authority faces a $1.2 billion deficit. And on Wednesday, the M.T.A. ratified a doomsday plan to increase the fare for a single ride by 50 cents, to $2.50, and to eliminate or reduce service on 100 bus and five subway lines. Three buses we regularly use—including the B75—were on the elimination list. When I found out, a wave of claustrophobia hit me. "Our bus!" rang Woolfie's little voice in my head.

In the weeks before the M.T.A. vote, the artist Jason Logan and I spent a lot of time on the buses and subways that, unless the state steps in with a last-minute rescue package, will soon be gone or severely cut back. We met people whose jobs or health depended on their routes; we met some who simply didn't want to walk far in the cold. Many—and it seemed often those most dependent—were unaware that their means of transportation could disappear.

Both Jason and I have always been drawn to this phenomenon of people, behaving for the most part civilly, getting from here to there, side by side. And we wanted to find some way to convey the less tangible costs of service cuts and fare hikes. Here, large X's are adults; small x's are children.

—Miranda Purves

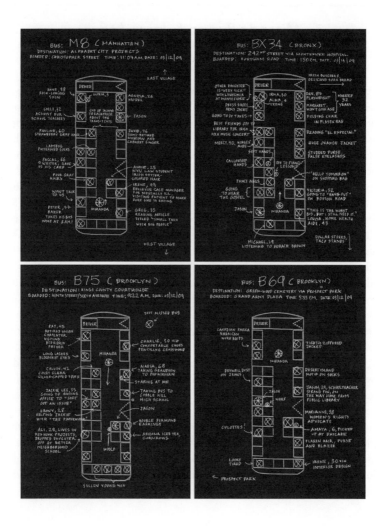

Knowledge Is Power

María Cristina Rangel

"It wasn't fair that welfare moms got to go to Smith College and idly pass their time studying such frivolities as literature and writing at the expense of the Commonwealth of Massachusetts."

"Well, what was it you majored in? And what were you planning to do with that? Didn't they encourage you to think ahead at all while you were at Smith? What *were* you thinking?" The social worker from the Transitional Services Unit of the Department of Transitional Assistance (a.k.a. Welfare) shook her head, and then paused, halted the scribbling on her notepad to scrutinize me, and waited for the response she wanted to hear, the one I would never give her. The one where I was supposed to say something like, oh, you're so right, I should have thought ahead. (But I guess I'm just not capable of that, being the fuck-up that I am.) It wasn't fair, after all, that welfare moms, so-called "gimme girls," got to go to Smith College and idly pass their time studying such frivolities as literature and writing at the expense of the Commonwealth of Massachusetts.

"I'm assuming that you were aware when you accepted the job that it required reliable transportation," was her response when she learned of my current transportation predicament. "What were you thinking?" she inquired again. She was referring to my barely functioning car with its several-years-expired inspection sticker, unreplaced since I could not afford the $500 in repairs the car needed in order to pass inspection. My inspection sticker, almost as old as my younger daughter, was infamous among the officers of the Northampton Police Department. Each time I saw the flash of blue lights in my rearview mirror, I would prepare to repeat my story one more time to one more unsympathetic officer. Did they really think I liked living like this? Or that I had much of a choice in the matter?

I knew that whatever answer I gave the social worker wouldn't matter, because it wouldn't be explanation enough. The Commonwealth had viewed me as an investment, feeding and sheltering me over the past four years. But their investment had failed them, miserably. I had failed them because after four years I still could not conform to the ideal they wanted me to conform to, or give them the answers they wanted to hear.

I had taken a thirty-hour-per-week job as a case coordinator for an agency that worked on behalf of low-income people in the area. I would make about nine dollars an hour, bring home a little over $1,000 a month and still live well below the poverty level. Most of my low-income clients would have bigger incomes than I would. So how could I begin to explain to the social worker that I had accepted this job not because I had reliable transportation, not because I thought it presented a great opportunity or livable wage or even because I felt that at the exact moment after graduation it was time for me to go from welfare to work, but because I *had* been thinking—plotting, actually, and very carefully. Had I not accepted the first job offered me, my children and I might have been homeless when "The Transition" was supposed to happen, upon my graduation. Because we were residing in college housing, I needed to find an apartment as soon as I graduated; in order to afford an apartment, I needed to secure a Job Link Section 8 voucher, which would grant me a subsidy enabling me to pay close to 30 percent of my total income in rent. The DTA had been dangling the Section 8 for months in an effort to entice me, and other recipients, to just get off our asses and work. Furthermore, to use my transitional childcare voucher I had to be employed. And I would need childcare when I went to work, would I not? While the Commonwealth did want me to take a job, they did not care about the circumstances of my situation or my impending homelessness, and did not want me to further "take advantage" of the system by utilizing available resources (such as Section 8 vouchers and childcare vouchers) and eating up more tax dollars.

It was the spring of 2000, the year I was to receive my degree. It had been four years since I had uprooted myself and moved to western Massachusetts in order to attend Smith College as an Ada Comstock Scholar (Smith's program for nontraditional students or those with families). It had also been four years since I had originally submitted my application for Transitional Aid to Families with Dependent Children (TAFDC) benefits.

The lullaby I remember singing most often to my older daughter during her infancy was, "Girl we've gotta get outta this place, if it's the last thing we ever do. Girl, there's a better life for me and you." In 1996, pregnant and with my three-year-old daughter in tow, I packed my life into four suitcases and fled the trap of poverty, tradition and culture that at that time signified home to me, and embarked on a journey to fulfill my academic dreams. I wanted a better life for myself and wanted to ensure that my daughters would know more than the rural, misogynistic, racist, homophobic area of Washington state I grew up in, where the only options for an uneducated Chicana single mother seemed to be migrant farm labor, factory work and marriage. I would be the first person in my family to attend college. And not only was I attending college, I was attending a college that was clear on the other side of the country, somewhere completely foreign to my family and me. A year's tuition at the college I chose to attend cost more than what most of my family members earned in a year.

I moved to Massachusetts in the fall. Because I submitted my application for public assistance right before the federal welfare reform law went into effect in December

1996, I was one of the last recipients not to have the dreaded twenty-four-month time limit imposed on them. Under welfare reform, recipients of TAFDC are able to receive only two years of benefits within a five-year period. Recipients are required to enroll in training or job-preparation activity in exchange for their benefits, and the pursuit of higher education does not qualify as valid training. In addition, if a recipient has a child over the age of six, she has to perform a certain number of hours of work per month, be it paid labor or unpaid community service. Recipients who wish to pursue higher education have only two years in which to complete their degrees while receiving benefits, and in addition are not eligible for childcare subsidies—which are available only to working recipients or working former recipients—making it impossible for a recipient to even think about entering a four-year program.

My original application for benefits was denied because I was not a Massachusetts resident—no matter that I had left everything behind to relocate. After an appeals process that took nearly three months, I was finally granted benefits. I was able to pay for my college-owned apartment and part-time daycare for my daughter through loans (there was no assistance through the Commonwealth or Smith for childcare costs incurred while attending a four-year college). However, because I did not receive benefits for the entire first semester, my daughter and I had very little to live on, and usually snuck into one of the dining halls for our meals. The next semester I opted to do mostly independent study in order to be home with Jordan, my younger daughter, when she arrived. The following year, I took a part-time job in order to secure a childcare subsidy.

As the semester progressed, I realized that the pressures of working, attending school, and parenting were too overwhelming. My grades were slipping, and the fact that my professors were used to dealing only with traditional students didn't help. I was exhausted. The time I would normally have utilized for class work was spent at my job, and I did most of my schoolwork late into the night. Just when I thought I was going to crack, my name came up on a waiting list for daycare subsidies through a nonprofit organization that worked to combat poverty locally; unlike the DTA, they *would* consider my education a worthwhile "training activity."

As a recipient of TAFDC, I had to report to my caseworker every few months to make sure my circumstances still made me eligible, or to fill out a patronizing Transition Plan that required me to describe my recent efforts made toward getting a job, my plans to get a job, and how I intended to support my family once we no longer received public benefits. I had to explain myself over and over again, always living with the fear that I would not be believed and my benefits would be cut as a result. After each humiliating, intimidating interrogation, I would make my way back through the waiting room and glance at the Welfare to Work posters hanging on the waiting room walls. "Mommy, will we always be on Welfare?" "Work Works!" "Think of your children. . . . Whose footsteps do you want to see them follow in?"

I was struck by how patronizing, how blaming these statements were, and how they were designed to inflict guilt on women because of the circumstances of our lives. Poverty is a matter of personal failure, they seemed to say, and ending poverty a matter of personal will. You have failed, but with our help you can become better, and then maybe your children won't be ashamed of you. Even the name of the welfare reform law hints at this blaming attitude: The Personal Responsibility and Work Opportunity Reconciliation Act. Implicit in the title is the assumption that welfare recipients refuse to accept responsibility for their lives.

During my four years as a TAFDC recipient, my relationship with the Commonwealth embodied our society's attitude of contempt, hostility, and distrust toward low-income people. The whole system is based on the assumption that you are trying to screw the DTA over. There are constant check-ins and impossibly long lists of "verifications" to submit to the state in order to back your story; inquisitions involving a battery of questions asked by countless supervisors behind closed doors when it appears that your story does not add up; rules that change rapidly (and for the most part, without your knowledge); and blatant economic abuse, since if you don't comply with whatever demand they place on you, be it submitting verifications that are impossible to get or participating in a job readiness program, your benefits can be cut.

During these years, all I could think about was making it out of Smith. Just getting by, getting out and going on. Surviving. And because of this, to me, *everything,* every single fucking thing, was at stake. If they took away my benefits, they took away my education. If they took away my car and I was not able to get my kids to daycare, they took away my education. When my housing was in jeopardy, so was my education. And if they took away my education, they took away everything I had worked for. They took away from me the life I was slowly and painfully carving out each day for my children and myself.

I didn't have the capability to think about *after* I made it out—just the getting there. But once some of the craziness began to subside from my life, it was time to think beyond just getting out. Women may become and stay poor due to life circumstances such as illness, death of a partner, domestic violence and abandonment; but their situation is also determined by systemic factors like poor public education, little job training for displaced workers, low wages and lack of affordable childcare— as well as the punitive nature of the welfare system itself. Why were things the way they were? I'd been so afraid of "them" for four years—but just who are "they" anyway? It was pondering these two questions that led me to combat the "theys" of the world: an abusive welfare system, a government that doesn't provide for its citizens and an education system that can only be accessed by the wealthy. I took a step beyond survival to work for justice.

With the assistance of other Ada Comstock Scholars who were experiencing similar challenges caused by poverty, welfare reform or both, I revived an organization, the Association of Low Income Students, that would become a forum to address issues surrounding poverty and class on the Smith campus and beyond. While the organization was initially founded to disperse discretionary funds to students in need who had no other resources, eventually the membership (which initially consisted of four Adas, but later included around twenty students, both traditional and Adas) started organizing on a multitude of issues: welfare reform, housing and tenants' rights (as

Smith was our landlord); the discrepancies between financial aid packages given to traditional students (with allowances for housing and meals) and those given to Adas (with none); and the sometimes blatant classism evident on our campus.

Because many of these issues exist well beyond the Smith bubble, for me the organization became a launching point to address, locally and at the state level, the issues that were central to my life as a recipient of TAFDC and a single parent living well under the poverty level. I began organizing, collaborating and advocating on behalf of other low-income women, while working toward being heard on the streets, in the courts and in the legislature. I became a member of a statewide organization—the Welfare, Education, Training and Access Coalition—which campaigns around issues of reform, strives to provide recipients facing impending time limits with strategies and options for expanding their time, and helps recipients in their efforts to obtain higher education and training. I have also developed a reputation for providing individual advocacy to low-income women with families who are trying to pursue education, and I currently sit on a panel that works to address housing problems locally.

Some people believe that welfare reform has been a huge success. If you can call disruption in the lives of countless women and children due to escalating homelessness, hunger, growing infant and maternal mortality rates, a workforce of underpaid women and the prevalence of women and children living under the poverty line a huge success, then, yes, it has succeeded. The current welfare system imposes a lifetime sentence on recipients, stipulating that they must become "self-sufficient," while at the same time barring access to adequate education and training opportunities. Imposed time limits and workfare have forced women out of the classroom and into minimum-wage jobs without benefits. According to data recorded by Massachusetts's fifteen community colleges, in 1997, one year after reform was enacted, enrollment of TAFDC recipients at community colleges throughout the Commonwealth decreased by an average of 47 percent. In Massachusetts, monthly monetary benefits for a woman with two dependents average around $579, while rents in the Northampton area run around $700 to $900 a month for a modest two-bedroom apartment (and in Boston, rents are anywhere from $1,200 up). The U.N. Declaration of Human Rights declares that each individual has the right to food, shelter, clothing, adequate work conditions and medical care, yet violations of these rights occur regularly against low-income individuals within our country, our states, our cities and our neighborhoods.

As I write this, I realize that this is the story of only *one* ex-welfare recipient—and the story of one who is privileged in ways that other recipients and ex-recipients might not be. I am English-fluent, and, as many barriers as there were for me, I had access to a four-year college education, something that is virtually impossible to obtain now under welfare reform. And as I write this I think about all the other stories that are not heard, all the other injustices that remain unresolved. I am reminded of how throughout history, slave owners would generally not allow their "property" to learn to read or write. Because what would happen if these slaves became literate? What would happen if low-income women had equal access to adequate training programs and education?

Maybe they would no longer be kept in the subordinate positions that our economy depends on—a large workforce who, with little education, can be hired at minimum wage with no benefits. Maybe then we would be more able to organize for economic justice.

Knowledge is power. It is in discovering this power that the true source of self-sufficiency and independence is found. And I assure you that, were it more easily accessible, this is what most "gimme girls" would opt for. The welfare system purports to encourage self-sufficiency and independence, but it refuses to offer recipients the tools and resources to escape the grind of poverty. The system's true, immediate goal is simply to reduce the number of welfare recipients, with little concern for the lives of the people who are cut off. Most women who reach the end of the two-year limit get off welfare, but remain in poverty.

It is time for reform to be unreformed, or at least modified. It is time for states to recognize that substantive education and training produce concrete and long-lasting effects. It is time to examine the limitations of work-first philosophies, which result at best in marginal and short-term improvements in income, and at worst in permanent displacement of women and their children. It is also long overdue that class be considered as much an issue of diversity as race or gender or sexual preference. It is time that institutions of higher learning be held accountable for their part in barring access to education for low-income women. And it is also time that institutions of higher learning recognize the fact that if they do not provide to low-income, nontraditional students the same benefits—such as food and shelter—that are granted to traditional students, then they are prohibiting access to higher education to a whole segment of the population.

So now, here I am. About $40,000 in debt to the government, and $10,000 in debt to Smith. Instead of receiving my diploma at graduation, I opened the cover to find a slip of paper reading "Your diploma will be mailed to you after your records are cleared [i.e. after you pay up what you owe]." It is this slip of paper that I framed and now display on my wall, a daily reminder of the need to advocate not only for economic justice, but also for access to higher education for low-income women. At this rate, when my monthly bill comes from Smith, and I am momentarily petrified at the balance stated, it's easy to feel as though I will never see my diploma. Sometimes I'm sure that hundreds of years from now someone will be conducting research and come across it in the school's archives.

There have been other costs associated with my education, some more significant than any price tag—in particular, leaving home and the people I love behind. As the years have passed, my education has become a sort of severing factor between my home and me; it grants me a privilege that nobody else has, and this privilege hurts. But whatever price I have paid for it, my education is priceless. From my example, my daughters will know what it is to struggle, to survive, to believe, to keep on rising. I think of the U.S.-Mexico border—not just as a geographic place, but as a space— and what a constant motif it has been throughout my life, a metaphor for every instance in which I have dared to cross into the unknown.

One quiet summer evening before I was to leave home yet again for another semester, I sat with my grandmother on her porch and asked her: Of all the things she had accomplished in her life, what did she feel was the most significant? She pondered my question for a few minutes before replying, "Coming to this country." I was confused, thinking of my transcultural childhood experience and all the hardships my family had endured trying to gain citizenship. I asked her why; squeezing my hand, she replied that, had she not come, none of us would be doing what we were at this moment. I realized that she had lived her entire life waiting for the day that I would pack my life into a few suitcases to make a new existence for myself, and cross my own *frontera*. And I know when it comes time for my daughters to cross theirs, that they will think back to this moment in my history, my crossing, and proceed carrying the strength of all those who have gone before them.

The North American

Richard Rodriguez

It is instinctive in humans, as it is in other warm-blooded creatures, to fear the swallower. I had an uncle who came from India and who feared being deported by U.S. immigration officials because he feared India would swallow him—consume, devour him again—without respect for his person or his life's journey, a journey that brought him to Sacramento, California, where he wished to remain. An American. Americans have lately taken up a Canadian word—multiculturalism—as a talisman against the notion of the swallower. But America has always been the swallower, our national culture has been omnivorous. I believe the United States of America swallowed me a long time ago. It may be that I am about to swallow you.

There is something unsettling about immigrants because they can seem to overturn America—or they can seem to undo America. At the very point at which Americans think we have a communal identity, at the very point at which we think we know who we are—we are Protestants, culled from Western Europe, are we not?—then new immigrants appear from Southern Europe or from Eastern Europe. Suddenly we don't know exactly what the latest comers mean to our community or our identity, how they fit. Thus are we led to question our identity. After a generation or two, the grandchildren or the great-grandchildren of immigrants to the United States will romanticize the immigrant, will see the immigrant as precisely the meaning of America, to see the immigrant—who comes and remakes herself in this new land—as the figure who teaches us most about what it means to be an American. The immigrant, in mythic terms, travels from the outermost rind of America to the very center of the country's mythology. None of this, of course, do we say to the Vietnamese immigrant who serves us our breakfast at the hotel. In another forty years, we will be prepared to say of the Vietnamese immigrant, that he, with his breakfast tray, with his intuition for travel, he alone realizes the meaning of America.

In 1997 the Gallup Poll conducted a survey on race relations in America. The pollster found that race relations in America strained as respondents ascended an economic ladder. For example, college-educated blacks were pessimistic about interracial relationships. But the poll was only concerned with white and black Americans. No question was asked of the Vietnamese man who served me breakfast today in the hotel. There was certainly no reference to the Chinese grocer at the corner. There was

"The North American," Richard Rodriguez, *Public Discourse in America: Conversation and Community in the 21st Century,* Judith Rodin & Stephan Steinberg, editors, Philadelphia, PA: University of Pennsylvania Press, 2003, pp. 60-70. Reprinted with permission of the University of Pennsylvania Press.

no reference to the Guatemalans in San Francisco or to the Salvadorans who re-roofed my Victorian house. None at all. That is because the American conversation about race has always been an abstract in white and black. What I represent, in my public life, is a kind of rude intrusion into the black-and-white conversation. Though I was born in San Francisco, I assume the outsider's task of unsettling the United States of America. I have listened to the black-and-white conversation for most of my life and it had nothing to do with me. I was supposed to attach myself to one side or the other, without asking the obvious questions: What is this white-and-black dialectic? Why does it admit so little reference to anyone else?

Brown does not represent a third race, but rather some blurring of racial distinction. I am speaking to you in American English that was taught me by Irish nuns, immigrant women, in California. I wear an Indian face; I answer to a Spanish surname as well as this California first name, Richard. You might wonder about the complexity of historical factors, the collision of centuries, that creates Richard Rodriguez. My brownness is the illustration of that collision, or the bland memorial of it. I stand before you as an impure-American. An ambiguous-American. I address you from the pride of my impurity. In the nineteenth century, Texans used to say that the reason that Mexicans were so easily defeated in battle was because we were so dilute, being neither pure Indian nor pure Spaniard. In the nineteenth century, Mexicans used to say that Mexico, the country of my ancestry, joined two worlds. José Vasconcelos, the Mexican educator and philosopher, famously described Mexicans as *la raza cosmica,* the cosmic race. In Mexico what one finds as early as the eighteenth century is a predominant population of mixed-race people. The *mestizo* predominated over the pure European and the pure Indian. Also, once the slave had been freed in Mexico, the intermarriage rate between the Indian and the African in Mexico was greater than in any other country in the Americas and has not been equaled since.

Race mixture has not been a point of pride in the United States. Americans speak more easily about diversity than we do about the fact that I might marry your daughter; you might become we; we might eat the same food. We settle more easily on the Canadian notion of diversity because it preserves the notion that we are separate, that our elbows do not have to touch, much less merge; that I need not become you, that I can remain Mexican, whatever that means, in the United States of America. I would argue that instead of adopting the Canadian model of multiculturalism, the United States might begin to imagine the Mexican alternative of a *mestizaje* society, and move away from the multicultural safety that Canada offers, and all fear of swallowing, of being swallowed.

I was born in Mexico, therefore—though I wasn't. I was born in San Francisco to Mexican immigrant parents. But I was reinvented in 1973 by Richard Nixon. Nixon had instructed the Office of Management and Budget to determine the major racial and ethnic groups in this country. (Can you imagine the bureaucratic deliberation over the phone books of America?) The Office of Management and Budget came up with five major ethnic or racial groups. The groups are, in no order of preference, white, black, Asian/Pacific Islander, American Indian, and Hispanic.

I call myself Hispanic.

The interesting thing about Hispanics is that you will never meet us in Latin America. You may meet Chileans and Peruvians and Mexicans. You will not meet Hispanics. If you inquire in Lima or Bogotá about Hispanics, you will be referred to Dallas. For "Hispanic" is a gringo contrivance, a definition of the world that suggests that I have more in common with Argentine Italians than I have with American Indians; that there is an ineffable union between the white Cuban and the mulatto Puerto Rican. Nixon's conclusion has become the basis for the way we now organize and understand our society. As a Hispanic, I will say with some irony that a recent statistic from the Census Bureau interests me very much. The Census Bureau tells us that by the year 2003 Hispanics will outnumber blacks to become the largest minority in the United States. While I admit a competition exists in America between Hispanic and black, I insist that the comparison of Hispanics to blacks will lead, ultimately, to complete nonsense. For there is no such thing as a Hispanic race. There is no Hispanic race in the world. In Latin America, you see every race of the world. You see white Hispanics, you see black Hispanics, you see brown Hispanics who are Indians, many of whom do not speak Spanish because they resisted. You see Asian Hispanics. To compare blacks and Hispanics, therefore, is to construct a fallacious equation.

Some Hispanics have accepted the fiction. Some Hispanics have too easily accustomed themselves to impersonating a third race, a great new third race in America. But Hispanic is an ethnic term. It is a term denoting culture. So when the Census Bureau says by the year 2060 one-third of all Americans will identify themselves as Hispanic, the Census Bureau is not speculating in pigment, but rather is predicting how by the year 2060 one-third of all Americans will identify themselves culturally. The black Dominican today who identifies himself as Hispanic is identifying himself in terms of culture rather than by race, and that is revolutionary. For a country that traditionally has taken its understandings of community from blood and color, to have so large a group of Americans identify themselves by virtue of language or fashion or cuisine or literature is an extraordinary change, and a revolutionary one.

Is there, in fact, a Hispanic culture? Henry Cisneros, the ex-mayor of San Antonio, gathered together a group of Hispanic politicians in the mid-1990s to try to determine whether there was a Hispanic political agenda, for, indeed, there is a Hispanic caucus in Washington modeled on the African American caucus in Washington. After two weeks the group that Henry Cisneros convened could not come up with an agenda. There is no Hispanic politics. What unites the eighth-generation New Mexican, who considers himself a Spaniard, with the white Republican Cuban with the black Puerto-Rican with the Guatemalan Indian who arrived in San Diego yesterday with the Mexican American gang kids who speak Spanglish in East L.A.? What singular culture is there in this diverse company?

Some Hispanics speak Spanish. Some do not. Some are Catholic. Many are becoming Evangelical Protestants. Some are white. Some are brown. Some are black. The more I think about it, the more I think there are only two considerations common to Hispanics. First, this business of impurity, that we are making America an impure place. The second thing that unites Hispanics is that we (those of us who are not of Europe) look south when we consider the past. That is our revolutionary gift to America, the cultural inheritance that we bring to this country. Hispanics are changing the contour of the United States because we are north-south people. The United States has traditionally written its history east to west, has begun its history at Plymouth Rock and has ended up at Venice Beach, a country that has always understood itself in one direction only. Suddenly, there are millions of Americans who see themselves along a north-south trajectory. That is a revolutionary regard.

After the North American Free Trade Agreement (NAFTA) was signed by the presidents of Mexico and the United States and the prime minister of Canada, the *New York Times* called me to ask if I would write something on NAFTA. I said I couldn't write anything on NAFTA, because I've never met a North American. But then I thought, actually, I do know one North American. He is a Mexican from the state of Oaxaca in southern Mexico. He impersonates an Italian chef in a restaurant in the Napa Valley for about nine months of the year. He is trilingual. He is a Mixteco Indian. His first language belongs to that tribe. His second language is Spanish, the language of his Colonial oppressors. His third language is a working knowledge of English, because, after all, he works here. He deals with two currencies, two codes of justice, two views of the human condition.

The North American knows thousands of miles of dirt roads and freeways. He knows where to hide in the United States, because he is, after all, illegal when he crosses the dangerous border. On the Mexican side, he knows how to hide from the Mexican federal police who are always trying to steal his money. He wires his money home by Western Union, he puts the rest in his shoes. In Mexico, he lives in a sixteenth-century village where the Virgen de Guadalupe floats over his wife's bed. In Napa Valley, too, he hears Madonna, "the material girl." He is the first North American. He sees this hemisphere whole. He is a peasant from Latin America. At the Harvard Business School, meanwhile, there is much talk about this new North American, this transborder reality. Harvard conceives the pan-American as a new idea, patented by MBAs, but the peasant has known the idea all his life.

There is a quarrel going on in California about mythology: Which myth applies? What does California mean? What is California? For a long time the United States labored under the impression that California was the Far West. "Go west, young man." Go west, young man, and change the color of your hair and go to Gold's Gym, get a new body, lose weight, become a movie star, Botox your name, become Rock Hudson. But, as early as the 1860s, California was finitude. We had come to the end of the road in California to discover that America was a finite idea. I think the innovation in California results from that idea of finitude—land's end. Americans have been trained by their maps to believe that everything will be OK if we move west. But having arrived at the end, what do we do? We look to the sky. It is no coincidence that so much technological innovation is happening along the strip of land that stretches from North County, San Diego, all the way to Redmond, Washington. Why there? Why are people entering cyberspace with such frenzy at the western portal? Because restlessness continues and because the land has come to an end. But has it? Today—in about an hour from now—a procession of planes will land at LAX from Asia. The flights originate in Asia. We are sort of glad to see Asians, but we don't have any more room in California. We've come to the end of things in California. But the Asian says, "Well, you know, I've always thought this was where America begins. I thought this was where the continent begins." What would the history of America look like if it were written in reverse, from west to east? Have we even imagined such a history?

People in Mexico go to el Norte not because they want to find a new future; they go to el Norte because they want a dreary job working at a dry cleaner's in L.A. They work to sustain the past. People climb to el Norte without experiencing the same sense of disconnection from the past that the Western traveler felt. If one travels east to west, one follows the light of day; one leaves the past behind. If one travels north and south, one begins to resemble a monarch butterfly or a whale. One moves with seasons. Laborers who worked six months of the year in the North and returned south every year infuriated Americans, because Americans didn't understand what that north-south journey might mean. Americans could only imagine disruption. Discontinuity. A new day, But now Americans are becoming north-south people. There are grandmothers in Minnesota who live not by some east-west calendar, but by a north-south calendar. They spend summer in Minneapolis and winter in Florida. All over the country I meet teenagers who are not traveling between coasts, as we used to imagine youth's journey in America, but between hot and cold, between desert and tundra—the new extremities of the country, the new way the country exists in the American imagination.

To my mind, nothing else Bill Clinton accomplished compares to NAFTA. The notion given to the United States by this trade agreement is that the United States is related to Canada, is related to Mexico. Northern Mexico looks like San Diego these days. Northern Mexico is filled with Gold's Gyms and Hard Rock Cafes, shopping centers. Everybody wants to be an American in northern Mexico. And South Texas is becoming very Mexican. That circumstance surprises Americans because our notion of community never extended beyond our borders and certainly never extended south. Look at the map now—the Hispanic map of the United States of America—and one of the weirdest things you will notice is the reconquest of the Spanish Empire. Florida, Colorado, New Mexico, Arizona, Texas, California, and Nevada are Hispanic—just as they were in the early eighteenth century.

I know there are concerns about diminished civility and social fragmentation in the United States, and especially in a city like Los Angeles. But there are uses of incivility, too. The formation of a society does not happen easily. It does not happen when all of us feel good about each other, and it does not happen because we all like each other. Coca-Cola commissioned a commercial to run at Christmas time wherein a Utopian population, in various ethnic costumes, in mutual respect and good will, sing a hymn to Coca-Cola. All of us in America have been encouraged thus to believe in a relative and banal multiculturalism. But the real working out of inevitability more often happens at some Frontage Road franchise where the red-headed waitress has to communicate with the Mexican fry-cook, and she doesn't have all the right words, and neither does he. And so their cooperation—entirely pragmatic—ends up sounding like this: "Dos huevos, over easy, side of salchiche!"

In 1992, Los Angeles endured one of the great urban riots of American history, a terrible event that began as a black-and-white altercation, but within hours drew Korean shopkeepers, then Salvadoran women who wrestled with Mexican women outside Kmart for looted boxes of Pampers. You cannot have a black-and-white riot in a multiracial city. The most interesting thing about that riot was the way the city got formed from the terror of those days and nights. On the West Side of the city, that first Thursday, one saw neighborhoods on television that one had never visited. L.A. was famous, after all, as the city of separate suburbs, and separate freeway exits. The interesting thing was the way those distant neighborhoods drew closer and closer and closer together. By about four A.M., people on the West Side began to hear fire sirens, began to smell smoke. For the first time, Los Angeles realized it was one city. This realization did not come from good feeling. It came from terror. People resorted to their closets for guns. People came to realize the street they live on is, in fact, connected to every other street.

Sometimes I stand on the line between San Diego and Tijuana, and I talk to the kids who are beginning their American lives. I do not talk to them about Benjamin Franklin or Tom Paine. They've never heard of the Bill of Rights. They are coming, they say—many of them illegally—because there is a job in Glendale waiting for them or there is a grower near Tracy who needs them to pick peaches. That's it. They are not coming for welfare. They are not coming for famous freedoms. There is no politician who will tell the truth about these young men and women. The truth is that we cannot stop them from coming. The fact is there is a 2,000-mile border that cannot be defended. Americans continue to worry about illegal immigration. But the poor cannot be stopped. The poor, worldwide, are mobile. We of the middle class do not know how to stop them, how to keep them out of our society, and the truth is that we don't want to keep them out of our society. These Mexican kids know that. They know we will hire them to sit patiently with our dying mother. They know we will hire them to spade the moats around our rose bushes. They know we will hire them. In Mexico, in the realm of the public, the politician will say one thing and everyone will assume the opposite to be true. The Mexican judge says, "five years"; the family of the defendant calculates one year or despair. The price of the jar of baby food says 50 pesos and it might be 50 pesos or it might be 10. Nothing is what it seems in the public realm. Mexicans transfer this knowledge to America. They know that public utterance of prohibition means one thing and private welcome means another. There is work in San Diego if you can make it across.

In the 1970s, people began to believe that L.A. might not be a West Coast city with palm trees and beachfront, but might, in fact, be a northern desert city with Indians, sand, sirocco. The moment the mythology of that city began to change from blond to brown—Los Angelinos began to make the best of inevitability. They began to bring cactus into the house. They took the curtains off the windows and extolled the beauty of desert light. By adopting a desert aesthetic, Los Angeles attempted to transform something fearful; to make beautiful something that was fearful. Fear is not always met with withdrawal; sometimes fear is met by a kind of seduction. One solution to the fear of the advent of a brown population is to cast the brown man or woman in a soap opera; to call him the newest, sexiest; to fall in love with her. We lock up black males at a disproportionate rate because we are afraid of black males and we don't know what to do with black males—that's why we dance to black music. We end up marrying Chinese women. We also don't know what to do with empowered Western women who are more like black males than they are like Chinese women. In the great ancient societies, France would marry England—the king would pawn his daughter to England—as a way of making England part of the family. We are giving each other our daughters. We are marrying each other as much out of fear as of yearning.

People ask me all the time, "Do you envision another Quebec forming in this country from all of this immigrant movement? Do you see a Quebec forming in the Southwest, for example?" No, I don't see that at all. I do see something different happening with the immigrant population, which is as much as ten years younger than the U.S. national population, and which is more fertile than the U.S. national population. I see the movement of the immigrant as the movement of youth into a country that is growing middle-aged. Immigrants are the archetypal Americans at a time when we—U.S. citizens—have become post-Americans.

Once more along the border: I met three boys from a group called Victory Outreach, an evangelical Protestant group that works with young people who have serious drug or gang problems. Here they were (five hundred years after Columbus), here were these three Indians who told me that they were coming to the United States of America to convert the United States of America to Protestantism. This doesn't sound like Quebec. This sounded like immigrants are bringing America to America—a gift.

I was at a small Apostolic Assembly in East Palo Alto a few years ago, a mainly Spanish-speaking congregation, along the freeway, near the heart of the Silicon Valley. This is the other side. It used to be black East Palo Alto. It's quickly becoming Asian and Hispanic Palo Alto—the same story. There was a moment in the service when newcomers to the congregation were introduced to the entire group. They brought letters of introduction from sister churches in Latin America. The minister read the various letters and announced the names and places of origin to the community. Everyone applauded. And I thought to myself: It's over. The border is over. These people were not being asked whether they had a green card. They were not being asked whether they're legally here or illegally here. They were being welcomed within this community for reasons of culture. There is now a north-south line that is theological, and it cannot be circumvented by the U.S. Border Patrol.

The deepest fear Americans conceive of the South right now is not of the separateness of the South, but that people of the South will replace us, that they want us, that they want to be us, that they want our food, that they want our culture, that we will be swallowed. One Monday, a few years ago, *Monday Night Football* originated from Monterrey, Mexico—a northern Mexican metropolis with all the charm of Pittsburgh in the 1930s. The pre-game show began with a serenade by a group of *mariachis,* singing in Spanish. What the *mariachis* sang was this: The Dallas Cowboys are our team. They are Mexico's team. And I thought, does anybody at ABC News know about this? Do any of us realize that the Dallas Cowboys are about to be devoured?

Americans continue to believe that Canadian multiculturalism is going to make everything come out all right. Multiculturalism is not going to make everything come out all right. You—here I address America—you are going to end up with Mexican grandchildren.

I was on a BBC interview show, and a woman introduced me as being "in favor" of assimilation. I am not in favor of assimilation any more than I am in favor of the Pacific Ocean. If I had a bumper sticker, it would read something like ASSIMILA-TION HAPPENS. One doesn't get up in the morning, as an immigrant child in America, and think to oneself, "How much of an American will I become today?" One doesn't walk down the street and decide to be 40 percent Mexican and 60 percent American. Culture is fluid. Culture is smoke in the air. You breathe it. You eat it. You notice culture or you don't. Elvis Presley goes in your ear and you cannot get Elvis Presley out of your mind. He's in there. I'm in favor of assimilation. I'm not in favor of assimilation. I recognize that it exists. L.A. has become Mexican, which is what it always was. L.A., this monstrous city that we identify now as the immigrant capital of America, has three times the miscegenation rate of the American average. I was in Merced, California, a few years ago, which is a town of about 75,000 people in the Central Valley of California. Merced's two largest immigrant groups now are Laotian Hmong and Mexicans. The Laotians have never in the history of the world, as far as I know, lived next to the Mexicans. But there they are in Merced, and they are living next to the Mexicans. They don't like each other. I was talking to the Laotian kids about why they don't like the Mexican kids. They were telling me this and that—the Mexicans do this and the Mexicans don't do that—when I suddenly realized these Laotian kids were speaking English with a Spanish accent.

I remember when once Bill Moyers asked me how I thought of myself, as an American or Hispanic. I said, "I'm Chinese." And that's because I live in a Chinese city and that's because I want to be Chinese. Well, why not?

Yes, I think it's a celebration of utopianism. I do think distinctions exist. I'm not talking about an America tomorrow in which we're going to find black and white no longer the distinguishing marks of separateness. But for many, many young people that I meet, it sounds almost Victorian to talk about their identity that way. They don't think of themselves in those terms. And they're already moving into a world in which skin or tattoo or ornament or movement or commune or sexuality or drug are the organizing principles of their identity. And the notion that they are white or black simply doesn't apply to them. And increasingly, of course, you meet children who really don't know how to say what they are anymore. They simply are too many things. We're in such a world, in such an America, already. What will we say—that we still live in a black and white America? I mean, what do we say to Tiger Woods, who insisted he's not African, because that would deny his mother's existence? I met a young girl in San Diego the other day at a convention of mixed race children, among whom the common habit is to define one parent over the other. In most white and black marriages, the habit is to define black over white. But this girl said that her mother was Mexican and her father was African. I said, "What are you?" She said,

"Black-xican." And I think to myself, "You know, the vocabulary that the Spanish empire has, the recognition of multiplicity of possibilities, we do not have in this society—we do not have words to describe who we are anymore. And I tell you, if we rely on the old vocabulary, we are doomed because no one is using it anymore. They're inventing their own words."

So, what myth do we tell ourselves? You know, I think the person who got closest to it was Karl Marx. Marx predicted that the discovery of gold in California would be a more central event to the Americas than the discovery of the Americas by Columbus. He goes on to write that the discovery of the Americas by Columbus was only the meeting of two tribes, essentially, the European and the Indian. But he said, "You know, when gold was discovered in California in the 1840s, the entire world met." For the first time in human history, all of the known world gathered. The Malaysian was in the gold fields alongside the African, alongside the Chinese, alongside the Australian, alongside the American pioneer, etc., etc., etc.

For the first time—and with calamitous results—the whole world was seeking gold in the same place at the same time, and they were at each other's throats. People were murdered and so forth. But that was an event without parallel, and it is, I think, the beginning of modern California and why California, today, really is our mythology. It provides the mythological structure for understanding how we might talk about the American experience as not being biracial, but the experience of the recreation of the known world in the New World.

Sometimes the truly revolutionary things that are going on in this society are happening almost regardless and almost without anybody being aware of them. We are going to wake up one day, and it's all going to be changed, and we're going to say, "When did it all change? Why didn't the *New York Times* tell us it was going to happen? Where was Maureen Dowd when we needed her?" She was going on about Bill Clinton's sex life.

There is no black race. There is no white race either. There are mythologies, and I'm in the business—insofar as I'm in any business at all—of demythologizing these identities, and suggesting their complexity and the dynamism of individuals to meet and learn and fall in love with people different from themselves.

So I come to you as a man of many cultures. I come to you as a Chinese, and unless you understand that I am Chinese, then you've not understood anything I've said.

More Equal Than Others
From a photo essay by Jan van Ijken, text by *Mother Jones*
Reprinted in *Mother Jones,* November/December, 2006
http://www.motherjones.com/photoessays/2006/10/more-equal-others

The photo essay "More Equal Than Others" is introduced with these words: "Dutch Photographer Jan van Ijken spent the past several years watching humans interact with animals in a range of settings—from research labs and factory farms to exotic bird shows. The result is a series of remarkable images documenting the shifting and ambivalent ways we value other creatures."

The particular image above is the twelfth in the essay. Its caption reads, "Poultry plant workers examine chicks for defects. (This one passed.)"

The Braindead Megaphone

George Saunders

1.

I find myself thinking of a guy standing in a field in the year 1200 doing whatever it is people in 1200 did while standing in fields. I'm thinking about his mind, wondering what's in it. What's he talking about in that tape-loop in his head? Who's he arguing with? From whom is he defending himself, to whom is he rationalizing his actions?

I'm wondering, in other words, if his mental experience of life is different in any essential way from mine.

What I have in common with this guy, I suspect, is that a lot of our mental dialogue is with people we know: our parents, wives, kids, neighbors.

Where I suspect we part ways is in the number and nature of the conversations we have with people we've never met.

He probably does some talking to his gods, his ancestors, mythological beings, historical figures. So do I. But there is a category of people I mentally converse with that he does not: people from far away, who've arrived in the mind, with various agendas, via high-tech sources.

I suspect that you also have these people in your mind; in fact, as you read this (sorry, sorry) I am become one of them.

Is this difference between us and Mr. or Ms. 1200 a good thing or a bad thing? I'm not sure. For now, let's just acknowledge it as a *difference;* a change in what human beings are asking their minds to do on a daily basis.

2.

Imagine a party. The guests, from all walks of life, are not negligible. They've been around: they've lived, suffered, own businesses, have real areas of expertise. They're talking about things that interest them, giving and taking subtle correction. Certain submerged concerns are coming to the surface and—surprise, pleasant surprise—being confirmed and seconded and assuaged by other people who've been feeling the same way.

Then a guy walks in with a megaphone. He's not the smartest person at the party, or the most experienced, or the most articulate.

But he's got that megaphone.

Say he starts talking about how much he loves early mornings in spring. What happens? Well, people turn to listen. It would be hard not to. It's only polite. And soon, in their small groups, the guests may find themselves talking about early spring mornings. Or, more correctly, about the validity of Megaphone Guy's ideas about early spring mornings. Some are agreeing with him, some disagreeing—but because he's so loud, their conversations will begin to react to what he's saying. As he changes topics, so do they. If he continually uses the phrase "at the end of the day," they start using it too. If he weaves into his arguments the assumption that the west side of the room is preferable to the east, a slow westward drift will begin.

These responses are predicated not on his intelligence, his unique experience of the world, his powers of contemplation, or his ability with language, but on the volume and omnipresence of his narrating voice.

His main characteristic is his *dominance.* He crowds the other voices out. His rhetoric becomes the central rhetoric because of its unavoidability.

In time, Megaphone Guy will ruin the party. The guests will stop believing in their value as guests, and come to see their main role as reactors-to-the-Guy. They'll stop doing what guests are supposed to do: keep the conversation going per their own interests and concerns. They'll become passive, stop believing in the validity of their own impressions. They may not even notice they've started speaking in his diction, that their thoughts are being limned by his. What's important to him will come to seem important to them.

We've said Megaphone Guy isn't the smartest, or most articulate, or most experienced person at the party—but what if the situation is even worse than this?

Let's say he hasn't carefully considered the things he's saying. He's basically just blurting things out. And even with the megaphone, he has to shout a little to be heard, which limits the complexity of what he can say. Because he feels he has to be entertaining, he jumps from topic to topic, favoring the conceptual-general ("We're eating more cheese cubes—and loving it!"), the anxiety- or controversy-provoking ("Wine running out due to shadowy conspiracy?"), the gossipy ("Quickie rumored in south bathroom!"), and the trivial ("Which quadrant of the party room do YOU prefer?").

We consider speech to be the result of thought (we have a thought, then select a sentence with which to express it), but thought also results from speech (as we grope, in words, toward meaning, we discover what we think). This yammering guy has, by forcibly putting his restricted language into the heads of the guests, affected the quality and coloration of the thoughts going on in there.

He has, in effect, put an intelligence-ceiling on the party.

3.

A man sits in a room. Someone begins shouting through his window, informing him of conditions in the house next door. Our man's mind inflects: that is, he begins imagining that house. What are the factors that might affect the quality of his imagining? That is, what factors affect his ability to imagine the next-door house as it actually *is?*

1. The clarity of the language being used by the Informant (the less muddled, inarticulate, or jargon-filled, the better);
2. The agenda of the Informant (*no agenda* preferable to *agenda-rich*);
3. The time and care the Informant has spent constructing his narrative (i.e., the extent to which his account was revised and improved before being transmitted, with *more* time and care preferable to *less*);
4. The time allowed for the communication (with *more* time preferable to *less,* on the assumption that more time grants the Informant a better opportunity to explain, explore, clarify, etc.).

So the best-case scenario for acquiring a truthful picture of that house next door might go something like this: Information arrives in the form of prose written and revised over a long period of time, in the interest of finding the truth, by a disinterested person with real-world experience in the subject area. The report can be as long, dense, nuanced, and complex as is necessary to portray the complexity of the situation.

The worst-case scenario might be: Information arrives in the form of prose written by a person with little or no firsthand experience in the subject area, who hasn't had much time to revise what he's written, working within narrow time constraints, in the service of an agenda that may be subtly or overtly distorting his ability to tell the truth.

Could we make this worst-case scenario even worse? Sure. Let it be understood that the Informant's main job is to entertain and that, if he fails in this, he's gone. Also, the man being informed? Make him too busy, ill-prepared, and distracted to properly assess what the Informant's shouting at him.

Then propose invading the house next door.

Welcome to America, circa 2003.

4.

To my way of thinking, something latent in our news media became overt and catastrophic around the time of the O. J. Simpson trial. Because the premise of the crime's national importance was obviously false, it had to be bolstered. A new style of presentation had to be invented. To wring thousands of hours of coverage from what could have been summarized in a couple of minutes every few weeks, a new rhetorical strategy was developed, or—let's be generous—evolved.

If someone has to lecture ten hours a day on a piece of dog crap in a bowl, adjustments will need to be made. To say the ridiculous things that will need to be said to sustain the illusion that the dog-crap story is serious news ("Dog-crap expert Jesse Toville provides his assessment of the probable size of the dog and its psychological state at time-of-crappage!"), distortions of voice, face, and format will be required.

This erosion continued through the Monica Lewinsky scandal ("More at five about The Stain! Have you ever caused a Stain? Which color do you think would most effectively hide a Stain? See what our experts predicted you would say!"), and dozens of lesser (?) cases and scandals, all morbid, sensational, and blown out of proportion, often involving minor celebrities—and then came 9/11.

By this time our national discourse had been so degraded—our national language so dumbed-down—that we were sitting ducks. In that hour of fear and need, finding in our hands the set of crude, hyperbolic tools we'd been using to discuss O.J., et al., we began using them to decide whether to invade another country, and soon were in Bagdhad, led by Megaphone Guy, via "Countdown to Slapdown in the Desert!" and "Twilight for the Evil One: America Comes Calling!" Megaphone Guy, it seemed, had gone a little braindead. Or part of him had. What had gone dead was the curious part that should have been helping us *decide* about the morality and intelligence of invasion, that should have known that the war being discussed was a real war, that might actually happen, to real, currently living people. Where was our sense of agonized wondering, of real doubt? We got (to my memory) a lot of discussion of tactics (which route, which vehicles) and strategy (how would it "play on the Arab street") but not much about the essential morality of invasion. (We did not hear, for example, "Well, Ted, as Gandhi once said, 'What difference does it make to the dead, the orphans, and the homeless, whether the mad destruction is wrought under the name of totalitarianism or the holy name of liberty or democracy?'")

Am I oversimplifying here? Yes. Is all our media stupid? Far from it. Were intelligent, valuable things written about the rush to war (and about O.J. and Monica, and then Laci Peterson and Michael Jackson, et al.)? Of course.

But: Is some of our media very stupid? Hoo boy. Does stupid, near-omnipresent media make us more tolerant toward stupidity in general? It would be surprising if it didn't.

Is human nature such that, under certain conditions, stupidity can come to dominate, infecting the brighter quadrants, dragging everybody down with it?

5.

Last night on the local news I watched a young reporter standing in front of our mall, obviously freezing his ass off. The essence of his report was, Malls Tend to Get Busier at Christmas! Then he reported the local implications of his investigation: (1) This Also True at Our Mall! (2) When Our Mall More Busy, More Cars Present in Parking Lot! (3) The More Cars, the Longer It Takes Shoppers to Park! and (shockingly): (4) Yet People Still Are Shopping, Due to, It Is Christmas!

It sounded like information, basically. He signed off crisply, nobody back at NewsCenter8 or wherever laughed at him. And across our fair city, people sat there and took it, and I believe that, generally, they weren't laughing at him either. They, like us in our house, were used to it, and consented to the idea that some Informing had just occurred. Although what we had been told, we already knew, although it had been told in banal language, revved up with that strange TV-news emphasis ("cold WEATHer leads SOME motorISTS to drive less, CARrie!"), we took it, and, I would say, it did something to us: made us dumber and more accepting of slop.

Furthermore, I suspect, it subtly degraded our ability to make bold, meaningful sentences, or laugh at stupid, ill-considered ones. The next time we felt tempted to say something like, "Wow, at Christmas the malls sure do get busier due to more people shop at Christmas because at Christmas so many people go out to buy things at malls due to Christmas being a holiday on which gifts are given by some to others"— we might actually say it, this sentiment having been elevated by our having seen it all dressed-up on television, in its fancy faux-Informational clothing.

And next time we hear someone saying something like, "We are pursuing this strategy because other strategies, when we had considered them, we concluded that, in terms of overall effectiveness, they were not sound strategies, which is why we enacted the one we are now embarked upon, which our enemies would like to see us fail, due to they hate freedom," we will wait to see if the anchorperson cracks up, or chokes back a sob of disgust, and if he or she does not, we'll feel a bit insane, and therefore less confident, and therefore more passive.

There is, in other words, a cost to dopey communication, even if that dopey communication is innocently intended.

And the cost of dopey communication is directly proportional to the omnipresence of the message.

6.

In the beginning, there's a blank mind. Then that mind gets an idea in it, and the trouble begins, because the mind mistakes the idea for the world. Mistaking the idea for the world, the mind formulates a theory and, having formulated a theory, feels inclined to act.

Because the idea is always only an approximation of the world, whether that action will be catastrophic or beneficial depends on the distance between the idea and the world.

Mass media's job is to provide this simulacra of the world, upon which we build our ideas. There's another name for this simulacra-building: storytelling.

Megaphone Guy is a storyteller, but his stories are not so good. Or rather, his stories are limited. His stories have not had time to gestate—they go out too fast and to too broad an audience. Storytelling is a language-rich enterprise, but Megaphone Guy does not have time to generate powerful language. The best stories proceed from a mysterious truth-seeking impulse that narrative has when revised extensively; they are complex and baffling and ambiguous; they tend to make us slower to act, rather than quicker. They make us more humble, cause us to empathize with people we don't know, because they help us imagine these people, and when we imagine them—if the storytelling is good enough—we imagine them as being, essentially, like us. If the story is poor, or has an agenda, if it comes out of a paucity of imagination or is rushed, we imagine those other people as essentially unlike us: unknowable, inscrutable, inconvertible.

Our venture in Iraq was a literary failure, by which I mean a failure of imagination. A culture better at imagining richly, three-dimensionally, would have had a greater respect for war than we did, more awareness of the law of unintended consequences, more familiarity with the world's tendency to throw aggressive energy back at the aggressor in ways he did not expect. A culture capable of imagining complexly is a humble culture. It acts, when it has to act, as late in the game as possible, and as cautiously, because it knows its own girth and the tight confines of the china shop it's blundering into. And it knows that no matter how well-prepared it is—no matter how ruthlessly it has held its projections up to intelligent scrutiny—the place it is headed for is going to be very different from the place it imagined. The shortfall between the imagined and the real, multiplied by the violence of one's intent, equals the evil one will do.

7.

So how did we get here? I think it went something like this: Elements on the right (Fox News, Rush Limbaugh, etc.) resuscitated an old American streak of simplistic, jingoistic, fear-based rhetoric that, in that post-9/11 climate of fear, infected, to a greater or lesser extent, the rest of the media. Remember Bill O'Reilly interrupting/chastising/misrepresenting Jeremy Glick, whose father died on 9/11, finally telling Glick to shut up, cutting off his microphone? And a few months later, Diane Sawyer's strange Mother Confessor interview/interrogation of the Dixie Chicks?

Ah, those were the days.

But also, those *are* the days, and the days yet to come. The basic illness in our media is not cured; it's only that our fear has subsided somewhat. When the next attack comes, the subsequent swing to the Stalinesque will be even more extreme, having, as it will, the additional oomph of retrospective repentance of what will then be perceived as a period (i.e., *now*) of relapse to softness and terror-encouraging open discourse.

Have we gone entirely to hell? No: the media, like life, is complex and stratified, filled with heroes holding the line. (All hail Bill Moyers; all hail Soledad O'Brien, post-Katrina, losing her temper with FEMA Director Michael Brown.) But if we define the Megaphone as *the composite of the hundreds of voices we hear each day that come to us from people we don't know, via high-tech sources,* it's clear that a significant and ascendant component of that voice has become bottom-dwelling, shrill, incurious, ranting, and agenda-driven. It strives to antagonize us, make us feel anxious, ineffective, and alone; convince us that the world is full of enemies and of people stupider and less agreeable than ourselves; is dedicated to the idea that, outside the sphere of our immediate experience, the world works in a different, more hostile, less knowable manner. This braindead tendency is viral and manifests intermittently; while it is the blood in the veins of some of our media figures, it flickers on and off in others. It frequently sheds its political skin for a stroll through Entertainment Park, where it leers and smirks and celebrates when someone is brought low by, say, an absence of underwear or a drunken evening.

But why should this tendency be ascendant? Fear, yes, fear is part of it. In a time of danger, the person sounding the paranoid continual alarm will eventually be right. A voice arguing for our complete rightness and the complete wrongness of our enemies, a voice constantly broadening the definition of "enemy," relieves us of the burden of living with ambiguity. The sensibility that generates a phrase like "unfortunate but necessary collateral damage" can, in the heat of the moment, feel like a kind of dark, necessary pragmatism.

But more than fear, our new braindeadedness has to do, I think, with commerce: the shift that has taken place within our major news organizations toward the corporate model, and away from the public-interest model. The necessity of profit is now assumed for our mass-media activities. This assumption has been shorn of all moral baggage: it is just something sophisticated people concede, so that other, more vital, discussions of "content" can begin.

Now, why aggressive, anxiety-provoking, maudlin, polarizing discourse should prove more profitable than its opposite is a mystery. Maybe it's a simple matter of drama: ranting, innuendo, wallowing in the squalid, the exasperation of the already-convinced, may, at some crude level, just be *more interesting* than some intelligent, skeptical human being trying to come to grips with complexity, especially given the way we use our media: as a time-killer in the airport, a sedative or stimulant at the end of a long day.

In any event, the people who used to ask, "Is it news?" now seem to be asking, "Will it stimulate?" And the change is felt, high and low, throughout the culture.

Imagine a village. A nearby village, having grown a surplus of a certain vegetable that, when eaten, turns the skin red, cuts our village a deal on this vegetable. Within a few months, the average color of the people in our village will have moved toward the Red end of the spectrum. Within that general trend will be all sorts of variations and exceptions: this guy eats as much as he likes of that vegetable but just goes a little Pink; this woman, who can't stand the taste of it, and never eats it, stays the same color as always. But in general, because of the omnipresence of that vegetable, the village is going to become Redder, and at the far end of the Gaussian curve folks will start looking downright demonic.

What, in this model, is the "vegetable"? What is "Red"?

The vegetable that has come to dominate our village is the profit motive.

"Red" is the resulting coarseness of our public rhetoric.

Now, profit is fine; economic viability is wonderful. But if these trump every other consideration, we will be rendered perma-children, having denied ourselves use of our higher faculties. With every grave-faced discussion of the disposition of the fetus within the body of its murdered mother, every interview with someone who knew the lawyer of an alleged close friend of some new Anna Nicole Smith, we become more clownish and bloated, and thereby more vulnerable.

In surrendering our mass storytelling function to entities whose first priority is profit, we make a dangerous concession: "Tell us," we say in effect, "as much truth as you can, *while still making money.*" This is not the same as asking: "Tell us the truth."

A culture's ability to understand the world and itself is critical to its survival. But today we are led into the arena of public debate by seers whose main gift is their ability to compel people to continue to watch them.

8.

The generalizing writer is like the passionate drunk, stumbling into your house mumbling: *I know I'm not being clear, exactly, but don't you kind of feel what I'm feeling?* If, generously overlooking my generalizations, your gut agrees with my gut in feeling that the nightly news may soon consist entirely of tirades by men so angry and inarticulate that all they do is sputter while punching themselves in the face, punctuated by videos of dogs blowing up after eating firecrackers, and dog-explosion experts rating the funniness of the videos—if you accept my basic premise that media is getting meaner and dumber—we might well ask, together: Who's running this mess? Who's making Sean Hannity's graphics? Who's booking the flights of that endless stream of reporters standing on the beach in the Bahamas, gravely speculating about the contents of a dead woman's stomach?

Well, that would be us. Who runs the media? Who *is* the media? The best and brightest among us—the most literate and ambitious and gifted, who go out from their homes and off to the best colleges, and from there to the best internships, and from there to offices throughout the nation, to inform us. They take the jobs they take, I suspect, without much consideration of the politics of their employer. What matters is the level of Heaven that employer occupies. The national is closer to God than the local; the large market looks down upon the small; the lately ratings-blessed floats slowly up, impressing the angels whose upward movement has fizzled out, because they work for losers.

There's no conspiracy at work, I don't think, no ill will, no leering Men Behind the Curtain: just a bunch of people from good universities, living out the dream, cringing a little at the dog-crap story even as they ensure that it goes out on time, with excellent production values.

How does such a harmful product emanate from such talented people? I'd imagine it has to do with the will to survive: each small piece of the machine doing what he or she must to avoid going home to Toledo, tail-between-legs, within the extant constraints of time and profitability, each deferring his or her "real" work until such time as he or she accumulates his or her nut and can head for the hills, or get a job that lets them honor their hearts. (A young friend who writes content for the news page of an online media giant, e-mails me: "I just wrote this news headline for my job: 'Anna Nicole's Lost Diary: "I Hate Sex."' If anyone wonders why Americans aren't informed with real news it's because of sell-out corporate goons like me who will do anything to never deliver a pizza again.")

An assistant to a famous conservative opinion-meister once described her boss to me, a little breathlessly and in the kind of value-neutral mode one hears in this milieu, as being one of the funniest, most intelligent, high-energy people she'd ever met. I believed her. To do what he does must take a special and terrifying skill set. Did she agree with his politics? She demurred—she did and she didn't. It was kind of beside the point. He was kicking much ass. I immediately felt a little gauche for asking about her politics, like a guy who, in the palace, asks how much the footman makes.

The first requirement of greatness is that one stay in the game. To stay in the game, one must prove viable; to prove viable, one has to be watched; to be watched, one has to be watchable, and, in the news business, a convention of Watchability has evolved—a tone, a pace, an unspoken set of acceptable topics and acceptable relations to these topics—that bears, at best, a peripheral relation to truth. What can be said on TV is circumscribed, subtly, by past performance, editing, and social cues, and, not so subtly, by whether one is invited back.

This entity I'm trying to unify under the rubric of The Megaphone is, of course, in reality, a community tens of thousands of people strong, and like all communities, it is diverse, and resistant to easy generality, and its ways are mysterious.

But this community constitutes a kind of *de facto* ruling class, because what it says we can't avoid hearing, and what we hear changes the way we think. It has become a kind of branch of our government: when government wants to mislead, it turns to the media; when media gets hot for a certain story (i.e., senses a ratings hot spot), it influences the government. This has always been true, but more and more this relationship is becoming a closed loop, which leaves the citizen extraneous. Like any ruling class, this one looks down on those it rules. The new twist is that this ruling class rules via our eyes and the ears. It fills the air, and thus our heads, with its priorities and thoughts, and its new stunted diction.

This is a ruling class made of strange bedfellows: the Conservative Opinion King has more in common with the Liberal Opinion King than either does with the liberal and conservative slaughterhouse workers toiling side by side in Wichita; the Opinion Kings have friends in common, similar ambitions, a common frame of reference (agents, expected perks, a knowledge of the hierarchy of success indicators, a mastery of insider jargon). What they share most is a desire not to be cast down, down from the realm of the rarefied air, back to where they came from.

There's a little slot on the side of the Megaphone, and as long as you're allowed to keep talking into it, money keeps dropping out.

Seasons pass. What once would have evoked an eye-roll evokes a dull blink. New truisms, new baselines, arise. A new foundation, labeled Our Basic Belief System, is laid, and on this foundation appear startling new structures: a sudden quasi acceptance of, say, the water-boarding of prisoners, or of the idea that a trial is a privilege we may choose to withhold if we deem the crime severe enough.

9.

At this point I hear a voice from the back of the room, and it is mine: "Come on, George, hasn't our mass media always been sensationalistic, dumb, and profit-seeking?"

Of course it has. If you want a tutorial on stupid tonality, watch an old newsreel ("These scrappy Southern Yanks are taking a brisk walk toward some Krauts who'll soon be whistling Dixie out of the other side of Das Traps!"). We were plenty able to whip ourselves into murderous frenzies even when the Megaphone was a baby, consisting of a handful of newspapers (Hi, Mr. Hearst!), and I suppose if we went back far enough, we'd find six or seven troglodytes madly projecting about a village of opposing troglodytes, then jogging down there, hooting pithy slogans, to eliminate it on the fallacious power of their collective flame-fanning.

But I think we're in an hour of special danger, if only because our technology has become so loud, slick, and seductive, its powers of self-critique so insufficient and glacial. The era of the jackboot is over: the forces that come for our decency, humor, and freedom will be extolling, in beautiful smooth voices, the virtue of decency, humor, and freedom.

Imagine that the Megaphone has two dials: One controls the Intelligence of its rhetoric and the other its Volume. Ideally, the Intelligence would be set on High, and the Volume on Low—making it possible for multiple, contradictory voices to be broadcast and heard. But to the extent that the Intelligence is set on Stupid, and the Volume on Drown Out All Others, this is verging on propaganda, and we have a problem, one that works directly against the health of our democracy.

Is there an antidote?

Well, there is, but it's partial, and may not work, and isn't very exciting. Can we legislate against Stupidity? I don't think we'd want to. Freedom means we have to be free to be Stupid, and Banal, and Perverse, free to generate both *Absalom, Absalom!,* and *Swapping Pets: The Alligator Edition.* Freedom means that if some former radio DJ can wrestle his way to the top of the heap and provoke political upheavals by spouting his lame opinions and bullying his guests, he too has a right to have a breakfast cereal named after him. American creative energy has always teetered on the brink of insanity. "Rhapsody in Blue" and "The Night Chicago Died" have, alas, common DNA, the DNA for "joyfully reckless confidence." What I propose as an antidote is simply: awareness of the Mega-phonic tendency, and discussion of same. Every well-thought-out rebuttal to dogma, every scrap of intelligent logic, every absurdist reduction of some bullying stance is the antidote. Every request for the clarification of the vague, every poke at smug banality, every pen stroke in a document under revision is the antidote.

This battle, like any great moral battle, will be won, if won, not with some easy corrective tidal wave of Total Righteousness, but with small drops of specificity and aplomb and correct logic, delivered titrationally, by many of us all at once.

We have met the enemy and he is us, yes, yes, but the fact that we have recognized ourselves as the enemy indicates we still have the ability to rise up and whip our own ass, so to speak: keep reminding ourselves that representations of the world are never the world itself. Turn that Megaphone down, and insist that what's said through it be as precise, intelligent, and humane as possible.

At the Edge of Poverty

David K. Shipler

Tired of wishes,
Empty of dreams

—Carl Sandburg

The man who washes cars does not own one. The clerk who files cancelled checks at the bank has $2.02 in her own account. The woman who copy-edits medical textbooks has not been to a dentist in a decade.

This is the forgotten America. At the bottom of its working world, millions live in the shadow of prosperity, in the twilight between poverty and well-being. Whether you're rich, poor, or middle-class, you encounter them every day. They serve you Big Macs and help you find merchandise at Wal-Mart. They harvest your food, clean your offices, and sew your clothes. In a California factory, they package lights for your kids' bikes. In a New Hampshire plant, they assemble books of wallpaper samples to help you redecorate.

They are shaped by their invisible hardships. Some are climbing out of welfare, drug addiction, or homelessness. Others have been trapped for life in a perilous zone of low-wage work. Some of their children are malnourished. Some have been sexually abused. Some live in crumbling housing that contributes to their children's asthma, which means days absent from school. Some of their youngsters do not even have the eyeglasses they need to see the chalkboard clearly.

This book is about a few of these people, their families, their dreams, their personal failings, and the larger failings of their country. While the United States has enjoyed unprecedented affluence, low-wage employees have been testing the American doctrine that hard work cures poverty. Some have found that work works. Others have learned that it doesn't. Moving in and out of jobs that demand much and pay little, many people tread just above the official poverty line, dangerously close to the edge of destitution. An inconvenience to an affluent family—minor car trouble, a brief illness, disrupted child care—is a crisis to them, for it can threaten their ability to stay employed. They spend everything and save nothing. They are always behind on their bills. They have minuscule bank accounts or none at all, and so pay more fees and higher interest rates than more secure Americans. Even when the economy is robust, many wander through a borderland of struggle, never getting very far from where they started. When the economy weakens, they slip back toward the precipice.

Millions have been pushed into a region of adversity by federal welfare reform's time limits and work mandates. Enacted in 1996 during an economic boom, the reform is credited by many welfare recipients for inducing them to travel beyond the stifling world of dependence into the active, challenging, hopeful culture of the workplace. They have gained self-confidence, some say, and have acquired new respect from their children. Those with luck or talent step onto career ladders toward better and better positions at higher and higher pay. Many more, however, are stuck at such low wages that their living standards are unchanged. They still cannot save, cannot get decent health care, cannot move to better neighborhoods, and cannot send their children to schools that offer a promise for a successful future. These are the forgotten Americans, who are noticed and counted as they leave welfare, but who disappear from the nation's radar as they struggle in their working lives.

Breaking away and moving a comfortable distance from poverty seems to require a perfect lineup of favorable conditions. A set of skills, a good starting wage, and a job with the likelihood of promotion are prerequisites. But so are clarity of purpose, courageous self-esteem, a lack of substantial debt, the freedom from illness or addiction, a functional family, a network of upstanding friends, and the right help from private or governmental agencies. Any gap in that array is an entry point for trouble, because being poor means being unprotected. You might as well try playing quarterback with no helmet, no padding, no training, and no experience, behind a line of hundred-pound weaklings. With no cushion of money, no training in the ways of the wider world, and too little defense against the threats and temptations of decaying communities, a poor man or woman gets sacked again and again—buffeted and bruised and defeated. When an exception breaks this cycle of failure, it is called the fulfillment of the American Dream.

As a culture, the United States is not quite sure about the causes of poverty, and is therefore uncertain about the solutions. The American Myth still supposes that any individual from the humblest origins can climb to well-being. We wish that to be true, and we delight in examples that make it seem so, whether fictional or real. The name of Horatio Alger, the nineteenth-century writer we no longer read, is embedded in our language as a synonym for the rise from rags to riches that his characters achieve through virtuous hard work. The classic immigrant story still stirs the American heart, despite the country's longstanding aversion to the arrival of "the wretched refuse" at "the golden door," in the words etched on the Statue of Liberty.[1] Even while resenting the influx of immigrants, we revel in the nobility of tireless labor and scrupulous thrift that can transform a destitute refugee into a successful entrepreneur. George W. Bush gave voice to the myth when he was asked whether he meant to send a message with the inclusion of two blacks, a Hispanic, and two women in the first senior appointments to his incoming administration. "You bet," the president-elect replied: "that people who work hard and make the right decisions in life can achieve anything they want in America."[2]

The myth has its value. It sets a demanding standard, both for the nation and for every resident. The nation has to strive to make itself the fabled land of opportunity; the resident must strive to use that opportunity. The ideal has inspired a Civil Rights Movement, a War on Poverty, and a continuing search for ways to ease the distress that persists in the midst of plenty.

But the American Myth also provides a means of laying blame. In the Puritan legacy, hard work is not merely practical but also moral; its absence suggests an ethical lapse. A harsh logic dictates a hard judgment: If a person's diligent work leads to prosperity, if work is a moral virtue, and if anyone in the society can attain prosperity through work, then the failure to do so is a fall from righteousness. The marketplace is the fair and final judge; a low wage is somehow the worker's fault, for it simply reflects the low value of his labor. In the American atmosphere, poverty has always carried a whiff of sinfulness. Thus, when Judy Woodruff of CNN moderated a debate among Republican presidential candidates in March 2000, she asked Alan Keyes why he thought morality was worsening when certain indicators of morality were improving: Crime was down, out-of-wedlock births were down, and welfare was down, she noted. Evidently, welfare was an index of immorality.

There is an opposite extreme, the American Anti-Myth, which holds the society largely responsible for the individual's poverty. The hierarchy of racial discrimination and economic power creates a syndrome of impoverished communities with bad schools and closed options. The children of the poor are funneled into delinquency, drugs, or jobs with meager pay and little future. The individual is a victim of great forces beyond his control, including profit-hungry corporations that exploit his labor.

In 1962, Michael Harrington's eloquent articulation of the Anti-Myth in his book *The Other America* heightened awareness; to a nation blinded by affluence at the time, the portrait of a vast "invisible land" of the poor came as a staggering revelation. It helped generate Lyndon B. Johnson's War on Poverty. But Johnson's war never truly mobilized the country, nor was it ever fought to victory.

Forty years later, after all our economic achievements, the gap between rich and poor has only widened, with a median net worth of $833,600 among the top 10 percent and just $7,900 for the bottom 20 percent.[3] Life expectancy in the United States is lower, and infant mortality higher, than in Japan, Hong Kong, Israel, Canada, and all the major nations of Western Europe.[4] Yet after all that has been written, discussed, and left unresolved, it is harder to surprise and shock and outrage. So it is harder to generate action.

In reality, people do not fit easily into myths or anti-myths, of course. The working individuals in this book are neither helpless nor omnipotent, but stand on various points along the spectrum between the polar opposites of personal and societal responsibility. Each person's life is the mixed product of bad choices and bad fortune, of roads not taken and roads cut off by the accident of birth or circumstance. It is difficult to find someone whose poverty is not somehow related to his or her unwise behavior—to drop out of school, to have a baby out of wedlock, to do drugs, to be chronically late to work. And it is difficult to find behavior that is not somehow related to the inherited conditions of being poorly parented, poorly educated, poorly housed in neighborhoods from which no distant horizon of possibility can be seen.

How to define the individual's role in her own poverty is a question that has shaped the debate about welfare and other social policies, but it can rarely be answered with certainty, even in a specific case. The poor have less control than the affluent over their private decisions, less insulation from the cold machinery of government, less agility to navigate around the pitfalls of a frenetic world driven by technology and competition. Their personal mistakes have larger consequences, and their personal achievements yield smaller returns. The interaction between the personal and the public is so intricate that for assistance such as job training to make a difference, for example, it has to be tailored to each individual's needs, which include not only such "hard skills" as using a computer or running a lathe, but also "soft skills" such as interacting with peers, following orders willingly, and managing the deep anger that may have developed during years of adversity. Job trainers are discovering that people who have repeatedly failed—in school, in love, in work—cannot succeed until they learn that they are capable of success. To get out of poverty, they have to acquire dexterity with their emotions as well as their hands.

An exit from poverty is not like showing your passport and crossing a frontier. There is a broad strip of contested territory between destitution and comfort, and the passage is not the same distance for everyone. "Comfortable is when I can pay my rent with one paycheck—I don't have to save for two weeks to pay one month's rent," said Tyrone Pixley, a slender man of fifty in Washington, D.C. He was especially undemanding, having emerged from a tough life as a day laborer and a heroin user. "I don't want to have to scuffle," he said simply. "I want to be able to live comfortable, even if it's in a ten-by-ten room. And in the course of a month I can pay all my bills out of my pay. I don't have to have anything saved. For me to be comfortable, I don't have to have a savings account."

In such a rich country, most people have more appetite than Tyrone Pixley. Surrounded by constant advertising from television sets that are almost always turned on, many Americans acquire wants that turn into needs. "You're living in the projects, your mom's on welfare, so if you got six kids or five or seven, eight kids growing up, you be wantin' things all your life, and you can't have," explained Frank Dickerson, a janitor who dealt drugs in Washington to get things he didn't have. "You got kids want to have the nice tennis shoes, the jackets; they can't get that with a mom with six, seven kids on welfare. How they gonna get it? They may be getting older, growing up, they want to have nice stuff, so the only way to get that is turn to drugs. That's right. You go out there, you deal, and you get the things that you need. Car, apartments, clothes." Frank Dickerson spent three years in prison, but he and his wife also bought a house in the Maryland suburbs with the money he made from drugs.

Poverty, then, does not lend itself to easy definition. It may be absolute—an inability to buy basic necessities. It may be relative—an inability to buy the lifestyle that prevails at a certain time and place. It can be measured by a universal yardstick or by an index of disparity. Even dictionaries cannot agree. "Want or scarcity of means of subsistence," one says categorically.[5] "Lack of the means of providing material needs *or comforts*," says another.[6] "The state of one who lacks *a usual or socially accept- able* amount of money or material possessions," says a third (emphases added).[7]

By global or historical standards, much of what Americans consider poverty is lux- ury. A rural Russian is not considered poor if he cannot afford a car and his home has no central heating; a rural American is. A Vietnamese farmer is not seen as poor because he plows with water buffalo, irrigates by hand, and lives in a thatched house; a North Carolina farmworker is, because he picks cucumbers by hand, gets paid a dollar a box, and lives in a run-down trailer. Most impoverished people in the world would be daz- zled by the apartments, telephones, television sets, running water, clothing, and other amenities that surround the poor in America. But that does not mean that the poor are not poor, or that those on the edge of poverty are not truly on the edge of a cliff.

"The American poor are not poor in Hong Kong or in the sixteenth century; they are poor here and now, in the United States," Michael Harrington wrote before Hong Kong's prosperity soared. "They are dispossessed in terms of what the rest of the nation enjoys, in terms of what the society could provide if it had the will. They live on the fringe, the margin. They watch the movies and read the magazines of affluent America, and these tell them that they are internal exiles. . . . To have one bowl of rice in a society where all other people have half a bowl may well be a sign of achievement and intelligence; it may spur a person to act and to fulfill his human potential. To have five bowls of rice in a society where the majority have a decent, balanced diet is a tragedy."[8]

Indeed, being poor in a rich country may be more difficult to endure than being poor in a poor country, for the skills of surviving in poverty have largely been lost in America. Visit a slum in Hanoi and you will find children inventing games with bot- tles and sticks and the rusty rims of bicycle wheels. Go to a slum in Los Angeles and you will find children dependent on plastic toys and video games. Living in Cambo- dia, my son Michael marveled at the ingenuity bred by necessity, the capacity to repair what would be thrown away at home; when his television remote stopped working in Phnom Penh, he got it fixed at the corner for a dollar.

In the United States, the federal government defines poverty very simply: an annual income, for a family with one adult and three children, of less than $19,223 in the year 2004. That works out to $9.24 an hour, or $4.09 above the federal mini- mum wage, assuming that someone can get a full forty hours of work a week for all fifty-two weeks of the year, or 2,080 working hours annually.[9] With incomes rising through the economic expansion of the 1990s, the incidence of official poverty declined, beginning the new decade at 11.3 percent of the population, down from 15.1 percent in 1993. Then it rose slightly in the ensuing recession, to 12.5 percent by 2003.

But the figures are misleading. The federal poverty line cuts far below the amount needed for a decent living, because the Census Bureau still uses the basic formula designed in 1964 by the Social Security Administration, with four modest revisions in subsequent years. That sets the poverty level at approximately three times the cost of a "thrifty food basket." The calculation was derived from spending patterns in 1955, when the average family used about one-third of its income for food. It is no longer valid today, when the average family spends only about one-sixth of its budget for food, but the government continues to multiply the cost of a "thrifty food basket" by three, adjusting for inflation only and overlooking nearly half a century of dramatically changing lifestyles.[10]

The result burnishes reality by underestimating the numbers whose lives can reasonably be considered impoverished. More accurate formulas, being tested by the Census Bureau and the National Academy of Sciences, would rely on actual costs of food, clothing, shelter, utilities, and the like. Under those calculations, income would include benefits not currently counted, such as food stamps, subsidized housing, fuel assistance, and school lunches; living costs would include expenditures now ignored, such as child care, doctor's bills, health insurance premiums, and Social Security payroll taxes. When the various formulas were run in 1998, they increased by about three percentage points the proportion of the population in poverty, from the official 34.5 million to a high of 42.4 million people.[11] A later variation raised the poverty rate in 2001 by 0.6 percent. [12] Such a change would presumably make more families eligible for benefits that are linked to the poverty level; some programs, including children's health insurance, already cover households with incomes up to 150 or 200 percent of the poverty threshold, depending on the state.

Even if revised methods of figuring poverty were adopted, however, they would provide only a still photograph of a family's momentary situation. In that snapshot, the ebb and flow of the moving picture is lost. By measuring only income and expenses during a current year and not assets and debts, the formulas ignore the past, and the past is frequently an overwhelming burden on the present. Plenty of people have moved into jobs that put them above the threshold of poverty, only to discover that their student loans, their car payments, and the exorbitant interest charged on old credit card balances consume so much of their cash that they live no better than before.

When the poor or the nearly poor are asked to define poverty, however, they talk not only about what's in the wallet but what's in the mind or the heart. "Hopelessness," said a fifteen-year-old girl in New Hampshire.

"Not hopelessness—helplessness," said a man in Los Angeles. "Why should I get up? Nobody's gonna ever hire me because look at the way I'm dressed, and look at the fact that I never finished high school, look at the fact that I'm black, I'm brown, I'm yellow, or I grew up in the trailer."

"The state of mind," said a man in Washington, D.C. "I believe that spirituality is way more important than physical."

"I am so rich," said a woman whose new job running Xerox machines was lifting her out of poverty, "because—not only material things—because I know who I am, I know where I'm going now."

Another woman, who fell into poverty after growing up middle class, celebrated her "cultural capital," which meant her love of books, music, ideas, and her close relationships with her children. "In some senses, we are not at all poor; we have a great richness," she said. "We don't feel very poor. We feel poor when we can't go to the doctor or fix the car."

For practically every family, then, the ingredients of poverty are part financial and part psychological, part personal and part societal, part past and part present. Every problem magnifies the impact of the others, and all are so tightly interlocked that one reversal can produce a chain reaction with results far distant from the original cause. A run-down apartment can exacerbate a child's asthma, which leads to a call for an ambulance, which generates a medical bill that cannot be paid, which ruins a credit record, which hikes the interest rate on an auto loan, which forces the purchase of an unreliable used car, which jeopardizes a mother's punctuality at work, which limits her promotions and earning capacity, which confines her to poor housing. If she or any other impoverished working parent added up all of her individual problems, the whole would be equal to more than the sum of its parts.

If problems are interlocking, then so must solutions be. A job alone is not enough. Medical insurance alone is not enough. Good housing alone is not enough. Reliable transportation, careful family budgeting, effective parenting, effective schooling are not enough when each is achieved in isolation from the rest. There is no single variable that can be altered to help working people move away from the edge of poverty. Only where the full array of factors is attacked can America fulfill its promise.

The first step is to see the problems, and the first problem is the failure to see the people. Those who work but live impoverished lives blend into familiar landscapes and are therefore overlooked. They make up the invisible, silent America that analysts casually ignore. "We all live in the suburbs now, not in the inner cities," proclaimed Professor Michael Goldstein of the University of Colorado, explaining on PBS why Woolworth's had been replaced by Wal-Mart in the Dow Jones Industrial Average.[13]

Tim Brookes, a commentator on National Public Radio, once did a witty screed against overpriced popcorn in movie theaters. Indignant at having been charged $5 for a small bag, he conducted research on the actual expenses. He calculated that the 5¼ ounces of popcorn he received cost 23.71875 cents in a supermarket but only 16.5 cents at prices theater managers paid for fifty-pound sacks. He generously figured 5 cents in electricity to cook the popcorn and 1 cent for the bag. Total cost: 22.5 cents. Subtracting sales tax, that left a profit of $4.075, or 1,811 percent.[14]

Evidently, the theater had the remarkable sense not to hire any workers, for Brookes gave no hint of having noticed any people behind the counter. Their paltry wages, which wouldn't have undermined the excessive profits, were absent from his calculation. The folks who popped the corn, filled the bag, handed the bag to him, and took his money must have been shrouded in an invisibility cloak. No NPR editor seemed to notice.

Notes

[1] From the poem by Emma Lazarus inscribed on the Statue of Liberty.

[2] Richard A. Oppel, Jr., *New York Times,* Dec. 18, 2000, p. A19.

[3] Albert B. Crenshaw, *Washington Post,* Jan. 23, 2003, p. E1.

[4] *World in Figures* (London: The Economist Newspaper, 2003), pp. 76, 79.

[5] *Webster's New International Dictionary,* 2nd ed., unabridged (Springfield, Mass.: Merriam, 1956), p. 1935.

[6]*American Heritage Dictionary of the English Language,* 3rd ed. (Boston: Houghton Mifflin, 1992), p. 1419.

[7]*Webster's Ninth New Collegiate Dictionary* (Springfield, Mass.: Merriam, 1983), P. 922.

[8]Michael Harrington, *The Other America* (Baltimore: Penguin, 1963), pp. 173–74.

[9]The Census Bureau "counts money income before taxes and does not include capital gains and noncash benefits (such as public housing, Medicaid, and food stamps)." The poverty threshold is adjusted annually on the basis of the consumer price index. See http://www.census.gov/hhes/poverty/povdef.html.

[10]For more on the history of the poverty index, see Gordon M. Fisher, "The Development of the Orshansky Poverty Thresholds and Their Subsequent History as the Official U.S. Poverty Measure," http://www.census.gov/hhes/poverty/povmeas/papers/orshansky.html.

[11]Kathleen Short, John Iceland, and Thesia I. Garner, *Experimental Poverty Measures,* 1998 (Washington, D.C.: U.S. Census Bureau), http://www.census.gov/hhes/poverty/povmeas/exppov/exppov.html.

[12]Institute for Research on Poverty, University of Wisconsin, http://www.ssc.wisc.edu/.irp/faqs/faq3.htm.

[13]*The NewsHour with Jim Lehrer,* Public Broadcasting System, Mar. 17, 1997.

[14]*Weekend Edition,* National Public Radio, Jan. 16, 2000.

Regarding the Pain of Others

Susan Sontag

Central to modern expectations, and modern ethical feeling, is the conviction that war is an aberration, if an unstoppable one. That peace is the norm, if an unattainable one. This, of course, is not the way war has been regarded throughout history. War has been the norm and peace the exception.

The description of the exact fashion in which bodies are injured and killed in combat is a recurring climax in the stories told in the *Iliad*. War is seen as something men do inveterately, undeterred by the accumulation of the suffering it inflicts; and to represent war in words or in pictures requires a keen, unflinching detachment. When Leonardo da Vinci gives instructions for a battle painting, he insists that artists have the courage and the imagination to show war in all its ghastliness:

> Make the conquered and beaten pale, with brows raised and knit, and the skin above their brows furrowed with pain . . . and the teeth apart as with crying out in lamentation . . . Make the dead partly or entirely covered with dust . . . and let the blood be seen by its color flowing in a sinuous stream from the corpse to the dust. Others in the death agony grinding their teeth, rolling their eyes, with their fists clenched against their bodies, and the legs distorted.

The concern is that the images to be devised won't be sufficiently upsetting: not concrete, not detailed enough. Pity can entail a moral judgment if, as Aristotle maintains, pity is considered to be the emotion that we owe only to those enduring undeserved misfortune. But pity, far from being the natural twin of fear in the dramas of catastrophic misfortune, seems diluted—distracted—by fear, while fear (dread, terror) usually manages to swamp pity. Leonardo is suggesting that the artist's gaze be, literally, pitiless. The image should appall, and in that *terribilità* lies a challenging kind of beauty.

That a gory battlescape could be beautiful—in the sublime or awesome or tragic register of the beautiful—is a commonplace about images of war made by artists. The idea does not sit well when applied to images taken by cameras: to find beauty in war photographs seems heartless. But the landscape of devastation is still a landscape. There is beauty in ruins. To acknowledge the beauty of photographs of the World Trade Center ruins in the months following the attack seemed frivolous, sacrilegious. The most people dared say was that the photographs were "surreal," a hectic euphemism behind which the disgraced notion of beauty cowered. But they *were* beautiful, many of them—by veteran photographers such as Gilles Peress, Susan Meiselas, and Joel Meyerowitz, among others. The site itself, the mass graveyard that had received the name "Ground Zero," was of course anything but beautiful. Photographs tend to transform, whatever their subject; and as an image something may be beautiful—or terrifying, or unbearable, or quite bearable—as it is not in real life.

Transforming is what art does, but photography that bears witness to the calamitous and the reprehensible is much criticized if it seems "aesthetic"; that is, too much like art. The dual powers of photography—to generate documents and to create works of visual art—have produced some remarkable exaggerations about what photographers ought or ought not to do. Lately, the most common exaggeration is one that regards these powers as opposites. Photographs that depict suffering shouldn't be beautiful, as captions shouldn't moralize. In this view, a beautiful photograph drains attention from the sobering subject and turns it toward the medium itself, thereby compromising the picture's status as a document. The photograph gives mixed signals. Stop this, it urges. But it also exclaims, What a spectacle!*

Take one of the most poignant images from the First World War: a line of English soldiers blinded by poison gas—each rests his hand on the left shoulder of the man ahead of him—shuffling toward a dressing station. It could be an image from one of the searing movies made about the war—King Vidor's *The Big Parade* (1925) or G. W. Pabst's *Westfront 1918*, Lewis Milestone's *All Quiet on the Western Front*, or Howard Hawks's *The Dawn Patrol* (all from 1930). That war photography seems, retroactively, to be echoing as much as inspiring the reconstruction of battle scenes in important war movies has begun to backfire on the photographer's enterprise. What assured the authenticity of Steven Spielberg's acclaimed re-creation of the Omaha Beach landing on D-Day in *Saving Private Ryan* (1998) was that it was based, among other sources, on the photographs taken with immense bravery by Robert Capa during the landing. But a war photograph seems inauthentic, even though there is nothing staged about it, when it looks like a still from a movie. A photographer who specializes in world misery (including but not restricted to the effects of war), Sebastião Salgado, has been the principal target of the new campaign against the inauthenticity of the beautiful. Particularly with the seven-year project he calls "Migrations: Humanity in Transition," Salgado has come under steady attack for producing spectacular, beautifully composed big pictures that are said to be "cinematic."

The sanctimonious Family of Man–style rhetoric that feathers Salgado's exhibitions and books has worked to the detriment of the pictures, however unfair this may

---

*The photographs of Bergen-Belsen, Buchenwald, and Dachau taken in April and May 1945 by anonymous witnesses and military photographers seem more valid than the "better" professional images taken by two celebrated professionals, Margaret Bourke-White and Lee Miller. But the criticism of the professional look in war photography is not a recent view. Walker Evans, for example, detested the work of Bourke-White. But then Evans, who photographed poor American peasants for a book with the heavily ironic title *Let Us Now Praise Famous Men*, would never take a picture of anybody famous.

be. (There is much humbug to be found, and ignored, in declarations made by some of the most admirable photographers of conscience.) Salgado's pictures have also been sourly treated in response to the commercialized situations in which, typically, his portraits of misery are seen. But the problem is in the pictures themselves, not how and where they are exhibited: in their focus on the powerless, reduced to their powerlessness. It is significant that the powerless are not named in the captions. A portrait that declines to name its subject becomes complicit, if inadvertently, in the cult of celebrity that has fueled an insatiable appetite for the opposite sort of photograph: to grant only the famous their names demotes the rest to representative instances of their occupations, their ethnicities, their plights. Taken in thirty-nine countries, Salgado's migration pictures group together, under this single heading, a host of different causes and kinds of distress. Making suffering loom larger, by globalizing it, may spur people to feel they ought to "care" more. It also invites them to feel that the sufferings and misfortunes are too vast, too irrevocable, too epic to be much changed by any local political intervention. With a subject conceived on this scale, compassion can only flounder—and make abstract. But all politics, like all of history, is concrete. (To be sure, nobody who really thinks about history can take politics altogether seriously.)

It used to be thought, when the candid images were not common, that showing something that needed to be seen, bringing a painful reality closer, was bound to goad viewers to feel more. In a world in which photography is brilliantly at the service of consumerist manipulations, no effect of a photograph of a doleful scene can be taken for granted. As a consequence, morally alert photographers and ideologues of photography have become increasingly concerned with the issues of exploitation of sentiment (pity, compassion, indignation) in war photography and of rote ways of provoking feeling.

Photographer-witnesses may think it more correct morally to make the spectacular not spectacular. But the spectacular is very much part of the religious narratives by which suffering, throughout most of Western history, has been understood. To feel the pulse of Christian iconography in certain wartime or disaster-time photographs is not a sentimental projection. It would be hard not to discern the lineaments of the Pietá in W. Eugene Smith's picture of a woman in Minamata cradling her deformed, blind, and deaf daughter, or the template of the Descent from the Gross in several of Don McGullin's pictures of dying American soldiers in Vietnam. However, such perceptions—which add aura and beauty—may be on the wane. The German historian Barbara Duden has said that when she was teaching a course in the history of representations of the body at a large American state university some years ago, not one student in a class of twenty undergraduates could identify the subject of any of the canonical paintings of the Flagellation she showed as slides. ("I think it's a religious picture," one ventured.) The only canonical image of Jesus she could count on most students being able to identify was the Crucifixion.

Photographs objectify: They turn an event or a person into something that can be possessed. And photographs are a species of alchemy, for all that they are prized as a transparent account of reality.

Often something looks, or is felt to look, "better" in a photograph. Indeed, it is one of the functions of photography to improve the normal appearance of things. (Hence, one is always disappointed by a photograph that is not flattering.) Beautifying is one classic operation of the camera, and it tends to bleach out a moral response to what is shown. Uglifying, showing something at its worst, is a more modern function: didactic, it invites an active response. For photographs to accuse, and possibly to alter conduct, they must shock.

An example: A few years ago, the public health authorities in Canada, where it had been estimated that smoking kills forty-five thousand people a year, decided to supplement the warning printed on every pack of cigarettes with a shock-photograph—of cancerous lungs, or a stroke-clotted brain, or a damaged heart, or a bloody mouth in acute periodontal distress. A pack with such a picture accompanying the warning about the deleterious effects of smoking would be sixty times more likely to inspire smokers to quit, a research study had somehow calculated, than a pack with only the verbal warning.

Let's assume this is true. But one might wonder, for how long? Does shock have term limits? Right now the smokers of Canada are recoiling in disgust, if they do look at these pictures. Will those still smoking five years from now still be upset? Shock can become familiar. Shock can wear off. Even if it doesn't, one can *not* look. People have means to defend themselves against what is upsetting—in this instance, unpleasant information for those wishing to continue to smoke. This seems normal, that is, adaptive. As one can become habituated to horror in real life, one can become habituated to the horror of certain images.

Yet there are cases where repeated exposure to what shocks, saddens, appalls does not use up a full-hearted response. Habituation is not automatic, for images (portable, insertable) obey different rules than real life. Representations of the Crucifixion do not become banal to believers, if they really are believers. This is even more true of staged representations. Performances of *Chushingura*, probably the best-known narrative in all of Japanese culture, can be counted on to make a Japanese audience sob when Lord Asano admires the beauty of the cherry blossoms on his way to where he must commit seppuku—sob each time, no matter how often they have followed the story (as a Kabuki or Bunraku play, as a film); the *ta'ziyah* drama of the betrayal and murder of Imam Hussayn does not cease to bring an Iranian audience to tears no matter how many times they have seen the martyrdom enacted. On the contrary. They weep, in part, because they have seen it many times. People want to weep. Pathos, in the form of a narrative, does not wear out.

But do people want to be horrified? Probably not. Still, there are pictures whose power does not abate, in part because one cannot look at them often. Pictures of the ruin of faces that will always testify to a great iniquity survived, at that cost: the faces of horribly disfigured First World War veterans who survived the inferno of the trenches; the faces melted and thickened with scar tissue of survivors of the American atomic bombs dropped on Hiroshima and Nagasaki; the faces cleft by machete blows of Tutsi survivors of the genocidal rampage launched by the Hutus in Rwanda—is it correct to say that people get *used* to these?

Indeed, the very notion of atrocity, of war crime, is associated with the expectation of photographic evidence. Such evidence is, usually, of something posthumous; the remains, as it were—the mounds of skulls in Pol Pot's Cambodia, the mass graves in Guatemala and El Salvador, Bosnia and Kosovo. And this posthumous reality is often the keenest of summations. As Hannah Arendt pointed out soon after the end of the Second World War, all the photographs and newsreels of the concentration camps are misleading because they show the camps at the moment the Allied troops marched in. What makes the images unbearable—the piles of corpses, the skeletal survivors—was not at all typical for the camps, which, when they were functioning, exterminated their inmates systematically (by gas, not starvation and illness), then immediately cremated them. And photographs echo photographs: it was inevitable that the photographs of emaciated Bosnian prisoners at Omarska, the Serb death camp created in northern Bosnia in 1992, would recall the photographs taken in the Nazi death camps in 1945.

Photographs of atrocity illustrate as well as corroborate. Bypassing disputes about exactly how many were killed (numbers are often inflated at first), the photograph gives the indelible sample. The illustrative function of photographs leaves opinions, prejudices, fantasies, misinformation untouched. The information that many fewer Palestinians died in the assault on Jenin than had been claimed by Palestinian officials (as the Israelis had said all along) made much less impact than the photographs of the razed center of the refugee camp. And, of course, atrocities that are not secured in our minds by well-known photographic images, or of which we simply have had very few images—the total extermination of the Herero people in Namibia decreed by the German colonial administration in 1904; the Japanese onslaught in China, notably the massacre of nearly four hundred thousand, and the rape of eighty thousand, Chinese in December 1937, the so-called Rape of Nanking; the rape of some one hundred and thirty thousand women and girls (ten thousand of whom committed suicide) by victorious Soviet soldiers unleashed by their commanding officers in Berlin in 1945—seem more remote. These are memories that few have cared to claim.

The familiarity of certain photographs builds our sense of the present and immediate past. Photographs lay down routes of reference, and serve as totems of causes: sentiment is more likely to crystallize around a photograph than around a verbal slogan. And photographs help construct—and revise—our sense of a more distant past, with the posthumous shocks engineered by the circulation of hitherto unknown photographs. Photographs that everyone recognizes are now a constituent part of what a society chooses to think about, or declares that it has chosen to think about. It calls these ideas "memories," and that is, over the long run, a fiction. Strictly speaking, there is no such thing as collective memory—part of the same family of spurious notions as collective guilt. But there is collective instruction.

All memory is individual, unreproducible—it dies with each person. What is called collective memory is not a remembering but a stipulating: that *this* is important, and this is the story about how it happened, with the pictures that lock the story in our minds. Ideologies create substantiating archives of images, representative images, which encapsulate common ideas of significance and trigger predictable thoughts, feelings. Poster-ready photographs—the mushroom cloud of an A-bomb test, Martin Luther King, Jr., speaking at the Lincoln Memorial in Washington, D.C., the astronaut walking on the moon—are the visual equivalent of sound bites. They commemorate, in no less blunt fashion than postage stamps, Important Historical Moments; indeed, the triumphalist ones (the picture of the A-bomb excepted) become postage stamps. Fortunately, there is no one signature picture of the Nazi death camps.

As art has been redefined during a century of modernism as whatever is destined to be enshrined in some kind of museum, so it is now the destiny of many photographic troves to be exhibited and preserved in museum-like institutions. Among such archives of horror, the photographs of genocide have undergone the greatest institutional development. The point of creating public repositories for these and other relics is to ensure that the crimes they depict will continue to figure in people's consciousness. This is called remembering, but in fact it is a good deal more than that.

The memory museum in its current proliferation is a product of a way of thinking about, and mourning, the destruction of European Jewry in the 1930s and 1940s, which came to institutional fruition in Yad Vashem in Jerusalem, the Holocaust Memorial Museum in Washington, D.C., and the Jewish Museum in Berlin. Photographs and other memorabilia of the Shoah have been committed to a perpetual recirculation, to ensure that what they show will be remembered. Photographs of the suffering and martyrdom of a people are more than reminders of death, of failure, of victimization. They invoke the miracle of survival. To aim at the perpetuation of memories means, inevitably, that one has undertaken the task of continually renewing, of creating, memories—aided, above all, by the impress of iconic photographs. People want to be able to visit—and refresh—their memories. Now many victim peoples want a memory museum, a temple that houses a comprehensive, chronologically organized, illustrated narrative of their sufferings. Armenians, for example, have long been clamoring for a museum in Washington to institutionalize the memory of the genocide of Armenian people by the Ottoman Turks. But why is there not already, in the nation's capital, which happens to be a city whose population is overwhelmingly African-American, a Museum of the History of Slavery? Indeed, there is no Museum of the History of Slavery—the whole story, starting with the slave trade in Africa itself, not just selected parts, such as the Underground Railroad—anywhere in the United States. This, it seems, is a memory judged too dangerous to social stability to activate and to create. The Holocaust Memorial Museum and the future Armenian Genocide Museum and Memorial are about what didn't happen in America, so the memory-work doesn't risk arousing an embittered domestic population against authority. To have a museum chronicling the great crime that was African slavery in the United States of America would be to acknowledge that the evil was *here*. Americans prefer to picture the evil that was *there*, and from which the United States—a unique nation, one without any certifiably wicked leaders throughout its entire history—is exempt. That this country, like every other country, has its tragic past does not sit well with the founding, and still all-powerful, belief in American exceptionalism. The national consensus on American history as a history of progress is a new setting for distressing photographs—one that focuses our attention on wrongs, both here and elsewhere, for which America sees itself as the solution or cure.

Even in the era of cybermodels, what the mind feels like is still, as the ancients imagined it, an inner space—like a theatre—in which we picture, and it is these pictures that allow us to remember. The problem is not that people remember through photographs, but that they remember only the photographs. This remembering through photographs eclipses other forms of understanding, and remembering. The concentration camps— that is, the photographs taken when the camps were liberated in 1945—are most of what people associate with Nazism and the miseries of the Second World War. Hideous deaths (by genocide, starvation, and epidemic) are most of what people retain of the whole clutch of iniquities and failures that have taken place in postcolonial Africa.

To remember is, more and more, not to recall a story but to be able to call up a picture. Even a writer as steeped in nineteenth-century and early modern literary solemnities as W. G. Sebald was moved to seed his lamentation-narratives of lost lives, lost nature, lost cityscapes with photographs. Sebald was not just an elegist, he was a militant elegist. Remembering, he wanted the reader to remember, too.

Harrowing photographs do not inevitably lose their power to shock. But they are not much help if the task is to understand. Narratives can make us understand. Photographs do something else: they haunt us. Consider one of the unforgettable images of the war in Bosnia, a photograph of which the *New York Times* foreign correspondent John Kifner wrote: "The image is stark, one of the most enduring of the Balkan wars: a Serb militiaman casually kicking a dying Muslim woman in the head. It tells you everything you need to know." But of course it doesn't tell us everything we need to know.

From an identification given by the photographer, Ron Haviv, we learn the photograph was taken in the town of Bijeljina in April 1992, the first month of the Serb rampage through Bosnia. From behind, we see a uniformed Serb militiaman, a youthful figure with sunglasses perched on the top of his head, a cigarette between the second and third fingers of his raised left hand, rifle dangling in his right hand, right leg poised to kick a woman lying face down on the sidewalk between two other bodies. The photograph doesn't tell us that she is Muslim, though she is unlikely to have been labeled in any other way, for why would she and the two others be lying there, as if dead (why "dying"?), under the gaze of some Serb soldiers? In fact, the photograph tells us very little—except that war is hell, and that graceful young men with guns are capable of kicking overweight older women lying helpless, or already killed, in the head.

The pictures of Bosnian atrocities were seen soon after the events took place. Like pictures from the Vietnam War, such as Ron Haberle's evidence of the massacre in March 1968 by a company of American soldiers of some five hundred unarmed civilians in the village of My Lai, they became important in bolstering the opposition to a war which was far from inevitable, far from intractable, and could have been stopped much sooner. Therefore one could feel an obligation to look at these pictures, gruesome as they were, because there was something to be done, right now, about what they depicted. Other issues are raised when we are invited to respond to a dossier of hitherto unknown pictures of horrors long past.

An example: a trove of photographs of black victims of lynching in small towns in the United States between the 1890s and the 1930s, which provided a shattering, revelatory experience for the thousands who saw them in a gallery in New York in 2000. The lynching pictures tell us about human wickedness. About inhumanity. They force us to think about the extent of the evil unleashed specifically by racism. Intrinsic to the perpetration of this evil is the shamelessness of photographing it. The pictures were taken as souvenirs and made, some of them, into postcards; more than a few show grinning spectators, good churchgoing citizens as most of them had to be, posing for a camera with the backdrop of a naked, charred, mutilated body hanging from a tree. The display of these pictures makes us spectators, too.

What is the point of exhibiting these pictures? To awaken indignation? To make us feel "bad"; that is, to appall and sadden? To help us mourn? Is looking at such pictures really necessary, given that these horrors lie in a past remote enough to be beyond punishment? Are we the better for seeing these images? Do they actually teach us anything? Don't they rather just confirm what we already know (or want to know)?

All these questions were raised at the time of the exhibition and afterward when a book of the photographs, *Without Sanctuary*, was published. Some people, it was said, might dispute the need for this grisly photographic display, lest it cater to voyeuristic appetites and perpetuate images of black victimization—or simply numb the mind. Nevertheless, it was argued, there is an obligation to "examine"—the more clinical "examine" is substituted for "look at"—the pictures. It was further argued that submitting to the ordeal should help us understand such atrocities not as the acts of "barbarians" but as the reflection of a belief system, racism, that by defining one people as less human than another legitimates torture and murder. But maybe they *were* barbarians. Maybe *this* is what most barbarians look like. (They look like everybody else.)

That being said, one person's "barbarian" is another person's "just doing what everybody else is doing." (How many can be expected to do better than that?) The question is, Whom do we wish to blame? More precisely, Whom do we believe we have the right to blame? The children of Hiroshima and Nagasaki were no less innocent than the young African-American men (and a few women) who were butchered and hanged from trees in small-town America. More than one hundred thousand civilians, three-fourths of them women, were massacred in the RAF firebombing of Dresden on the night of February 13, 1945; seventy-two thousand civilians were incinerated in seconds by the American bomb dropped on Hiroshima. The roll call could be much longer. Again, Whom do we wish to blame? Which atrocities from the incurable, past do we think we are obliged to revisit?

Probably, if we are Americans, we think that it would be morbid to go out of our way to look at pictures of burnt victims of atomic bombing or the napalmed flesh of the civilian victims of the American war on Vietnam, but that we have a duty to look at the lynching pictures—if we belong to the party of the right-thinking, which on this issue is now very large. A stepped-up recognition of the monstrousness of the slave system that once existed, unquestioned by most, in the United States is a national project of recent decades that many Euro-Americans feel some tug of obligation to join. This ongoing project is a great achievement, a benchmark of civic virtue. The acknowledgment of the American use of disproportionate firepower in war (in violation of one of the cardinal laws of war) is very much not a national project. A museum devoted to the history of America's wars that included the vicious war the United States fought against guerrillas in the Philippines from 1899 to 1902 (expertly excoriated by Mark Twain), and that fairly presented the arguments for and against using the atomic bomb in 1945 on the Japanese cities, with photographic evidence that showed what those weapons did, would be regarded—now more than ever—as a most unpatriotic endeavor.

A Time To Serve

Richard Stengel

*As the Constitutional Convention of 1787 came to a close, after three and a half months of delib-
eration, a lady asked Dr. Franklin, "Well, Doctor, what have we got, a republic or a monarchy?"
"A republic," replied the Doctor, "if you can keep it."*

—Anecdote From *The Records of The Federal Convention of 1787*,
ed., Max Farrand, vol. 3, Appendix A, 1911

A republic, if you can keep it. The founders were not at all optimistic about the future
of the Republic. There had been only a handful of other republics in all of human history, and most were small and far away. The founders' pessimism, though, came not
from history but from their knowledge of human nature. A republic, to survive,
needed not only the consent of the governed but also their active participation. It was
not a machine that would go of itself; free societies do not stay free without the
involvement of their citizens.

Today the two central acts of democratic citizenship are voting and paying taxes.
That's basically it. The last time we demanded anything else from people was when
the draft ended in 1973. And yes, there are libertarians who believe that government
asks too much of us—and that the principal right in a democracy is the right to be
left alone—but most everyone else bemoans the fact that only about half of us vote
and don't do much more than send in our returns on April 15. The truth is, even the
archetype of the model citizen is mostly a myth. Except for times of war and the colonial days, we haven't been all that energetic about keeping the Republic.

When Americans look around right now, they see a public-school system with
38% of fourth graders unable to read at a basic level; they see the cost of health insurance escalating as 47 million people go uninsured; they see a government that
responded ineptly to a hurricane in New Orleans; and they see a war whose ends they
do not completely value or understand.

But there is something else we are seeing in the land. Polls show that while confidence in our democracy and our government is near an all-time low, volunteerism
and civic participation since the '70s are near all-time highs. Political scientists are
perplexed about this. If confidence is so low, why would people bother volunteering?
The explanation is pretty simple. People, especially young people, think the government

"A Time to Serve." by Richard Stengel, *Time*, September 10, 2007. Reprinted by permission.

and the public sphere are broken, but they feel they can personally make a difference through community service. After 9/11, Americans were hungry to be asked to do something, to make some kind of sacrifice, and what they mostly remember is being asked to go shopping. The reason private volunteerism is so high is precisely that confidence in our public institutions is so low. People see volunteering not as a form of public service but as an antidote for it.

That is not a recipe for keeping a republic.

Another reality the founders could not have possibly foreseen was that a country that originally enslaved African Americans would be a majority non-white nation by 2050. Robert Putnam, the famed Harvard political scientist who wrote about the decline of civic engagement in *Bowling Alone,* recently released a new study that showed the more diverse a community is, the less people care about and engage with that community. Diversity, in fact, seems to breed distrust and disengagement. The study lands in the midst of a rackety immigration debate, but even if all immigration were to cease tomorrow, we would still be diverse whether we liked it or not. Yet the course of American history, Putnam writes, has always given way to "more encompassing identities" that create a "more capacious sense of 'we.'"

But at this moment in our history, 220 years after the Constitutional Convention, the way to get citizens involved in civic life, the way to create a common culture that will make a virtue of our diversity, the way to give us that more capacious sense of "we"—finally, the way to keep the Republic—is universal national service. No, not mandatory or compulsory service but service that is in our enlightened self-interest as a nation. We are at a historic junction; with the first open presidential election in more than a half-century, it is time for the next President to mine the desire that is out there for serving and create a program for universal national service that will be his—or her—legacy for decades to come. It is the simple but compelling idea that devoting a year or more to national service, whether military or civilian, should become a countrywide rite of passage, the common expectation and widespread experience of virtually every young American.

In 2006 more than 61 million Americans dedicated 8.1 billion hours to volunteerism. The nation's volunteer rate has increased by more than 6 percentage points since 1989. Overall, 27% of Americans, engage in civic life by volunteering. Dr. Franklin would be impressed. The service movement itself began to take off in the 1980s, and today there is a renaissance of dynamic altruistic organizations in the U.S., from Teach for America to City Year to Senior Corps, many of them under the umbrella of AmeriCorps.

In a 2002 poll, 70% of Americans thought universal service was a good idea. And while it's easy to sit back and say this to a pollster, the next President can harness the spirit of volunteerism that already exists and make it a permanent part of American culture.

At various times in American history, public service and private effort went arm in arm. After Pearl Harbor, Rosie the Riveter and Uncle Sam exhorted people to help the war effort, and Americans responded. But since F.D.R., and especially since J.F.K's launching of the Peace Corps, national service has been seen by some as a Democratic or liberal idea. In the '90s, Newt Gingrich argued that the rise of big government programs robbed people of their initiative to volunteer. After Bill Clinton signed the bill to create AmeriCorps in 1993, then Senator John Ashcroft called it "welfare for the well-to-do."

But these days there is a growing consensus on Capitol Hill that the private and public spheres can be linked. Democrats understand the need to support programs outside of government; Republicans understand that voluntary programs can be helped by government. In his first State of the Union address after 9/11, President George W. Bush called for Americans to give 4,000 hours of service and established the USA Freedom Corps. One of the early critics of AmeriCorps, John McCain, has since become a devout supporter. "National service is an issue that has been largely identified with the Democratic Party and the left of the political spectrum," McCain wrote in a 2001 *Washington Monthly* essay. "That is unfortunate, because duty, honor and country are values that transcend ideology . . . National service is a crucial means of making our patriotism real, to the benefit of both ourselves and our country."

It may seem like a strange moment to make the case for national service for young Americans when so many are already doing so much. Young men and women have made their patriotism all too real by volunteering to fight two wars on foreign soil. But we have battlefields in America, too—particularly in education and health care—and the commitment of soldiers abroad has left others yearning to make a parallel commitment here at home.

The Plan

So what would a plan for universal national service look like? It would be voluntary, not mandatory. Americans don't like to be told what they have to do; many have argued that requiring service drains the gift of its virtue. It would be based on carrots, not sticks—"doing well by doing good," as Benjamin Franklin, the true father of civic engagement, put it. So here is a 10-point plan for universal national service. The ideas here are a mixture of suggestions already made, revised versions of other proposals and a few new wrinkles.

1. Create a National-Service Baby Bond

Every time an American baby is born, the Federal Government would invest $5,000 in that child's name in a 529-type fund—the kind many Americans are already using for college savings. At a rate of return of 7%—the historic return for equities—that money would total roughly $19,000 by the time that baby reaches age 20. That money could be accessed between the ages of 18 and 25 on one condition: that he or she commits to at least one year of national or military service. Like the old GI Bill, the money must be used to fund education, start a business or make a down payment on a home. The bond would preserve the voluntary nature of the service but offer a strong incentive for young people to sign up for it. Says City Year CEO and co-founder Michael Brown: "It's a new kind of government philosophy about reciprocity. If you invest in your country, your country will invest in you."

2. Make National Service a Cabinet-Level Department

Right now, the Corporation for National and Community Service—created in 1993 to manage AmeriCorps, Senior Corps and Learn and Serve America—is a small, independent federal agency. Find a catchier name, streamline its responsibilities and bring it up to Cabinet level. This would show that the new President means business when it comes to national service and would recognize that service is integral to how America thinks of itself—and how the President thinks of America. And don't appoint a gray bureaucrat to this job; make it someone like Arnold Schwarzenegger or Mike Bloomberg, who would capture the imagination of the public. In fact, the next President—whatever party—should set a goal to enlist at least 1 million Americans annually in national service by the year 2016.

3. Expand Existing National-Service Programs Like AmeriCorps and the National Senior Volunteer Corps

Since 1994, 500,000 people have gone through AmeriCorps programs tutoring and teaching in urban schools; managing after-school programs; cleaning up playgrounds, schools and parks; and caring for the elderly. After Katrina, AmeriCorps participants descended on the Gulf Coast within 24 hours and have since contributed more than 3 million hours of service. AmeriCorps members earn a small stipend for their volunteering and receive education awards of up to $4,725 per year. Right now, says David Eisner, CEO of the Corporation for National and Community Service, "AmeriCorps is the best-kept secret in America." But under this national-service proposal, the program would more than triple in size, from 75,000 members each year to approximately 250,000. "We don't need to reinvent this nascent infrastructure," says Brown. "We need to take it to scale."

Presently, AmeriCorps is a catch-all initiative for a variety of different programs. Here are four new branded corps and other programs that could come under the new Department of National Service.

4. Create an Education Corps

The idea here is to create a cadre of tutors, teachers and volunteers who can help the 38% of fourth-graders who can't read at a basic level. The members of the Education Corps would also lead after-school programs for the 14 million students—a quarter of all school-age kids—who do not have a supervised activity between 3 and 6 p.m. on schooldays. Studies show that students who spend no time in after-school programs are almost 50% more likely to have used drugs and 37% more likely to become teen parents than students who spend one to four hours a week in an extracurricular activity. The Corps members would also focus on curbing America's dropout epidemic. Right now, 50% of the dropouts come from 15% of the high schools in the U.S., most of them located in high-poverty city neighborhoods and throughout the South. The Education Corps would focus on those troubled school districts.

5. Institute a Summer of Service

For many teenagers, the summer between middle school and high school is an awkward time. They're too young to get a real job and too old to be babysat. Well-to-do families can afford summer camps and exotic learning opportunities, but they're a minority. Shirley Sagawa, an expert on youth policy and an architect of the AmeriCorps legislation, is proposing a Summer of Service. One hundred thousand students would volunteer for organizations like City Year, a national volunteering program and think tank, or Citizen Schools, which organizes after-school activities for middle schoolers, and run summer programs for younger students in exchange for a $500 college scholarship. Senators Christopher Dodd (Democrat, Conn.) and Thad Cochran (Republican, Miss.) and Representative Rosa DeLauro (Democrat, Conn.) have sponsored a bill that would support a service "rite of passage" for students before they begin high school.

6. Build a Health Corps

There are nearly 7 million American children who are eligible for but not enrolled in government-sponsored health-insurance programs. Health Corps volunteers would assist the mostly low-income families of these children in accessing available public insurance offerings like the Children's Health Insurance Program. These volunteers could also act as nonmedical support staff such as caseworkers and community education specialists in underserved rural health clinics—which have less than three-quarters of the nonmedical staffing they need, according to Voices for National Service, a coalition of service organizations that advocates expanding federal service programs. The one-year experience in the Health Corps could lead these volunteers toward careers in nursing or medicine, helping to redress gaps that have left the U.S. with a dearth of qualified nurses and medical professionals.

7. Launch a Green Corps

This would be a combination of F.D.R.'s Civilian Conservation Corps—which put 3 million "boys in the woods" to build the foundation of our modern park system—and a group that would improve national infrastructure and combat climate change. When Roosevelt created the CCC, there were 25 million young Americans who were unemployed. Today there are 1.5 million Americans between 18 and 24 who are neither employed nor in school. These young men and women could address America's well-documented infrastructure problems. The Green Corps could reclaim polluted streams and blighted urban lots; repair and rehabilitate railroad lines, ports, schools and hospitals; and build energy-efficient green housing for elderly and low-income people.

8. Recruit a Rapid-Response Reserve Corps

The disarray and lack of a coordinated response to 9/11 and Katrina tell us there is a role volunteers play in responding quickly to disasters and emergencies. The new

Rapid-Response Reserve Corps would consist of retired military and National Guard personnel as well as national- and community-service program alumni to focus on disaster preparedness and immediate response to local and national disasters. The program would initially train 50,000 members, who could be deployed for two-week periods in response to emergencies and serve under the guidance of the Federal Emergency Management Agency.

9. Start a National-Service Academy

Picture West Point, but instead of learning how to fire an M-4 and reading *The Art of War*, students would be studying the *Federalist* papers and learning how to transform a failing public school. Conceived by two former Teach for America corps members, Chris Myers Asch and Shawn Raymond, the U.S. Public Service Academy would give undergraduates a four-year education in exchange for a five-year commitment to public service after they graduate. The idea is to provide a focused education for people who will serve in the public sector—either the federal, state or local government—and thereby create a new generation of civic leaders. Asch and Raymond were so dismayed by the government's response to Katrina that they wanted to create a new generation of people who were idealistic about government. "We need an institution that systematically develops leadership," says Asch. "We need to elevate it in the eyes of young people so we can attract the best and the brightest." The idea has been endorsed by Hillary Clinton and Pennsylvanian Republican Senator Arlen Specter, who are co-sponsors of legislation that would allocate $164 million per year for the envisioned 5,000-student academy.

10. Create a Baby-Boomer Education Bond

Over the next 20 years, 78 million baby boomers will be eligible to retire. That is, if they can afford to—and if they want to. According to an AARP survey, 80% of Americans between 50 and 60 said they were planning to work during retirement. "Many seniors are interested in careers that are influenced by a spirit of service. Over half want to work in the education, health-care and nonprofit sector," says Marc Freedman, founder and CEO of Civic Ventures and co-founder of Experience Corps. Experience Corps is the largest AmeriCorps program for people over 55; it consists of teams of 10 to 15 people working to improve reading for students in kindergarten through third grade. Just as AmeriCorps members receive scholarships, baby-boomer volunteers would be able to designate a scholarship of $1,000 for every 500 hours of community service they complete. The $1,000 would be deposited into an education savings account or a 529 fund to be used by the volunteer's children or grandchildren or a student they designate. "There is a whole trend of people starting second careers with a focus on service," says Freedman. "National service is not just for young people. This is the generation that national service was created for in the first place, whom J.F.K. called on to help and for whom we created the Peace Corps. Many missed their chance and are now getting a second opportunity to ask what they can do for their country."

The Cost

So how much would all this cost? There are about 4 million babies born each year, and if each receives a $5,000 baby bond, that would be about $20 billion a year; that is, roughly two months of funding for the Iraq war and about half what the government spends per year on the federal prison system. The government would get $1 billion in dividends from the investment and would be able to cash in the bonds that people don't use. At the same time, corporate America would need to play a critical role in a plan for universal national service. The private sector has contributed more than $1 billion to AmeriCorps. The private sector must step up to the plate in funding national service—after all, it benefits too.

People are often skeptical of calls for service, especially from politicians, as they see them as crowd-pleasing rhetoric or a way of avoiding asking people to make a true sacrifice. But Americans are ready to be asked to do something. "People understand the idea that this is a great country, and that greatness isn't free," says Zach Maurin, the co-founder of ServeNext.org, which has launched a campaign to get the presidential candidates to endorse national service.

Between 1944 and 1956, 8 million returning veterans received debt-free education, low-interest mortgages or small-business loans. The GI Bill helped assimilate those young men into a new postwar society and helped turn America into a middle-class nation. A new GI Bill for national service involving men and women, young and old, could help secure America for the future and turn every new generation into a Greatest Generation. The courageous souls who signed the Declaration of Independence pledged "our Lives, our Fortunes and our sacred Honor." The least we can do to keep the Republic is to pledge a little time.

With reporting by Jeremy Caplan and Kristina Dell/New York.

Comfort Women
© Chris Steele-Perkins / Magnum Photos
Published January 13, 2009, in *Slate*
http://todayspictures.slate.com/20090113/

The photo essay "Comfort Women" is introduced with these words: "In 1992, Japan issued an apology for having forced tens of thousands of Korean women into sexual slavery during its colonial period and World War II, 1931 to 1945. Recently, the government again denied its culpability. An estimated 200,000 were taken into sexual slavery, many also from China, Taiwan, the Philippines, and Singapore. Chris Steele-Perkins interviewed these survivors, who are still boldly fighting for recognition." In a statement at mag-numphotos.com, Steele-Perkins writes, "I wanted to photograph these women as I fundamentally saw them: strong women who had survived the most degrading atrocities unbroken and with dignity. Women I admired."

The particular image above, from 2006, is the eighth in the essay. Its caption reads, "KOREA—Kim Soon Ak, born in 1928, was the eldest child and only daughter of poor farmers. She remembers she was wearing a white top and black skirt when she was taken to work, she was told, in a thread factory, She was taken on a four-day journey to Mongolia and forced to work in a sex station at age 17. On weekends, even when she had her period, she had to have sex with 20 to 30 soldiers who stood in line outside. When she came home, she learned her father had died of grief over losing her. Until the Comfort Women movement started, she told no one of her past. She still wishes she could have worn the wedding veil."

Why I Blog

Andrew Sullivan

The word *blog* is a conflation of two words: *Web* and *log*. It contains in its four letters a concise and accurate self-description: it is a log of thoughts and writing posted publicly on the World Wide Web. In the monosyllabic vernacular of the Internet, *Web log* soon became the word *blog*.

This form of instant and global self-publishing, made possible by technology widely available only for the past decade or so, allows for no retroactive editing (apart from fixing minor typos or small glitches) and removes from the act of writing any considered or lengthy review. It is the spontaneous expression of instant thought—impermanent beyond even the ephemera of daily journalism. It is accountable in immediate and unavoidable ways to readers and other bloggers, and linked via hypertext to continuously multiplying references and sources. Unlike any single piece of print journalism, its borders are extremely porous and its truth inherently transitory. The consequences of this for the act of writing are still sinking in.

A ship's log owes its name to a small wooden board, often weighted with lead, that was for centuries attached to a line and thrown over the stern. The weight of the log would keep it in the same place in the water, like a provisional anchor, while the ship moved away. By measuring the length of line used up in a set period of time, mariners could calculate the speed of their journey (the rope itself was marked by equidistant "knots" for easy measurement). As a ship's voyage progressed, the course came to be marked down in a book that was called a log.

In journeys at sea that took place before radio or radar or satellites or sonar, these logs were an indispensable source for recording what actually happened. They helped navigators surmise where they were and how far they had traveled and how much longer they had to stay at sea. They provided accountability to a ship's owners and traders. They were designed to be as immune to faking as possible. Away from land, there was usually no reliable corroboration of events apart from the crew's own account in the middle of an expanse of blue and gray and green; and in long journeys, memories always blur and facts disperse. A log provided as accurate an account as could be gleaned in real time.

As you read a log, you have the curious sense of moving backward in time as you move forward in pages—the opposite of a book. As you piece together a narrative that was never intended as one, it seems—and is—more truthful. Logs, in this sense, were a form of human self-correction. They amended for hindsight, for the ways in which human beings order and tidy and construct the story of their lives as they look back on them. Logs require a letting-go of narrative because they do not allow for a knowledge of the ending. So they have plot as well as dramatic irony—the reader will know the ending before the writer did.

Anyone who has blogged his thoughts for an extended time will recognize this world. We bloggers have scant opportunity to collect our thoughts, to wait until events have settled and a clear pattern emerges. We blog now—as news reaches us, as facts emerge. This is partly true for all journalism, which is, as its etymology suggests, daily writing, always subject to subsequent revision. And a good columnist will adjust position and judgment and even political loyalty over time, depending on events. But a blog is not so much daily writing as hourly writing. And with that level of timeliness, the provisionality of every word is even more pressing—and the risk of error or the thrill of prescience that much greater.

No columnist or reporter or novelist will have his minute shifts or constant small contradictions exposed as mercilessly as a blogger's are. A columnist can ignore or duck a subject less noticeably than a blogger committing thoughts to pixels several times a day. A reporter can wait—must wait—until every source has confirmed. A novelist can spend months or years before committing words to the world. For bloggers, the deadline is always now. Blogging is therefore to writing what extreme sports are to athletics: more free-form, more accident-prone, less formal, more alive. It is, in many ways, writing out loud.

You end up writing about yourself, since you are a relatively fixed point in this constant interaction with the ideas and facts of the exterior world. And in this sense, the historic form closest to blogs is the diary. But with this difference: a diary is almost always a private matter. Its raw honesty, its dedication to marking life as it happens and remembering life as it was, makes it a terrestrial log. A few diaries are meant to be read by others, of course, just as correspondence could be—but usually posthumously, or as a way to compile facts for a more considered autobiographical rendering. But a blog, unlike a diary, is instantly public. It transforms this most personal and retrospective of forms into a painfully public and immediate one. It combines the confessional genre with the log form and exposes the author in a manner no author has ever been exposed before.

I remember first grappling with what to put on my blog. It was the spring of 2000 and, like many a freelance writer at the time, I had some vague notion that I needed to have a presence "online." I had no clear idea of what to do, but a friend who ran a Web-design company offered to create a site for me, and, since I was technologically clueless, he also agreed to post various essays and columns as I wrote them. Before too long, this became a chore for him, and he called me one day to say he'd found an online platform that was so simple I could henceforth post all my writing myself. The platform was called Blogger.

As I used it to post columns or links to books or old essays, it occurred to me that I could also post new writing—writing that could even be exclusive to the blog. But what? Like any new form, blogging did not start from nothing. It evolved from various journalistic traditions. In my case, I drew on my mainstream-media experience to navigate the virgin sea. I had a few early inspirations: the old Notebook section of *The New Republic*, a magazine that, under the editorial guidance of Michael Kinsley, had introduced a more English style of crisp, short commentary into what had been a more high-minded genre of American opinion writing. *The New Republic* had also pioneered a Diarist feature on the last page, which was designed to be a more personal, essayistic, first-person form of journalism. Mixing the two genres, I did what I had been trained to do—and improvised.

I'd previously written online as well, contributing to a listserv for gay writers and helping Kinsley initiate a more discursive form of online writing for *Slate*, the first magazine published exclusively on the Web. As soon as I began writing this way, I realized that the online form rewarded a colloquial, unfinished tone. In one of my early Kinsley-guided experiments, he urged me not to think too hard before writing. So I wrote as I'd write an e-mail—with only a mite more circumspection. This is hazardous, of course, as anyone who has ever clicked Send in a fit of anger or hurt will testify. But blogging requires an embrace of such hazards, a willingness to fall off the trapeze rather than fail to make the leap.

From the first few days of using the form, I was hooked. The simple experience of being able to directly broadcast my own words to readers was an exhilarating literary liberation. Unlike the current generation of writers, who have only ever blogged, I knew firsthand what the alternative meant. I'd edited a weekly print magazine, *The New Republic*, for five years, and written countless columns and essays for a variety of traditional outlets. And in all this, I'd often chafed, as most writers do, at the endless delays, revisions, office politics, editorial fights, and last-minute cuts for space that dead-tree publishing entails. Blogging—even to an audience of a few hundred in the early days—was intoxicatingly free in comparison. Like taking a narcotic.

It was obvious from the start that it was revolutionary. Every writer since the printing press has longed for a means to publish himself and reach—instantly—any reader on Earth. Every professional writer has paid some dues waiting for an editor's nod, or enduring a publisher's incompetence, or being ground to literary dust by a legion of fact-checkers and copy editors. If you added up the time a writer once had to spend finding an outlet, impressing editors, sucking up to proprietors, and proofreading edits, you'd find another lifetime buried in the interstices. But with one click of the Publish Now button, all these troubles evaporated.

Alas, as I soon discovered, this sudden freedom from above was immediately replaced by insurrection from below. Within minutes of my posting something, even in the earliest days, readers responded. E-mail seemed to unleash their inner beast. They were more brutal than any editor, more persnickety than any copy editor, and more emotionally unstable than any colleague.

Again, it's hard to overrate how different this is. Writers can be sensitive, vain souls, requiring gentle nurturing from editors and oddly susceptible to the blows delivered by reviewers. They survive, for the most part, but the thinness of their skins is legendary. Moreover, before the blogosphere, reporters and columnists were largely shielded from this kind of direct hazing. Yes, letters to the editor would arrive in due course and subscriptions would be canceled. But reporters and columnists tended to operate in a relative sanctuary, answerable mainly to their editors, not readers. For a long time, columns were essentially monologues published to applause, muffled murmurs, silence, or a distant heckle. I'd gotten blowback from pieces before—but in an amorphous, time-delayed, distant way. Now the feedback was instant, personal, and brutal.

And so blogging found its own answer to the defensive counterblast from the journalistic establishment. To the charges of inaccuracy and unprofessionalism, bloggers could point to the fierce, immediate scrutiny of their readers. Unlike newspapers, which would eventually publish corrections in a box of printed spinach far from the original error, bloggers had to walk the walk of self-correction in the same space and in the same format as the original screwup. The form was more accountable, not less, because there is nothing more conducive to professionalism than being publicly humiliated for sloppiness. Of course, a blogger could ignore an error or simply refuse to acknowledge mistakes. But if he persisted, he would be razzed by competitors and assailed by commenters and abandoned by readers. In an era when the traditional media found itself beset by scandals as disparate as Stephen Glass, Jayson Blair, and Dan Rather, bloggers survived the first assault on their worth. In time, in fact, the high standards expected of well-trafficked bloggers spilled over into greater accountability, transparency, and punctiliousness among the media powers that were. Even *New York Times* columnists were forced to admit when they had been wrong.

The blog remained a *superficial* medium, of course. By superficial, I mean simply that blogging rewards brevity and immediacy. No one wants to read a 9,000-word treatise online. On the Web, one-sentence links are as legitimate as thousand-word diatribes—in fact, they are often valued more. And, as Matt Drudge told me when I sought advice from the master in 2001, the key to understanding a blog is to realize that it's a broadcast, not a publication. If it stops moving, it dies. If it stops paddling, it sinks.

But the superficiality masked considerable depth—greater depth, from one perspective, than the traditional media could offer. The reason was a single technological innovation: the hyperlink. An old-school columnist can write 800 brilliant words analyzing or commenting on, say, a new think-tank report or scientific survey. But in reading it on paper, you have to take the columnist's presentation of the material on faith, or be convinced by a brief quotation (which can always be misleading out of context). Online, a hyperlink to the original source transforms the experience. Yes, a few sentences of bloggy spin may not be as satisfying as a full column, but the ability to read the primary material instantly—in as careful or shallow a fashion as you choose—can add much greater context than anything on paper. Even a blogger's chosen pull quote, unlike a columnist's, can be effortlessly checked against the original. Now this innovation, pre-dating blogs but popularized by them, is increasingly central to mainstream journalism.

A blog, therefore, bobs on the surface of the ocean but has its anchorage in waters deeper than those print media is technologically able to exploit. It disempowers the writer to that extent, of course. The blogger can get away with less and afford fewer pretensions of authority. He is—more than any writer of the past—a node among other nodes, connected but unfinished without the links and the comments and the track-backs that make the blogosphere, at its best, a conversation, rather than a production.

A writer fully aware of and at ease with the provisionality of his own work is nothing new. For centuries, writers have experimented with forms that suggest the imperfection of human thought, the inconstancy of human affairs, and the humbling, chastening passage of time. If you compare the meandering, questioning, unresolved dialogues of Plato with the definitive, logical treatises of Aristotle, you see the difference between a skeptic's spirit translated into writing and a spirit that seeks to bring some finality to the argument. Perhaps the greatest single piece of Christian apologetics, Pascal's *Pensées*, is a series of meandering, short, and incomplete stabs at arguments, observations, insights. Their lack of finish is what makes them so compelling—arguably more compelling than a polished treatise by Aquinas.

Or take the brilliant polemics of Karl Kraus, the publisher of and main writer for *Die Fackel,* who delighted in constantly twitting authority with slashing aphorisms and rapid-fire bursts of invective. Kraus had something rare in his day: the financial wherewithal to self-publish. It gave him a fearlessness that is now available to anyone who can afford a computer and an Internet connection.

But perhaps the quintessential blogger *avant la lettre* was Montaigne. His essays were published in three major editions, each one longer and more complex than the previous. A passionate skeptic, Montaigne amended, added to, and amplified the essays for each edition, making them three-dimensional through time. In the best modern translations, each essay is annotated, sentence by sentence, paragraph by paragraph, by small letters (A, B, and C) for each major edition, helping the reader see how each rewrite added to or subverted, emphasized or ironized, the version before. Montaigne was living his skepticism, daring to show how a writer evolves, changes his mind, learns new things, shifts perspectives, grows older—and that this, far from being something that needs to be hidden behind a veneer of unchanging authority, can become a virtue, a new way of looking at the pretensions of authorship and text and truth. Montaigne, for good measure, also peppered his essays with myriads of what bloggers would call external links. His own thoughts are strewn with and complicated by the aphorisms and anecdotes of others. Scholars of the sources note that many of these "money quotes" were deliberately taken out of context, adding layers of irony to writing that was already saturated in empirical doubt.

To blog is therefore to let go of your writing in a way, to hold it at arm's length, open it to scrutiny, allow it to float in the ether for a while, and to let others, as Montaigne did, pivot you toward relative truth. A blogger will notice this almost immediately upon starting. Some e-mailers, unsurprisingly, know more about a subject than the blogger does. They will send links, stories, and facts, challenging the blogger's view of the world, sometimes outright refuting it, but more frequently adding context and nuance and complexity to an idea. The role of a blogger is not to defend against this but to embrace it. He is similar in this way to the host of a dinner party. He can provoke discussion or take a position, even passionately, but he also must create an atmosphere in which others want to participate.

That atmosphere will inevitably be formed by the blogger's personality. The blogosphere may, in fact, be the least veiled of any forum in which a writer dares to express himself. Even the most careful and self-aware blogger will reveal more about himself than he wants to in a few unguarded sentences and publish them before he has the sense to hit Delete. The wise panic that can paralyze a writer—the fear that he will be exposed, undone, humiliated—is not available to a blogger. You can't have blogger's block. You have to express yourself now, while your emotions roil, while your temper flares, while your humor lasts. You can try to hide yourself from real scrutiny, and the exposure it demands, but it's hard. And that's what makes blogging as a form stand out: it is rich in personality. The faux intimacy of the Web experience, the closeness of the e-mail and the instant message, seeps through. You feel as if you know bloggers as they go through their lives, experience the same things you are experiencing, and share the moment. When readers of my blog bump into me in person, they invariably address me as Andrew. Print readers don't do that. It's Mr. Sullivan to them.

On my blog, my readers and I experienced 9/11 together, in real time. I can look back and see not just how I responded to the event, but how I responded to it at 3:47 that afternoon. And at 9:46 that night. There is a vividness to this immediacy that cannot be rivaled by print. The same goes for the 2000 recount, the Iraq War, the revelations of Abu Ghraib, the death of John Paul II, or any of the other history-making events of the past decade. There is simply no way to write about them in real time without revealing a huge amount about yourself. And the intimate bond this creates with readers is unlike the bond that the The Times, say, develops with its readers through the same events. Alone in front of a computer, at any moment, are two people: a blogger and a reader. The proximity is palpable, the moment human—whatever authority a blogger has is derived not from the institution he works for but from the humanness he conveys. This is writing with emotion not just under but always breaking through the surface. It renders a writer and a reader not just connected but linked in a visceral, personal way. The only term that really describes this is *friendship*. And it is a relatively new thing to write for thousands and thousands of friends.

These friends, moreover, are an integral part of the blog itself—sources of solace, company, provocation, hurt, and correction. If I were to do an inventory of the material that appears on my blog, I'd estimate that a good third of it is reader-generated, and a good third of my time is spent absorbing readers' views, comments, and tips. Readers tell me of breaking stories, new perspectives, and counterarguments to prevailing assumptions. And this is what blogging, in turn, does to reporting. The traditional method involves a journalist searching for key sources, nurturing them, and sequestering them from his rivals. A blogger splashes gamely into a subject and dares the sources to come to him.

Some of this material—e-mails from soldiers on the front lines, from scientists explaining new research, from dissident Washington writers too scared to say what they think in their own partisan redoubts—might never have seen the light of day before the blogosphere. And some of it, of course, is dubious stuff. Bloggers can be spun and misled as easily as traditional writers—and the rigorous source assessment that good reporters do can't be done by e-mail. But you'd be surprised by what comes unsolicited into the in-box, and how helpful it often is.

Not all of it is mere information. Much of it is also opinion and scholarship, a knowledge base that exceeds the research department of any newspaper. A good blog is your own private Wikipedia. Indeed, the most pleasant surprise of blogging has been the number of people working in law or government or academia or rearing kids at home who have real literary talent and real knowledge, and who had no outlet—until now. There is a distinction here, of course, between the edited use of e-mailed sources by a careful blogger and the often mercurial cacophony on an unmediated comments section. But the truth is out there—and the miracle of e-mail allows it to come to you.

Fellow bloggers are always expanding this knowledge base. Eight years ago, the blogosphere felt like a handful of individual cranks fighting with one another. Today, it feels like a universe of cranks, with vast, pulsating readerships, fighting with one another. To the neophyte reader, or blogger, it can seem overwhelming. But there is a connection between the intimacy of the early years and the industry it has become today. And the connection is human individuality.

The pioneers of online journalism—*Slate* and *Salon*—are still very popular, and successful. But the more memorable stars of the Internet—even within those two sites—are all personally branded. Daily Kos, for example, is written by hundreds of bloggers, and amended by thousands of commenters. But it is named after Markos Moulitsas, who started it, and his own prose still provides a backbone to the front-page blog. The biggest news-aggregator site in the world, the Drudge Report, is named after its founder, Matt Drudge, who somehow conveys a unified sensibility through his selection of links, images, and stories. The vast, expanding universe of The Huffington Post still finds some semblance of coherence in the Cambridge-Greek twang of Arianna; the entire world of online celebrity gossip circles the drain of Perez Hilton; and the investigative journalism, reviewing, and commentary of Talking Points Memo is still tied together by the tone of Josh Marshall. Even *Slate* is unimaginable without Mickey Kaus's voice.

What endures is a human brand. Readers have encountered this phenomenon before—*I.F. Stone's Weekly* comes to mind—but not to this extent. It stems, I think, from the conversational style that blogging rewards. What you want in a conversationalist is as much character as authority. And if you think of blogging as more like talk radio or cable news than opinion magazines or daily newspapers, then this personalized emphasis is less surprising. People have a voice for radio and a face for television. For blogging, they have a sensibility.

But writing in this new form is a collective enterprise as much as it is an individual one—and the connections between bloggers are as important as the content on the blogs. The links not only drive conversation, they drive readers. The more you link, the more others will link to you, and the more traffic and readers you will get. The zero-sum game of old media—in which *Time* benefits from *Newsweek*'s decline and vice versa—becomes win-win. It's great for *Time* to be linked to by *Newsweek* and the other way round. One of the most prized statistics in the blogosphere is therefore not the total number of readers or page views, but the "authority" you get by being linked to by other blogs. It's an indication of how central you are to the online conversation of humankind.

The reason this open-source market of thinking and writing has such potential is that the always adjusting and evolving collective mind can rapidly filter out bad arguments and bad ideas. The flip side, of course, is that bloggers are also human beings. Reason is not the only fuel in the tank. In a world where no distinction is made between good traffic and bad traffic, and where emotion often rules, some will always raise their voice to dominate the conversation; others will pander shamelessly to their readers' prejudices; others will start online brawls for the fun of it. Sensationalism, dirt, and the ease of formulaic talking points always beckon. You can disappear into the partisan blogosphere and never stumble onto a site you disagree with.

But linkage mitigates this. A Democratic blog will, for example, be forced to link to Republican ones, if only to attack and mock. And it's in the interests of both camps to generate shared traffic. This encourages polarized slugfests. But online, at least you see both sides. Reading *The Nation* or *National Review* before the Internet existed allowed for more cocooning than the wide-open online sluice gates do now. If there's more incivility, there's also more fluidity. Rudeness, in any case, isn't the worst thing that can happen to a blogger. Being ignored is. Perhaps the nastiest thing one can do to a fellow blogger is to rip him apart and fail to provide a link.

A successful blog therefore has to balance itself between a writer's own take on the world and others. Some bloggers collect, or "aggregate," other bloggers' posts with dozens of quick links and minimalist opinion topspin: Glenn Reynolds at Instapundit does this for the right-of-center; Duncan Black at Eschaton does it for the left. Others are more eclectic, or aggregate links in a particular niche, or cater to a settled and knowledgeable reader base. A "blogroll" is an indicator of whom you respect enough to keep in your galaxy. For many years, I kept my reading and linking habits to a relatively small coterie of fellow political bloggers. In today's blogosphere, to do this is to embrace marginality. I've since added links to religious blogs and literary ones and scientific ones and just plain weird ones. As the blogosphere has expanded beyond anyone's capacity to absorb it, I've needed an assistant and interns to scour the Web for links and stories and photographs to respond to and think about. It's a difficult balance, between your own interests and obsessions, and the knowledge, insight, and wit of others—but an immensely rich one. There are times, in fact, when a blogger feels less like a writer than an online disc jockey, mixing samples of tunes and generating new melodies through mashups while also making his own music. He is both artist and producer—and the beat always goes on.

If all this sounds postmodern, that's because it is. And blogging suffers from the same flaws as postmodernism: a failure to provide stable truth or a permanent perspective. A traditional writer is valued by readers precisely because they trust him to have thought long and hard about a subject, given it time to evolve in his head, and composed a piece of writing that is worth their time to read at length and to ponder. Bloggers don't do this and cannot do this—and that limits them far more than it does traditional long-form writing.

A blogger will air a variety of thoughts or facts on any subject in no particular order other than that dictated by the passing of time. A writer will instead use time, synthesizing these thoughts, ordering them, weighing which points count more than others, seeing how his views evolved in the writing process itself, and responding to an editor's perusal of a draft or two. The result is almost always more measured, more satisfying, and more enduring than a blizzard of posts. The triumphalist notion that blogging should somehow replace traditional writing is as foolish as it is pernicious. In some ways, blogging's gifts to our discourse make the skills of a good traditional writer much more valuable, not less. The torrent of blogospheric insights, ideas, and arguments places a greater premium on the person who can finally make sense of it all, turning it into something more solid, and lasting, and rewarding.

The points of this essay, for example, have appeared in shards and fragments on my blog for years. But being forced to order them in my head and think about them for a longer stretch has helped me understand them better, and perhaps express them more clearly. Each week, after a few hundred posts, I also write an actual newspaper column. It invariably turns out to be more considered, balanced, and evenhanded than the blog. But the blog will always inform and enrich the column, and often serve as a kind of free-form, free-associative research. And an essay like this will spawn discussion best handled on a blog. The conversation, in other words, is the point, and the different idioms used by the conversationalists all contribute something of value to it. And so, if the defenders of the old media once viscerally regarded blogging as some kind of threat, they are starting to see it more as a portal, and a spur.

There is, after all, something simply irreplaceable about reading a piece of writing at length on paper, in a chair or on a couch or in bed. To use an obvious analogy, jazz entered our civilization much later than composed, formal music. But it hasn't replaced it; and no jazz musician would ever claim that it could. Jazz merely demands a different way of playing and listening, just as blogging requires a different mode of writing and reading. Jazz and blogging are intimate, improvisational, and individual—but also inherently collective. And the audience talks over both.

The reason they talk while listening, and comment or link while reading, is that they understand that this is a kind of music that needs to be engaged rather than merely absorbed. To listen to jazz as one would listen to an aria is to miss the point. Reading at a monitor, at a desk, or on an iPhone provokes a querulous, impatient, distracted attitude, a demand for instant, usable information, that is simply not conducive to opening a novel or a favorite magazine on the couch. Reading on paper evokes a more relaxed and meditative response. The message dictates the medium. And each medium has its place—as long as one is not mistaken for the other.

In fact, for all the intense gloom surrounding the news-paper and magazine business, this is actually a golden era for journalism. The blogosphere has added a whole new idiom to the act of writing and has introduced an entirely new generation to nonfiction. It has enabled writers to write out loud in ways never seen or understood before. And yet it has exposed a hunger and need for traditional writing that, in the age of television's dominance, had seemed on the wane. Words, of all sorts, have never seemed so now.

The Language of Discretion

Amy Tan

Once, at a family dinner in San Francisco, my mother whispered to me: "Sau-sau [Brother's Wife] pretends too hard to be polite! Why bother? In the end, she always takes everything."

My mother acted like a *waixiao,* an expatriate, temporarily away from China since 1949, no longer patient with ritual courtesies. As if to prove her point, she reached across the table to offer my elderly aunt from Beijing the last scallop from the Happy Family seafood dish.

Sau-sau scowled. *"B'yao, zhen b'yao!"* she cried, patting her plump stomach. I don't want it, really I don't!

"Take it! Take it!" my mother scolded in Chinese.

"Full, I'm already full," Sau-sau protested weakly, eyeing the beloved scallop.

"Ai!" exclaimed my mother, exasperated. "Nobody else wants it. If you don't take it, it will only rot!"

Sau-sau sighed, acting as if she were doing my mother a big favor by taking the wretched scrap off her hands.

My mother turned to her brother, a high-ranking Communist official who with Sau-sau was visiting her in California for the first time: "In America a Chinese person could starve to death. If you say you don't want it, they won't ask you again forever."

My uncle nodded and said he understood fully: Americans take things quickly because they have no time to be polite.

I thought about this misunderstanding again—of social contexts failing in translation— when a friend sent me an article from *The New York Times Magazine.* The article, on changes in New York's Chinatown, made passing reference to the inherent ambivalence of the Chinese language.

Chinese people are so "discreet and modest," the article stated, that there aren't even words for "yes" and "no."

That's not true, I thought, although I could see why an outsider might think that. I continued reading.

If one is Chinese, the article went on, "one compromises, one doesn't hazard a loss of face by an overemphatic response."

My throat seized. Why do people keep saying these things? As though we were like those little dolls sold in Chinatown tourist shops, heads bobbing up and down in complacent agreement to anything said!

I worry about the effect of one-dimensional statements on the unwary and guileless. When they read about this so-called vocabulary deficit, do they also conclude that Chinese people evolved into a mild-mannered lot because their language allowed them only to hobble forth with minced words?

Something enormous is always lost in translation. Something insidious seeps into the gaps, especially when amateur linguists continue to compare, one for one, language differences and then put forth notions wide open to misinterpretation: that Chinese people have no direct linguistic means to make decisions, assert or deny, affirm or negate, just say no to drug dealers, or behave properly on the witness stand when told, "Please answer yes or no."

Yet one can argue, with the help of renowned linguists, that the Chinese are indeed up a creek without "yes" and "no." Take any number of variations on the old language-and-reality theory stated years ago by Edward Sapir: "Human beings . . . are very much at the mercy of the particular language which has become the medium of expression for their society. . . . The fact of the matter is that the 'real world' is to a large extent unconsciously built up on the language habits of the group."*

This notion was further bolstered by the famous Sapir–Whorf hypothesis, which states roughly that one's perception of the world and how one functions in it depends a great deal on the language used. As Sapir, Benjamin Whorf, and new carriers of the banner would have us believe, language shapes our thinking, channels us along certain patterns embedded in words, syntactic structures, and intonation patterns. Language has become the peg and the shelf that enable us to sort out and categorize the world. In English, we see "cats" and "dogs"; what if the language had also specified *glatz,* meaning "animals that leave fur on the sofa," and *glotz,* meaning "animals that leave fur and drool on the sofa"? How would language, the enabler, have changed our perceptions with slight vocabulary variations?

And if this were the case—if language were the master of destined thought—think of the opportunities lost from failure to evolve two little words, "yes" and "no," the simplest of opposites! Genghis Khan could have been sent back to Mongolia. Opium wars might have been averted. The Cultural Revolution could have been sidestepped.

There are still many, from serious linguists to pop psychology cultists, who view language and reality as inextricably tied, one being the consequence of the other. We have traversed the range from Sapir–Whorf to est to neurolinguistic programming, which tell us that "you are what you say."

I too have been intrigued by the theories. I can summarize, albeit badly, ages-old empirical evidence: of Eskimos and their infinite ways to say "snow," their ability to *see* differences in snowflake configurations, thanks to the richness of their vocabulary,

---

* *Selected Writings of Edward Sapir in Language, Culture and Personality,* ed. D. G. Mandelbaum (Berkeley and Los Angeles: University of California Press, 1949).

while non-Eskimos like me founder in "snow," "more snow," and "lots more where that came from."

I too have experienced dramatic cognitive awakenings via the word. Once I added "mauve" to my vocabulary, I began to see it everywhere. "When I learned how to pronounce "prix fixe," I ate French food at prices better than the easier-to-say "à la carte" choices.

But just how seriously are we supposed to take this?

Sapir said something else about language and reality. It is the part that often gets left behind in the dot-dot-dots of quotations: "No two languages are ever sufficiently similar to be considered as representing the same social reality. The worlds in which different societies live are distinct worlds, not merely the same world with different labels attached."

When I first read this, I thought, Here at last is validity for the dilemmas I felt growing up in a bicultural, bilingual family! As any child of immigrant parents knows, there's a special kind of double bind attached to knowing two languages. My parents, for example, spoke to me in both Chinese and English; I spoke back to them in English.

"Amy-ah!" they'd call to me.

"What?" I'd mumble back.

"Do not question us when we call," they'd scold in Chinese. "It is not respectful."

"What do you mean?"

"Ai! Didn't we just tell you not to question?"

To this day, I wonder which parts of my behavior were shaped by Chinese, which by English. I am tempted to think that if I am of two minds on some matter, it is due to the richness of my linguistic experiences, not to any personal tendencies toward wishy-washiness. But which mind says what?

Was it perhaps patience—developed through years of deciphering my mother's fractured English—that had me listening politely while a woman announced over the phone that I had won one of five valuable prizes? Was it respect—pounded in by the Chinese imperative to accept convoluted explanations—that had me agreeing that I might find it worthwhile to drive seventy-five miles to view a time-share resort? Could I have been at a loss for words when asked, "Wouldn't you like to win a Hawaiian cruise or perhaps a fabulous Star of India designed exclusively by Carter and Van Arpels?"

And when this same woman called back a week later, this time complaining that I had missed my appointment, obviously it was my type A language that kicked into gear and interrupted her. Certainly, my blunt denial—"Frankly I'm not interested"— was as American as apple pie. And when she said, "But it's in Morgan Hill," and I shouted back, "Read my lips. I don't care if it's Timbuktu," you can be sure I said it with the precise intonation expressing both cynicism and disgust.

It's dangerous business, this sorting out of language and behavior. Which one is English? Which is Chinese? The categories manifest themselves: passive or aggressive, tentative or assertive, indirect or direct. And I realize they are just variations of the same theme: that Chinese people are discreet and modest.

Reject them all!

If my reaction seems overly strident, it is because I cannot come across as too emphatic. I grew up listening to the same lines over and over, like so many rote expressions repeated in an English phrasebook. And I too almost came to believe them.

Yet if I consider my upbringing more carefully, I find there was nothing discreet about the Chinese language I grew up with. My parents made everything abundantly clear. Nothing wishy-washy in their demands, no compromises accepted: "Of course you will become a famous neurosurgeon," they told me. "And yes, a concert pianist on the side."

In fact, now that I remember, it seems that the more emphatic outbursts always spilled over into Chinese: "Not that way! You must wash rice so not a single grain is lost."

I do not believe that my parents—both immigrants from mainland China—are the sole exceptions to the discreet-and-modest rule. I have only to look at the number of Chinese engineering students skewing minority ratios at Berkeley, MIT, and Yale. Certainly they were not raised by passive mothers and fathers who said, "It's up to you, my daughter. Writer, welfare recipient, masseuse, or molecular engineer—you decide."

And my American mind says, See, those engineering students weren't able to say no to their parents' demands. But then my Chinese mind remembers: Ah, but those parents all wanted their sons and daughters to be *pre-med.*

Having listened to both Chinese and English, I tend to be suspicious of any comparisons made between the two languages. Typically, one language—that of the person who is doing the comparing—is used as the standard, the benchmark for a logical form of expression. And so the other language is in danger of being judged by comparison deficient or superfluous, simplistic or unnecessarily complex, melodious or cacophonous. English speakers point out that Chinese is extremely difficult because it relies on variations in tone barely discernible to the human ear. By the same token, Chinese speakers tell me English is extremely difficult because it is inconsistent, a language of too many broken rules, of Mickey Mice and Donald Ducks.

Even more dangerous, in my view, is the temptation to compare both language and behavior *in translation.* To listen to my mother speak English, one might think she has no concept of past or future, that she doesn't see the difference between singular and plural, that she is gender blind because she refers to my husband as "she." If one were not careful, one might also generalize, from how my mother talks, that all Chinese people take a circumlocutory route to get to the point. It is, rather, my mother's idiosyncratic behavior to ramble a bit.

I worry that the dominant society may see Chinese people from a limited—and limiting—perspective. I worry that seemingly benign stereotypes may be part of the reason there are few Chinese in top management positions, in mainstream political roles. I worry about the power of language: that if one says anything enough times—in *any* language—it might come true.

Could this be why Chinese friends of my parents' generation are willing to accept the generalizations?

"Why are you complaining?" one of them said to me. "If people think we are modest and polite, let them think that. Wouldn't Americans be pleased to be thought of as polite?"

And I do believe that anyone would take the description as a compliment—at first. But after a while, it annoys, as if the only things that people heard one say were phatic remarks: I'm so pleased to meet you. I've heard many wonderful things about you. For me? You shouldn't have!

These remarks are not representative of new ideas, honest emotions, or considered thought. They are what is said from the polite distance of social contexts: greetings, farewells, wedding thank-you notes, convenient excuses, and the like.

I wonder, though. How many anthropologists, how many sociologists, how many travel journalists have documented so-called natural interactions in foreign lands, all observed with spiral notebook in hand? How many cases are there of long-lost "primitive" tribes, people who turned, out to be sophisticated enough to put on the stone-age show that ethnologists had come to see?

And how many tourists fresh off the bus have wandered into Chinatown expecting the self-effacing shopkeeper to admit under duress that the goods are not worth the price asked? I have witnessed it:

"I don't know," a tourist told the shopkeeper, a Cantonese woman perhaps in her fifties. "It doesn't look genuine to me. I'll give you three dollars."

"You don't like my price, go somewhere else," answered the shopkeeper.

"You are not a nice person," cried the shocked tourist, "not a nice person at all!"

"Who say I have to be nice," snapped the shopkeeper.

So how does one say 'yes' and 'no' in Chinese?" my friends ask a bit warily.

And here I do agree in part with the *New York Times Magazine* article. There is no one word for "yes" or "no"—but not out of necessity to be discreet. If anything, I would say the Chinese equivalent of answering "yes" or "no" is dis*crete,* that is, specific to what is asked.

Ask a Chinese person if he or she has eaten, and he or she might say *chrle* (eaten already) or *meiyou* (have not).

Ask, "So you had insurance at the time of the accident?" and the response would be *dwei* (correct) or *meiyou* (did not have).

Ask, "Have you stopped beating your wife?" and the answer refers directly to the proposition being asserted or denied: stopped already, still have not, never beat, have no wife.

What could be clearer?

As for people who are still wondering how to translate the language of discretion, I offer this personal example.

My aunt and uncle were about to return to Beijing after a three-month visit to the United States. On their last night I announced I wanted to take them out to dinner.

"Are you hungry?" I asked in Chinese.

"Not hungry," my uncle said promptly—the same response he once gave me ten minutes before suffering a low-blood-sugar attack.

"Not too hungry," said my aunt. "Perhaps you're hungry?"

"A little," I admitted.

"We can eat, we can eat, then," they both consented.

"What kind of food?" I asked.

"Oh, doesn't matter. Anything will do. Nothing fancy, just some simple food is fine."

"Do you like Japanese food?" I suggested. "We haven't had that yet."

They looked at each other.

"We can eat it," said my uncle bravely, this survivor of the Long March.

"We have eaten it before," added my aunt. "Raw fish."

"Oh, you don't like it?" I said. "Don't be polite. We can go somewhere else."

"We are not being polite. We can eat it," my aunt insisted.

So I drove them to Japantown and we walked past several restaurants featuring colorful displays of plastic sushi in the windows.

"Not this one, not this one either," I continued to say, as if searching for a certain Japanese restaurant. "Here it is," I finally said', in front of a Chinese restaurant famous for its fish dishes from Shandong Province.

"Oh, Chinese food!" cried my aunt, obviously relieved.

My uncle patted my arm. "You think like a Chinese."

"It's your last night here in America," I said. "So don't be polite. Act like an American."

And that night we ate a banquet.

Ask Not What You Can Do For Your University, But What Your University Can Do For You

UCLA Student WebZine

In recent decades, a shift has occurred within the structure of the American university system. This change, however, did not come as the direct result of educational reform; instead, the nation's higher learning facilities adapted their ethos to fit society's new model of the university as a business enterprise. Once heralded as a high-brow institute of knowledge, the university has since been absorbed by the ubiquitous commerce industry. Many contemporary scholars have critiqued the university for adopting business-like procedures and focusing their policy-making decisions on economic considerations. The new university weighs not only which administrative choices are best for their students, but also which are the most cost-efficient. While many critical analyses of such university funding and administration issues are visible, the flip-side of this educational problem is often overlooked. The university functions as a business with monetary considerations, and concurrently, students at these institutions assume the role of customers. Young adults attending college view their university education not as a valuable opportunity to gain knowledge, but rather as a purchase. Undergraduates invest tuition money to attend classes and, in turn, expect to receive a degree that will then precipitate a financially successful career. Since the university has morphed into a business enterprise, the student's love of learning has been overturned by a desire for money-making. According to a survey of university students cited in the LA Times, the number one priority of entering college freshman is earning money after graduation. Young men and women enrolled in the contemporary university curriculum often express attitudes of apathy toward the academic material presented because they view their college classes as a capital investment instead of a window to knowledge. In turn, students exhibiting this prevalent attitude of educational ambivalence and economic emphasis become individual customers, who remain aloof from their university system.

"Ask Not What You Can Do For Your University, But What Your University Can Do For You: The New Student-Consumer Attitude," as appeared in *The Daily Brewin'*, http://english.ttu.edu. Reprinted by permission of Robert D. Samuels.

   This lack of student motivation characteristic to the new university is illustrated in an online guide for instructors at the University of California, Santa Barbara. The section of this advice manual for instructors entitled "Teaching Undergraduates: Student Attitudes" depicts the majority of contemporary university students as overly casual, disinterested, and unenthusiastic. The site explains how American college coeds may often arrive late to class and then leave early; while they are in lecture, students can be seen eating, drinking, and chatting. "Teaching Undergraduates" identifies the most debilitating element of the students' learning process as the general attitude of apathy, which has washed over university campuses not only in beach-side Santa Barbara, but also nation-wide. As the guide warns, "students may show little motivation for the course other than the motivation to receive a passing grade." Undergraduates have an interest in absorbing class material only so that they may complete their required courses and ultimately receive a degree. This indifferent attitude is demonstrated by the typical college study style of cramming; students memorize necessary class information the night before an exam and then this knowledge fades away soon after it has been regurgitated onto the test pages. For the normal university undergrad, learning functions more as a temporary obstacle to reach the real goal of graduating and advancing a career than as a motivating force to discover new knowledge. Furthermore, this callous attitude toward the learning process appears to be at the root of other unfortunate student issues such as cheating, which bypasses knowledge acquisition all together.

   While the UCSB teaching guide does illuminate the common condition of apathy affecting American university students, this online resource offers excuses for the undergraduates' lackadaisical attitudes and actions. The site explains that many students have lax attendance records because they have obligations outside of the classroom, such as work or family. Although this reasoning might be accurate in some cases, it represents a minority of college students and gives the benefit of the doubt to the lazy undergrad who wanders into class twenty minutes late and leaves before the professor finishes speaking. "Teaching Undergraduates" further explains that students lack enthusiasm about their general education coursework because such varied and broad subject matter does not pertain to their major field. In addition, the typical eighteen to twenty-two year old university student is young and thus lacks the clear future goals that would drive him or her to learn class material. However, even a student with a focused educational aim of, for example, becoming a doctor would be motivated to learn pertinent information to fulfill the ultimate end of attending medical school and entering into the profession, not to enjoy learning for the sake of knowledge acquisition. While an attitude of apathy and disregard for the act of learning by no means represents every single student currently enrolled in the country's universities, this mind-set is increasingly becoming the norm. The UCSB website, then, treats the issue with a narrow and forgiving stance. Since this guide is intended for university teaching faculty, the manual portrays the problem of educational indifference so that the predicament may seem justifiable and surmountable. If teachers saw student apathy as a situation that they can neither fix nor understand, then they too would approach educational curricula with unconcern.

A more thorough and widely applicable analysis of contemporary student attitudes toward the university system can be found in the online article "Pedagogy and Students" by Rob Roy Kelly. Here, Kelly not only identifies the same phenomenon of undergraduate apathy that is described in the UCSB site, but also links this shift in student attitude to the recent businessization of American universities. In this article, Kelly points out that "Between the 1940s and 1990s, there have been significant shifts in student attitudes toward education and teachers," and these changing outlooks have, in turn, shaped contemporary student motivation and behavior. Kelly believes that the new undergraduate mind-set places unrealistic demands on teachers because students expect the incentive for learning to come from their instructors instead of from themselves. As a result of these expectations, university students lack the self-motivation to learn. Kelly's web article describes "student perception of teachers as shifting from authority figures to service persons." Undergraduates no longer see their instructors as respected intellectuals and mentors but instead as servers obliged to hand them educational inspiration and career opening diplomas. If a student does not feel stimulated by his or her coursework or does not receive passing grades, then these shortcomings are labeled as teaching deficiencies instead of student failures. This shift of blame is often evidenced in student evaluations, which commonly berate professors and TAs who give low grades to their students.

As Kelly explains, "Students believe that if they pay tuition, they should be able to do what, how and when they want, and it is the teacher's responsibility to assist them in the task." Here, Kelly perceptively points to the business transaction of receiving a university education; students purchase their place in a college class and then feel entitled to a bachelor's degree in return. Undergrads become customers at a university-company where they may buy their ticket to a high-income career. The new student-customers invests money in this system with the hopes of gaining a profit after graduation. However, the actual learning process and acquisition of knowledge, once central to the university education, now gets shoved aside. Rob Roy Kelly writes, "Students tend to view education as grades and a diploma rather than what they learn. Most students do not understand what education is, the educational process, or their role in the process." College undergraduates believe that they receive an education merely by enrolling in classes and forget that a real scholar is one who seeks new information and understanding with interest and enthusiasm. In the past, society valued education with high regard and viewed this process of seasoned intellectuals passing their knowledge onto younger minds as imperative to the advancement of the community at large. However, since the university has become identified and treated as a business by politicians and industrial leaders, "education" is a commodity which can be bought and sold. Kelly's article declares that students should realize that "education is not something given to them but something they must obtain by aggressively availing themselves of every opportunity." While this prescription certainly represents an educational ideal, it does not reflect a current reality. Contemporary university students, whether consciously or not, see themselves as consumer investors and, resultantly, remain largely apathetic toward an education of true learning and thinking. This debilitating economic model of the university system is echoed in several other scholarly writings, notably including Paul Trout's "Student Anti-Intellectualism and the Dumbing Down of the University," which suggests that the students are not only apathetic but also resistant to their higher education.

The prevalent attitude of educational indifference and economic entitlement amongst American undergraduates places these students as individual customers seeking benefits for themselves. Students, by and large, are no longer motivated members of their academic community, nor are they innovative scholars seeking to make important advances for their greater society. According to a Clarion University survey, nearly half of undergraduates do not feel a part of a community at their university, and over one-third do not understand their role in the education process. They have become autonomous investors, trading tuition money for later financial security. This perspective, though obviously flawed, has become ingrained into the commerce-oriented consciousness of contemporary America. Consequently, a change in this educational ethos must come not only from university reforms but from a revaluation of societal values.

1983: New York

Kurt Vonnegut

Cure for an Addiction

I am not an alcoholic. If I was, I would go before the nearest A.A. meeting and say, "My name is Kurt Vonnegut. I am an alcoholic." God willing, that might be my first step down the long, hard road back to sobriety.

The A.A. scheme, which requires a confession like that, is the first to have any measurable success in dealing with the tendency of some human beings, perhaps 10 percent of any population sample anyone might care to choose, to become addicted to substances that give them brief spasms of pleasure but in the long term transmute their lives and the lives of those around them into ultimate ghastliness.

The A.A. scheme, which, again, can work only if the addicts regularly admit that this or that chemical is poisonous to them, is now proving its effectiveness with compulsive gamblers, who are not dependent on chemicals from a distillery or a pharmaceutical laboratory. This is no paradox. Gamblers, in effect, manufacture their own dangerous substances. God help them, they produce chemicals that elate them whenever they place a bet on simply anything.

If I was a compulsive gambler, which I am not, I would be well advised to stand up before the nearest meeting of Gamblers Anonymous and declare, "My name is Kurt Vonnegut. I am a compulsive gambler."

Whether I was standing before a meeting of Gamblers Anonymous or Alcoholics Anonymous, I would be encouraged to testify as to how the chemicals I had generated within myself or swallowed had alienated my friends and relatives, cost me jobs and houses, and deprived me of my last shred of self-respect.

I now wish to call attention to another form of addiction, which has not been previously identified. It is more like gambling than drinking, since the people afflicted are ravenous for situations that will cause their bodies to release exciting chemicals into their bloodstreams. I am persuaded that there are among us people who are tragically hooked on preparations for war.

Tell people with that disease that war is coming and we have to get ready for it, and for a few minutes there, they will be as happy as a drunk with his martini breakfast or a compulsive gambler with his paycheck bet on the Super Bowl.

Let us recognize how sick such people are. From now on, when a national leader, or even just a neighbor, starts talking about some new weapons system which is going to cost us a mere $29 billion, we should speak up. We should say something on the order of, "Honest to God, I couldn't be sorrier for you if I'd seen you wash down a fistful of black beauties with a pint of Southern Comfort."

I mean it. I am not joking. Compulsive preparers for World War III, in this country or any other, are as tragically and, yes, as repulsively addicted as any stockbroker passed out with his head in a toilet in the Port Authority Bus Terminal.

If we know a compulsive gambler who is dead broke, we can probably make him happy with a dollar to bet on who can spit farther than someone else. For us to give a compulsive war-preparer a fleeting moment of happiness, we may have to buy him three Trident submarines and a hundred intercontinental ballistic missiles mounted on choo-choo trains.

If Western Civilization were a person—

If Western Civilization, which blankets the world now, as far as I can tell, were a person—

If Western Civilizations, which surely now includes the Soviet Union and China and India and Pakistan and on and on, were a person—

If Western Civilization were a person, we would be directing it to the nearest meeting of War-Preparers Anonymous. We would be telling it to stand up before the meeting and say, "My name is Western Civilization. I am a compulsive war-preparer. I have lost everything I ever cared about. I should have come here long ago. I first hit bottom in World War I." Western Civilization cannot be represented by a single person, of course, but a single explanation for the catastrophic course it has followed during this bloody century is possible. We the people, because of our ignorance of the disease, have again and again entrusted power to people we did not know were sickies.

And let us not mock them now, any more than we would mock someone with syphilis or smallpox or leprosy or yaws or typhoid fever or any of the other diseases to which the flesh is heir. All we have to do is separate them from the levers of power, I think.

Most addictions start innocently enough in childhood, under agreeable, reputable auspices— a sip of champagne at a wedding, a game of poker for matchsticks on a rainy afternoon. Compulsive war-preparers may have been encouraged as infants to clap their hands with glee at a campfire or a Fourth of July parade.

Not every child gets hooked. Not every child so tempted grows up to be a drunk or a gambler or a babbler about knocking down the incoming missiles of the Evil Empire with laser beams. When I identify the war-preparers as addicts, I am not calling for the exclusion of children from all martial celebrations. I doubt that more than one child in a hundred, having seen fireworks, for example, will become an adult who wants us to stop squandering our substance on education and health and social justice and the arts and food and shelter and clothing for the needy, and so on—who wants us to blow it all on ammunition instead.

And please understand that the addiction I have identified is to *preparations* for war. I repeat: to *preparations* for war, addiction to the thrills of demothballing battleships and inventing weapons systems against which there cannot possibly be a defense, supposedly, and urging the citizenry to hate this part of humanity or that one, and knocking over little governments that might aid and abet an enemy someday, and so on. I am not talking about an addiction to war itself, which is a very different matter. A compulsive preparer for war wants to go to big-time war no more than an alcoholic stockbroker wants to pass out with his head in a toilet in the Port Authority Bus Terminal.

Should addicts of any sort hold high office in this or any other country? Absolutely not, for their first priority will always be to satisfy their addiction, no matter how terrible the consequences may be—even to themselves.

Suppose we had an alcoholic president who still had not hit bottom and whose chief companions were drunks like himself. And suppose it were a fact, made absolutely clear to him, that if he took just one more drink, the whole planet would blow up.

So he has all the liquor thrown out of the White House, including his Aqua Velva shaving lotion. So late at night he is terribly restless, crazy for a drink but proud of not drinking. So he opens the White House refrigerator, looking for a Tab or a Diet Pepsi, he tells himself. And there, half-hidden by a family-size jar of French's mustard, is an unopened can of Coors beer.

What do you think he'll do?

Consider the Lobster

David Foster Wallace

The enormous, pungent, and extremely well-marketed Maine Lobster Festival is held every late July in the state's midcoast region, meaning the western side of Penobscot Bay, the nerve stem of Maine's lobster industry. What's called the midcoast runs from Owl's Head and Thomaston in the south to Belfast in the north. (Actually, it might extend all the way up to Bucksport, but we were never able to get farther north than Belfast on Route 1, whose summer traffic is, as you can imagine, unimaginable.) The region's two main communities are Camden, with its very old money and yachty harbor and five-star restaurants and phenomenal B&Bs, and Rockland, a serious old fishing town that hosts the festival every summer in historic Harbor Park, right along the water.[1]

Tourism and lobster are the midcoast region's two main industries, and they're both warm-weather enterprises, and the Maine Lobster Festival represents less an intersection of the industries than a deliberate collision, joyful and lucrative and loud. The assigned subject of this *Gourmet* article is the 56th Annual MLF, 30 July– 3 August 2003, whose official theme this year was "Lighthouses, Laughter, and Lobster." Total paid attendance was over 100,000, due partly to a national CNN spot in June during which a senior editor of *Food & Wine* magazine hailed the MLF as one of the best food-themed galas in the world. 2003 festival highlights: concerts by Lee Ann Womack and Orleans, annual Maine Sea Goddess beauty pageant, Saturday's big parade, Sunday's William G. Atwood Memorial Crate Race, annual Amateur Cooking Competition, carnival rides and midway attractions and food booths, and the MLF's Main Eating Tent, where something over 25,000 pounds of fresh-caught Maine lobster is consumed after preparation in the World's Largest Lobster Cooker near the grounds' north entrance. Also available are lobster rolls, lobster turnovers, lobster sauté, Down East lobster salad, lobster bisque, lobster ravioli, and deep-fried lobster dumplings. Lobster thermidor is obtainable at a sit-down restaurant called the Black Pearl on Harbor Park's northwest wharf. A large all-pine booth sponsored by the Maine Lobster Promotion Council has free pamphlets with recipes, eating tips, and Lobster Fun Facts. The winner of Friday's Amateur Cooking Competition prepares Saffron Lobster Ramekins, the recipe for which is now available for public downloading at www.mainelobsterfestival.com. There are lobster T-shirts and lobster

---

[1]There's a comprehensive native apothegm: "Camden by the sea, Rockland by the smell."

bobblehead dolls and inflatable lobster pool toys and clamp-on lobster hats with big scarlet claws that wobble on springs. Your assigned correspondent saw it all, accompanied by one girlfriend and both his own parents—one of which parents was actually born and raised in Maine, albeit in the extreme northern inland part, which is potato country and a world away from the touristic midcoast.[2]

For practical purposes, everyone knows what a lobster is. As usual, though, there's much more to know than most of us care about—it's all a matter of what your interests are. Taxonomically speaking, a lobster is a marine crustacean of the family Homaridae, characterized by five pairs of jointed legs, the first pair terminating in large pincerish claws used for subduing prey. Like many other species of benthic carnivore, lobsters are both hunters and scavengers. They have stalked eyes, gills on their legs, and antennae. There are a dozen or so different kinds worldwide, of which the relevant species here is the Maine lobster, *Homarus americanus.* The name "lobster" comes from the Old English *loppestre,* which is thought to be a corrupt form of the Latin word for locust combined with the Old English *loppe,* which meant spider.

Moreover, a crustacean is an aquatic arthropod of the class Crustacea, which comprises crabs, shrimp, barnacles, lobsters, and freshwater crayfish. All this is right there in the encyclopedia. And arthropods are members of the phylum Arthropoda, which phylum covers insects, spiders, crustaceans, and centipedes/millipedes, all of whose main commonality, besides the absence of a centralized brain-spine assembly, is a chitinous exoskeleton composed of segments, to which appendages are articulated in pairs.

The point is that lobsters are basically giant sea insects.[3] Like most arthropods, they date from the Jurassic period, biologically so much older than mammalia that they might as well be from another planet. And they are—particularly in their natural brown-green state, brandishing their claws like weapons and with thick antennae awhip—not nice to look at. And it's true that they are garbagemen of the sea, eaters of dead stuff,[4] although they'll also eat some live shellfish, certain kinds of injured fish, and sometimes one another.

But they are themselves good eating. Or so we think now. Up until sometime in the 1800s, though, lobster was literally low-class food, eaten only by the poor and institutionalized. Even in the harsh penal environment of early America, some colonies had laws against feeding lobsters to inmates more than once a week because it was thought to be cruel and unusual, like making people eat rats. One reason for their low status was how plentiful lobsters were in old New England. "Unbelievable abundance" is how one source describes the situation, including accounts of Plymouth Pilgrims wading out and capturing all they wanted by hand, and of early

---

[2]N.B. All personally connected parties have made it clear from the start that they do not want to be talked about in this article.

[3]Midcoasters' native term for a lobster is, in fact, "bug," as in "Come around on Sunday and we'll cook up some bugs."

[4]Factoid: Lobster traps are usually baited with dead herring.

Boston's seashore being littered with lobsters after hard storms—these latter were treated as a smelly nuisance and ground up for fertilizer. There is also the fact that premodern lobster was cooked dead and then preserved, usually packed in salt or crude hermetic containers. Maine's earliest lobster industry was based around a dozen such seaside canneries in the 1840s, from which lobster was shipped as far away as California, in demand only because it was cheap and high in protein, basically chewable fuel.

Now, of course, lobster is posh, a delicacy, only a step or two down from caviar. The meat is richer and more substantial than most fish, its taste subtle compared to the marine-gaminess of mussels and clams. In the US pop-food imagination, lobster is now the seafood analog to steak, with which it's so often twinned as Surf 'n' Turf on the really expensive part of the chain steakhouse menu.

In fact, one obvious project of the MLF, and of its omni-presently sponsorial Maine Lobster Promotion Council, is to counter the idea that lobster is unusually luxe or unhealthy or expensive, suitable only for effete palates or the occasional blow-the-diet treat. It is emphasized over and over in presentations and pamphlets at the festival that lobster meat has fewer calories, less cholesterol, and less saturated fat than chicken.[5] And in the Main Eating Tent, you can get a "quarter" (industry shorthand for a 1¼-pound lobster), a four-ounce cup of melted butter, a bag of chips, and a soft roll w/ butter-pat for around $12.00, which is only slightly more expensive than supper at McDonald's.

Be apprised, though, that the Maine Lobster Festival's democratization of lobster comes with all the massed inconvenience and aesthetic compromise of real democracy. See, for example, the aforementioned Main Eating Tent, for which there is a constant Disneyland-grade queue, and which turns out to be a square quarter mile of awning-shaded cafeteria lines and rows of long institutional tables at which friend and stranger alike sit cheek by jowl, cracking and chewing and dribbling. It's hot, and the sagged roof traps the steam and the smells, which latter are strong and only partly food-related. It is also loud, and a good percentage of the total noise is masticatory. The suppers come in styrofoam trays, and the soft drinks are iceless and flat, and the coffee is convenience-store coffee in more styrofoam, and the utensils are plastic (there are none of the special long skinny forks for pushing out the tail meat, though a few savvy diners bring their own). Nor do they give you near enough napkins considering how messy lobster is to eat, especially when you're squeezed onto benches alongside children of various ages and vastly different levels of fine-motor development—not to mention the people who've somehow smuggled in their own beer in enormous aisle-blocking coolers, or who all of a sudden produce their own plastic tablecloths and spread them over large portions of tables to try to reserve them (the tables) for their own little groups. And so on. Any one example is no more than a petty inconvenience, of course,

---

[5]Of course, the common practice of dipping the lobster meat in melted butter torpedoes all these happy fat-specs, which none of the council's promotional stuff ever mentions, any more than potato industry PR talks about sour cream and bacon bits.

but the MLF turns out to be full of irksome little downers like this—see for instance the Main Stage's headliner shows, where it turns out that you have to pay $20 extra for a folding chair if you want to sit down; or the North Tent's mad scramble for the Nyquil-cup-sized samples of finalists' entries handed out after the Cooking Competition; or the much-touted Maine Sea Goddess pageant finals, which turn out to be excruciatingly long and to consist mainly of endless thanks and tributes to local sponsors. Let's not even talk about the grossly inadequate Port-A-San facilities or the fact that there's nowhere to wash your hands before or after eating. What the Maine Lobster Festival really is is a midlevel county fair with a culinary hook, and in this respect it's not unlike Tidewater crab festivals, Midwest corn festivals, Texas chili festivals, etc., and shares with these venues the core paradox of all teeming commercial demotic events: It's not for everyone.[6] Nothing against the euphoric senior editor of *Food & Wine,* but I'd be surprised if she'd ever actually been here in Harbor Park, amid crowds of people slapping canal-zone mosquitoes as they eat deep-fried Twinkies and watch Professor Paddywhack, on six-foot stilts in a raincoat with plastic lobsters protruding from all directions on springs, terrify their children.

---

[6]In truth, there's a great deal to be said about the differences between working-class Rockland and the heavily populist flavor of its festival versus comfortable and elitist Camden with its expensive view and shops given entirely over to $200 sweaters and great rows of Victorian homes converted to upscale B&Bs. And about these differences as two sides of the great coin that is US tourism. Very little of which will be said here, except to amplify the above-mentioned paradox and to reveal your assigned correspondent's own preferences. I confess that I have never understood why so many people's idea of a fun vacation is to don flip-flops and sunglasses and crawl through maddening traffic to loud, hot, crowded tourist venues in order to sample a "local flavor" that is by definition ruined by the presence of tourists. This may (as my festival companions keep pointing out) all be a matter of personality and hardwired taste: the fact that I do not like tourist venues means that I'll never understand their appeal and so am probably not the one to talk about it (the supposed appeal). But, since this FN will almost surely not survive magazine-editing anyway, here goes:

As I see it, it probably really is good for the soul to be a tourist, even if it's only once in a while. Not good for the soul in a refreshing or enlivening way, though, but rather in a grim, steely-eyed, let's-look-honestly-at-the-facts-and-find-some-way-to-deal-with-them way. My personal experience has not been that traveling around the country is broadening or relaxing, or that radical changes in place and context have a salutary effect, but rather that intranational tourism is radically constricting, and humbling in the hardest way—hostile to my fantasy of being a true individual, of living somehow outside and above it all. (Coming up is the part that my companions find especially unhappy and repellent, a sure way to spoil the fun of vacation travel:) To be a mass tourist, for me, is to become a pure late-date American: alien, ignorant, greedy for something you cannot ever have, disappointed in a way you can never admit. It is to spoil, by way of sheer ontology, the very unspoiledness you are there to experience. It is to impose yourself on places that in all non-economic ways would be better, realer, without you. It is, in lines and gridlock and transaction after transaction, to confront a dimension of yourself that is as inescapable as it is painful: As a tourist, you become economically significant but existentially loathsome, an insect on a dead thing.

Lobster is essentially a summer food. This is because we now prefer our lobsters fresh, which means they have to be recently caught, which for both tactical and economic reasons takes place at depths less than 25 fathoms. Lobsters tend to be hungriest and most active (i.e., most trappable) at summer water temperatures of 45–50 degrees. In the autumn, most Maine lobsters migrate out into deeper water, either for warmth or to avoid the heavy waves that pound New England's coast all winter. Some burrow into the bottom. They might hibernate; nobody's sure. Summer is also lobsters' molting season—specifically early- to mid-July. Chitinous arthropods grow by molting, rather the way people have to buy bigger clothes as they age and gain weight. Since lobsters can live to be over 100, they can also get to be quite large, as in 30 pounds or more—though truly senior lobsters are rare now because New England's waters are so heavily trapped.[7] Anyway, hence the culinary distinction between hard- and soft-shell lobsters, the latter sometimes a.k.a. shedders. A soft-shell lobster is one that has recently molted. In midcoast restaurants, the summer menu often offers both kinds, with shedders being slightly cheaper even though they're easier to dismantle and the meat is allegedly sweeter. The reason for the discount is that a molting lobster uses a layer of seawater for insulation while its new shell is hardening, so there's slightly less actual meat when you crack open a shedder, plus a redolent gout of water that gets all over everything and can sometimes jet out lemonlike and catch a tablemate right in the eye. If it's winter or you're buying lobster someplace far from New England, on the other hand, you can almost bet that the lobster is a hard-shell, which for obvious reasons travel better.

As an à la carte entrée, lobster can be baked, broiled, steamed, grilled, sautéed, stir-fried, or microwaved. The most common method, though, is boiling. If you're someone who enjoys having lobster at home, this is probably the way you do it, since boiling is so easy. You need a large kettle w/ cover, which you fill about half full with water (the standard advice is that you want 2.5 quarts of water per lobster). Seawater is optimal, or you can add two tbsp salt per quart from the tap. It also helps to know how much your lobsters weigh. You get the water boiling, put in the lobsters one at a time, cover the kettle, and bring it back up to a boil. Then you bank the heat and let the kettle simmer—ten minutes for the first pound of lobster, then three minutes for each pound after that. (This is assuming you've got hard-shell lobsters, which, again, if you don't live between Boston and Halifax is probably what you've got. For shedders, you're supposed to subtract three minutes from the total.) The reason the kettle's lobsters turn scarlet is that boiling somehow suppresses every pigment in their chitin but one. If you want an easy test of whether the lobsters are done, you try pulling on one of their antennae—if it comes out of the head with minimal effort, you're ready to eat.

A detail so obvious that most recipes don't even bother to mention it is that each lobster is supposed to be alive when you put it in the kettle. This is part of lobster's modern appeal—it's the freshest food there is. There's no decomposition between harvesting and eating. And not only do lobsters require no cleaning or dressing or plucking, they're relatively easy for vendors to keep alive. They come up alive in the

---

[7]Datum: In a good year, the US industry produces around 80,000,000 pounds of lobster, and Maine accounts for more than half that total.

traps, are placed in containers of seawater, and can—so long as the water's aerated and the animals' claws are pegged or banded to keep them from tearing one another up under the stresses of captivity[8]—survive right up until they're boiled. Most of us have been in supermarkets or restaurants that feature tanks of live lobsters, from which you can pick out your supper while it watches you point. And part of the overall spectacle of the Maine Lobster Festival is that you can see actual lobstermen's vessels docking at the wharves along the northeast grounds and unloading fresh-caught product, which is transferred by hand or cart 150 yards to the great clear tanks stacked up around the festival's cooker—which is, as mentioned, billed as the World's Largest Lobster Cooker and can process over 100 lobsters at a time for the Main Eating Tent.

So then here is a question that's all but unavoidable at the World's Largest Lobster Cooker, and may arise in kitchens across the US: Is it all right to boil a sentient creature alive just for our gustatory pleasure? A related set of concerns: Is the previous question irksomely PC or sentimental? What does "all right" even mean in this context? Is the whole thing just a matter of personal choice?

As you may or may not know, a certain well-known group called People for the Ethical Treatment of Animals thinks that the morality of lobster-boiling is not just a matter of individual conscience. In fact, one of the very first things we hear about the MLF . . . well, to set the scene: We're coming in by cab from the almost indescribably odd and rustic Knox County Airport[9] very late on the night before the festival opens, sharing the cab with a wealthy political consultant who lives on Vinalhaven Island in the bay half the year (he's headed for the island ferry in Rockland). The consultant and cabdriver are responding to informal journalistic probes about how people who live in the midcoast region actually view the MLF, as in is the festival just a big-dollar tourist thing or is it something local residents look forward to attending, take genuine civic pride in, etc. The cabdriver (who's in his seventies, one of apparently a whole platoon of retirees the cab company puts on to help with the summer rush, and wears a US-flag lapel pin, and drives in what can only be called a very *deliberate* way) assures us that locals do endorse and enjoy the MLF, although he himself hasn't gone in years, and now come to think of it no one he and his wife know has, either. However, the demilocal consultant's been to recent festivals a couple times (one gets the impression

---

[8]N.B. Similar reasoning underlies the practice of what's termed "debeaking" broiler chickens and brood hens in modern factory farms. Maximum commercial efficiency requires that enormous poultry populations be confined in unnaturally close quarters, under which conditions many birds go crazy and peck one another to death. As a purely observational side-note, be apprised that debeaking is usually an automated process and that the chickens receive no anesthetic. It's not clear to me whether most *Gourmet* readers know about debeaking, or about related practices like dehorning cattle in commercial feed lots, cropping swine's tails in factory hog farms to keep psychotically bored neighbors from chewing them off, and so forth. It so happens that your assigned correspondent knew almost nothing about standard meat-industry operations before starting work on this article.

[9]The terminal used to be somebody's house, for example, and the lost-luggage-reporting room was clearly once a pantry.

it was at his wife's behest), of which his most vivid impression was that "you have to line up for an ungodly long time to get your lobsters, and meanwhile there are all these ex-flower children coming up and down along the line handing out pamphlets that say the lobsters die in terrible pain and you shouldn't eat them."

And it turns out that the post-hippies of the consultant's recollection were activists from PETA. There were no PETA people in obvious view at the 2003 MLF,[10] but they've been conspicuous at many of the recent festivals. Since at least the mid-1990s, articles in everything from the *Camden Herald* to the *New York Times* have described PETA urging boycotts of the Maine Lobster Festival, often deploying celebrity spokesmen like Mary Tyler Moore for open letters and ads saying stuff like "Lobsters are extraordinarily sensitive" and "To me, eating a lobster is out of the question." More concrete is the oral testimony of Dick, our florid and extremely gregarious rental-car liaison,[11] to the effect that PETA's been around so much during recent years that a kind of brittlely tolerant homeostasis now obtains between the activists and the festival's locals, e.g.: "We had some incidents a couple years ago. One lady took most of her clothes off and painted herself like a lobster, almost got herself arrested. But for the most part they're let alone. [Rapid series of small ambiguous laughs, which with Dick happens a lot.] They do their thing and we do our thing."

This whole interchange takes place on Route 1, 30 July, during a four-mile, 50-minute ride from the airport[12] to the dealership to sign car-rental papers. Several

---

[10]It turned out that one Mr. William R. Rivas-Rivas, a high-ranking PETA official out of the group's Virginia headquarters, was indeed there this year, albeit solo, working the festival's main and side entrances on Saturday, 2 August, handing out pamphlets and adhesive stickers emblazoned with "Being Boiled Hurts," which is the tagline in most of PETA's published material about lobsters. I learned that he'd been there only later, when speaking with Mr. Rivas-Rivas on the phone. I'm not sure how we missed seeing him *in situ* at the festival, and I can't see much to do except apologize for the oversight—although it's also true that Saturday was the day of the big MLF parade through Rockland, which basic journalistic responsibility seemed to require going to (and which, with all due respect, meant that Saturday was maybe not the best day for PETA to work the Harbor Park grounds, especially if it was going to be just one person for one day, since a lot of diehard MLF partisans were off-site watching the parade (which, again with no offense intended, was in truth kind of cheesy and boring, consisting mostly of slow homemade floats and various midcoast people waving at one another, and with an extremely annoying man dressed as Blackbeard ranging up and down the length of the crowd saying "Arrr" over and over and brandishing a plastic sword at people, etc.; plus it rained)).

[11]By profession, Dick is actually a car salesman; the midcoast region's National Car Rental franchise operates out of a Chevy delership in Thomaston.

[12]The short version regarding why we were back at the airport after already arriving the previous night involves lost luggage and a miscommunication about where and what the midcoast's National franchise was—Dick came out personally to the airport and got us, out of no evident motive but kindness. (He also talked nonstop the entire way, with a very distinctive speaking style that can be described only as manically laconic; the truth is that I now know more about this man than I do about some members of my own family.)

irreproducible segues down the road from the PETA anecdotes, Dick—whose son-in-law happens to be a professional lobsterman and one of the Main Eating Tent's regular suppliers—explains what he and his family feel is the crucial mitigating factor in the whole morality-of-boiling-lobsters-alive issue: "There's a part of the brain in people and animals that lets us feel pain, and lobsters' brains don't have this part."

Besides the fact that it's incorrect in about nine different ways, the main reason Dick's statement is interesting is that its thesis is more or less echoed by the festival's own pronouncement on lobsters and pain, which is part of a Test Your Lobster IQ quiz that appears in the 2003 MLF program courtesy of the Maine Lobster Promotion Council:

> The nervous system of a lobster is very simple, and is in fact most similar to the nervous system of the grasshopper. It is decentralized with no brain. There is no cerebral cortex, which in humans is the area of the brain that gives the experience of pain.

Though it sounds more sophisticated, a lot of the neurology in this latter claim is still either false or fuzzy. The human cerebral cortex is the brain-part that deals with higher faculties like reason, metaphysical self-awareness, language, etc. Pain reception is known to be part of a much older and more primitive system of nociceptors and prostaglandins that are managed by the brain stem and thalamus.[13]

On the other hand, it is true that the cerebral cortex is involved in what's variously called suffering, distress, or the emotional experience of pain—i.e., experiencing painful stimuli as unpleasant, very unpleasant, unbearable, and so on.

Before we go any further, let's acknowledge that the questions of whether and how different kinds of animals feel pain, and of whether and why it might be justifiable to inflict pain on them in order to eat them, turn out to be extremely complex and difficult. And comparative neuroanatomy is only part of the problem. Since pain is a totally subjective mental experience, we do not have direct access to anyone or anything's pain but our own; and even just the principles by which we can infer that other human beings experience pain and have a legitimate interest in not feeling pain involve hardcore philosophy—metaphysics, epistemology, value theory, ethics. The fact that even the most highly evolved nonhuman mammals can't use language to communicate with us about their subjective mental experience is only the first layer of additional complication in trying to extend our reasoning about pain and morality to animals. And everything gets progressively more abstract and convoluted as we move farther and farther out from the higher-type mammals into cattle and swine and dogs and cats and rodents, and then birds and fish, and finally invertebrates like lobsters.

---

[13]To elaborate by way of example: The common experience of accidentally touching a hot stove and yanking your hand back before you're even aware that anything's going on is explained by the fact that many of the processes by which we detect and avoid painful stimuli do not involve the cortex. In the case of the hand and stove, the brain is bypassed altogether; all the important neurochemical action takes place in the spine.

The more important point here, though, is that the whole animal-cruelty-and-eating issue is not just complex, it's also uncomfortable. It is, at any rate, uncomfortable for me, and for just about everyone I know who enjoys a variety of foods and yet does not want to see herself as cruel or unfeeling. As far as I can tell, my own main way of dealing with this conflict has been to avoid thinking about the whole unpleasant thing. I should add that it appears to me unlikely that many readers of *Gourmet* wish to think about it, either, or to be queried about the morality of their eating habits in the pages of a culinary monthly. Since, however, the assigned subject of this article is what it was like to attend the 2003 MLF, and thus to spend several days in the midst of a great mass of Americans all eating lobster, and thus to be more or less impelled to think hard about lobster and the experience of buying and eating lobster, it turns out that there is no honest way to avoid certain moral questions.

There are several reasons for this. For one thing, it's not just that lobsters get boiled alive, it's that you do it yourself—or at least it's done specifically for you, on-site.[14] As mentioned, the World's Largest Lobster Cooker, which is highlighted as an attraction in the festival's program, is right out there on the MLF's north grounds for everyone to see. Try to imagine a Nebraska Beef Festival[15] at which part of the festivities is watching trucks pull up and the live cattle get driven down the ramp and slaughtered right there on the World's Largest Killing Floor or something—there's no way.

The intimacy of the whole thing; is maximized at home, which of course is where most lobster gets prepared and eaten (although note already the semiconscious euphemism "prepared," which in the case of lobsters really means killing them right there in our kitchens). The basic scenario is that we come in from the store and make our little preparations like getting the kettle filled and boiling, and then we lift the lobsters out of the bag or whatever retail container they came home in . . . whereupon some

---

[14]Morality-wise, let's concede that this cuts both ways. Lobster-eating is at least not abetted by the system of corporate factory farms that produces most beef, pork, and chicken. Because, if nothing else, of the way they're marketed and packaged for sale, we eat these latter meats without having to consider that they were once conscious, sentient creatures to whom horrible things were done. (N.B. "Horrible" here meaning really, really horrible. Write off to PETA or peta.org for their free "Meet Your Meat" video, narrated by Mr. Alec Baldwin, if you want to see just about everything meat-related you don't want to see or think about. (N.B.$_2$ Not that PETA's any sort of font of unspun truth. Like many partisans in complex moral disputes, the PETA people are fanatics, and a lot of their rhetoric seems simplistic and self-righteous. But this particular video, replete with actual factory-farm and corporate-slaughterhouse footage, is both credible and traumatizing.))

[15]Is it significant that "lobster," "fish," and "chicken" are our culture's words for both the animal and the meat, whereas most mammals seem to require euphemisms like "beef" and "pork" that help us separate the meat we eat from the living creature the meat once was? Is this evidence that some kind of deep unease about eating higher animals is endemic enough to show up in English usage, but that the unease diminishes as we move out of the mammalian order? (And is "lamb"/"lamb" the counterexample that sinks the whole theory, or are there special, biblico-historical reasons for that equivalence?)

uncomfortable things start to happen. However stuporous a lobster is from the trip home, for instance, it tends to come alarmingly to life when placed in boiling water. If you're tilting it from a container into the steaming kettle, the lobster will sometimes try to cling to the container's sides or even to hook its claws over the kettle's rim like a person trying to keep from going over the edge of a roof. And worse is when the lobster's fully immersed. Even if you cover the kettle and turn away, you can usually hear the cover rattling and clanking as the lobster tries to push it off. Or the creature's claws scraping the sides of the kettle as it thrashes around. The lobster, in other words, behaves very much as you or I would behave if we were plunged into boiling water (with the obvious exception of screaming[16]). A blunter way to say this is that the lobster acts as if it's in terrible pain, causing some cooks to leave the kitchen altogether and to take one of those little lightweight plastic oven-timers with them into another room and wait until the whole process is over.

There happen to be two main criteria that most ethicists agree on for determining whether a living creature has the capacity to suffer and so has genuine interests that it may or may not be our moral duty to consider.[17] One is how much of the neurological hardware required for pain-experience the animal comes equipped with—nociceptors, prostaglandins, neuronal opioid receptors, etc. The other criterion is whether the animal demonstrates behavior associated with pain. And it takes a lot of intellectual gymnastics and behaviorist hairsplitting not to see struggling, thrashing, and lid-clattering as just such pain-behavior. According to marine zoologists, it usually takes lobsters between 35 and 45 seconds to die in boiling water. (No source I could find talks about how long it takes them to die in superheated steam; one rather hopes it's faster.)

There are, of course, other ways to kill your lobster on-site and so achieve maximum freshness. Some cooks' practice is to drive a sharp heavy knife point-first into a spot just above the midpoint between the lobster's eyestalks (more or less where the

---

[16]There's a relevant populist myth about the high-pitched whistling sound that sometimes issues from a pot of boiling lobster. The sound is really vented steam from the layer of seawater between the lobster's flesh and its carapace (this is why shedders whistle more than hard-shells), but the pop version has it that the sound is the lobster's rabbit like death-scream. Lobsters communicate via pheromones in their urine and don't have anything close to the vocal equipment for screaming, but the myth's very persistent—which might, once again, point to a low-level cultural unease about the boiling thing.

[17]"Interests" basically means strong and legitimate preferences, which obviously require some degree of consciousness, responsiveness to stimuli, etc. See, for instance, the utilitarian philosopher Peter Singer, whose 1974 *Animal Liberation* is more or less the bible of the modern animal-rights movement:

It would be nonsense to say that it was not in the interests of a stone to be kicked along the road by a schoolboy. A stone does not have interests because it cannot suffer. Nothing that we can do to it could possibly make any difference to its welfare. A mouse, on the other hand, does have an interest in not being kicked along the road, because it will suffer if it is.

Third Eye is in human foreheads). This is alleged either to kill the lobster instantly or to render it insensate, and is said at least to eliminate some of the cowardice involved in throwing a creature into boiling water and then fleeing the room. As far as I can tell from talking to proponents of the knife-in-head method, the idea is that it's more violent but ultimately more merciful, plus that a willingness to exert personal agency and accept responsibility for stabbing the lobster's head honors the lobster somehow and entitles one to eat it (there's often a vague sort of Native American spirituality-of-the-hunt flavor to pro-knife arguments). But the problem with the knife method is basic biology: Lobsters' nervous systems operate off not one but several ganglia, a.k.a. nerve bundles, which are sort of wired in series and distributed all along the lobster's underside, from stem to stern. And disabling only the frontal ganglion does not normally result in quick death or unconsciousness.

Another alternative is to put the lobster in cold saltwater and then very slowly bring it up to a full boil. Cooks who advocate this method are going on the analogy to a frog, which can supposedly be kept from jumping out of a boiling pot by heating the water incrementally. In order to save a lot of research-summarizing, I'll simply assure you that the analogy between frogs and lobsters tarns out not to hold—plus, if the kettle's water isn't aerated seawater, the immersed lobster suffers from slow suffocation, although usually not decisive enough suffocation to keep it from still thrashing and clattering when the water gets hot enough to kill it. In fact, lobsters boiled incrementally often display a whole bonus set of gruesome, convulsionlike reactions that you don't see in regular boiling.

Ultimately, the only certain virtues of the home-lobotomy and slow-heating methods are comparative, because there are even worse/crueler ways people prepare lobster. Time-thrifty cooks sometimes microwave them alive (usually after poking several vent-holes in the carapace, which is a precaution most shellfish-microwavers learn about the hard way). Live dismemberment, on the other hand, is big in Europe—some chefs cut the lobster in half before cooking; others like to tear off the claws and tail and toss only these parts into the pot.

And there's more unhappy news respecting suffering-criterion number one. Lobsters don't have much in the way of eyesight or hearing, but they do have an exquisite tactile sense, one facilitated by hundreds of thousands of tiny hairs that protrude through their carapace. "Thus it is," in the words of T. M. Prudden's industry classic *About Lobster,* "that although encased in what seems a solid, impenetrable armor, the lobster can receive stimuli and impressions from without as readily as if it possessed a soft and delicate skin." And lobsters do have nociceptors,[18] as well as invertebrate versions of the prostaglandins and major neurotransmitters via which our own brains register pain.

Lobsters do not, on the other hand, appear to have the equipment for making or absorbing natural opioids like endorphins and enkephalins, which are what more

---

[18]This is the neurological term for special pain-receptors that are "sensitive to potentially damaging extremes of temperature, to mechanical forces, and to chemical substances which are released when body tissues are damaged."

advanced nervous systems use to try to handle intense pain. From this fact, though, one could conclude either that lobsters are maybe even *more* vulnerable to pain, since they lack mammalian nervous systems' built-in analgesia, or, instead, that the absence of natural opioids implies an absence of the really intense pain-sensations that natural opioids are designed to mitigate. I for one can detect a marked upswing in mood as I contemplate this latter possibility. It could be that their lack of endorphin/enkephalin hardware means that lobsters' raw subjective experience of pain is so radically different from mammals' that it may not even deserve the term "pain." Perhaps lobsters are more like those frontal-lobotomy patients one reads about who report experiencing pain in a totally different way than you and I. These patients evidently do feel physical pain, neurologically speaking, but don't dislike it—though neither do they like it; it's more that they feel it but don't feel anything *about* it—the point being that the pain is not distressing to them or something they want to get away from. Maybe lobsters, who are also without frontal lobes, are detached from the neurological-registration-of-injury-or-hazard we call pain in just the same way. There is, after all, a difference between (1) pain as a purely neurological event, and (2) actual suffering, which seems crucially to involve an emotional component, an awareness of pain as unpleasant, as something to fear/dislike/want to avoid.

Still, after all the abstract intellection, there remain the facts of the frantically clanking lid, the pathetic clinging to the edge of the pot. Standing at the stove, it is hard to deny in any meaningful way that this is a living creature experiencing pain and wishing to avoid/escape the painful experience. To my lay mind, the lobster's behavior in the kettle appears to be the expression of a *preference;* and it may well be that an ability to form preferences is the decisive criterion for real suffering.[19] The logic of this (preference → suffering) relation may be easiest to see in the negative case. If you cut certain kinds of worms in half, the halves will often keep crawling around and going about their vermiform business as if nothing had happened. When we assert, based on their post-op behavior, that these worms appear not to be suffering, what we're really saying is that there's no sign the worms know anything bad has happened or would *prefer* not to have gotten cut in half.

Lobsters, though, are known to exhibit preferences. Experiments have shown that they can detect changes of only a degree or two in water temperature; one reason for their complex migratory cycles (which can often cover 100-plus miles a year) is to pursue the temperatures they like best.[20] And, as mentioned, they're bottom-dwellers and do not like bright light—if a tank of food-lobsters is out in the sunlight or a store's fluorescence, the lobsters will always congregate in whatever part is darkest. Fairly solitary in the ocean, they also clearly dislike the crowding that's part of their captivity in

---

[19]"Preference" is maybe roughly synonymous with "interests," but it is a better term for our purposes because it's less abstractly philosophical—"preference" seems more personal, and it's the whole idea of a living creature's personal experience that's at issue.

[20]Of course, the most common sort of counterargument here would begin by objecting that "like best" is really just a metaphor, and a misleadingly anthropomorphic one at that. The

tanks, since (as also mentioned) one reason why lobsters' claws are banded on capture is to keep them from attacking one another under the stress of close-quarter storage.

In any event, at the MLF, standing by the bubbling tanks outside the World's Largest Lobster Cooker, watching the fresh-caught lobsters pile over one another, wave their hobbled claws impotently, huddle in the rear corners, or scrabble frantically back from the glass as you approach, it is difficult not to sense that they're unhappy, or frightened, even if it's some rudimentary version of these feelings . . . and, again, why does rudimentariness even enter into it? Why is a primitive, inarticulate form of suffering less urgent or uncomfortable for the person who's helping to inflict it by paying for the food it results in? I'm not trying to give you a PETA-like screed here—at least I don't think so. I'm trying, rather, to work out and articulate some of the troubling questions that arise amid all the laughter and saltation and community pride of the Maine Lobster Festival. The truth is that if you, the festival attendee, permit yourself to think that lobsters can suffer and would rather not, the MLF begins to take on the aspect of something like a Roman circus or medieval torture-fest.

Does that comparison seem a bit much? If so, exactly why? Or what about this one: Is it possible that future generations will regard our present agribusiness and eating practices in much the same way we now view Nero's entertainments or Mengele's experiments? My own initial reaction is that such a comparison is hysterical, extreme—and yet the reason it seems extreme to me appears to be that I believe animals are less morally important than human beings;[21] and when it comes to defending such a belief, even to myself, I have to acknowledge that (a) I have an obvious selfish interest in this belief, since I like to eat certain kinds of animals and want to be able to keep doing it,

---

counterarguer would posit that the lobster seeks to maintain a certain optimal ambient temperature out of nothing but unconscious instinct (with a similar explanation for the low-light affinities upcoming in the main text). The thrust of such a counterargument will be that the lobster's thrashings and clankings in the kettle express not unpreferred pain but involuntary reflexes, like your leg shooting out when the doctor hits your knee. Be advised that there are professional scientists, including many researchers who use animals in experiments, who hold to the view that nonhuman creatures have no real feelings at all, merely "behaviors." Be further advised that this view has a long history that goes all the way back to Descartes, although its modern support comes mostly from behaviorist psychology.

To these what-looks-like-pain-is-really-just-reflexes counterarguments, however, there happen to be all sorts of scientific and pro-animal rights counter-counterarguments. And then further attempted rebuttals and redirects, and so on. Suffice it to say that both the scientific and the philosophical arguments on either side of the animal-suffering issue are involved, abstruse, technical, often informed by self-interest or ideology, and in the end so totally inconclusive that as a practical matter, in the kitchen or restaurant, it all still seems to come down to individual conscience, going with (no pun) your gut.

[21]Meaning a *lot* less important, apparently, since the moral comparison here is not the value of one human's life vs. the value of one animal's life, but rather the value of one animal's life vs. the value of one human's taste for a particular kind of protein. Even the most diehard carniphile will acknowledge that it's possible to live and eat well without consuming animals.

and (b) I haven't succeeded in working out any sort of personal ethical system in which the belief is truly defensible instead of just selfishly convenient.

Given this article's venue and my own lack of culinary sophistication, I'm curious about whether the reader can identify with any of these reactions and acknowledgments and discomforts. I'm also concerned not to come off as shrill or preachy when what I really am is more like confused. For those *Gourmet* readers who enjoy well-prepared and -presented meals involving beef, veal, lamb, pork, chicken, lobster, etc.: Do you think much about the (possible) moral status and (probable) suffering of the animals involved? If you do, what ethical convictions have you worked out that permit you not just to eat but to savor and enjoy flesh-based viands (since of course refined *enjoyment,* rather than mere ingestion, is the whole point of gastronomy)? If, on the other hand, you'll have no truck with confusions or convictions and regard stuff like the previous paragraph as just so much fatuous navel-gazing, what makes it feel truly okay, inside, to just dismiss the whole thing out of hand? That is, is your refusal to think about any of this the product of actual thought, or is it just that you don't want to think about it? And if the latter, then why not? Do you ever think, even idly, about the possible reasons for your reluctance to think about it? I am not trying to bait anyone here—I'm genuinely curious. After all, isn't being extra aware and attentive and thoughtful about one's food and its overall context part of what distinguishes a real gourmet? Or is all the gourmet's extra attention and sensibility just supposed to be sensuous? Is it really all just a matter of taste and presentation?

These last few queries, though, while sincere, obviously involve much larger and more abstract questions about the connections (if any) between aesthetics and morality—about what the adjective in a phrase like "The Magazine of Good Living" is really supposed to mean—and these questions lead straightaway into such deep and treacherous waters that it's probably best to stop the public discussion right here. There are limits to what even interested persons can ask of each other.

Intersections

[body]

Against Ordinary Language • Orchids: Half Sacred, Half Profane • Emily & Heather • Consider the Lobster • Gender and Videogames • The Last Bus Home • One Sentence • My Memory and Witness

[language & writing]

The Vocabulary of Comics • Against Ordinary Language • One Sentence • My Metaphor Weighs Tons • The Braindead Megaphone • Is Google Making Us Stupid? • Why I Blog • Regarding the Pain of Others • The Language of Discretion

[identity]

Orchids: Half Sacred, Half Profane • My Memory and Witness • Leaving Babylon • My Metaphor Weighs Tons • One Sentence • The Homeland, Aztlán / El otro México • The North American • The Language of Discretion • Emily & Heather • Consider the Lobster • Human Restoration

[work]

Brick Wall • Ask Not What You Can Do For Your University • Against Ordinary Language • At the Edge of Poverty • A Time to Serve • The Last Bus Home • My Memory and Witness • Why I Blog • Is Whole Foods Wholesome? • Knowledge is Power

[invisibility]

What About the Boys? • Knowledge is Power • At the Edge of Poverty • One Sentence • Against Ordinary Language • Orchids: Half Sacred, Half Profane • A Small Place • My Memory and Witness • The Vocabulary of Comics • Gender and Videogames • Is Whole Foods Wholesome?

[place]

Human Restoration • A Small Place • Life in the Dorms • The Homeland, Aztlán / El otro México • The Last Bus Home • Brick Wall • Thirteen More Ways of Looking at a Blackbird • Leaving Babylon • Is Whole Foods Wholesome? • The North American

[perspective]

Is Whole Foods Wholesome? • Ask Not What You Can Do For Your University • Human Restoration • Regarding the Pain of Others • 1983: New York • Consider the Lobster • Thirteen More Ways of Looking at a Blackbird • Why Bother? • The Homeland, Aztlán / El otro México • Emily & Heather • The Vocabulary of Comics • The Braindead Megaphone

[new media]

Is Google Making Us Stupid? • The Braindead Megaphone • Why I Blog • The Vocabulary of Comics • Gender and Videogames • Regarding the Pain of Others

[community]

Human Restoration • Life in the Dorms • Why Bother? • A Time to Serve • Leaving Babylon • The Language of Discretion • Ask Not What You Can Do for Your University • The Last Bus Home

[borderlands]

Emily & Heather • Orchids: Half Sacred, Half Profane • The Homeland, Aztlán / El otro México • My Memory and Witness • Leaving Babylon • A Small Place • Knowledge is Power • The North American • At the Edge of Poverty • The Language of Discretion • One Sentence

[education]

What About the Boys? • Knowledge is Power • Gender and Videogames • Ask Not What You Can Do For Your University • A Time to Serve • Is Google Making Us Stupid? • Life in the Dorms • My Memory and Witness • Emily & Heather • Orchids: Half Sacred, Half Profane • Leaving Babylon

[relationships]

Emily & Heather • My Memory and Witness • The Homeland, Aztlán / El otro México • Leaving Babylon • Human Restoration • Life in the Dorms • The Last Bus Home • A Time to Serve • Orchids: Half Sacred, Half Profane • One Sentence • Consider the Lobster • Gender and Videogames

[the American Dream]

The Homeland, Aztlán / El otro México • At the Edge of Poverty • The North American • Knowledge is Power • Regarding the Pain of Others • 1983: New York • A Time to Serve • Consider the Lobster • Human Restoration

[nature]

Thirteen More Ways of Looking at a Blackbird • Human Restoration • Why Bother? • Consider the Lobster • A Small Place • Is Whole Food Wholesome? • The Braindead Megaphone • The Last Bus Home • The Homeland, Aztlán / El otro México

[race, class, gender]

Orchids: Half Sacred, Half Profane • Knowledge is Power • The Homeland, Aztlán / El otro México • My Memory and Witness • At the Edge of Poverty • The North American • Brick Wall • The Last Bus Home • Emily & Heather • A Small Place • Gender and Videogames • What About the Boys? • One Sentence • Against Ordinary Language

Biographies

Heather Abel earned her master's degree in fiction writing at the New School in New York City. She has been a reporter and an editor for the *High County News* and the *San Francisco Bay Guardian*. She is currently working on a novel about faith, place, and family set in Colorado and California. She lives in Northampton, Massachusetts.

Kathy Acker was born in 1947 and raised in New York City. She attended Brandeis University before moving to the west coast to study writing with the poets David Antin and Jerome Rothenberg at the University of California, San Diego. She did postgraduate work at City University of New York. She worked at a range of jobs (file clerk, secretary, stripper, and porn performer) which leaked into her writing. She was and remains a controversial figure, a writer whose work is not easy to classify, who confronts the reader with difficult issues of identity and sexuality, who provokes mixed reactions from critics and feminists alike. She taught at several schools, including the San Francisco Art Institute. Shortly after her death in 1997 from breast cancer, her friend Richard Kadrey wrote that, more than anything, Acker cared "about the power of words to define the world and shape our thoughts. Whoever controlled the words controlled thought, Kathy knew. She set out to understand and liberate words (and herself) by direct action: She'd seize control of language and reinvent it in her work."

"Orchids: Half Sacred, Half Profane" is from **Faith Adiele's** travel memoir *Meeting Faith: An Inward Odyssey,* winner of the PEN Beyond the Margins Award. The PBS documentary "My Journey Home" is based on her life growing up in a Nordic-American family and then traveling to Nigeria to meet her father and siblings. She is co-editor of *Coming of Age Around the World: A Multicultural Anthology* and co-author, under the pen name Jane Harvard, of *The Student Body,* a scorching campus bestseller. She is currently working on a memoir about growing up Nigerian-Nordic-American. She holds degrees from Harvard, Lesley University, and the University of Iowa. She teaches creative non-fiction at the University of Pittsburgh. To learn more about Adiele and to read her blog, visit: http://www.adiele.com/home.html.

Mexican American author **Gloria Anzaldúa** intermingles Englishes and Spanishes in her writing as a single, cohesive system of expression. The fluid incorporation illustrates Anzaldúa's most significant contribution to academic discourse, her application of the term "mestizaje," which indicates the state of being beyond the binary oppositions inherent in the nationalist labels "Chicano" and "Mexican." Anzaldúa's work calls us to embrace a more fluid sense of identity that is not limited by social and territorial borders and is, therefore, rife with the possibility for creativity. Her works include *Borderlands/La Frontera: The New Mestiza* (recognized as one of the 38 Best Books of

1987 by *Library Journal)*, poetry, fiction, and children's books. She has won the National Endowment for the Arts fiction award, the Lesbian Rights Award, and the Sappho Award of Distinction.

Dorie Bargmann grew up in Athens, Georgia, where she attended the University of Georgia as an undergraduate. After receiving the master's degree in International Affairs from the University of Denver, she spent five years directing potable water projects in Central America. Upon returning to the United States, she pursued a second master's degree in Nonfiction Writing at the Johns Hopkins Writing Seminars. Presently she lives in Austin, Texas, where she works as an investigator for the Federal Public Defender's office. Writing non-fiction is her area of expertise. In addition to "Thirteen More Ways of Looking at a Blackbird," she has published two other essays: "Lionbird" and "After the Ceasefire." The latter won an award at the Mayborn Literary Nonfiction Writers Conference of the Southwest in 2006. "Thirteen Ways" has also been reprinted in *The Best Creative Nonfiction,* Volume 1.

Nicholas Carr has written a personal blog, Rough Type, since 2005, and has also written a number of "essay blogs" (both of which can be found at www.nicholasgcarr.com). Carr has the knack for stirring debate. In 2005, he posted on Rough Type "The Amorality of Web 2.0," which criticized the quality of digital information projects such as Wikipedia, arguing that they have a net negative effect on society. Wikipedia co-founder Jimmy Wales disagreed with much of Carr's critique but did admit that the two examples Carr put forward were "a horrific embarrassment, and are nearly unreadable crap." Carr's book *Does IT Matter?* (2004), which is about the role of computers in business, was hotly contested by technology giants Microsoft and Intel, among other companies and critics.

Emily Chenoweth holds the M.F.A. from Columbia University. She is the former fiction editor of *Publisher's Weekly.* Her work has appeared in *Tin House, Bookforum, People,* and other publications. Her first novel, *Hello Goodbye,* about friendship, loyalty, and growing up, has recently been published by Random House.

Charles D'Ambrosio, a short story writer and essayist, grew up in Seattle with an "obscure desire to write." After graduating from Oberlin College, he attended the Iowa Writers' Workshop. His stories and essays have been published in *The New Yorker* and *Paris Review,* among other periodicals. His first collection of stories, *The Point* (1995), was a finalist for the Pen/Hemingway Award and was a *New York Times* Notable Book of the Year; his essay collection *Orphans* was also a finalist for the PEN/Faulkner Award. He has been a visiting faculty member at the Iowa Writers' Workshop, as well as an instructor at the Tin House Summer Writers' Workshop and the Warren Wilson MFA Program for Writers. He has been the recipient of several prestigious awards, including the Whiting Writers Award and a USA Rasmuson Fellowship in Literature. He now lives in Portland, Oregon, with his wife.

Lis Goldschmidt grew up in rural Virginia. She is a visual artist whose work has appeared in the Pocket Myths zine series, including *Cupid + Psyche* and *Persephone,* and the zine *Manifixation*. She currently lives in San Francisco and is a graduate student studying Traditional Chinese Medicine. Her favorite number is five.

Judyth Har-Even is the pseudonym used by Ohio native and Jerusalem resident (since 1966) Judy Labensohn. She has been teaching creative writing in informal settings around Israel to both Israelis and tourists since 1992. She teaches in both Hebrew and English and believes the collaboration of group strengths in the writing process can help members to overcome creative blocks. Labensohn's writing has appeared in *Creative Nonfiction, Kenyon Review, Lilith, Hadassah Magazine, Fourth Genre,* and various American and Canadian Jewish newspapers.

Michael S. Kimmel is one of the leading researchers in the world on masculinity. Author of over twenty books, he wrote the landmark *Manhood in America: A Cultural History* (1996), which critics hailed as the definitive work on the subject. A professional speaker as well, Kimmel has been a vocal advocate of seeing manhood as combining "strength with nurturing, personal accountability, compassion and egalitarianism" *(Publishers' Weekly)*. In 2004, he co-edited the *Encyclopedia on Men and Masculinities* and *The Handbook of Studies on Men and Masculinities.*

Jamaica Kincaid was born in St. John's, Antigua, in 1949. At about the age of sixteen, she moved to New York to pursue a career as an au pair. After leaving the family for which she worked, she studied photography at the New York School for Social Research and also briefly attended Franconia College in New Hampshire. She became a writer for *The New Yorker,* to which she contributed for about twenty years. Kincaid is the author of nonfiction texts, short stories, and novels, including *The Autobiography of My Mother,* a novel of a 70-year-old woman looking back on her life in Dominica. In 2000, she was awarded the Prix Femina Étranger for *My Brother.* She now lives in Bennington, Vermont, with her husband and children.

William Davies King is a professor of theater at the University of California, Santa Barbara. King is a self-proclaimed collector of nothing. His enormous collection of ephemera is economically valueless and lacks currency even in collector circles. The value King recognizes in his collecting is a connection to the creative process as he must make decisions about what to collect and how to present a collection. King's book *Collections of Nothing* is a memoir of his life through collecting.

Jason Logan is an illustrator, based in Toronto, and the author of *If We Ever Break Up, This is My Book.* He has been scribbling away in notebooks on public transportation for a long time.

Field Maloney has written for *Slate, The New York Times,* and *The New Yorker.* He comes from a hard-cider-making family and is writing a book about wine in America. He likes to drink beer.

Scott McCloud has been both a theorist and creator of comics since the publication of his first comic, *Zot!,* in 1984. Active in the comics community throughout his career, he drafted a "Creator's Bill of Rights" in 1988 to help creators retain the rights to characters they develop. Also an early supporter of webcomics, McCloud is fascinated by the possibilities created by the "infinite canvas" of the web browser, a medium that has fewer spatial limitations than the pages of a book. In 2008, McCloud created a 38-page comic that serves as the user's manual for Google's web browser, Chrome.

Bill McKibben grew up in Lexington, Massachusetts, and was president of the *Harvard Crimson* newspaper in college. He later moved to the Adirondack Mountains of upstate New York. His first book, *The End of Nature,* was published in 1989 and has since appeared in more than 20 languages. He now lives in Ripton, Vermont, with his wife and daughter and is scholar in residence at Middlebury College. *Deep Economy: The Wealth of Communities and the Durable Future* was published in 2007 and *The Bill McKibben Reader* in 2008. McKibben is co-founder and director of 350.org, an international movement to unite the world around solutions to the climate crisis (350 parts per million is the safe upper limit for CO_2 in our atmosphere, a level we've already surpassed).

John Medeiros' nonfiction, fiction, and poetry can be found in a broad range of publications, such as *Gents, Badboys, and Barbarians: New Gay Male Poetry* (1995), *Writers against War* (2005), and *Sport Literate* (2008). For Medeiros, writing nonfiction is "often a rebellious act—because we are constantly asked to seek new logic. [And] because of poetry's sensuous and lyrical effect, the stories that have remained with me are those that carry a certain cadence." "One Sentence" won the *Gulf Coast* nonfiction prize in 2005.

Maja Mikula is a Senior Lecturer in Italian Studies at the University of Technology Sydney. With research interests in popular culture, cultural studies, and gender, Mikula is also affiliated with the University's Contesting Euro Visions Research Group—a group that claims to take "a radically different approach to European cultural identities, concentrating on the popular, the contested, the transcultural and the marginal."

Rebekah Nathan is the pseudonym of cultural anthropologist Cathy A. Small. A 1967 graduate of the University of Massachusetts Amherst, Small has a lifelong interest in the South Pacific and is the author of *Voyages: From Tongan Villages to American Suburbs* (Cornell, 1997). In 2002, after fifteen years of teaching in American universities, she took a sabbatical and enrolled as a freshman at her own university, moving into a dorm and taking a full course load. The result was *My Freshman Year: What A Professor Learned by Becoming a Student,* published in 2005 by Cornell University Press. Small is currently professor of anthropology at Northern Arizona University, where she has been active in mentoring and scholarship programs for low-income youth.

Michael Pollan currently serves as the Knight Professor of Science and Environmental Journalism at the University of California, Berkeley. He has published several books on food, agriculture, gardening, and architecture, including *In Defense of Food: An Eater's Manifesto* and the award-winning *The Omnivore's Dilemma: A Natural History of Four Meals.* He is also a contributing writer to *The New York Times Magazine.*

To see pictures of the one-room cabin Pollan constructed as a space for writing, check out his website at http://www.michaelpollan.com / writing_house.php.

Miranda Purves, 38, is an editor at *Elle* magazine in New York City. Among her heroes are the Linux creator Linus Torvalds, environmental crusaders everywhere, and Virginia Woolf, after whom she named her son.

Maria Cristina Rangel grew up in Washington state, the daughter of migrant farm workers. She is an alumna of Smith College and has received the Gertrude Posner Spencer Prize for excellence in writing both fiction and nonfiction and the Premio El Andar for creative nonfiction. As a Queer Chicana activist, writer, feminist, and Malinchista, she fights for economic justice for women, children, and people of color. Rangel lives with her daughters in Western Massachusetts.

Richard Rodriguez grew up in Sacramento, California, the son of Mexican immigrant parents. He went on to study at Stanford University and Columbia. As an essayist and journalist, Rodriguez often writes about the intersections between his personal experiences and the larger social issues in the Americas. His work challenges hegemonic ideas about race, democracy, purity, identity, geography, and religion. His books include *The Hunger of Memory: The Education of Richard Rodriguez, Days of Obligation: An Argument with my Father,* and *Brown: The Last Discovery of America.* This last book proposes a new racial politics of confusion, contradiction, and impurity in order to undermine old ideas about race and identity.

George Saunders was raised on the south side of Chicago. In 1981, he received the B.S. in Geophysical Engineering from Colorado School of Mines in Golden, Colorado. He has worked as a technical writer, geophysical engineer, doorman, roofer, convenience store clerk, guitarist in a country-and-western band, and knuckle-puller in a slaughterhouse. He has been teaching in the Syracuse University Creative Writing Program since 1997. He is the author of *The Brief and Frightening Reign of Phil; Pastoralia;* and *The Braindead Megaphone* among others. In 2006, he was awarded a MacArthur Foundation Genius Grant.

Award-winning journalist and author **David K. Shipler** graduated from Dartmouth College in 1964 before serving as a navel officer on a destroyer. During his time at *The New York Times,* Shipler reported from New York, Saigon, Moscow, and Jerusalem, and served as chief diplomatic correspondent in Washington, D.C. His books include *The Working Poor: Invisible in America* (2004); *A Country of Strangers: Black and Whites in America* (1998); the Pulitzer Prize-winning *Arab and Jew: Wounded Spirits in a Promised Land* (1986); and *Russia: Broken Idols, Solemn Dreams* (1983). Shipler has received the Martin Luther King Jr. Social Justice Award from Dartmouth College as well as honorary degrees from numerous universities. He has taught at several universities including Princeton, American University, and Dartmouth. He lives in Chevy Chase, Maryland.

Susan Sontag (1933–2004) was an author, filmmaker, and political activist who wrote voluminously. Her notable works include *Against Interpretation* (1966),

On Photography (1977), and *Regarding the Pain of Others* (2003). *On Photography* broke new ground in conceptualizing photography as an art form that interprets the world as much as painting and drawing do. She was also an outspoken activist and a critic of western imperialism. Her final nonfiction work, *Regarding the Pain of Others,* re-examined art and photography from a moral standpoint.

Dean Spade is an Assistant Professor of Law at Seattle University School of Law. In 2002, he founded the Sylvia Rivera Law Project (www.srlp.org), a non-profit law collective that provides free legal services to transgender, intersex and gender non-conforming people who are low-income and/or people of color. Spade's current research interests include the impact of the War on Terror on transgender rights, the bureaucratization of trans identities, and models of non-profit governance in social movements.

Richard Stengel is the managing editor of *Time* magazine. After graduating in 1977 from Princeton University, where he played on the basketball team, Stengel was a Rhodes Scholar at Oxford University in England. In 1993, he collaborated with Nelson Mandela on the latter's autobiography, *Long Way to Freedom;* he is also author of *January Sun: One Day, Three Lives, A South African Town.* Since writing "A Time to Serve," Stengel has become active in the national service movement. For more information on that movement, visit the website of ServiceNation, a coalition of organizations dedicated to volunteerism (http://www.bethechangeinc.org/servicenation/).

Andrew Sullivan is a British-born journalist, blogger, and political commentator. An openly gay Roman Catholic living as an expatriate in the U.S., Sullivan's unique personal-political identity has helped make him a prominent critic of American politics and culture. The former editor of *The New Republic* and current blogger for *The Atlantic,* Sullivan was one of the first mainstream journalists to embrace the blogging medium. His blog "Daily Dish" can be found at andrewsullivan.com and is updated daily.

Amy Tan was born in Oakland, California, in 1952, after her parents immigrated from China. After receiving her B.A. and M.A. in Linguistics from San Jose University, Tan worked for programs that aid children with developmental disabilities. She also worked as a business writer for large corporations such as IBM until pursuing a career as a freelance writer. Her most notable novels include the following: *The Joy Luck Club, The Kitchen God's Wife, The Hundred Secret Senses,* and *The Bonesetter's Daughter.* Tan's essays have appeared in *The New Yorker* and *Harper's.* She has also written several children's books, and her memoir, *The Opposite of Fate: Memories of a Writing Life,* was published in 2003. Her work has been translated into more than 25 languages.

Kurt Vonnegut was a prolific and provocative American novelist and essayist. He became known for his commingling of satire, black comedy, and science fiction (in 1999, the main-belt asteroid 25399 Vonnegut was named in his honor). Vonnegut's genre-bending fiction can be seen in such works as *Cat's Cradle* (1963) and

Slaughterhouse-Five (1969). The latter is a memorial to his experiences as a World War II POW in Dresden, Germany, during the Allied fire-bombing of that city. After writing for nearly half a century, he began to find the "labor" of it disagreeable, choosing instead to focus his creative energies on his artwork, which lingered for years as doodling on the edges of manuscripts. His "felt tip calligraphs" have been likened to his honed writing style. Vonnegut taught writing at Harvard, CUNY, and Smith College. In 2000, he was named State Author of New York. He died in 2007 at the age of 84.

David Foster Wallace was born in Ithaca, New York, but was raised in Philo, Illinois. He received the B.A. from Amherst College in 1985. He is the author of *Infinite Jest* and *A Supposedly Fun Thing I'll Never Do Again,* among other works. He most recently taught at Pomona College in Claremont, California. He was awarded a MacArthur Foundation Genius Grant in 1997. "I received 500,000 discrete bits of information today," he once said, "of which maybe twenty-five are important. My job is to make some sense of it."